Globalization's Co

Since the 1980s, globalization and neoliberalism have brought about a comprehensive restructuring of everyone's lives. People are being 'disciplined' by neoliberal economic agendas, 'transformed' by communication and information technology changes, global commodity chains and networks, and in the Global South in particular, destroyed livelihoods, debilitating impoverishment and disease pandemics, among other disastrous disruptions, are also globalization's legacies.

This collection of geographical treatments of such a complex set of processes unearths the contradictions in the impacts of globalization on peoples' lives. *Globalization's Contradictions* firstly introduces globalization in all its intricacy and contrariness, followed by substantive coverage of globalization's dimensions. Areas that are covered in depth are:

- globalization's macroeconomic faces
- globalization's unruly spaces
- globalization's geopolitical faces
- ecological globalization
- globalization's cultural challenges
- globalization from below
- fair globalization

Globalization's Contradictions is a critical examination of the continuing role of international and supranational institutions and their involvement in the political and economic management and determination of global restructuring. Deliberately, this collection raises questions, even as it offers geographical insights and thoughtful assessments of globalization's multifaceted 'faces and spaces'.

Dennis Conway is Professor of Geography and Latin American and Caribbean Studies at Indiana University, Bloomington, Indiana.

Nik Heynen is an Assistant Professor in the Department of Geography at the University of Georgia, Athens, Georgia.

Globalization's Contradictions

Geographies of discipline, destruction and transformation

**Edited by
Dennis Conway and Nik Heynen**

LONDON AND NEW YORK

First published 2006
by Routledge
2 Park Square, Milton Park, Abingdon, Oxon OX14 4RN

Simultaneously published in the USA and Canada
by Routledge
270 Madison Ave, New York, NY 10016

Routledge is an imprint of the Taylor & Francis Group, an informa business

© 2006 Dennis Conway and Nik Heynen

Typeset in Times New Roman by
Book Now Ltd
Printed and bound in Great Britain by
MPG Books Ltd, Bodmin

All rights reserved. No part of this book may be reprinted or reproduced or utilised in any form or by any electronic, mechanical, or other means, now known or hereafter invented, including photocopying and recording, or in any information storage or retrieval system, without permission in writing from the publishers.

Every effort has been made to ensure that the advice and information in this book is true and accurate at the time of going to press. However, neither the publisher nor the authors can accept any legal responsibility or liability for any errors or omissions that may be made. In the case of drug administration, any medical procedure or the use of technical equipment mentioned within this book, you are strongly advised to consult the manufacturer's guidelines.

British Library Cataloguing in Publication Data
A catalogue record for this book is available from the British Library

Library of Congress Cataloging in Publication Data
Conway, Dennis, 1941–
Globalization's contradictions: geographies of discipline, destruction, and transformation/Dennis Conway and Nik Heynen.
    p. cm.
Includes bibliographical references and index.
1. Globalization. 2. Neoliberalism. I. Heynen, Nik, 1973– II. Title.

JZ1318.C6578 2006
303.48'2–dc22   2006005462

ISBN10: 0–415–77061–0 (hbk)
ISBN10: 0–415–77062–9 (pbk)

ISBN13: 978–0–415–77061–3 (hbk)
ISBN13: 978–0–415–77062–0 (pbk)

For Kira, Riley, Fletcher and Birkley
May they grow up in a more socially just world

Contents

List of illustrations x
List of contributors xi
Preface xiii

PART I
Globalization and neoliberalism: dominating disciplines 1

1 **Globalization's dimensions** 3
 DENNIS CONWAY AND NIK HEYNEN

2 **The ascendancy of neoliberalism and emergence of contemporary globalization** 17
 DENNIS CONWAY AND NIK HEYNEN

PART II
Globalization's many dimensions 35

Globalization's macroeconomic faces 37

Financial globalization

3 **Global financial architecture transitions: mutations through "roll-back" neoliberalism to technocratic fixes** 39
 ADAM TICKELL

Corporate globalization

4 **Multi-local global corporations: new reach – same core locations** 49
 SUSAN M. WALCOTT

Technological globalization

5 **Systems of production and international competitiveness: prospects for the developing nations** 65
 DANIEL C. KNUDSEN AND MOLLY KOTLEN

Globalization's unruly spaces 77

The globalization of labor

6 **Globalization of labor: increasing complexity, more unruly** 79
   DENNIS CONWAY

Illegal globalization

7 **Unruly spaces: globalization and transnational criminal economies** 95
   CHRISTIAN ALLEN

Globalization's geopolitical faces 107

Political globalization

8 **Geopolitical globalization: from world systems to global city systems** 109
   DENNIS CONWAY AND RICHARD WOLFEL

Geographical globalization

9 **Globalization has a home address: the geopolitics of globalization** 127
   JOHN AGNEW

Cultural globalization

10 **The globalization of culture: geography and the industrial production of culture** 144
    DON MITCHELL AND CLAYTON ROSATI

The globalization of fear

11 **The globalization of fear: fear as a technology of governance** 161
    BYRON MILLER

PART III
Alternative visions: constructive, democratic and hopeful 179

Ecological globalization

12 **The neoliberalization of the global environment** 181
    NIK HEYNEN AND JEREMIA NJERU

Globalization's cultural challenges

13 Globalization's cultural challenges: homogenization, hybridization and heightened identity   196
NANDA R. SHRESTHA AND DENNIS CONWAY

Globalization from below

14 Globalization from below: coordinating global resistance, alternative social forums, civil society and grassroots networks   212
DENNIS CONWAY

Towards "fair globalization"

15 Towards "fair globalization": opposing neoliberal destruction, relying on democratic institutions and local empowerment, and sustaining human development   226
DENNIS CONWAY AND NIK HEYNEN

References   242
Index   281

Illustrations

Tables

1.1	A hyperactive, runaway world: a new form of global capitalism?	5
1.2	Indicators of globalization, 1980–2003	10
4.1	Top 500 global companies by country	51
4.2	Industries by country and average profit ($US million)	51
4.3	US foreign direct investment in China	58
8.1	International organizations	112
11.1	US foreign policy and the war on terror: countries of the Global South (2002)	173
11.2	Middle East/Asia Minor opinions on the United States	174
11.3	Muslims' views of democracy (2003 and 2002)	175

Figures

4.1	Location and amount of foreign direct investment in China	56
4.2	Location of national-level high- and new-technology parks in China	60
4.3	Profit centers for high-technology exports	61
9.1	Twenty-five years of declining rates of profit for firms in major industrialized countries, 1955–1980	136
9.2	How average plant size in the United States has shrunk, 1967–1999	137
9.3	World net migration by country, 2000	140

Contributors

John Agnew is a Professor in the Department of Geography at the University of California, Los Angeles, with research interests in Political Geography, International Political Economy, European Urbanization, and Italy.

Christian Allen is a Franklin Fellow in the Department of Geography at the University of Georgia, Athens, with research interests in Economic Geography, Political Economy, and Transnational Crime.

Dennis Conway is a Professor in the Department of Geography at Indiana University, Bloomington, with research interests in Migration, Development, Urbanization-housing and Land Markets, and Caribbean Small Island Development Problems.

Nik Heynen is an Assistant Professor in the Department of Geography at the University of Georgia, Athens, Georgia, with research interests in Urban Political Ecology, Political Economy, and Social Theory.

Daniel C. Knudsen is a Professor in the Department of Geography at Indiana University, Bloomington, with research interests in Economic Geography, Cultural Geography, and Landscape and Tourism Geography.

Molly Kotlen is an MA candidate in the Department of City and Regional Planning at the University of Pennsylvania, Philadelphia, with research and career interests in City Planning.

Byron Miller is a Professor in the Department of Geography at the University of Calgary, Canada, with research interests in Urban Political Geography and Social Theory.

Don Mitchell is a Professor in the Department of Geography at Syracuse University and Director of the People's Geography Project. His research interests include Economic Geography, Cultural Geography, and the Production of Landscape.

Jeremia Njeru is a PhD candidate in the Department of Geography at the University of Wisconsin-Milwaukee, with research interests in Urban Political Ecology and Sub-Saharan African Geography.

xii *Contributors*

Clayton Rosati is a Visiting Research Associate and Lecturer in the Department of Geography at the University of Vermont, Burlington, with research interests in Economic Geography and Cultural Geography.

Nanda R. Shrestha is a Professor in the School of Business at Florida A&M University, Tallahassee, with research interests in Economic Development and Cultural Change, and the Political Economy of Nepal.

Adam Tickell is a Professor in the School of Geographical Sciences at the University of Bristol, UK, with research interests in Economic Geography and Political Economy.

Susan M. Walcott is a Professor in the Department of Anthropology and Geography at Georgia State University, Atlanta, with research interests in Urban Geography, Economic Geography, and East Asia.

Richard Wolfel is an Assistant Professor in the Department of Geography at Southern Illinois University, Edwardsville, with research interests in Political Geography, Migration, and Post-soviet Geography.

Preface

This collection has been long in coming, evolving from an initial project in 1999 supported by Indiana University's Center on Global Change and Multidisciplinary Ventures Fund to its present form as a collection of originally commissioned articles on the varying dimensions of globalization's reach. Two successive meetings in 1999 – the first a mini-conference, the second a follow-up author's meeting and discussion of common issues – brought colleagues and experts together in the summer and autumn of 1999 to share their views on globalization and neoliberalism's disturbingly disastrous effects on Latin American, Caribbean and African societies. Over the next two years, other scholars were invited to participate in a project that had broadened its agenda to provide a fuller and more comprehensive account of globalization's transformative power. Mindful that the literature on globalization was growing rapidly, we challenged our contributors to be critical and insightful, even provocative if necessary, so that the readers would be similarly challenged to take a much more careful look at the forces that were swirling around them, bringing tremendous changes to their lives and the lives of others.

In 2004, two panels were organized and held at the 100th Annual Meeting of the Association of American Geographers in Philadelphia by one of the editors, Dennis Conway, and one of our contributors, Christian Allen, to appraise the wider geography community of our project and its breadth of coverage of globalization's many dimensions. A year later, the collection has finally come to fruition, and we are as excited about the collection's messages now as we were when we embarked upon it over five years ago. We have endeavored to keep current with the rapidly changing global situation, but as with all contemporary accounts, we are sure there will be unpredictable turns of events, surprises, and unforeseen changes. Because globalization is such a fickle entity, and the complex of forces we are examining are anything but steady or conformable, we know new, current events will change the stories, and qualify our conclusions. We insist that there are essential geographies of globalization and geographies in globalization's dynamic processes, which give a fuller account of "the beast," albeit a spatially uneven explanation and exposition. That said, we remain convinced that globalization and neoliberalism, and their impacts and influences, are contradictory, unruly, unprecedented and elusive to grasp in their entirety. But, that is the challenge we took on, and that is the excitement we have experienced while putting together this collection, sharing ideas, synthesizing points of view and better informing each other. We trust readers will be similarly enthused and stimulated to search for clearer answers to the troubling questions of today's disorderly world, and how we might fashion – or move towards – a more socially just and equitable world that will sustain and enrich the lives of future generations – including our children's and grandchildren's globalized world.

Dennis Conway and Nik Heynen

Part I
Globalization and neoliberalism

Dominating disciplines

1 Globalization's dimensions

Dennis Conway and Nik Heynen

Introduction

Since the "long sixteenth century," the growth of European mercantilism and the onset of industrial capitalism in Britain, Europe and the Western world (Wallerstein 1976, 1980, 1989), the uneven development and evolution of our world system is replete with episodes of global strategies, global penetrations of local, national and regional systems, and globalizing forces and movements (Amin 1997). Though not without its "nay-Sayers," who question its contemporary identity (for example, Hirst and Thompson 1999; Sen 2002), today's era of globalization has been characterized as a "new, informational global economy and new culture" (Castells 1998) and the product of a new "knowledge-based economy" (Thurow 2000). To many, including the authors of this collection, today's globalization era appears to be globally more comprehensive and interdependent, and fundamental in its restructuring of national economies and societies (Held *et al.* 1999; Henderson 1999).

Globalization in the first decade of the 21st millennium is, therefore, in Dicken's (2004: 6, 8) words, "a syndrome of *material processes and outcomes* ... that are manifested very unevenly, in both time and space." Providing more specificity to this redefinition of global-to-local interactions and circulatory influences, Held (1995) centers the spatiality of the contemporary global system on social meanings of place and space and the time–space nexus of social relations and transactions. Accordingly, he characterizes globalization as:

> the stretching and deepening of social relations and institutions across space and time, such that, on the one hand, day-to-day activities are increasingly influenced by events happening on the other side of the globe and, on the other hand, the practices and decisions of local groups can have significant global reverberations.
>
> (Held 1995: 20)

There appears to be considerable agreement that today's globalization refers to the processes and consequences of two interrelated phenomena that have helped bring about the "time–space compression of global interactions" (Harvey 1989a), whereby global production, communication, travel, and exchange processes are increasing in rapidity, transferability and spatial scope. The first is technological changes in processing and disseminating information related to finance, production, logistical systems of transportation, information services and consumption. The second is the international spread of technical competence and educational advancement worldwide (Ferleger and Mandle 2000). What Thurow (2000) sees as a post-1980s "knowledge-based economy" depends upon this global technical and linguistic reach, however unevenly diffused and culturally contested it might be.

On the one hand, there is an apparent global acceptance of English as the language of science, technology, international business, information dissemination, record-keeping, financial accounting and media coverage, among others. But, as Cassen (2005: 14) points out, "Anglophone domination is a fashion, not a necessity," and furthermore, that English is a central cultural icon of the neoliberal globalization system, as central and advantageous to US imperial power as the US dollar is to the international monetary system. Cassen (2005), importantly, reminds us that Chinese, Romance-language speakers, and Arabic speakers, as well as English-speakers, all equally qualify to occupy a central role in the global linguistic universe. Indeed, other global languages are finding their niches in the rapidly growing spread of internet communication systems, and competing with this Western, modernizing, educational icon (Guillén 2001). For example, fewer than 50 percent of world users of the internet know English as their first language and the proportion is dropping as the new medium diffuses into Asia (China, especially) and Latin America. Even in English-speaking cultural realms, Romance languages such as Spanish challenge English in parts of North America, and in Asia, Mandarin Chinese is an emerging important second language in Korea. Rather than a monolingual global world, we should expect considerable variety in shared languages of groups, communities and population strata, with English, Chinese, Spanish, Russian, Arabic, French and Kiswahili emerging as internationally shared languages (Cassen 2005; Guillén 2001). Perhaps, we might more realistically hypothesize that globalization will foster multilingual knowledge- and information-sharing, rather than perpetuate the imperialistic monolingual dominance of "English-as-the-global-language" (Mazlish 1993).

Distinguishing this contemporary era of globalization from its imperial, mercantile and early capitalist forerunners is its "hyperactivity," the "hyper-mobility" of people, capital, information, ideas, and its greater degree of interconnectedness, complexity and volatility (Giddens 2003; Thrift 1989; Dicken 2003). Thrift (2002) offers us a challenging set of new global spaces, or "cartographies of global capitalism," that demonstrate the comprehensive restructuring of our global world, and depict a new world order undergoing rapid and unpredictable change. In his depiction of globalization's "new clothes," Thrift was at pains to demonstrate the partiality in any explanation of globalization which privileges one determining factor, or feature, or attempts to explain globalization's emergence as a consequence of one major transformation. Rather, conflicting views are interrogated, and three "cartographies of global capitalism" were found to have substance and significance: Jameson's (1991) post-structuralist position, Castells' (1989) technological answer, and Harvey's (1989) geographical point; each being representative, yet partial "maps" of the current global system's transformative nature. In addition to adding more complexity to the dimensions of globalization of Thrift's "hyperactive world," we add our own "cartography of global capitalism" to those of Castells (1989) and Harvey (1989), and so characterize globalization's inherent contradictory character as "unruly, volatile and unpredictable" (see Table 1.1).

Declaring the need to better understand our "runaway world," in 1999 Giddens had this to say about its complexity and its transformative dynamic:

> This is not – at least at the moment – a global order driven by collective human will. Instead, it is emerging in an anarchic, haphazard, fashion, carried along by a mixture of economic, technological and cultural imperatives. It is not settled or secure, but fraught with anxieties, as well as scarred by deep divisions. Many of us feel in the grip of forces over which we have no control. Can we re-impose our will upon them? I believe we can. The powerlessness we experience is not a sign of personal failings, but reflects the incapacities of our institutions. We need to reconstruct those we have, or create new ones, in

Table 1.1 A hyperactive, runaway world: a new form of global capitalism?

- Globalization of spheres of production, commerce and logistical systems
- Globalization of financial systems: "soft-capitalism," "fictitious capital"
- Globalization of corporate power – mega-mergers, oligopolies: "predatory capitalism"
- Globalization of communication and information technology: "digital divide"
- Globalization of employment, work and migration
- Globalization of human effects on biosphere/environmental degradation
- Globalization of supranational, geopolitical conflict over regulatory and legal authority
- "Globalization from below": global, national and local resistance and human rights movements
- Globalization of consumption, "homogenization" of international culture, cultural challenges
- Globalization of militarization, conflict and "fear": post-Cold War continuity, post-9/11 tensions
- Globalization of underground economy: narcotrade, money-laundering, human trafficking

...

- *The accelerated internationalization of economic processes*
- *A frenetic international financial system – "insider" controlled and managed*
- *The use of new information technologies – urban-based, urbanization-driven*
- *Increasing involvement (interpretation) of culture as a factor in and of production → hybridization*

...

Three "cartographies" of global capitalism
- Capitalism's "hyper-mobility": new kinds of (economic) mobile space of flows (Castells 1989)
- Capitalism's "time–space compression": annihilation of space and time (Harvey 1989)
- Capitalism's contradictions: its unruliness, volatility and unpredictable global-to-local effects (Conway and Heynen 2006)

ways appropriate to the global age. We should and we can look to achieve greater control over our runaway world. We shan't be able to do so if we shirk the challenges, or pretend that all can go on as before. For globalization is not incidental to our lives today. It is a shift in our very life circumstances. It is the way we now live.

(Giddens 2003)

Globalization's contradictory complexity and consequences

The main debates over globalization's existence, definitional characterization, historical prominence, and societal contribution(s), not to mention its processes of incorporation and the resultant complex and contradictory outcomes, need to be briefly introduced here because they provide a theoretical backdrop to what will follow in the main body of the collection.

Reviewing the authoritative range of assessments of globalization's particular characteristics that have blossomed in an outpouring of academic and populist interest, Held *et al.* (1999) distinguish three schools of thought, each with distinctly different assessments of globalization's virtues, strengths and weaknesses.

Hyperglobalizers such as Ohmae (1995) argue that a new era has dawned in which global forces supercede nation-states, and a much more efficient "borderless" global economy emerges through the establishment of transnational networks of production, finance and commerce in which corporate capital thrives, achieves efficiencies and encourages accumulation and "progress." Another, Greider (1997), warns that contemporary globalization represents an unwelcome triumph of supranational global capital, and this argumentative group of hyperglobalizers, regardless of their relatively extreme right-wing or left-wing ideological persuasions, all tend to agree that globalization is a process driven and dominated by macroeconomic forces.

Skeptics such as Hirst and Thompson (1996), on the other hand, oppose the hyperglobalist view and argue that today's era does not represent a new characterization of global capitalism, but a "myth." All the claims for a more globally interconnected world are refuted, or disputed, and skeptics especially point to geographical differences of experience and the continuation of deeply embedded social and economic inequalities, as their proof that the world hasn't fundamentally changed under globalization's umbrella.

Transformationalists, one of whom is Giddens (1990, 1996), are convinced that globalization is an unprecedented major force causing the rapid social, economic and political restructuring of our "runaway world." For Rosenau (1997) also, the domestic–foreign frontier is an expanding set of intertwined spaces of interchange and exchange, such that globalization is not only not diminishing the authority of national governments, but is in fact helping to reconstitute and restructure national/civil power and influence, as adaptations to the growing complexity of supranational governance, regulation and global consensus-building in an ever-increasingly, interconnected world. Convinced that globalization needs situating in its sociohistorical context and explained in terms of its contingent structural processes, "transformationists" argue that explanations of contemporary globalization's open-ended trajectory need to deal with a complex and dynamic set of changing interrelationships between causal factors – economic, technological, political and sociocultural. Commentators of this persuasion are neither so extremely positive about globalization's effects, nor are they as extremely critical of globalization's oppressive, structural dominance as are the left-wing advocates of the "hyperglobalizers." Rather, "transformationalists" are optimists, but pragmatic in their assessments, that the global processes which have been charted by the current groups of influential actors can be re-charted, refocused and restructured by influential stakeholders, if the political and economic will is present.

Although Dicken (2004) complained that geographers have not been fully engaged in the earlier debates on globalization's influences, we beg to differ. We feel we can add a fifth school of thought – *global geographies* – in which political- and economic-geographers have engaged globalization as a scale-sensitive process of geographical processes and patterns, and have theorized on their geographical consequences as well as their time–space interconnections (Peck 2002; Swyngedouw 1997). Not only have geographers paid close attention to the many varied scalar connections which occur when global processes cascade from the global to the local, but there is a growing recognition of the significance of global geographical differences in outcomes and consequences. Johnston *et al.* (2002: 3) put it succinctly when they note there is "geography *and* globalization," "geography *in* globalization," "geography *of* globalization," and "geography *for and against* globalization."

Globalization's impacts are unevenly distributed geographically. Neoliberalism's messages and capitalist models vary geographically, so that decidedly different versions of advanced capitalist governmental regimes emerge; contrast US and Canadian versions for their different treatments of public social welfare provision, or contrast the US and German economic democratic regimes with the social democratic regimes of Scandinavia. Then there are contrasts between Japanese, Korean and Malaysian capitalist regimes and between this group's practices of public–private partnerships with China's and India's as they all pursue their own paths of export-oriented economic growth and expansion. In Latin America, Cuban, Venezuelan and Brazilian models of capitalist enterprise and social democratic priorities are similar in some general respects, yet different in many ways. The "globalization story" for other global regions could be expanded to further exemplify geographical/territorial difference, but let these aforementioned examples suffice to demonstrate the point that geopolitical, global–cultural processes and their unruly antitheses concentrate and disperse across different "spaces" and "localities." And, different experiences and practices are the rule not the exception.

Global technological diffusion is uneven, geographically concentrated, and as such it geographically divides the world into "haves" and "have-nots," "insiders" and "outsiders" – with digital divides, technological advantages and innovations privileging and depriving simultaneously. Destructive, disciplinary and transformative geographies cause spatial and societal vulnerabilities, as much as they

8   *Dennis Conway and Nik Heynen*

contribute to the centralization and concentration of wealth and power in the hands of an elite minority and the increasing global social divide of "winners" and "losers" in the neoliberal capitalist model of unbridled free marketeering and privatization. Globalization's contradictory impacts are felt at many geographical scales, in widely varying geographical locations, regions and communities, and in evolving global, national, regional and local social systems of information, knowledge and communication exchange.

Amin (2002) and Dicken (2004) add to the theoretical depth of these geographical conceptualizations of globalization, by stressing the importance of actor networks in the global-to-local hierarchies of interconnected influences and outcomes, thereby providing a balance to the more familiar spatial emphases on scalar and territorial relationships and connections. Amin (2002), Amin and Graham (1997), Sassen (2002) and Taylor (2004) also make the important point that globalization networks have provided a new dynamic to city growth and global city interactions. Indeed, the growing importance of global cities – *and globalizing cities* – as the "new" and "renewed" sites for globalization's geographical expressions means our collection visits and revisits this transformative urban dimension as much as it visits and revisits nation-state and regional geographies.

That said, we prefer to examine "geographies of globalization and their contradictory tendencies" because this keeps us firmly focused on the real world of peoples' experiences and the divisions and divisiveness that is globalization's legacy. At the same time, such a "geographical optic" enables us to assess the power and influences of structural forces and the accompanying agency interactions, which make many of globalization's consequences and neoliberalism's effects so disquieting as well as unpredictable, volatile and dehumanizing. Viewed from a behavioral perspective which privileges agency and peoples' actions, global structural forces and the structural imperatives of network embeddedness need no longer be conceived as immutable forces, but rather they can be considered as modifiable, open to re-evaluation, and subject to reappraisal, re-regulation, renewal or reversal.

Other geographers with regional interests and with an intent to insure that geographical diversity and subnational and regional processes are given the notice they deserve have dealt substantively with "alternative capitalisms" as a framework for identifying the varying consequences of global forces in emerging regions, and the changing regional worlds beyond the Western advanced capitalist Cores (Gwynne *et al.* 2003). And, as our collection will attest, macroeconomic geography, geopolitics, sociocultural geographical diversity, global-to-local scalar and relational interconnectedness, and geographies *of, in* and *for and against* globalization are all dimensions of considerable analytical significance. So, political and economic geographers and their geographical perspectives on global change and global transformations have their place in the debating contest, even though they might be considered latecomers (Dicken 2004).

The positions taken in our collection are, in effect, part "hyperglobalizers" and part "transformationalists" in their conception and their critical viewpoints, as well as in their concluding optimistic stance. Agreeing with Sklair (2002), we acknowledge the global diffusion of generic globalization, the dominance of neoliberal capitalist globalization, and the possibility that progressive change can be forthcoming with the growth of alternative globalizations. Where we go beyond that position is to insist that globalization's dimensions are fundamentally geographical in their scalar interconnections and spatial embeddedness; i.e. global "geographical knowledges" (Johnston et al. 2002).

Embracing the essential need to situate our explanation of contemporary globalization in its sociohistorical context, we argue that the neoliberal economic project is a primary, but not exclusive, feature of globalization's combinatory character. Understanding how the macroeconomic faces, the geopolitical spaces, the sociocultural and ideological dimensions intersect and combine thereby becomes a worthy goal of this collection. Global shifts are highly uneven geographically, global production and commodity chains are geographically dispersed, yet technologically integrated, global capital and global labor continue to be at odds with each other and the former is increasingly hypermobile. Transnational networks and nation-states are not supplanting each other, but rather operating in interactive, mutual systems. Cultural challenges, and local hybrid globalizations, broaden the range of geographical globalization so that the hegemonic Western and modernist model of a US-advocated neoliberal globalization project is not at all an inevitable consequence.

Contemporary globalization's rapid transformations

As Guillén (2001: 239) reminds us, contemporary "globalization is an incomplete, discontinuous, contingent, and in many ways contradictory and puzzling process." Dicken (2003: 12) adds to this characterization by emphasizing that contemporary "globalization tendencies can occur without this resulting in an all-encompassing end-state – a globalized economy – in which all unevenness and difference is ironed out, market forces are rampant and uncontrollable and the nation-state merely passive and supine." Despite these salutary qualifications, there is considerable empirical verification of the rapidity of globalization's current "tendencies" to be found in the following set of 1980–2003 indicators that Guillén (2001, 2005) provides (Table 1.2).

The volume's critical perspective

The aim of this collection is to both conduct a detailed examination of the varying and interconnected globalization processes, and to delineate the resultant outcomes – in particular the effects of globalization and neoliberalism on ordinary peoples' lives in general, and the poor in Third World/Global South countries in particular. Highlighted are the punitive and destructive characteristics of these global and supranational disciplinary forces and their contradictory characteristics. Broad-ranging questions emerging from this critical examination seek to understand the multifaceted nature of global restructuring, and its effects upon particular regional and local geographies.

Table 1.2 Indicators of globalization, 1980–2003

Indicators	1980	1990	1995	2000	2003
A. Economic					
Inward FDI stock (% world GDP)	6.7	9.3	10.3	19.6	22.9
Developed countries (% GDP)	4.9	8.2	8.9	16.5	20.7
Developing countries (% GDP)	12.6	14.8	16.6	31.1	31.4
Exports of foreign affiliates (% total world exports)	–	27.5	32.3	33.3	–
Exports + imports of goods (% world goods GDP)	77.7	80.2	96.9	117.8	152.1
Developed countries (% goods GDP)	78.6	80.9	96.8	119.0	156.4
Developing countries (% goods GDP)	72.8	74.5	80.9	111.2	134.0
B. Financial					
Daily currency exchange turnover (% world GDP)	0.7	3.8	5.6	6.8	3.8
Cross-border bank credit stock (% world GDP)	13.9	34.3	33.1	37.6	45.2
Cross-border banking assets (% world GDP)	13.7	28.1	28.5	34.2	41.2
C. Social and political					
International tourist arrivals (% world population)	3.5	8.6	9.9	11.6	10.0
Stock of international migrants (% world population)	2.3	2.9	–	2.9	–
International telephone calls (minutes per capita)	–	7.1	11.1	19.5	21.8
Nation-states with UN membership	154	159	185	189	191
International organizations					
Inter-governmental	337	300	–	243	245
Non-governmental	4,265	4,621	–	6,357	7,261

Source: *Mauro Guillén's Indicators of Globalization, 1980–2003* (2005), http://www.management.wharton.upenn.edu/guillen/files/Global.Table.1980-2003.pdf

Notable in the debate in this volume is a critical examination of the continuing role of international and supranational institutions and their involvement in the political economic management and determination of global restructuring. Is neoliberalism and advanced capitalism's "Washington consensus" moving the world along a destructive neoliberal path? We believe so. Is the neoliberal and Structural Adjustment (SAP) "solution" meted out to Third World countries more punishment than therapy? Are the WTO and GATT policies leading the world towards a more unequal future? We think so. Not only is this solution inappropriate and unsuccessful as a development path to follow, it is indeed perpetuating the problems it claims to address; i.e. continued immiseration, increases in impoverishment, greater dependency on the exploitation of the periphery's extractive resources, and continued iniquities in their comparative advantages *vis-à-vis* the advanced capitalist Cores of Europe and North America, Japan, and their transnational corporate partners.

Is the current era of globalization favoring transnational corporate interests and the interests of the elite capitalist classes at the expense of labor and the poorer classes? We are more and more convinced of this iniquitous reality. We observe transnational mergers and mega-mergers of the larger and largest corporations in the name of "downsizing" and for supposedly competitive reasons, with the antitrust commissions and peoples' protection mechanisms operating at the national level routinely acquiescent and unresponsive. Such tendencies as this centralization of capitalist power in corporate hands not only elevates these supranational bodies above and beyond national reaches in terms of capital stocks. It also reduces many a national government's bargaining power, and renders the smaller and poorer countries of the Third World/Global South even more helpless in a world where capital and money talks most authoritatively.

Today's world is a global domain where bribery, corruption, organized crime and the underworld of criminal activity is more and more involved with, and scarcely indistinguishable from, political patronage, party donations, influence-pedaling and the bankrolling of national and international political candidates for positions of authority and power in the new globalizing order. Corruption appears to be indistinguishable from "smart business practice," or so it seems as practiced at home and abroad, East or West, North or South, Core or Periphery. Capitalism's underside is seamlessly interwoven with its praxis globally.

In this chapter, therefore, we provide a brief introduction of contemporary globalization's many interwoven dimensions, to set the agenda for the critical commentary that follows. Grouped into sets of overlapping and confirmatory chapters, the heart of this collection is the set of original contributions written by the authorities we have marshaled together; critical political–economic geographers by theoretical persuasion and passion.

To provide a macro-structural accounting of how this new era came into being, in the second part of this introductory part, Chapter 2, we trace how the post-1980 ascendancy of neoliberal capitalism occurred. This is followed by a condensed accounting of major features in globalization's emergence and consolidation and neoliberalism's growing dominance as a global ideology in the 1980s and 1990s and into the twenty-first century – to the year 2005. Most importantly, we focus upon the increasingly contradictory nature of this latest "unregulated" and volatile capitalist model of centralized and destructive power – a US-led "new imperialism" is one critic's opinion (Harvey 2003). Agnew and Miller in Chapters 9 and 11, respectively, also argue this geopolitical point forcefully and successfully. But, before we set the stage, globalization's interwoven and multidimensional nature needs to be more formally introduced, and detailed.

Globalization's many dimensions

The determining, destructive and contradictory forms of globalization's complexity and transformative power are to be found in macroeconomic, technological, geopolitical, societal, cultural and ideological spheres. Change is occurring almost everywhere, it seems. Change and restructuring is occurring at all scalar levels; globally worldwide, in hemispheres and world regions, in global urban systems, national urban systems, even small towns, agrarian landscapes and rural frontiers. Changes in the spatial organization of social, economic, political and cultural relationships and transactions are "generating transcontinental or interregional flows and networks of activity, interaction and the exercise of power" (Held *et al.* 1999: 16). Neoliberal capitalism is the dominant (some would say, "triumphant") economic model and ideological project holding sway over globalization's all-powerful reach, though it manifests itself in several different structural versions according to geographical, geopolitical and macroeconomic origins and practices – Japanese, European and North American versions, as well as Asian "emerging market" versions (Chinese and Indian, Malaysian and Korean, for example). Core–periphery nation-state relationships are being paralleled by intercity systems of interaction, thereby changing *and diversifying* the contexts in which transnational interactions and interconnections occur.

It would be impossible to provide adequate, in-depth coverage of all of globalization's many interactive dimensions in one collection, without oversimplifying the growing complexity of our world's transformations today. Accordingly, we focus our attention on those dimensions of globalization that are changing the scale of influence on, and political economic power over, people's livelihoods and their interactions. All of these dimensions constitute overlapping and intersecting "faces" and "spaces" of globalization, which can be categorized and grouped around a nexus of global geographical knowledge; namely, macroeconomic faces, unruly spaces, geopolitical faces, and alternative vistas. Our choice to focus on macroeconomic and geopolitical spaces of geographical knowledge is deliberate, because it highlights the fundamental importance of these two perspectives to a better understanding of globalization's workings. Associated complex and contradictory forces are also unleashed, and we have characterized these as "unruly spaces" and "alternative visions." Together, they constitute an ensemble of extremely important, interconnected dimensions.

Globalization's macroeconomic faces

Dicken (2004) provides us with a useful encapsulation of the macro-economic structures at work in our globalizing world:

> The macro-structures of the global economy are essentially the institutions, conventions and rules of the capitalist market system. These are, of course, not naturally given, but socially constructed – in their present form predominantly as a neo-liberal political-economic ideology. The rules and conventions of the capitalist market economy relate to such phenomena as private property, profit-making, resource allocation on the basis of market signals, and the consequent commodification of production inputs (including labour). The IMF, the WTO and the World Bank, together with various "G" meetings, are the most obvious manifestations of global institutions, although there is of course a myriad other, more specific, bodies such as industry-specific regulatory bodies. What we do not have is a coherent system of global governance, but rather a "confusion" of institutions.... Virtually, the entire world economy is now a market economy. Yet, despite the normative prescriptions of the neo-liberals, institutions and conventions continue to be manifest in *specific configurations and varieties* in specific places (notable within national-states, but not only at that scale). In other words, they too are *territorially embedded*.
> (Dicken 2004: 11–12)

The post-1980s resurgence of global capital and its neoliberal formulas, and this emergent, advanced capitalist project's attendant restructuring of the political–economic (and ecological) landscapes of the world, are evidence of the historical and geographical significance of macroeconomic forces in such a restructuring process. International finance, transnational corporate behavior, the restructuring of global production and commodity chains, the innovative role(s) of technology and advanced communication and transport logistical support systems; all feature in this macroeconomic project. "Soft capitalism" and global producer services are willing company to this neoliberal economic project, which favors and privileges private capital, while challenging public collective power, whether it is the state, civil society or communal interest (Thrift 1998). In recognition of its fundamental role in the restructuring of our world, we first deal with these *macroeconomic dimensions* – specifically examining international finance's growing role, corporate power's consolidation and industrial restructuring's consequences (Chapters 3, 4 and 5, respectively).

Globalization's unruly spaces

While the ease at which capital crosses international borders has been well treated within the globalization literature, there has been relatively little discussion of the other main component of global economic activity – labor – within the same context. Not only has there been an international division of labor with corporations using global relocation to achieve reductions in their labor costs of production, but labor has also responded to capital's movements and moved nationally and internationally. In many Western, advanced capitalist economies, labor's collective power to oppose, or counter, capital's dictates in the workplace through union activity, strike action and collective bargaining has been under assault, in both the political and industrial spheres (Ross 2000). Although internal and international migration has become a strategic option for increasing numbers of the world's population, labor immobility as well as its mobility are both parts of the livelihood and labor recruitment equations. And, not only is labor less mobile than capital in today's globalizing world, but it is less predictable, more unruly and less easy for advanced capitalism's institutions to direct spatially, or locationally.

Today's new international migrants retain considerable flexibility to be deliberately "unruly" in response to the destination country's immigration policies and practices. Internal movements are, by contrast, continuities of earlier massive rural-to-urban transfers that began in the 1960s, whereby rural peripheral sectors continue to be enmeshed in depressing and irreversible conditions of stagnation and neglect, while rapid urbanization in Third World city after Third World city continues its unruly transformational process, still uncontrolled, unregulated and seemingly unstoppable. Today's complex (unruly and new) patterns of international and transnational movement, on the other hand, are a diverse mixture of formal and informal modes, of legally sanctioned and illegally practiced entry strategies, as well as a means for diversifying the survival strategies of many of the world's poor and powerless. Chapter 6 details these unruly happenings.

Transnational organized crime is a "postmodern" security threat which flourishes in the unruly spaces and places generated by globalization processes. It is a trans-sovereign problem, crossing state boundaries in ways that individual nation-states cannot control. Unlike Cold War era security threats, it is diffuse, dominated by non-state actors, and motivated by entrepreneurial interests. State institutions are increasingly challenged by a tension between promoting free markets while simultaneously restricting the flow of drugs, arms, prostitutes, "conflict" diamonds, or other undesirable commodities. Because the regulatory mechanisms of globalized markets are highly fragmented, criminal actors can exploit legal, economic and cultural asymmetries that stimulate demand for illicit commodities or reduce the capacity of the state to respond to such activities. Indeed, globalization rhetoric commonly portrays the state as marginalized or even irrelevant. This consideration of globalization's *unruly spaces* deals substantively with international migration and illegal global activities (Chapters 6 and 7, respectively).

Globalization's geopolitical faces

The long-established field of geopolitics considers spatial relations as integral to the critical examination of global power relations, nation-state identity formation, territoriality and sovereignty, border issues and international, political–economic relationships. Critical geopolitics goes further to investigate globalization's supranational influences, the emergence of symbolic boundaries, deterritorialization dangers and cross-boundary network formations (Dodds 2000; Ó'Tuathail and Dalby 1998). The geopolitical faces of globalization are diverse, in large part because they revolve around global hegemonic relationships, the decline and fall of nation-state regimes, the new challenges to existing hegemonic power, and the global nature of supranational and national institution-building, territorialization, extra-territorialization, and new political allegiances (Flint 2002, 2004). Economic, cultural and political forces are at (inter)play in today's restructuring world. So, in our contributions to this global theme, four geopolitical issues are given in-depth treatments – the global political systems' urbanization dynamic and urban reconstitution (Chapter 8), globalization's roots in American/US geopolitics (Chapter 9), the politicization of global culture (Chapter 10) and the contemporary state of uncertainty since "9/11"; to wit, the globalization of fear (Chapter 11). Elsewhere in the collection, geopolitical and macroeconomic issues surface time and time again, which is as much an apt demonstration of the interconnected nature of globalization's influences and outcomes as a realization that not every globalization dimension can be isolated, or singularly treated. The geopolitical foci, here, address major themes, but there is insufficient space in our collection for a full, comprehensive coverage of all critical geopolitical perspectives. There are other, more specialist anthologies which attempt that academic objective (Herod *et al.* 1998; O'Loughlin *et al.* 2004).

Globalization's rapid spread, its restructuring directives, destructive tendencies and overwhelming disciplinary authority has also generated both academic and activist/populist "discontent" and opposition (Burbeck *et al.* 2000; Gills 2000; Sassen 1998; Stiglitz 2002), and the pros and cons of this complex transformation of our world deserve a comprehensive assessment, if not a rethink (see Aulakh and Schechter 2000). Indeed, these twenty-first century counter-arguments directly challenged what appeared to be in the 1990s a comfortable acceptance of globalization's inevitability, and of advanced capitalism's triumphant ascendancy (Fukuyama 1992). Accordingly, we are emboldened by these scholars' "discontent" and critical assessments, and firmly believe this collection can add to the groundswell of critical rethinking, while at the same time offering some hopeful and progressive signs for a way forward.

Alternative visions

The themes which emerge within and across these aforementioned in-depth treatments of globalization's faces and spaces are then "counterbalanced" in our concluding part, which presents "alternative visions" in four chapters. The first (Chapter 12) throws down the gauntlet, and theoretically uncovers the social roots of the growing environmental crisis our globe faces under the ravages of neoliberal capitalism. The second (Chapter 13) revisits the cultural faces of globalization and the contradictory cross-currents of social and cultural transfers and transformations that globalization both fosters and opposes, as local resistances and hybridization results from homogenization pressures, and multiple identity formation and other synergistic outcomes occur regionally, locally and unevenly. The third (Chapter 14) explicitly introduces and characterizes the growing global opposition to unfettered globalization and neoliberal capitalism and to the destructive and disciplinary impacts of this "globalization from above." Notably, this chapter on "globalization from below" returns the debate to themes of social justice, global justice, equity, activism and advocacy, and to questions of societal and ecological sustainability. It portrays the growing activism and resistance to globalization, not only because of its many destructive forms, but also because it encourages (and even rewards) antisocial, dehumanizing traits of "individualism" – mean-spiritedness, arrogance, selfishness and greed, and a callous disregard for the plight of others who are less fortunate or less privileged. Everyone's sense of social responsibility must be rekindled, or energized, globally, nationally, regionally and locally. A final concluding Chapter 15 builds upon the critical appraisals of earlier chapters but finishes on a positive note, seeking to answer the following questions: Can "fair globalization" be possible? Is global justice possible? Can globalization deliver sustainability? People around the world are questioning (quite rightly so in our opinion) globalization's potential, if it remains in its present form, with macroeconomic forces so dominant, and people's democratic power and authority so subordinated or weakened in the name of free trade, privatization, neoliberalism and post-modernity.

An alternative prescription which seeks a fair globalization and global justice for all – decent work, social democratic processes, local empowerment and sustainable systems – is advocated. Good governance, with responsible regulatory authority, is critical, at both the global and national levels. Upholding everyone's human rights and the redressing of injustices wrought under this most recent harsh disciplinary variant of advanced capitalism is a must. Sustainable systems of our life-worlds must be sought – in urban living, transportation systems, rural livelihoods, work regimes, health services, food and water provision, resource management and environmental stewardship (though no order is implied in this listing – each and every one of these domains is equally important). At this juncture, and at this critical time of reflection on the unsustainable paths global forces and neoliberal capitalism are taking us, participating in the social democratic process to forge a more socially just and truly humane path is everyone's global, national, regional and local responsibility. Now the world's people need their representatives – intellectuals, academics and teachers, representative governments, NGOs, public citizenry, philanthropists, communal organizations and the like – to have the political will to chart such a new path (Henderson 1999; New Economics Foundation 2003b).

Where there's life there's hope

Such is the strength and authority of global forces today that we may be examining a process of transformation that is already so well advanced it cannot be easily diverted or turned aside. Nevertheless, a thoughtful examination of the many "geographies of globalization" and a purposeful critique of neoliberal capitalism is warranted, if we are to look to a more sustainable and viable future for the world's people, and the world's ecumene. As the last part of four chapters will attest, there are hopeful signs that progressive institutional structures both need to be – and are being – promoted, tested and presented. Peoples' rights are being better defended, there are some visions for the future that are hopeful, and there are promising signs that the overwhelming (and dominating) nature of neoliberal capitalism's macro-structural forces can be refashioned, even re-regulated.

Environmental sustainability is gaining global acceptance as a viable objective, especially at local communal levels. Cultural resistance has gained in strength and resourcefulness, Western ideas and modernist ideologies have not swept away regional and local practices, hybridization and cross-border transfers are building transnational cultural bridges, cultural synergy, and revived cultural strengths. The "developmental state" may be down, but it is not out! Supranational institutional and regulatory capacities are expanding, and growing in authority. Corporate power's authority and self-regulatory image has been tarnished by scandal, corruption and devious accounting practices, so that unfettered privatization no longer goes unchallenged; it is no longer a "sacred cow." The ascendancy of neoliberal capitalism has brought hardship, immiseration, widening inequality, and much more, but tomorrow's geopolitical era can emerge from its ashes, and from the lessons learnt, so that social democratic futures can be popularly assured.

We sincerely hope the youthful readers of this collection will be energized to become politically active and engaged. We hope the critical views presented in our collection go some way to mobilizing them to become involved in participatory, social democratic thought and praxis, thereby adding immeasurably to the collection's educational value. We are hopeful that a better, sustainable future can be attained. Globalization's paths can be redirected, and her projects given a much more humane face.

2 The ascendancy of neoliberalism and emergence of contemporary globalization

Dennis Conway and Nik Heynen

Introduction

The world is becoming more and more interconnected, interdependent and interrelated. This we can agree upon. How did contemporary globalization and neoliberalism materialize? What brought about this most recent restructuring of the world system? Surprisingly, globalization's emergence is usually taken for granted, or critics/analysts isolate what they consider the important *new* features of the phenomenon. Missing from most examinations is a detailed account of neoliberalism's central role in contemporary globalization's emergence and consolidation in the second half of the twentieth century. Although other major structural transformations – such as technological change, social and cultural transformations, geopolitical crises and dynamics – are also significant, neoliberal capitalism and neoliberal modernization deserve special attention because, as our latest macroeconomic doctrine, "neoliberalism" has grown to become an unchallenged ideology; nothing short of an overwhelming, mind-controlling ethic. Yet, as today's current global ideology and market faith, it has ascended from its roots in the contradictions of previous eras of advanced capitalism, and its accompanying restructuring imperatives are in response to the crises and obstacles of these earlier projects. The consummate power of market exchange, privatization and capital accumulation as *the* defining features of human action and activity has been raised to unprecedented levels, so that neoliberalism disciplines, destroys, dehumanizes and destabilizes, while such outcomes are rationalized as social inevitabilities, and people – especially the poor, weak and powerless (and, by definition, 'uncompetitive') – become the disposable assets of today's uneven globalizing world.

In this chapter, therefore, we provide a sociohistorical account of the ascendancy of neoliberal capitalism from the 1970s to the present; as it emerged out of the ashes of Keynesian economic thinking to become recast as a supply-side, neoliberal alternative. More specifically, we establish neoliberalism's roots during the post-World War II period, then outline the structural transformations accompanying neoliberalism's post-1980 ascendancy. This is "narrated" in an historical accounting of major features in globalization's consolidation in the 1990s and early twenty-first century, and, most importantly, the growing contradictory nature of this latest "unregulated," volatile and unsustainable capitalist model of centralized and destructive power. "Predatory globalization" is one recent author's critical condemnation of the era, which appears to be in a perpetual state of global crisis (Falk 1999).

Before going into more detail on its historical trajectory, however, it would be helpful to delineate what neoliberalism is essentially about.

Neoliberalism's roots

Addressing the definitional roots of neoliberal capitalism, and neoliberalism writ large, Martinez and Garcia (1997) remind us that "neo" means we are talking about the new kind of liberalism that has emerged during the last 25 years – the post-1980 era. English economist Adam Smith's 1776 *Wealth of Nations* text was the exemplary benchmark of this first liberal school of economics, which advocated the abolition of government intervention in economic matters and promoted a free market ideology with no restrictions on manufacturing, no barriers to trade and commerce and no tariff barriers as the best way for a national economy to grow efficiently. And, Imperial Great Britain certainly practiced this economic liberalism to great effect, as it expanded its global reach beyond its colonies into Latin America, East Asia and beyond. Such economic liberalism was also the favored national economic policy of the rapidly industrializing United States through much of the nineteenth century and into the third decade of the twentieth. Challenging British economic influence in Latin America was part and parcel of this hegemonic struggle.

The 1930's Great Depression, however, exposed this ideological model's shortcomings, so that in accordance with the structural prerogatives such a crisis in capitalism brings, a new national economic orthodoxy came to the fore. John Maynard Keynes was as influential in the 1940s and 1950s as Adam Smith had been in the 1780s and beyond, in convincing economic policy-makers that liberalism was no longer the best policy for national growth and well-being. "Keynesianism," in contrast to liberalism, argued for a much more central role for government (and central bank) intervention, and furthermore argued that full employment was necessary for capitalism to grow and for people to prosper. The belief that the government should intervene where the private market was loath to go, subsidize capital, provide public welfare services and support a social safety net for the citizenry at large, was a dramatic pendulum swing in economic thinking and practice. But, these state-interventionist and regulatory ideas greatly influenced political and economic agendas in Europe and North America during the post-World War II period – President Roosevelt's "New Deal" and President Johnson's "Great Society Program," for example.

Keynesianism and its fellow institutional programs like the Bretton Woods Agreement, the financial aid portfolios of the International Bank for Reconstruction and Development (later to become the World Bank), the Alliance for Progress, among many others, might have underpinned the post-war economic expansion and spread of capitalism from the world's Core countries to their peripheries, but it too would experience its own economic contradictions, structural limitations and resultant financial crises. Accordingly, by the late 1970s, supply-side economics solutions to economic recovery and the basic tenets of economic liberalism underwent a revival, and a re-assertion into economic policy circles. Britain's Margaret Thatcher would jubilantly trumpet her convincing acronym, TINA, or "*There Is No Alternative*," in defense of this pendulum swing to the conservative right. In the United States, Ronald Reagan's succession to the presidency in 1981 also signaled the ascension of his brand of "pragmatic conservatism" and Washington's ideological right-turn away from Keynesianism and its state-intervention practices.

The essence of neoliberalism "unpacked"

Unpacking its essentials, Bourdieu (1998: 2) enables us to see this current economic neoliberal theory as a *political project*, which "aims to create the conditions under which the 'theory' can be realized and can function: *a programme of the methodological destruction of collectives*." He further elaborates on this by observing that:

> [T]he neoliberal programme draws its social power from the political and economic power of those whose interests it expresses: stockholders, financial operators, industrialists, conservatives or social–democratic politicians who have been converted to the reassuring lay-offs of laissez-faire, high-level financial officials eager to impose policies advocating their own extinction because, unlike the managers of firms, they run no risk of having to eventually pay the consequences. Neoliberalism tends on the whole to favour severing the economy from social realities and thereby constructing, in reality, an economic system conforming to its description in pure theory, that is a sort of logical machine that presents itself as a chain of constraints regulating economic agents.
>
> (Bourdieu 1998: 2–3)

In terms of national or international conflict relationships between capital and labor, Bourdieu (1998: 6) ridicules neoliberalism as a free market system built upon the *structural violence* of unemployment, of the insecurity of job tenure and the menace of the layoff:

> [The neoliberal utopia] evokes powerful belief – *the free trade faith* – not only among those who live off it, such as financiers, the owners and managers of large corporations, etc., but also among those, such as high-level government officials and politicians, who derive their justification for existing from it. For they sanctify the power of markets in the name of economic efficiency, which requires the elimination of administrative or political barriers capable of inconveniencing the owners of capital in their individual quest for the maximization of individual profit, which has been turned into a model of rationality. They want independent central banks. And they preach the subordination of nation-states to the requirements of economic freedom for the masters of the economy, with the suppression of any regulation of any

market, beginning with the labour market, the prohibition of deficits and inflation, the general privatization of public services, and the reduction of public and social expenses.

(Bourdieu 1998: 4)

If we are to characterize neoliberalism by its impacts on those outside the privileged elites, who have been the project's beneficiaries these past 25 years or so, then this global economic and political project has not only perpetuated previous inequalities, but it has exacerbated the global divide. The poor and "new poor" of the peripheral Third World – Latin America and the Caribbean, Africa, the Middle East, East Asia, Southeast Asia, South Asia – are being made to suffer through another round of the same bitter medicine they suffered under colonialism and post-colonialism; namely a neoliberal modernization version of Samir Amin's (1974) and André Gunder Frank's (1978) "development of underdevelopment."

The common collective interest and the public good has been negotiated away by ideological, political, social and economic power-plays, which privilege individual accumulation and self-interest among internal elites over communal obligation and societal responsibility for one's fellow human beings – neighbors, citizens and guests alike. The global majority (labor and dependents together), on the other hand, are being duped, co-opted and coerced by the power and persuasion of this new free market project and its theological messages (Cox 1999). Neoliberalism, as globalization's most powerful ideological persuasion, subordinates collective, communal rights to the dominant power of market exchange, which favors individualistic accumulation of wealth, selfishness, greed, and even underwrites justification for excessive militarism and war-mongering (Amin 2003; Hardt and Negri 2004).

Neoliberal capitalism's ascendance

We start our time–space journey in the 1950s, though undoubtedly important changes had their incubation either during World War II, or even prior to that catastrophic event – in manufacturing and technology spheres, for instance. The post-World War II period is, however, a useful temporal window in which to examine and explain contemporary globalization's emergence and the concomitant ascendance of neoliberal capitalism and neoliberal modernization. Note, we do not bind the emergence of globalization to a particular threshold or benchmark, but rather view it as a dynamic and still-changing global-to-local process which has its structural roots in global capitalism's evolution and a multiplicity of strands/ dimensions undergoing political, economic, societal, cultural and spatial transformations. Notably, the time–space modulation of these transformations is not even-paced, nor convergent. Characterizing globalization as a uni-linear system of space–time, or of time–space convergence, as if everything is changing in step with the other, is scarcely credible given the inherent unevenness of the dynamic process. Neoliberalism's disciplinary reach is also not unequivocally, globally hegemonic, nor without its contradictions and crises.

That said, the ascendance of neoliberalism as the ideological basis for restructuring the global economic system from the late 1970s onwards, and especially its political economic "coming of age" in the 1980s decade, does provide a temporal benchmark of considerable significance. Neoliberalism and contemporary globalization's consolidation can be situated in the post-1980 period, and the subsequent contradictory and uneven tendencies that grow stronger during the following 25 years or so are major features of the examination we intend to undertake in this chapter. Certainly, the end of this contemporary era is not in sight, globalization's transformative reach has by no means run out of steam, and neoliberal capitalism and neoliberal modernization are not under serious challenge. Its ideological power is still the dominant "new economic faith" (Cox 1999), its ascendance is still on an upswing, and perhaps we are among a minority of discontented progressives who call for a return to Keynesian social responsibility and accountability (Daly 2003; George 1999; Sassen 1998; Stiglitz 2002). Now, let us set the emergence of contemporary globalization and the ascendancy of neoliberalism as the new disciplinary project for the capitalist world in its historical perspective, and explain this global transformation more fully.

Post-World War II reconstruction and capitalist expansion

World War II left only one of the major industrial economies intact, that of the United States. Not surprisingly therefore, the US's early dominance of the Western world was assured. Despite the eventual successful reconstruction of the German and Japanese economies under Marshall Plan directives, it would not be until the late 1960s that the US's hegemonic position came under challenge. The 1950s was a decade of growth, expansion and social progress for the advanced capitalist economies of the Global North, and even the peripheral states of the Global South received some of the benefits of the world's economic expansion. Of course, the 1950s decade was not without its social divisions (racism, class warfare, ethnic strife), nor without warfare (civil wars, communist insurgencies, military dictatorships), nor without geopolitical tensions (rise of the Cold War and hard-line East–West relationships). Generally, however, national economies expanded, decolonialization got under way, and nation-states and nationalism consolidated sovereign identities, while building their institutional capacities.

The postwar reconstruction of war-torn infrastructures and economic systems was to be partnered by "development and modernization" of the less developed world, with President Roosevelt setting the tone and delivering the message for First World assistance to be disbursed to the underdeveloped Third World (Sachs 1992). The Marshall Plan rebuilt Western European capacities and a similar initiative rebuilt Japan under US occupation, while the USSR assumed political control over the partitioned Eastern European countries to form a communist trading bloc. Rapidly growing to become a global "superpower" in terms of its military capabilities and industrial/technological advances, the Soviet Union supported socialist and communist regimes in these satellites, and imposed Soviet-style, central-state economic programs to rapidly develop and exploit resource bases, build industrial capacity, and develop state farming with the express purpose of providing cheap food for their urban industrial workforces.

The late 1940s and 1950s witnessed the creation of several "global institutions," many of which would eventually serve the causes of globalization and neoliberalism from the 1980s onward. The Bretton Woods agreements undertaken by the Western Allies in 1944 saw to the creation of the International Monetary Fund (IMF) and the International Bank of Reconstruction and Development (IBRD) – which would later "morph" into the World Bank – and both were designed to be progressive financial institutions. IBRD would lend capital for reconstruction and development, while the IMF was a short-term loan facility to enable indebted countries to smooth over temporary balance of payments problems. In 1948, after attempts to create a third Bretton Woods institution, the International Trade Organization failed, 50 countries signed on to the first "provisional" General Agreement on Tariffs and Trade (GATT), which began what would become a "50 years and counting" project for greater levels of trade liberalization.

Geopolitical rivalries accelerated in this postwar rebuilding period, however, prompting the Cold War and a hardening of East–West political positions. This led to the emergence of the communist block of core and satellite countries – the Soviet Union, Poland, Hungary, Czechoslovakia, Yugoslavia, Romania, Bulgaria – the consolidation of the Western alliance between the United States and her West European allies, and an arms race between the two superpowers and their allies. Nuclear weaponry was developed and stockpiled as the superpowers sought to outplay each other in building these weapons of mass destruction as an effective deterrent against each other's "first strike" capabilities. Accompanying this military escalation was a space race, with technological advances in space exploration pitting the two superpowers, America and Russia, in races to be first – first man in space, first orbiting satellite, first man on the moon, etc.

The world was geopolitically and economically split into East and West market systems; the two very much in conflict with each other, as both exported their development models, their modernization messages, and their geopolitical "influences" on the world stage to bring new post-colonial states into their respective capitalist or socialist spheres of influence. China turned to Maoism as its communist ideology and centralized government system, and India was instrumental in forging a Non-Aligned Movement among post-colonial states that sought independence and neutrality from the Cold War camps.

Such were the hardened ideological currents behind the Cold War that dictators were as commonly supported by Western governments, as much as centralized authoritarian regimes were encouraged by the communist/Soviet block. Social democracy was often compromised, with legitimately elected premiers and presidents overthrown by interventions, subversive activities, even assassinations on behalf of "freedom," or to reassert Marxist/Leninist "discipline." The Soviet Union invaded Hungary in 1956, then Czechoslovakia in 1968, when popular uprisings threatened to destabilize these countries' communist regimes. President Lyndon Johnston sent troops into the Dominican Republic to counter the election of a left-leaning premier. Haiti's corrupt Duvalier regimes, Papa Doc and Baby

Doc, were actively supported by US administrations because of their avowed opposition to communism. Fidel Castro's communist regime in Cuba became a symbol of confrontation between the two superpowers in the US's "backyard," with the missile crisis of 1961, and the brinkmanship politics of the Castro regime being equally opposed by hard-line positions from successive US administrations, from President Kennedy to today.

The increased military involvement of the United States in Southeast Asia, the escalation of the Vietnam War into a fully-fledged military engagement, the repercussions of conscription (the draft) domestically and among the youth of the country, not to mention the body-bags returning from this distant conflict, and the student "anti-war" protests, eventually took their toll on the US's geopolitical Cold War policies. US hegemony was under challenge, and suffering such a humiliating military defeat in this theater of war led to fundamental soul-searching among the American people about their government's geopolitical policies. Domestic upheavals concerning the basic civil rights of black Americans in the 1960s only increased the disquiet about the directions of US government policies at home and abroad. Global geopolitical considerations were to take a back seat to domestic and internal considerations. Then, to make matters more complicated, and difficult, the economic growth that had bestowed benefits on most of the country's people also slowed. Significantly, by the early 1970s inflation rates were increasing throughout the Western economies – in Europe, Japan and the USA – production outstripped consumption, world commodity prices dropped and the next crisis of capitalism was imminent.

Mid-1970s crisis

The crisis of the mid-1970s was brought on by changes in domestic economic policies, by changes wrought by governments – singularly and in cartels – and through decisions made by state leaders at the scale of the nation-state. More fundamentally, the economic and social contradictions of advanced capitalism's expansion, which had built up through this latest era of "mature, industrial-monopoly capitalism" since World War II, began to assert themselves as the "good times" of the "swinging sixties" came to an end. However, it was international events and international affairs that brought the crisis to a head, and helped bring this long wave of capitalist expansion to its "recessional" conclusion. There was "an unusual bunching of unfortunate disturbances" in the financial and production sectors. There was the collapse of Keynesian stability – the bankruptcy of New York City in 1973 being one indicator of this. There was the unraveling of the 1948 Bretton Woods currency agreement of fixed exchange rates when, in response to the burgeoning trading of euro-dollars, President Nixon took the US dollar off the gold standard in 1971 and major currencies became speculative commodities. In the major Core countries, inflationary pressures, government overspending, high taxation rates, continued high military budgets, and general downturns in consumer confidence were some of the main features of this long wave's stagnation. Keynesianism – especially its imperative for state intervention in economic matters

– was discredited. Finally, two OPEC-driven oil price hikes in 1974–5 and again in 1978–9 effectively raised the price of a barrel of oil eight-fold, dramatically raising energy costs and contributing to widespread indebtedness.

A much more select and powerful institution, the Group of Seven (now G-8 with Russia as its newest member), had its roots in the 1974–5 oil crisis and its reverberations that threatened the economic health of the richest Western countries. In 1975, the heads of state of six major industrialized democracies – France, West Germany, Italy, Japan, the United Kingdom and the United States – agreed to an annual meeting organized under a rotating presidency, forming what was dubbed the Group of Six (G-6). The following year it became the G-7 when Canada joined, and President Clinton would then invite Russia to join in 1998 to form today's G-8. Another business-friendly global institution, the World Economic Forum, or "Davos Symposium," was incorporated as a foundation in 1971, based in Geneva and under the supervision of the Swiss Federal Government, with the patronage of the Commission of the European Communities, as well as the encouragement of Europe's industry associations. From the start, the World Economic Forum fostered advanced capitalism's goals for economic expansion, political stability and wealth creation as its rationale and agenda. From 1982 onwards, the World Economic Forum's annual summit in Davos became a regular platform for world leaders and the international corporate business world to meet and forge international and regional capitalist coalitions to further the neoliberal cause, and advance public–private partnership notions, export-oriented industrialization and technological and logistical efficiency (*Wall Street Journal* 2003).

The role of the Chicago School of Monetarists, especially the "economic-evangelism" of the likes of leading supply-side economists Friedrich von Hayek and Milton Friedman, cannot be left out of the discussion, far from it! Both were vehemently opposed to socialism, dismissive of Keynesianism, against organized labor to the core, and passionate "true believers" in the power of the free market, the unfettered power of the capitalist entrepreneurial spirit, and the individual's right to economic wealth creation. As monetarist gurus, these neoliberal thinkers and ideologues provided conservative leaders like Margaret Thatcher and Ronald Reagan with a new economic model that promised renewed and rekindled economic expansion, wealth creation, public sector efficiencies, private sector enhancement, deregulation, and state withdrawal from burdensome welfare responsibilities. It also stressed the need for the disempowerment of organized labor so that wages could be brought under control; in every way – a right-wing political Nirvana! In addition, as Susan George (1999: 2–3) so insightfully observed:

> Starting from a tiny embryo at the University of Chicago with the philosopher–economist Friedrich von Hayek and his students like Milton Friedman at its nucleus, the neoliberals and their funders have created a huge international network of foundations, institutes, research centers, publications, scholars, writers and public relations hacks to develop, package and push their ideas and doctrine relentlessly. ... So, from a small, unpopular sect with virtually no influence, neoliberalism has become the major world religion with its

dogmatic doctrine, its priesthood, its law-giving institutions and perhaps most important of all, its hell for heathen and sinners who dare to contest the revealed truth.

Three groups of major players in the major Core economies of the Global North were the public and private institutions involved either in attempting to react to this looming economic crisis, or were actively seeking ways to avoid bankruptcy and financial default; namely, state governments, banks and corporate industry. All designed strategies or paths that led to international solutions, or policies designed to diversify their economic plans to embrace international or global solutions. National industrial corporations looked beyond domestic fields of opportunity to forge multinational or transnational linkages. Banks, no longer content to invest solely in domestic ventures, expanded their loan portfolios into international markets. Governments concerned with bloated budgets and declining revenues turned to supply-side economics to rationalize their roll-back of welfare services, and Keynesian solutions of state intervention were cast aside in favor of neoliberal formulas – free-marketeering, privatization, deregulation.

Globalization's emergence in the late 1970s and 1980s decade

Internationalization of capital

Faced with falling rates of profit, industrial corporations were forced to "automate, emigrate or evaporate" (Thrift 1983). There was a massive divestment of capital in dated manufacturing plants in the older industrial regions of Britain, the USA, Germany, Belgium and France, and considerable restructuring of methods of mass-production to follow Japanese or Volvo-style restructuring of industrial organization – from the mass-production model of Henry Ford, with its hierarchical Taylorist operational structure, to the just-in-time "flexible" model of customized production lines of Toyota, Honda or Toshiba. A New International Division of Labor (NIDL) emerged as an outcome of this era's global industrial restructuring, in which global core and periphery production relationships and capital–labor relationships were comprehensively reconfigured. Drawing upon the insights of Sayer and Walker (1992), Frobel *et al.* (1980) and Massey (1984), Wright summarizes the changes in NIDL:

> A process of vertical uncoupling, subdivision and/or sub-contracting of production results in the periphery developing low-skilled, standardized operations such as manufacturing assembly and routine date entry, while the global core retains high-skilled knowledge- and technology-intensive industries and occupations. Through deskilling labor, and the functional and physical separation of various tasks in the corporation, this process creates "roles" for places in the world economy.
>
> Wright (2002: 73)

(Much more on this industrial restructuring of the world's production systems is provided in the part on globalization's macroeconomic spaces, in Chapters 3, 4 and 5.)

There were major changes in the origins and destinations of foreign direct investment (FDI), from the patterns of the 1970s. Private and public capital that had flowed freely from the Global North to the Global South, from US banks to South America, or from European banks to their previous colonial territories in Africa and Asia, now was more likely to be redirected to flow between Global North/Core economies. For example, more British private capital flowed into the US economy than was invested in the island's domestic sectors in the early 1980s. Japanese capital flowed into the US also. European capital circulated within that common market's boundaries. In short, while Latin American countries were especially hard hit by a debt crisis and capital shortage, the flows of private capital in the 1980s largely avoided what now appeared to be risky markets. Latin American governments were forced to appeal to the IMF for financial help to pay their loans, and in return were obligated to agree to a set of restrictive "conditionalities" which imposed neoliberal economic reforms.

There was the internationalization of finance, with many of the major banks expanding their operations into international fields. For example, two of the largest US banks at the time, Chase-Manhattan and City Bank, belatedly emulated the colonial strategies of such London-based banks as Barclays, Lloyds and Midland Bank and expanded their reach to deal in foreign markets. European and Japanese banks, as well as investing in their own expanding realms, also invested heavily in some of the newly industrializing countries (NICs), such as Spain, Korea, Taiwan, Malaysia and Indonesia. There was the internationalization of domestic currencies and the trading of such uncontrolled hard currencies as the euro-dollar, and the internationalization of capital trading markets, with the integration of the world's stock markets, which accelerated capital circulation as well as thrust stock and fund investment considerations to the fore of corporate decision-making.

International finance not only reinvented itself, but it changed its character under deregulation. Its authority grew with its global reach, and the accompanying growth of global accounting giants who served the interests of their corporate partners with the management of their portfolios, their capital transfers and the like effectively centralized global financial power, providing oligarchic alliances that promised security to international capital interests, but less accountability to nation-states and state legislative authority. Thrift (1998) has demonstrated very persuasively the ways in which the international business and finance communities have come to practice institutional and managerial knowledge-based, self-regulatory authority, where their claims for caring and sharing, accountability and transparency, are in reality dubious covers for pursuing their shared interests in capital accumulation, profit and wealth creation. Data management and manipulation, corporate-controlled "science" and R&D, as well as fraudulent financial accounting practices, find their way into this interconnected morass of academics and public/private sector assessment institutions. "Soft capitalism" is his label for this deceptive and increasingly self-serving, global enterprise.

Internationalization of the state

With Keynesian economic solutions discredited, state governments adopted supply-side economic policies in which they sought to derive efficiencies in service delivery and efficiencies in government expenditures. Major leaders such as Margaret Thatcher of Britain and President Ronald Reagan promoted these more right-wing agendas, and under their administrations these global Core countries restructured, adopted more center-right policies, and attempted to thoroughly discredit the left, with its social democratic ideals of equality, of labor rights. Privatization of public services was on the Thatcher agenda in Britain, and a sell-off of government industries and services was accomplished. In the US, union power was aggressively challenged, the public provision of health and welfare services was rolled back, deregulation of industries continued apace, and state responsibilities were substantially redefined.

There were state–capital alliances in national trading policies controlling commodity flows, and a dual package of protectionism *plus* enabling packages helped (and subsidized) US and international corporate business immensely. There were state negotiations in international spheres in which the economic and commercial interests of multinational and transnational corporations were as often as not defined in terms of national interests. The era saw the genesis and growth of business and commerce forums in which international agreements were organized and finalized, sometimes quite openly and shamelessly conducted in "smoked-filled rooms."

There were also, however, more open and democratic global debates on peoples' issues, on human rights, the global environment, on the plight of children, etc. As a foil to the aforementioned business and commerce forums, the United Nations was a wider forum. The Non-Aligned movement was a place where alternative viewpoints could be expressed and shared. The International Labor Organization, the International Red Cross, and the many UN agencies sought to provide guidelines for the equitable treatment of people, regardless of their material well-being or state power. Importantly, the many non-governmental organizations (NGOs) that had grown internationally also served as supranational platforms for progressive action and activism.

New international division of labor (NIDL)

International labor markets became the opportunity fields for industrial corporations seeking efficiencies on labor costs, flexibility in production systems and diversification in plant investments. Transportation costs no longer were defining limits to production location decisions. Global production systems were established that spanned continents and the beneficiaries appeared to be the consumers of the major Core societies who experienced increased choice of commodities, increased internationalization of sources of food, clothing and consumer durables, while cost of these commodities remained relatively low. In peripheral states offering low-wage regimes, export-oriented industrial production as *the* development strategy was not only promoted and subsidized but was "forced" upon countries as the only capitalist path to take by IMF austerity measures and World Bank conditionalities, and by government aid agencies, such as the US Agency for International Development (USAID), or Britain's Ministry of Overseas Development (ODM). Europe, North America, Japan and the emerging NICs of the Pacific Rim – South Korea, Taiwan, Malaysia and Indonesia – also were the target consumer markets for these international commodities. "Emerging markets" was to be their metaphorical label.

Another dimension of the restructuring of the international division of labor was the growing volume of the international migration of "skilled" workers as well as of "unskilled" labor. With manufacturing reorganized internationally, there was also the rise of a new international services economic sector, with producer services also seeking low-wage regimes. Eventually, an interrelated set of international financial, producer and information technology services surfaced as a relatively unregulated global industrial ensemble. Global production systems diversified, they spread geographically, and logistics delivery systems – and their centralized (and merged) corporations – were restructured to meet the growing demands of global commerce. National boundaries no longer defined the economic landscapes of commerce, and even hemispheric trade regions – such as NAFTA, MERCOSUR and CARICOM – were opened up to global players, global corporation penetration and foreign/external commercial influences.

Contradictory tendencies in the 1990s and the twenty-first century downturn

Neoliberalism as an ideological, right-wing discourse and narrative and as an unchallenged model of economic efficiency and capitalist enterprise prevailed through the 1980s and into the 1990s, as the globalization era came of age. Blind faith in the market was preached with a religious fervour that resonated well in the USA (Cox 1999). In this now sole-remaining superpower (with the geopolitical demise of the USSR and its break-up), the Clinton administration's embracing of neoliberalism appeared to be a resounding political economic success. His Democratic administration's move to the center-right in ideological terms and the resultant 1990s economic boom and unprecedented growth of "American-style capitalism" were trumpeted as triumphs. Other capitalist models' performances in this boom decade – European and East Asian – paled by comparison. The emerging markets of the Global South had only to follow America's lead, to participate in the fruits of globalization.

The seven-and-a-half-year marathon of the Uruguay round of talks on General Agreements on Tariffs and Trade (GATT) – started in 1986 and concluded in 1994 – brought about the biggest "liberal" reform of the world's trading system since this international trade-negotiating institution was created at the end of World War II (actually in 1948). It also called for the establishment of a World Trade Organization as its successor to manage the growing multilateral world trade system, and the WTO was formally established the following year, in 1995. As the world's largest Core economy, albeit restructuring from its manufacturing base to a services-based economy, the US neoliberal "express" was expected to reap healthy profits from this global free-trade initiative, and so it did. The North American Free Trade Agreement (NAFTA) promised to bring high returns to Mexico as well as the US and Canada, but time would tell otherwise for the poorer people "south of the border." The 1990s, for many in the US, were good. Job creation was appreciable, inflation was kept in check by Alan Greenspan's policies at the Fed, economic expansion in many productive sectors received the benefits of technological innovations and logistics development, and a "culture of contentment" appeared to embrace the society (Galbraith 1992). Given the "globalization boom" under way, there was even speculation that the US, with the rest of the world following suit, could look to a "new economic future" in which stock prices would continue to soar, incomes would also continue to rise, and the capitalist world would no longer need to worry about a downturn in this never-ending business cycle (Stiglitz 2003).

Then in the early 2000s came the first of several huge corporate bankruptcy scandals, with the Enron scandal leading the way. Not only did rampant malfeasance abound among the executives and accounting managers of this energy conglomerate, the rhetoric of Enron's corrupt CEOs and the amoral defense of their contemptible corporate practices were exposed as a lethal mixture of religiosity and selfishness (*Le Monde* 2002). The list of other corporate miscreants who followed Enron into the disgrace of bankruptcy, stock and share price crashes, Security and Exchange Commission investigations into criminal accounting procedures etc. demonstrates there was a culture of arrogance, greed and dishonesty that had become "normal business practice" in the corporate America of the 1990s – Qwest, Tyco International, Adelphia Communications, Global Crossing, and WorldCom. Even among the "Big Five" international accounting firms that were supposed to be the regulatory environment for corporate America, one – Arthur Anderson LLP – was firmly implicated in the Enron cover-up, and is now no more (NEF 2002). Corporate abuses of power, corrupt practices, CEO scandals, stock-market insider-trading and the like might have been exposed by investigative vigilance, but the rapid centralization of corporate wealth and power, and the accumulation of more and more capital in the hands of fewer and fewer capitalists, continues unabated (DeLong 1998; Mokhiber 2004; Mokhiber and Weissmann 2004; Ransom 1994).

Through the 1990s, ultra-conservative and conservative/right-wing political ideologies dominated socialist and left-wing platforms, and very much determined national political scenes in Europe, Asia and Latin America. The political spectrum in these "economic democracies" continued to swing to the right of center, in large part because the elite class of leaders, government heads, technocrat supporters and neoliberal modernists in the Global South's "emerging markets" as well as the Global North's Core economies all chased the promise that economic growth and expansion would come from privatization, export-oriented industrialization, technology transfers and opening their protected landscapes to natural resource extraction.

Center-left administrations prevailed in Europe up to the turn of the millennium, with Blair's New Labour government being a characteristic archetype of this revisionist, centrist political platform, which embraced neoliberalism and globalization's commercial and industrial visions, but continued to embrace socialist agendas in their domestic policy frameworks. This was further typecast (and identified) as a "Third Way," hybrid social–democratic option; a new middle-ground of political negotiation in which left-wing, domestic social welfare agendas could be pursued, while the right-wing tenets of globalization and neoliberalism could be embraced in matters of free marketeering, economic growth and revenue accumulation and private–public partnerships in the efficient management of public services (Kiely 2005). By 2003, however, only Blair's government in the UK had survived, with social democratic parties being replaced in Italy, Norway, Denmark and the Netherlands, by another political swing of the European pendulum to the center-right (Watkins 2004).

In Asia, the end of the 1990s saw the burst of the bubble in many countries – with the exception of China and India. The dramatic termination of that region's economic "miracle" in countries such as Indonesia, Korea and Thailand in 1998–9 also witnessed the overturning of autocratic regimes that had been partners to the rapid economic expansion of export-oriented industrial growth and domestic capital's adventurism. Neoliberal capitalism, however, was not discredited, but rather this late-nineties crisis was interpreted, either as a problem of external interference, of the domestic banking sector's malfeasance, of government corrupt practices and inefficiencies, and other internally generated, management failures. Only in South America has there been an appreciable swing to the left of center in political ideologies of sitting governments and their democratic supporters – in Brazil, Venezuela, Uruguay and Bolivia – by the early part of the twenty-first century. Right-wing and center-right governments and administrations continue to be in the majority whether in the global core or global periphery, as the solidarity of international socialism is under severe challenge and organized labor no longer enjoys its former political power and international strength (Herod 2002).

The IMF, the WTO and the World Bank (though to a lesser degree) did their part in this "pact with the neoliberal devil," by continuing to impose their agendas of "conditionalities" and "structural adjustment programs" on the indebted governments in the Global South, and continued to promote the opening-up of countries to more free trade and corporate penetration. This disciplinary rigidity never wavered, despite the outcries of a more forceful and internationally coordinated civil society's campaign for global justice and social justice for the world's oppressed and impoverished, and despite their arguments for strengthening social democracy and providing social safety nets for all, not only the materially wealthy (Danaher 1994; Jubilee 2000). Even as global institution after global institution called for more free trade and more market openness, the self-serving regimes of the Core nations – the G-8, the European Union and the USA – continued to practice government subsidization, impose discretionary protective tariffs, and maintain unfair, "unfree" rules of commerce and trade. The WTO increasingly became an arbiter of US–EU "battles" over subsidies, in which the losing side invariably managed to negotiate itself out of strict compliance, with this arbitration rarely changing the domestic situation in these Core countries' governmental support for its protected, or highly subsidized, industries/agricultural sectors/airplane producers/luxury exports, among others.

Then, in the latter half of the decade – starting in 1997 and rapidly growing into a full-blown financial crisis in the early months of 1998 – what was supposed to be a never-ending neoliberal capitalist "boom" received its first "shock therapy" with the East Asian "meltdown." Like dominos, first Thailand, then Indonesia, Malaysia and Korea, saw international financial capital withdrawn at such a pace that their national economies collapsed one after the other. Further capital flight, government paralysis (except in the case of Malaysia) and widespread bankruptcy in the domestic financial and industrial sectors of these exposed economies followed, with the IMF unable to intervene sufficiently to stem the hemorrhaging. Japan's financial sector, as the holder of much of the debt in these shell-shocked economies, also took a major hit during this "meltdown" and Japan's efforts to rebound from its economy's already sluggish levels of expansion in the 1990s suffered a major setback, driving it into a recession within a couple of months. Across the world, the Russian economic restructuring project was also hit by mass capital flight, and the ensuing stock market volatility reverberated to seriously affect several Latin American countries' financial stability – namely, Argentina, Ecuador and Brazil. Global bickering between US, European and Japanese financiers over fiscal solutions to this poorly predicted yet devastating crisis for the working people in these afflicted societies characterized the multipolar tensions between the three major contenders' capitalist models, and brought into the light the fragility and unpredictability of the new world (dis)order that globalization has fostered.

The Uruguay GATT round of negotiations eventually forged general agreement on international trade liberalization for a multitude of commodities. This gave the "undemocratic" World Trade Organization (run by member state designates) a global legitimacy it wielded on behalf of the privileged and powerful. Transnational corporations and client Global North administrations working in partnership more often than not got used to WTO decisions going their way, when the opening up of Global South territories for resource extraction was at issue, or when these latter nations' protectionist policies over basic food products hindered external penetration, or disadvantaged North-to-South export opportunities. Its global authority, however, came under challenge in Seattle in 1999, when its annual meeting was disrupted and pilloried by activist momentum in the "Battle for Seattle," and nothing came of the Doha meeting of the WTO in 2001, in large part because of leadership squabbles. It was then dealt an even more severe blow in Cancun in 2003, when internal differences and hardened positions on many sides over agricultural commodity subsidies, among other protected industries of the Global North, caused the meeting to disband in disarray. Unlike the IMF and the World Bank, its Bretton Woods partners of long ago, the WTO has not maintained the same degree of disciplinary authority over trade dispute resolution, as the former two US-based institutions have wielded over international financial matters; and in particular, over indebtedness and debt-repayment mandates. The IMF has been especially unyielding and particularly harsh and dogmatic in its resistance to international calls for debt forgiveness, thereby demonstrating an ideological firmness worthy of von Hayekian's blessing, if it wasn't so blind-sighted in its neoliberal rigidity!

Concluding musings: bringing cities into the picture, among other "global-to-local" geographies of neoliberalism

Neoliberalism's "makeovers"

Neoliberalism's disciplinary severity as well as its policy agendas has undergone transformation, in large part because of its contingent, interactional relations within and between its predecessor's institutional landscapes, local and regional contexts and public–private power configurations. From a relatively abstract macroeconomic doctrine, which Thatcher and Reagan administrations embraced as a substitute for Keynesian statist policies, neoliberalism "morphed" into Blair, Clinton and Schroeder's "Third Way" of socially moderate policy formulation and center-right, market-guided regulation in the 1990s (Kiely 2005), only to further evolve and move more drastically in the US to a neoconservative genre dogmatically practiced and promoted by George W. Bush in the twenty-first century. Peck and Tickell (2002) quite perceptively note that these transformations of neoliberalism in the advanced industrial economies of North America and Europe from the 1970s to present constitute path-dependent adjustments which are significantly constrained in scope and trajectory because of place-based, well-established institutional arrangements.

After all, as a capitalist model of accumulation for accumulation's sake and of uneven/unequal social impacts, this reconstitution of neoliberal strategies, and their attendant repositioned ideological platforms, are evolving responses to their own disruptive, dysfunctional sociopolitical effects. Neoliberalism is both rooted in its predecessor's contradictions, as well as a producer of its own contradictions, crises and dysfunctionalities. Neoliberalism is also place-based and place-contingent, so that *where* its policy agendas unfold is as important as *when* and *how*. Brenner and Theodore (2002a), for example, examine the "geographies of actual existing neoliberalism," arguing persuasively that neoliberalism's influences are manifesting themselves in the entrepreneurialism of city management and the resultant sociospatial restructuring of metropolitan North America and Europe. This topic is revisited in Chapter 8, where urban entrepreneurialism and geoeconomic competitiveness are conceptualized both in geopolitical terms as well as an integral part of the global neoliberal project (Kiely 2005). Here, the section that follows summarizes the urban face of neoliberalism's global-to-local unevenness, competitiveness and social divisiveness.

"Global-to-local" spaces of neoliberalism

This chapter's charting of the ascendancy of neoliberalism, as the underlying dogma and macroeconomic calculus behind this most recent transformative phase of global capitalism's evolution, has primarily focused on the structural and agency interactions at the national (nation-state) and international (supranational) scales. There are, of course, other complexes of political economic/ecological interactions and interactive processes among and between scales, from the global to the local, and among and between locations, places and spaces (Swyngedouw 1997) – to wit, "global-to-local" geographies of neoliberalism. Importantly, scale, "spaces" and "places" are contested, defined and redefined in geographically diverse ways. Influential global processes such as neoliberalism cascade through interlinked hierarchies and networks, within and between city systems, within formal and informal transnational networks and between societies.

As a result, we should expect contemporary neoliberal constructions of space, place and scale to be always in states of flux and continually being "structured and restructured" by global, national and local social forces which are always contradictory, often conflictual and capable of being resisted or contested from below by "locals." Indeed, "transnational urbanism" is the metaphor coined by Michael Peter Smith (2001: 67) to "reconfigure 'the city' from a global phenomenon to a fluid site of contested social relations of meaning and power." In Smith's case, he is referring to transnational social practices of immigrant communities, local grassroots political maneuvering, informal networks of economic activity among transnational communities, street-spaces, and the whole gamut of peoples' resistance actions, which contest the restructuring of their urban life-spaces by the formal public and private institutional authorities and the dominant and dominating global forces of neoliberal capitalism – economic, sociocultural and geopolitical "structuration" processes. This topic is taken up later in Chapter 14, where "globalization from below" is debated and detailed.

Although this chapter has focused on the political economic restructuring and institution-building of the neoliberal capitalist project, it should never be forgotten that new imperialistic agendas of domination and subservience have been "essential" (though scarcely welcomed) accompaniments to the global transformation that has occurred (Harvey 2003b). Most alarmingly, the new imperialist agendas of the Global North "Triad" – the public–private partnerships of client governments and their corporate and financial elites in the US, Europe and Japan – and their promotions of neoliberal modernization, neoliberal free-trade marketeering and global corporate capitalist enterprise, have all too often been accompanied by *neoliberal militarism* (Amin 2003; Choudry 2003).

Pre-emptive military interventions, pre-emptive wars, war-mongering, saber-rattling and verbal threats of retribution, gunboat diplomacy, and declarative utterances of hegemonic power's response to national peoples' challenges – "interventional actions," "contra-fighters," "wars on drugs," the "war on terror" and "in defense of national security" – have taken on added meanings since the

1980s. Much more on this theme is forthcoming in Chapter 11. Neoliberalism's ascendancy and globalization's emergence and consolidation was, and is, the sociohistorical path that has led us to our present state of global crisis; its unacceptable levels of social inequality, of poverty and social insecurity, and its lack of comprehensive healthcare delivery systems, its lack of gainful employment opportunities, and its lack of social responsibility for the powerless, the needy – the "losers."

Part II
Globalization's many dimensions

Globalization's macroeconomic faces

3 Global financial architecture transitions

Mutations through "roll-back" neoliberalism to technocratic fixes

Adam Tickell

Introduction

Over the past 40 years, a complex series of interlinked policy decisions and economic circumstances has led us to the point where the health (or problems) of the global economy rely more and more upon the stability (or instability) of the financial sector. Furthermore, as was so evident in the 1998 fears for the global economy at the time of the Asian crisis (Wade 1998, 2000; Wade and Veneroso 1998; Fitzgerald 1999; Eichengreen 1999; Noble and Ravenhill 2000), or the collapse of key institutions such as Long Term Capital Management or Barings Bank (Tickell 1996, 1999, 2001; Mackenzie 2000; Edwards 1999; de Goede 2001), an (infectious) crisis in one part of the international financial system is highly contagious. As financial markets and financial institutions have become more interlinked, and more international in reach, so too have their influences on national economies. The financial sector has become *intellectually influential* too, in large part because the conservative ideological persuasion of its practitioners blends so comfortably with capitalism's ideologies of market power and dominance (Cox 1999). For example, advocates of (the neoliberal variant of) globalization have argued that the liquidity and efficiency gains from unrestricted financial markets pave the way to a liberal globalized future of unlimited promise (Bryan and Farrell 1996).

This chapter explores the recent history of international finance. The degree of policy convergence among the developed countries of the Global North is more acute than in any other economic sector and the degree of harmonization is on an upward curve. In most accounts of this regulatory harmonization the roles of formal, inter-governmental organizations and agreements in promulgating regulatory reform and policy change are emphasized, to reflect the current geopolitical and economic realities of globalization. As argued below, the decision of the IMF to develop a financial stability monitoring capability of the landmark Basel capital adequacy accords, for example, demonstrates the extent to which the simple ideologically inscripted wave of "roll-back" neoliberal deregulation (Peck and Tickell 2002) has transmogrified into a more technocratic regime that privileges "what works." Furthermore, the key institutions and agreements of the international financial regime possess both key discursive (and decision-making) powers and also, in their interactions with recipient nation-states, a brutal economic structural power (Pauly 1997, Taylor 1997, Rugman 1999).

Unfortunately, or unpromisingly, an undue emphasis on the behaviour and decision-making of core institutions of the financial architecture only gives us a partial explanation of the processes of international policy change and interaction. Claims about the development of global financial regulation, which stress the loss of state power in the face of financial market deregulation, are problematic (Walker 1999a; Jessop 1997, 1999; Cerny 1997, 1998a,b). I also have problems with economic analyses that propose construction of a simple, technocratically rational financial architecture. Instead, I argue that – in tandem with broader changes in neoliberalism – today's financial architecture might be coming technocratically more effective, while at the same time being open to "soft-capitalist" influences from the private sector to an enormous degree (Thrift 1998).

The globalization of finance

It was not until the nineteenth century that international banks became a permanent feature in national and international economic affairs. From the 1830s onwards there was a growth in the international representation of British banks, primarily in British colonies, in order to provide funds for imperial development (Jones 1990; Gardener and Molyneux 1990). During this period there was intense competition for international financial supremacy. London and Paris vied with each other for superiority as the leading European/international financial center (Morgenstern 1959; Kindleberger 1974, 1984).

Then, for a short while after World War I, the USA became the principal source of capital in the world, with US "money center" banks expanding their operations into Europe (Huertas 1990). However, these banks were hit by large defaults on overseas loans and by the collapse of both financial institutions and confidence in their domestic market during the 1930s Depression. Accordingly, US banks went into retreat, heralding "an era of extreme conservatism in international banking. ... a long period of quiescence" (Gardener and Molyneux 1990: 129).

After World War II, the capitalist world economy came to be (re)directed by the Bretton Woods framework. In 1944, negotiators for the "Allies" met at Bretton Woods to map out the postwar architecture of trade and finance with explicit aims to provide a stable and relatively equitable system that would help insure international political stability. The negotiators, Harry Dexter White for the US and John Maynard Keynes for the UK, agreed to develop a tripartite international system based upon the International Monetary Fund (to provide short-term funding), the World Bank (to provide longer-term funding) and the International Trade Organization (to regulate trade relationships). The ITO was rejected by the US Congress, however, so the Bretton Woods negotiators created a framework for financial regulation and determination which was overwhelmingly oriented around the primacy of national institutions and national regulatory instruments.

Governments retained effective control over their interest rates *and* exchange rates. (Today, governments can usually control either interest rates or exchange rates, but not both.) Critically, too, in this pre-1970s national regulatory environment, governments maintained strict controls over the activities of financial institutions.

Until the early 1960s, finance remained *largely* confined within the borders of the nation-state: in 1960 there were only 202 foreign affiliates of OECD-headquartered banks (Dicken 1992a). However, during the 1960s the banking industry was transformed from one with few multinational banks into a fully internationalized sector. During this decade, finance moved to become a truly international, and subsequently global, pillar of the world economy. The internationalization of banking was stimulated particularly by the rapid growth of the Eurocurrency markets during the 1960s. These markets first appeared in the late 1950s when the USSR feared that its dollar-denominated assets were vulnerable to US political control. To escape American regulatory jurisdiction, the USSR and its satellite COMECON countries moved their dollar accounts to banks in London and Switzerland, so that before long these (extra-national) "Euro-dollars" had become a competitive global currency. Bankers in general soon became aware that London-based dollar balances were free not only of American political control, but also of US domestic banking laws which stipulated minimum reserve balances and interest controls (Rabino 1984; Strange 1986; Lewis and Davis 1987).

The regulatory authorities in London developed a lax attitude towards the growing Eurocurrency markets, which grew from US$11 billion in 1965 to US$661 billion in 1981 (Stafford 1992). Eurocurrency markets, therefore, developed an "offshore" status, because they were regulated neither by the host country nor the Bretton Woods' currency rates of exchange mechanisms. In the discourse of liberal and neoliberal economic thinking this development was regarded as a positive move, because it restored freedom and market-objectivity to the financial sector.

From the late 1960s onwards, international banks became involved in trade finance, in servicing their domestic customers overseas, in retail banking, in complex derivatives markets and, most recently, in the processing of information in off-shore back-offices. During the 1960s the surge in international activity of banks mostly involved US money center institutions – Bank of America, Citibank, Chase Manhattan, for example – opening up branches both to operate in the Euromarkets and to serve multinational clients who had, in the aftermath of World War II, indulged in an enormous growth of overseas manufacturing investment (Sassen 1991; Dicken 2002). During the 1970s, smaller US regional banks internationalized as a response to slackening growth, regulatory restrictions and credit ceilings in their domestic markets. Furthermore, as Germain has argued, we need to be aware that these internationalization activities are exporting more than US institutional architectures, but US capitalist mores: "economic expertise, social norms and cultural habits are transmitted by the investing firm which tie the recipient economies into the broader social totality out of which the investment has come" (Germain 1997: 82).

The following decade – the 1970s – saw the start of a fundamental political and economic sea-change. Supporting, or defending, the integrity of the national economy and decision-making on behalf of a collective national interest was being challenged ideologically, and undermined experientially, by relative economic decline. In short, the Keynesian social democratic political platform was withering in the face of neoliberal political critiques (Desai 1994; Peck and Tickell 2002; Tickell and Peck 2003). Change in approach to international finance in the United States was perhaps the most significant outcome of this global sea-change. Within the US, the New York Stock Exchange tore up many of its regulatory controls in 1975 in what turned out to be a successful attempt to increase its share of American financial transactions. While it is too simplistic to point to this moment as leading to the dominance of finance in the US economy (on which, see Krippner 2003), it certainly was an appropriate symbolic achievement and singular signal of intent, heralding the arrival of neoliberal capitalist priorities that have since increasingly dominated the global economy, both intellectually and methodologically.

In the face of an international "threat" from the London Euromarkets, and the domestic "threat" of an enlivened deregulating stock market, the large American banks lobbied Congress heavily to persuade the Federal Reserve Board to remove their regulatory "burden" (Helleiner 1994; Hawley 1984). By the early 1980s, two key pieces of legislation that reduced bank regulation and supervision were introduced as a consequence. The two proved to be key moments in the recent history of international finance because they demonstrated that powerful financial institutions could exercise considerable power over the regulatory authorities. More importantly, these deregulatory "moments" contributed to a wave of regulatory reform in international finance across the capitalist world (Helleiner 1994; Tickell 1999).

Furthermore, while some nations were reluctant to embrace neoliberalization of finance, most were unable to resist it completely for a number of reasons, including: (i) the emergence of new financial products and a renewed economic and discursive centrality for the financial sector; (ii) developments in computing and communications technologies which enabled the almost instantaneous transmission of money between financial centers; (iii) the emergence of truly transnational financial conglomerates; (iv) the virtual disappearance of capital controls; (v) the blurring of long-standing boundaries between different types of financial firms (Group of Thirty 1997; Eatwell and Taylor 2000; Hills *et al.* 1999);[1] and (vi) the neoliberalization of international organizations.

For the Global South, the brutal medicine imposed by the IMF's "structural adjustment programs" imposed a harsh disciplinary logic of accountability to privatization's penetration. For such "emerging markets," free capital markets and flows were a *sine qua non* for access to the vast reserves in the capital markets, while the US used its uniquely-strong bargaining power to make access to international bodies conditional upon market liberalization (Kristof and Sanger 1999; Wade 2001). At the same time, Core countries (and their financial institutions) utilized the ossification of regional trade blocs to their mutual advantage, because their increasingly internalizing neoliberal logics allowed (the former's) penetration and dominance by the back door (Brenner and Theodore 2002; Tickell and Peck 2002).[2]

Increased risk in international finance

In the euphoria that accompanied the 1990s "boom," the aforementioned financial liberalization processes appeared to be phenomenally successful. Stock markets boomed and the rich capitalist countries enjoyed a period of such sustained economic growth that some commentators began to speculate that the age-old laws of a "boom–bust" economic cycle had been overcome (Bootle 1996; see also Woodward 2000). It appeared to be so "triumphant" because international finance had become the dominant driver of the contemporary capitalist world economy (Krippner 2003; Germain 1997).

While financial markets across the capitalist world liberalized during the 1980s and 1990s, the "success story" was not without its contradictory counterpoint. In particular, the peculiarly risk-laden nature of finance meant that the theoretical limitations of neoliberal deregulation would be experienced and learned by central bankers earlier than in other arenas (cf. Wacquant 2000; Peck 2001; Brenner and Theodore 2002; Peck and Tickell 2002; Tickell and Peck 2002). The resultant interconnectivity of global financial markets, for example, meant that local perturbations were being rapidly transmitted throughout the world; witness, the case of successive bursts in the bubble economies of East and Southeast Asia in late 1997 and again in 1998. A "domino effect" ensued when shares on the Hong Kong stock market collapsed, precipitating large falls in all the world's stock exchanges and stimulating fears of a global financial meltdown (Noble and Ravenhill 2000).

Equally troubling, deregulation led to a series of fundamental changes to the structure of international finance that have exacerbated the levels of systemic risk in the international financial system. First, there has been the emergence of large, integrated financial conglomerates with highly complex financial and corporate structures that are anything but transparent, or accountable. One of the contributory factors in the collapse of Barings Bank, for example, was the lack of clarity in the reporting lines engendered by the complex nature of the bank's corporate structure (Board of Banking Supervision 1995; Ministry of Finance 1995). Second, an increasing share of international financial transactions is dominated by a small number of merged institutions – mostly headquartered in G-8 countries – which have the geographical networks, specialist knowledge and technological expertise to command market power and manage internal risk. Furthermore, the trend is towards greater institutional concentration via mergers or buyouts, as the costs of running an integrated global presence (in terms of technology and labor costs) squeeze out smaller participants. Such concentration contributes to instability because if one of the dominant institutions gets into difficulty the contagion effect is likely to be more serious than in a more diverse, competitive market.

These, apparently unavoidable, increases in systemic risk eventually stimulated some modest growth in international cooperation over global financial regulation. Under the auspices of the Bank for International Settlements (BIS), central bank supervisors came to an agreement about where the ultimate responsibility for international banks lay under the Basel Concordat of 1975 (Kapstein 1998; Helleiner 1994; Roberts 1998; Fratianni and Pattison 2001). More importantly, concern that the quality of bank assets had deteriorated as a result of liberalization and the developing country debt crisis led the UK and US governments to draw up proposals for banks to hold proportions of their reserves in less risky investments (the so-called minimum capital adequacy standards). And, since the global cities of London and New York are home to the bulk of international financial activity, the two countries were able to use the BIS to normalize these minimum standards in the 1987 Basel Accord (BIS 1997) which, according to Kapstein (1991, 1994), became the "cornerstone of a new regulatory order."

On the other hand, it is important not to overestimate the (regulatory) functionality of the 1987 Accord (subsequently known as Basel I). First, it only came about because two of the key nation states in international finance – the US and the UK – were able to impose an agreement on standards on which there was little international consensus, and whose detailed architecture reflected the specific geo-economic interests of their own particular financial institutions, not necessarily the global system writ large. Second, Basel I was very much the regulatory analogue of roll-back neoliberalism, underwriting the "pro-market" nature of international regulatory cooperation (Kroszner 1999). It is a supervisory regime that embodies a broadly neoliberal assessment of how governments *can* intervene in an era of financial openness and also how they *should* intervene. The Basel I regime accepts as axiomatic, however, that in an era of open financial markets, regulatory arbitrage pretty much insures that unilateral intervention is unlikely to be effective. Third, Basel I introduced a "one-size-fits-all" regime which was crudely geographically discriminatory, because banks had to set aside capital equivalent to 100 percent of their exposure to non-OECD governments, while trade with OECD governments was judged to be risk-free. According to King (2000), this Core state bias was very much implicated in the conditions that led to the Asian "melt-down" of 1998.[3]

Structural "reality-checks" in the international financial sector during the latter part of the 1990 decade led to greater international cooperation in financial regulation as attempts were made to strengthen its resilience against unpredictable shocks of capital flight (Kenen 2000; Crockett 2001). The threats to the integrity of the global financial system engendered by the events at Barings and the Asian financial "melt-down" in 1998 truly shook the mantra/faith of neoliberal economists. By the end of 1998, the builders of the international disorder were falling all over themselves with calls for a "new architecture for the international financial system" (see, for example, Greenspan [Chair of the US Federal Reserve Board] 1998; Michel Camdessus [Managing Director of the IMF] 1998; Robert Rubin [US Treasury Secretary] 1998).

Yet it is important to understand that there is an imbalance in the new financial architecture. Whilst the response to the so-called national fiscal crises in Mexico, Southeast Asia's Thailand, Indonesia, and Malaysia, and East Asia's Korea was swift and profound, the response to the institutional crises at Barings, Long Term Capital Management and so on was, I would argue, far more desultory. For the markets outside North America and the European Union, a reorientation of their financial infrastructures along Western lines was required. Financial supervisors would be trained to emulate Anglo-American practice; accounting practices, codes of financial supervision, insurance conventions, stock market oversight and so on all apparently needed fundamental reorganization and harmonization according to Western criteria (see, for example, Clark *et al.* 2001, 2002). Critically, the IMF and the World Bank underwrote this restructuring imperative with their Financial Sector Assessment Program (FSAP) and the Report on the Observation of Standards and Codes (ROSC). Although non-observance with the codes carries no formal sanctions, the FSAP and ROSC programs serve as powerful disciplinary procedures because non-compliance chokes off access to international capital markets and, potentially, to the resources of the IMF and the World Bank.

At the same time, when collapses of English and American *institutions* have the capacity to undermine financial stability, central bank supervisors – Greenspan among others – counsel cautionary measures, if any, and argue instead that regulation should allow greater variability depending on the risk-weighting of an institution. Furthermore, where there might appear to be room for a wider and more inclusive debate among stakeholders about the future shape of the global regulatory environment of finance, this is not the reality. It is in fact a "closed shop," conducted within and between North America, Europe and Australasia (but most commonly between and within the US and the UK). Years of critiques by development charities about the functioning of the IMF has had little effect. Neoliberal premises are not to be challenged, or their basic philosophies reframed. Instead, neoliberal "solutions" to the systems' excesses and fractures were to be the guiding principles of any reform (Hills *et al.* 1999).

Yet, there are important tactical shifts in (de)regulatory policy-making under way. Unlike the overtly politicized moves towards neoliberal deregulation in the 1980s, the broad parameters of the emergent ruling regime in finance are in many ways anti-ideological, emphasizing *technocratic* solutions to sophisticated and complex problems in three main ways. First, national regulators have built upon the experience of cooperation with agreements to share information about banks with large exposures in order to gain a global picture of firms' activities. At a minimum, such cooperation should insure that, if banks are honest in their reporting, supervisors are aware of any potential problems before they arise. Implicit in regulatory cooperation is that regulators should eventually begin to harmonize their approaches, in much the same way as the capital adequacy accord led to a *de facto* norm (Clark *et al.* 2001).

Second, supervisors are increasingly emphasizing risk management systems (see, for example, BIS and IOSCO 1995; BIS 2001). This approach attempts to quantify all the risks held by a financial institution in order to assess the net value of the firm's exposure that would be jeopardized in the event of credit, liquidity or market problems. In the current proposals to replace the Basel I accord with new capital standards, banks with lower risk portfolios will be able to set aside less capital, whereas higher risk portfolios will be penalized (BIS 2001). Third, the financial markets and private actors play an increasing role in policing financial institutions as firms need to disclose pertinent information.

There is, then, an imbalance in the new financial architecture of the twenty-first century. The explanation for this is partly institutional: the international regulatory procedures for national currency crises are located in the framework of large intergovernmental institutions such as the IMF and World Bank as well as smaller more exclusive bodies such as the OECD and the G-8 group. On the financial industry side, markets are regulated on a national basis with international policy and standards developed through the various committees of the Bank for International Settlements (BIS) and the International Organization of Securities Commissions (IOSCO): agencies that have very little power to enforce measures. The work done through these organizations develops international agreements on standards that are then enforced by national regulators. So, on the one hand, the regulation of the monetary system is framed through inter-governmental agencies, while on the other, in the banking system, the architecture is developed through quasi-governmental agencies.

Although institutional capacity matters, so does ideology. The *form* of neoliberalism might have undergone change and mutations (even if many neoliberal economists appear in denial), but the persistence of beliefs and practice of policies which accept unquestionably that markets are the most effective resource-allocation mechanisms is deeply embedded in the international financial sector's architecture. Unquestioned is the conviction that the private sector is better able to efficiently deliver social outcomes than the public sector. Globalization is viewed as unchallengeable, and (horror of horrors?) "micro-economic rationality [is] the validating criterion for all aspects of social life" (van der Pijl 1998, 2001). All are testament to the endurance of the ideology (Peck and Tickell 2002) and its "faith-based" creed (Cox 1998).

This new mutant form of neoliberalism, in addition, raises questions about the behavior of the state in the regulation of finance. I agree with political economic analyses that the transformation of international and national financial markets during the 1980s diminished the power and authority of the state. Emphatically (or unfortunately), faced with the globalization of finance, nation-states lost their nerve and responded by reducing the regulatory "burden" on financial firms. However, these analyses (particularly Helleiner 1996) are careful to stress that since these processes were enabled by the state they may also be undone through concerted state action. I would argue, also, that there is a tendency for scholarship to unwittingly "naturalize" the evisceration of state power (for parallel arguments, see Dicken *et al.* 1997; Piven 1995; Peck and Tickell 2002).

More importantly, the globalization of finance occurred along with two other key geopolitical changes. First, during the 1980s and into the 1990s there *was* an effective *reduction* in many forms of financial regulation (alongside a bureaucratization of other forms). Of equal importance was the emergence of a technocratic re-regulation, as embodied in the Basel I capital accord, or as represented by the frequent meetings between the regulators and finance ministers to share information and ward off crises (Mansfield *et al.* 2001). Second, as nation-states saw financial markets grow in size, global reach and autonomy beyond national boundaries, they lost vital elements of their rhetorical authority over national financial management, and more and more looked to private sector actors to provide legitimization for their financial actions and policies.

Conclusions

I have argued in this chapter that, as neoliberalism in general has mutated, so too have neoliberal approaches to international financial regulation. Neoliberalism has become more deeply embedded in international (de)regulatory frameworks through the expanded disciplinary role of the IMF and with the transformation of the GATT into the World Trade Organization in 1995.[4] It is also important to recognize that the contemporary form of neoliberalism appears to be mutating to mitigate some of the excesses of roll-back neoliberalism. The neoliberalization of international finance, for example, brought on the series of financial crises of the late 1990s – Barings, the Asian melt-down, Ecuador's default. While the specificities of each crisis differed, their common parentage was clearly apparent. The liberalization of financial markets and loosening of regulation stimulated and permitted increasingly risky trading (sometimes, but by no means always, this was legally dubious as well). Financial regulators and supervisors were unable (and sometimes unwilling) to adequately police this trading; and the onset of adverse "external" circumstances contributed to the potential for a system-wide crisis in the entire financial system (Eatwell and Taylor 2000).

In this examination of financial globalization, I have explained how the new architecture of international finance is a response to the "illogics of roll-back neoliberalism." Although it is early days in the design of this revised architecture, two key features are already apparent: (i) while it is a response to the contradictions of roll-back neoliberalization of finance, the new architecture actively extends and deepens the role of the market in regulation (with an enhanced role for "market discipline"); and (ii) countries with financial structures dissimilar to the Anglo-American model are encouraged to converge to these norms via both potentially strong policing (via the IMF/ World Bank's Financial Sector Assessment Program) and the setting of internationally agreed standards and codes (Tickell 2000). Thus, the financial system of a country as economically powerful and politically robust as Germany is adopting US accounting standards and reducing pension entitlements in the face of pressure from the capital markets (Clark 2000; Clark et al. 2001; Toporowski 2000). In none of these changes is there any restructuring or "re-imagination" which might undermine the supremacy of financial markets and bring national accounts back to being accountable to people's productivity and creativity. Nor is there any movement to reduce the power of financial centers, or even reduce the influence of uttering of governors of central banks and to return the regulatory authority and power of financial systems to nation-states. Finance is being used, like other economic tools, to discipline errant governments, while it privileges the insiders – the Euro-American/G-8 brotherhood of "fixers" (Thrift 1987).

Always remember, first, that technocratic management embodies neoliberalized rationalities which are themselves ideologically constructed. Second, technocratic management becomes a dominant mechanism in political and economic regimes and sectors where the technocratic framers – public and private "entrepreneurs" – share the same ideological beliefs. And, third, that technocratic managerialism may have been successful at managing meso-level crises because these have not tested the limits of the system.

By privileging non-state authority, the international finance policy community has internalized an assessment of the difficulties of reining in the markets and their belief in the desirability and rationality of efficient markets, and concluded that strong regulation is impossible. Ultimately, however, the "worth" of neo-liberalized regulation should not be judged solely on the basis of its economic rationalities and effectiveness. Regulation is a means to achieve geopolitical and geo-economic outcomes (whether these are explicitly recognized or not). While financial stability is more than just a desirable outcome (without financial stability other outcomes are impossible), it should never be the *sole* desired outcome.

Notes

1 For example, in the UK until the 1980s banks, building societies, insurance companies, stockbrokers and so on all occupied specific niches and did not tend to compete out of sector (in some cases this was prescribed by law). After a raft of regulatory reforms and cultural shifts the UK has developed a model where firms operate in all these markets (e.g. Moran 1990; see also Tickell 2000 on Canada).

2 For example, one former Reagan White House staffer explained in an interview with me that:

> At the same time, you had the European single market program ... and this picked up on many of the ideas ... actually it was a deregulation program under the guise of regulatory harmonization. Once again there was little evidence to support [the logic of deregulation], but I suspect these people got their ideas from the US and the UK and things spread quickly. *So Europe had basically one of the most powerful deregulation programs in the world and didn't know it.*
>
> (interviewed November 2000 by Adam Tickell)

3 Thus Turkish government debt carried no risk, but lending to the Singaporean government was deemed to be highly risky (e.g. White 1996; Fratianni and Pattison 2001).

4 As Mark Rupert (2000: 49) has argued, one effect of this is that:

> Even as people in locations around the globe are increasingly integrated into – and affected by – transnational social relations, neoliberalism seeks to remove these relations from the public sphere – where they might be subjected to the norms of democratic governance – and subject them to the power of capital as expressed through the discipline of the market.

4 Multi-local global corporations
New reach – same core locations

Susan M. Walcott

Introduction

This chapter examines the development of global economic forces within corporations in the late twentieth century and the political–economic consequences of their increasingly global integration. As the spatial scale of firms' economic activity expands to encompass the globe, the roles of other political economic actors (communities, states, and even nations) seem to diminish. The strategies of corporations increasingly reflect the prospects of their stock value, which in turn impact the wealth and health of nations. Geopolitical colonization and neocolonialism has been replaced (though not completely) by geo-economic interdependency; substantial "economic clout" still resides in the most advanced countries, with emerging developing nations – China, Indonesia and India, for example – competing to perform more routine, low-cost and lower-order manufacturing and producer service tasks.

This chapter discusses first the interpenetrating scales of geo-economic relationships (nation-states, location of corporate headquarters in developed countries, global capital and flows to specific sites within less developed areas), and defines the major components of this new global structure. It then looks at how the new international economic order (NIEO) plays out globally, with case studies in Asia and Africa. The high-technology sector in China, and the role of global capital fueling the economic development of that country, provides pertinent examples contrasted briefly with India's development pattern. The following section examines corporate power consolidation and the major actors involved: the formerly all-powerful nation-state, the rapidly ascendant stock market representing global capital, and the cross-cutting effect of global business organizations representing self-regulatory authority.

Overview

A concern with "what firms do, where they do it, why they do it, why they are allowed to do it, and how they organize the doing of it across different geographic scales" (Henderson *et al.* 2002: 5) is a cross-disciplinary subject involving politics, economics and business as well as its geographic domains. Emergence of the transnational (or "*multi-local*") corporation in the late twentieth century constitutes an indisputably important force; only its implications remain controversial (Dicken 2000). Geography focuses on the importance of the location of economic activity, examining elements rooted in the context of a particular place (micro-scale firm level) as well as transnational operational factors such as the exchanges of technology and information vital to corporate well-being. The increased importance of information projection across globe-spanning distances arguably creates international "flows through place" of information (Dicken 2000). The degree to which a local place is part of this information exchange constitutes the "space of place" in what has been termed the new *space of flows* (Castells 1996), thereby prioritizing particular areas of value creation. Although mega-corporations are credited for creating the spaces they inhabit (Schoenberger 2000), forcing localities to construct factors suitable for global corporations to inhabit if they wish to attract these powerful job-creating entities, place-based contingencies constrict or accelerate widely dispersed networks of communication and transactions (Sheppard 2001). A later section examines these corporate considerations and their geographic implications in more detail.

National significance redefined

National characteristics attach to firms primarily based on their headquarters, and secondarily based on their operational location(s). This observation confirms the continuing importance of geographic characteristics, as well as the relevance of general economic theory and management variations for each firm. The availability of products via the worldwide web makes the market more global (Wrigley 2000), but increases the search for local places of unique advantage in order to secure a competitive advantage or niche for production and supply factors. A ranking of "Fortune 500" corporations indicates the retained importance of Global North/ developed world headquarters sites, the ascendancy of a few new locations, and the related importance of technology as a profit generator (Table 4.1). When ranked further by profitability, the predominance of the United States as a headquarters location in the most highly profitable industrial sectors becomes even clearer, particularly in the financial and computer areas for mega-corporations (Table 4.2).

The well-established attractiveness of *clustering* in local *agglomerations* with firms in similar fields and their related suppliers (Porter 1990, 2000) now reflects global ties. Firms interacting in *production chains* around the world are compelled to follow the major customer firm wherever it sees a locational advantage anywhere in the world. Car manufacturers from many countries, for example, can be seen with their related suppliers and new local connections throughout the midwestern and southeastern United States, coastal China, Mexico, and Europe. Porter's (1990) informative diamond graphic of factor and demand conditions supporting global and locally competing industries functions in innumerable widely scattered locations. The four major points in this *"diamond"* consist of: (i) a suitably trained workforce, (ii) a profitable home market sustaining global expansion, (iii) competitively affordable suppliers with reliable quality, undergirded by a trust-based relationship and rapid information exchange aided by locational proximity,

Multi-local global corporations 51

Table 4.1 Top 500 global companies by country

Country	Number of companies	Rank	Country	Number of companies	Rank
United States	198	1	Belgium	4	15
Japan	87	2	Brazil	4	15
France	37	3	Finland	2	17
Britain	35	4	Luxembourg	2	17
Germany	35	4	Mexico	2	17
Canada	16	6	Norway	2	17
South Korea	12	7	Russia	2	17
China	11	8	Taiwan	2	17
Switzerland	11	8	Denmark	1	23
Netherlands	9	10	India	1	23
Italy	8	11	Malaysia	1	23
Australia	6	12	Singapore	1	23
Spain	5	13	Venezuela	1	23
Sweden	5	13			

Source: Calculated based on www.fortune.com

Notes
(a) Belgium and the Netherlands own the same company: Fortis. (b) Britain and the Netherlands own both Royal Dutch/Shell Group and Unilever NV/ Unilever PLC.

Table 4.2 Industries by country and average profit ($US million)

Industry	Average profit	Number of companies	Number from US
Diversified financials	6847.67	6	6
Computer software	4953.50	2	2
Pharmaceuticals	3786.31	13	8
Tobacco	3436.33	3	1
Petroleum refining	2761.15	26	8
Securities	1914.75	4	4
Food consumer products	1725.40	5	2
Chemicals	1717.17	6	4
Beverages	1651.67	6	4
Household personal products	1534.25	4	2
Gas and electric utilities	1086.47	19	7
Banks: commercial/savings	911.19	62	10
Computer office equipment	693.22	9	6
Computer and data services	853.50	2	2
Energy	804.88	17	12
Totals		184	78

Source: Calculated from www.fortune.com

and (iv) domestic competition among similar firms honing their competitive advantage to a world class level. (More coverage of this restructuring process is provided in Chapter 5.)

Each decade since the 1960s has witnessed an ever larger and broader accumulation of corporate power and decreasing ability (in many cases a decreasing desire) of political intermediaries such as nation-state governments to intervene in this process of power accumulation. International competition instead has become an ongoing scramble to attract "a piece of the action" by becoming a location for international capital or foreign direct investment (FDI). Corporate consolidation along both *vertical* axes (production functions within the firm) and *horizontal* axes (with suppliers) increased its pace at a global scale in the 1970s with the expansion of companies to global production sites – primarily in order to take advantage of low wage rates and more lax production (and environmental) regulations in other countries (Warf 2000). In the next decade, corporate executive administration consolidated via mergers, buyouts – with the occasional unfriendly "takeover" in the mix – to form larger transnational companies, seeking economies in a trimmer institutional management model and leaner governance structures.

The restructuring also led to more powerful corporate entities at a broader global scale, with a focused mission on profit maximization often at odds with local and national political authorities. Post-Fordist *"flexible production"* arrangements permitted high geographic mobility of production sites, leading to the rampant outsourcing of work and domestic job loss in traditional "industrial heartlands" such as the US MidWest. The 1990s saw the rise of *"multi-local"* corporations, permitting cost savings by hiring more local management and relying on a corresponding competitive sensitivity to local market conditions. Deeper penetration of local labor and commodity markets became possible due to better human networks built with local powers and better understanding of production and market conditions within each country. Closer ties to the local political situation encouraged competition for special privileges from the local elite, setting up a complex internal dynamic that continues to play out on a multinational scale (Dunning 1993). The competition over securing closer ties to local political authorities brought instances of corporate bribery, public–private partnerships to promote business interests in overseas markets and the imperative for companies large and small to engage in international ventures and seek opportunities in overseas markets.

Three major challenges

The rapid growth of corporate globalization's capital worth, both individually and collectively, poses challenges in three major respects:

1   Who benefits from this restructuring of economic relations, at whose expense, and where are the players located in relation to each other?
2   How sustainable is this situation, in light of historical experiences, resource utilization, and the shift of power from political to economic actors?
3   The roles and increasing powers of Core-country political regimes, internal and external business elites, development agencies and consultants in relation to the power and functions of nations and non-economic elites, via internationalization of suppliers, production, promotion and markets, need to be considered.

These shifts come about through the transition toward privatization of formerly public service functions to global firms through sale of the provision contract and existing facilities. Additionally, the drive to raise financial capital through global stock market participation increases the short-term pressures and instabilities of a stock market-driven international economy. The following sections explore the effects of these contestations in major economic sectors and regions of the developing world.

Corporate globalization impacts on economic sectors

Global corporations exert their self-serving, profit-maximizing influences in the three main economic sectors of *primary* (natural resource extractive), *secondary* (manufacturing), and *tertiary* (services) activities. The ways in which such non-local power functions with deleterious local consequences varies by product and location and is examined in the following subsections.

Primary extractive activities

The fate of countries with commercially attractive natural resource endowments, whether in the Global North/First-World or Global South/Third-World, fluctuates in boom and bust cycles, that increasingly channel profits into foreign corporate hands. This "*resource curse*" occurs in stages as a market opens and increases for the fixed location resource, which first channels investment in the new and inflationary commodity (Hanink 2000). More sustainable economic investments suffer in comparison, and long-term investments are made in anticipation of long-term revenues, which often fail to develop as forecast. Workers retain simple extractive skills, or immigrants are employed to do the basic tasks.

A *technological treadmill* develops to hold down costs through advancing production and distribution technologies. The search for new resources to exploit, at greater amounts and cheaper costs, leads to a global shift of sites at a pace more rapid than expected. Because they control the R&D side of the production process, the profit-creating technology invariably remains in the hands of the First World-based corporations, who also arrange for the transportation and marketing (Hotz-Hart 2000). The costs of thwarted development, and over-extended credit, remain with the penetrated and still impoverished resource supplying nations, with local communities particularly hard hit. Specific examples can be found in various industries, from lumber in Canada, South America, and Southeast Asia, to oil in Nigeria and Mexico.

Secondary manufacturing activities

The operation and effect of global commodity chains display a recurring picture played out across the world, involving the manufacture in Global South developing world countries of various low-cost high-demand items principally for First World markets (Gereffi *et al.* 1994). Arrangements are made by First World corporate giants and executed by globally situated branches or often subcontractors, frequently of a different national affiliation from either maker or purchaser, to *outsource* work done less profitably in the headquarter country. Due to its global network and its pre-eminence as the American high-demand athletic footwear producer, the Nike shoe corporation served as an examination target for several studies (a good read is Wright and Austen 1993).

Focusing on the whole series of steps and relationships involved in the manufacture of a product, referred to as a *commodity chain*, heightens an appreciation for the global range of these operations – and the unequal distribution of power and benefits among countries on the periphery, semiperiphery, and core of the world economy. The linked effect also demonstrates the complex and reinforcing interplay between local culture, business culture and competitive pressure for technological upgrades that act to perpetuate the unequal power and geographic relationship along the commodity chain. Indeed, Nike sees itself as primarily "marketers and designers" (Korzeniewicz 1993: 159), outsourcing the highly competitive (and less savory) manufacturing piece through a global network in shifting locations. Nike rose to prominence by mastering a fitness marketing strategy in the 1970s and 1980s, and accompanying arrangements with retail outlets to feature its products.

Since the 1960s, manufacturing shifted offshore to the Pacific Rim newly industrializing "tiger" economies (NIEs) of Japan, Taiwan and South Korea. As these countries profited and gained experience through broad participation in the global economic network, they in turn moved production facilities further offshore, subcontracting under their own nationally affiliated companies to even lower-wage countries on the Asia–Pacific periphery – such as China and Indonesia. Labor in these factories often consisted of marginal populations migrating from impoverished rural areas to peri-urban towns in outlying urban development rings.

Tertiary services

The global reach and growing importance of international financing operations and information technology attract the attention of numerous studies examining the expansion and restructuring of corporate globalization. The production and logistic technologies which have been crucial bases of the functions of the range of services so vital to the operation of modern industries were invented in First World countries. These R&D industrial ensembles (including contracted university research institutes) employ a preponderance of highly paid workers in these countries, and underwrite the globalization of corporate activities (Reddy 2000; Warf 2000). Internet operations have in turn permitted the outsourcing of *producer services*, back-office and secretarial functions to second-tier countries such as Ireland and India, where there are relatively lower-paid native English-speaking populations conversant with business practices in the more developed countries of the Global North-Europe and North America in particular.

The concentration of highest order activities in global cities such as New York and London has correspondingly increased, along with the geographic diffusion of second-order supporting activities through tertiary operation chains in far-flung global locations (see Chapter 8 for more detail of the diverse roles of global cities). A new hierarchy of global corporate activities is thus created, with relationships built on logistical attributes such as language and training facilities rather than as a response to distance-costs. The geographic legacy of colonial conquest networks is reasserted in new value-added respects, as profits flow even faster and in greater volume to traditional headquarters locations in this new geopolitical information-systems reordering process. While the highest value-added function of innovative knowledge is kept in the more highly developed headquarter location (US, Europe, Taiwan), lower-order more routine maintenance, service and manufacturing functions are redeployed to locations with lower labor costs (China, India). The amount of total FDI in China in a typical benchmark year is displayed in Figure 4.1. Clearly, global capital is primarily attracted to, and enriches, pre-existing advantaged locations. The following section provides some illustrative examples of this process currently at work in corresponding global locations.

Global case studies

The effects – contradictory in social cost–benefit terms – of corporate globalization fall particularly heavily on newly developing countries attempting the precarious climb from dependency to being more fully fledged players in the global economy. This section examines the situation in two regions of the world where the local political structure currently struggles to utilize its economy as a development engine for attaining self-sufficiency and asserting a role on the world stage. The difficulties – in the face of oft-vaunted opportunities – posed by the structure of corporate globalization appear more clearly when examining specific national cases.

Asia: China, India and Malaysia

The arena for global corporate profit-seeking penetration moved in the mid-1990s from offshore to more inland Asia–Pacific nation-states. As the newest "frontier," the effects continue to ripple inland, rearranging Chinese, Indian and Malaysian domestic locational fortunes. Premier Deng Xiaoping's proclamation that "to get rich is glorious," and corresponding "Opening and Reform" movement to make China more hospitable for foreign corporations, signaled a post-Mao sea-change. His successor Jiang Zemin's proclamation of "develop the West" attempted to lure foreign corporations such as Ford and Japanese auto makers to inner China, supplying jobs to stem the migratory flood to the cities of the east coast. Developing countries compete with struggling states in lagging regions to offer incentives for global corporations seeking low-cost production sites, trading in non-pecuniary interdependencies to create additional place-based advantages (Storper 1997).

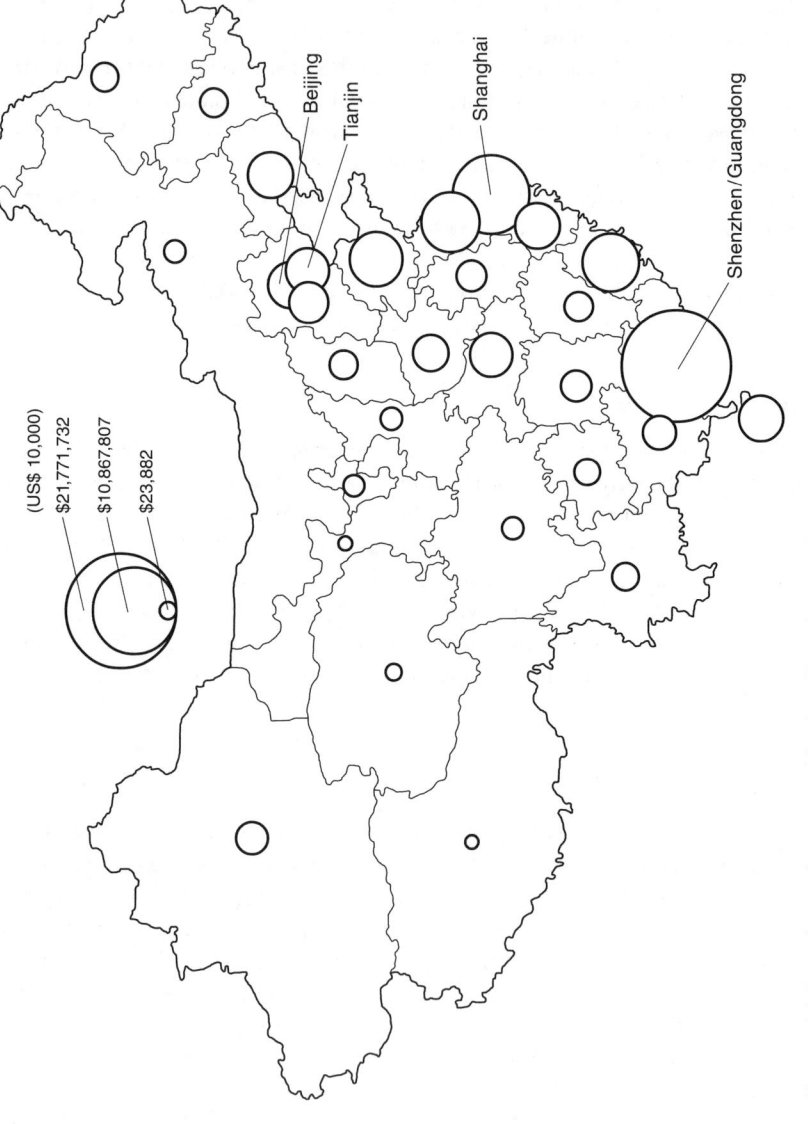

Figure 4.1 Location and amount of foreign direct investment in China

Source: *Chinese Statistical Yearbook 1998*

Mahathir's Malaysia entered "the game" by attracting global giants like Motorola to early industrial park islands of privileged production, by offering locational and industrial sector-targeted fiscal and physical infrastructure incentives. The relationship with foreign companies often begins through foreign direct investment and/or joint ventures with local companies, offering transitional learning opportunities for both. These frequently develop through a separation process to freestanding "wholly foreign-owned entities." In a newly established science and technology industrial park on the southeastern outskirts of Beijing, Motorola is developing its own park-within-a-park, clustering its global and local suppliers in close proximity to the main manufacturing facility (Walcott 2003).

In both countries, the relationship between advantage-granting locations and advantage-taking corporations threatens to flounder due in part to the failure for technology transfer to develop at the hoped-for pace, quality and quantity. Predictably, corporations keep their "cutting edge" competitive technology confined to the home country (suffering *reverse engineering* or intellectual property purloining, otherwise). A wary dance of mutual distrust and need ensues between foreign corporations and domestic producers, each angling for production advantage (Zhou 2005). A local overabundance of highly trained technicians often ends up underemployed at lower skilled tasks, or competing with even lower-wage locations such as in job-hungry India (Greider 2000). Both India and China began their high-tech globalization as players in the computer industry – "body shopping" utilization of transnational workers and satellite dish transactions via Bangalore in the former, through marketing and technology transfer from Peking University in the latter (Zhou 2005). The subsequent insertion of global capital created stark islands of affluence in both countries; in India the contrast with the common fate proved glaring enough to doom the re-election of the ruling party banking on "Shining India" pride. The nation-state retains the reins over global corporations in both countries, but their grip loosens with each entangling engagement (Box 4.1).

Box 4.1 China's science and technology industrial parks

China's experience with development led by the economic penetration of global capital began in the mid-1800s with the British takeover of Hong Kong (known by the name of Xiang Gang, in the national dialect, since its reversion to mainland Chinese control in 1997) as an island outpost at the mouth of the Pearl River delta (PRD). The cautiously gradual opening of China to foreign investment, as the supplier of desperately needed capital, formed a key component of Deng Xiaoping's "Opening and Reform" policy begun in the late 1970s. The initial "Special Economic Zones" (SEZ) cities offering specific areas with tax and regulations incentives for foreign investment were all in the PRD. Proclamation in 1984 of "Open Coastal Cities" along the south and eastern coast formed the next step widening the range for global capital. By 1990 the depositional land of Pudong to the east of Shanghai became a "Super SEZ" mecca for foreign corporations, cityscapes and capitalists, designed by a foreign team of city planners and boasting Shanghai's role of "Dragonhead of the Yangtze Delta" in the vanguard of China's modernization movement based on "other people's money." US investment in China's development is diverse as well as significant (Table 4.3).

Table 4.3 US foreign direct investment in China

Sector	Investment (US$ billion)	Percentage of total	Increase (1994–2000) (%)
Electrical equipment manufacturing	3.2	33.5	1,787
Petroleum	1.8	19.3	106
Financial services	1.1	11.6	179
Machinery manufacturing	0.93	9.7	–
Chemical manufacturing	0.24	2.6	11
Metals manufacturing	0.18	1.9	76
Food manufacturing	0.18	1.8	38
NEC manufacturing	0.77	8.0	252
Wholesale trade	0.36	3.8	168
Other	0.59	6.2	357
Totals	9.57	100	275

Source: US-CSRC 2002, based on US Bureau of Economic Analysis

Beginning in 1984, China's State Council approved the establishment of 54 "Economic and Technological Development Zones" (ETDZs) and 54 (ever-increasing in number) national-level "science and technology industrial parks" (STIPs). The latter specifically seek to leverage their location near to leading research universities in major cities throughout China to promote a blend of domestic research and highly trained labor and foreign manufacturing expertise to catapult China's modernization and high-level job growth. The government works through major universities to support both acquisition and generation of intellectual property in novel ways. In China only two basic sources of investment capital exist: foreign funds and the Chinese government. With the realization by China's leadership under Deng Xiaoping in the late 1970s that modernization meant globalization, economic efficiency demanded transitioning of the huge, financially unsound State Owned Enterprises (SOEs) to (hopefully) clusters of smaller, more enterprising and responsible companies. Foreign manufacturers, both as joint venture enterprises or (less common) wholly foreign-owned enterprises, were seen as providing jobs, investment funds and training for transitioning this period. The map of Chinese STIPs indicates the political considerations leading to distribution of these intended spatial development engines in each province, with some natural clumping near the major cities of Shanghai, Beijing and Hong Kong. The fall of the Soviet Union in 1990, and US military engagement that same year in Iraq, rekindled China's urge to rapidly modernize in order to self-strengthen economically and, as a consequence, militarily.

The current era characterized by globalization is only the latest stage in this political–economic positioning of corporate capital. Cities experience spatial reorganization to accommodate the demands of global corporations and their expatriate workers (similar to Shanghai's development of Pudong for this purpose). Similar experiences in global "gateway cities" reflect local historical experiences and embedded distinct cultural contexts. The differential strengths of these cities to wager with developed world corporations – and their own national elites – influence the outcome for their local workers and citizens (Drakakis-Smith 1996; Dicken and Malmberg 2001).

Roles of major political–economic actors

The ever-changing, uneven powers (and location) of key forces in the geography of corporate capitalism create a dynamic imbalance. Corporations seek to take advantage of locations where profit can be extracted due to a (however short-lived) advantage granted them in return for a potential tax benefit to the territorial power in which they are located. The cross-cutting role of corporations adds an additional dynamic and global scale to competition for political advantage, pitting local entities against each other as well as the interloper. This section examines the roles and influences of several major players in the ensuing scramble for (disorderly) capital accumulation.

Nation-states

Territorially distinct legal bodies set and control regulatory policies within their borders. They can also decide to delegate or subordinate some of these powers to other entities. Creation of regional bodies such as the European Union, North American Free Trade Area, and overarching arrangements such as the General Agreement on Tariffs and Trade, extend the territoriality of economic sanctions to a regional scale, thereby affecting economic entities such as corporations (Dicken 1992a, 1998). China asserts its control over foreign corporate location decisions within its borders by providing a narrow (or no) range of high-tech-industry park choices. Foreign capital locations constitute an extension of regional development policy, with parks scattered throughout the country offering incentives reflecting national policy (Figure 4.2).

The political influence of affluent businesses exerting pressure on legislative bodies to craft favorable agreements, either individually or as an industry, blurs in some countries what otherwise would appear as a case of contending national interest versus individual business interests. The entanglement of companies headquartered in one country with their corporate interest in doing business under favorable circumstances in another country also blunts the advocacy of national interests in the global corporate arena. On a topographically uneven playing field, nations appear to scramble for ever larger pieces of the profitable high-technology export pie represented in Figure 4.3. The point to keep in mind in this case concerns the fact that these figures represent business done by companies headquartered in

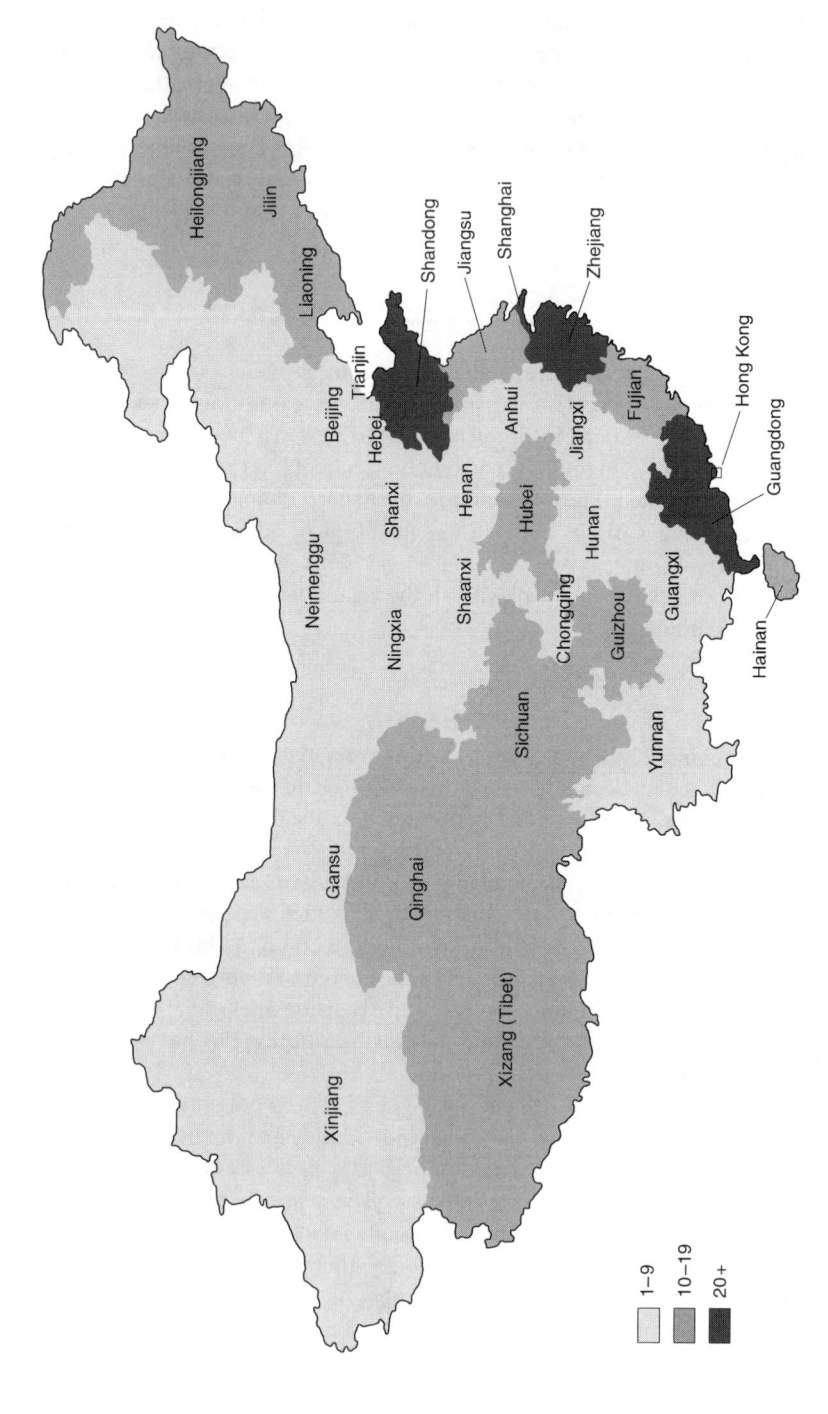

Figure 4.2 Location of national-level high- and new-technology parks in China

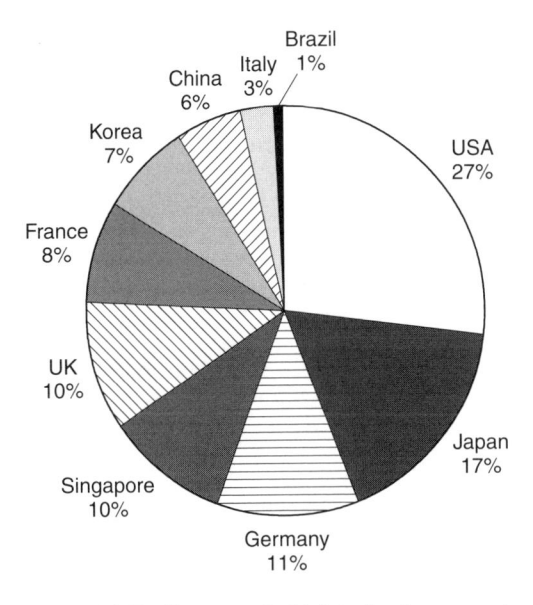

Figure 4.3 Profit centers for high-technology exports
Source: *China Statistics Yearbook on High Tech Industry* 2003

the indicated country – subsuming the strength of its global subsidiaries and tentacled connections at various stages of the production process.

Stock markets

Corporations raise vital working capital through the sale of their stock – pieces of the company that are owned by individuals and/or other separate entities. Two factors create crucial time-delimited considerations on the value of stock: the ability to trade any amount of stock at virtually any time, from anywhere, and the required quarterly reporting of earnings by public companies. Major stock exchanges are located in a globe-spanning overlap of time zones from New York to London and Paris, Shanghai, Hong Kong and Tokyo. The globalization of ownership, whereby an individual in one country can hold stock in companies headquartered in many different countries, increases the sensitivity of one market to fluctuations in another, given the relative attraction that generates selling in a descending value, less stable environment and purchases in a rising value, more stable market. Global connectivity thus increases susceptibility to a stampede effect, or avalanche of transactions across national markets, reflecting value relative to "predicted earnings" as well as actual corporate performance.

Business decisions that seek to improve profits, thus rewarding stockholders who often reap a designated percentage, are rewarded by an increase in stock value. Layoffs of workers, for example, meet with a predictable rise in value irrespective of the subsequent negative impact on human well-being or the increase in welfare rolls and tax burden. The business-oriented response of corporations to economic value fluctuations occurs irrespective of political or social considerations, with potentially strong cross-border as well as domestic national ramifications. Since annual compensation packages of top corporate officials such as chief executive officers and chief financial officers reflect the performance of company stock, market considerations of profitability, rather than longer range or more complicated strategy, frequently dictate corporate actions such as downsizing, mergers and acquisitions. The tail increasingly wags the dog.

Global business organizations

Perceptions of nation-states rendered less powerful in the face of resurgent world-spanning corporations, and the move to regional organizations often-as-not funded mainly by G-8 and other similarly wealthy countries, led to the establishment of many supporting organizations that were decidedly "business friendly," such as the Organization for Economic Co-operation and Development (OECD), the European Round Table of Industrialists, the World Business Council for Sustainable Development and the World Economic Forum. Executives from the boards of major global corporations were therefore able to communicate with each other, organize and lobby against government regulatory limits (which were believed to be costs to them) and join their supposed competitors in lobbying efforts to further their mutual interests. The cross-cutting of the agendas of these global and regional influence groups sometimes brought them into conflict with each other; but they invariably joined together to uphold common causes of furthering capitalist principles of accumulation and profit-generation, in the face of the agendas of global institutions such as the UN, or ILO or UNEP, whose responsibility was to safeguard social health, welfare and justice principles.

Corporate capital power

Corporate capital power now exceeds most national economies, except the largest European and US domestic accounts. The rise of global corporate power has been phenomenal. A recent report by Corporate Watch provides alarming signs of the growing concentration of capital and financial power in corporate institutions:

1. Of the 100 largest economies in the world, 51 are now global corporations, only 49 are nation-states. For example, Wal-Mart – the number 12 corporation – is bigger than 161 countries, including Israel, Poland and Greece, Toyota is bigger than Denmark, Ford is bigger than South Africa, and Philip Morris is larger than New Zealand while operating in 170 countries.
2. The combined sales of the world's Top 200 corporations are far greater than a quarter of the world's economic activity.
3. The Top 200 corporations' combined sales (over $7 trillion) are bigger than the combined economies of all countries, minus the biggest 9 – the

United States, Japan, Germany, France, Italy, the United Kingdom, Brazil, Canada and China; i.e. they surpass the combined economic wealth of 182 countries.

4   The Top 200 have almost twice the economic clout of the poorest four-fifths of humanity.

5   The Top 200 have been "net job-destroyers" in recent years, energetically "downsizing" their workforces as they merge, or consolidate, to enhance their CEOs' stock-options packages. Their combined global employment is only 18.8 million, which is less than a third of one one-hundredth of one percent of the world's people.

6   While downsizing and merging, fewer than half realize increased profits for their increases in corporate mixtures, but most CEOs on the other hand benefit substantially from mergers and acquisitions and the resultant stock-market effects.

7   Over half of the sales of the Top 200 are in just five economic sectors – trading, automobiles, banking and insurance, retailing and electronics. The concentrated economic power of a few firms in such sectors is enormous. For example, in the automobile industry the top five firms account for 60 percent of global sales; in electronics, the top five firms have garnered over half of global sales.

8   Access to global banking is scarcely equal, or just. The 31 banks in the Top 200 may have combined assets of $10 trillion and sales of more than $800 billion, but the majority of humankind – 4.8 out of the world's 5.6 billion – do not have access to these transnational financial coffers.

(Anderson and Cavanagh 2000)

Corporate reorganization of their manufacturing systems to "flexible regimes" has globalized the process and thereby undercut the power of labor, weakened the negotiating power of labor unions, as well as weakened or circumvented, the authority of political regulatory mechanisms. This is especially the case in the globalization of labor-intensive assembly where the deregulatory environments of EPZs and similar export-oriented manufacturing zones, such as Mexico's *maquiladores*, have led to dangerous working conditions, unregulated environmental regimes, and waged-labor exploitation (Fernandez-Kelly 1982).

Conclusion: summary of issues

The neoliberal disengagement of the nation-state from economic management in the 1980s paved the way in the following decade for new forms of regulation – such as global entities – rather than the supposed reassertion of market mechanisms. Free-trade agreements such as NATFA and GATT, and decisions favoring deregulated markets and the repeal of protective tariff structures by the World Trade Organization, supplant the old "Keynesian" Bretton Woods system. Global lending organizations such as the International Monetary Fund and World Bank impose rules of restructuring national and local economies from above, rather than responding to local exigencies and contexts (and Chapter 2 has explained how this "corporate-friendly" climate came about). The sub-global political economy – nation-states, regional groupings of states, even the last vestiges of European colonial empires – has become "hollowed out," as corporate-directed capital flits around the world, out of "old sites" and into new sites as comparative advantages occur, or are offered (by government subsidies, tax holidays and incentive packages).

Two key issues posed early in this chapter concerned the location of major beneficiaries and profit extraction sites in the new hierarchical reaches of global corporations. Subsequent examination revealed that the widened scale of linked world economic activity served also to concentrate power and wealth in the same core locations. Beyond the corporate centers in the Global North, areas of "comparative advantage" continue to be exploited further afield and further down the scales of national, regional and local market development, engaging local actors – local or urban governments – in a "race to the bottom" scramble to attract jobs. The sustainability of these arrangements, the second major issue raised, remains in doubt as old patterns are reasserted in different locations within global production chains.

The seeming deprioritization of location inherent in globalization's creation of world-wide commodity chains has nevertheless resulted in "agglomerative re-groupings" of regional and local corporate clusters of companies. These maintain a vital production relation to the anchoring firm, wherever in the world that key corporate component happens to be (Brown and McNaughton 2002). The drive for cost-minimization through decreasing the space needed for transactions to span – which is well documented from Marshallian theory and practice through the most recent centuries – reasserts itself, along with the continuing importance of local factors in a globalized corporate world.

5 Systems of production and international competitiveness
Prospects for the developing nations

Daniel C. Knudsen and Molly Kotlen

Introduction

The purpose of this chapter is to examine the problems of and prospects for developing countries to become technologically and industrially competitive in the current period of global capitalism. One economic reality in our globalizing world is that this "development" hinges on the international competitiveness of nations and regions. International competitiveness has been defined as: "The degree to which a nation can ... *produce* goods and services that meet the test of *international markets* while simultaneously *maintaining and expanding the real income of its citizens*" (Hart 1992: 5). Thus, economic development involves production and trade. However, for production and trade to qualify as "development" and not simply capitalism, it must be beneficial to a nation's citizens.

In successive sections of the chapter we discuss production, trade and development, respectively. In the section on production, we juxtapose two archetypical approaches to production: capital-intensive and labor-intensive production. We provide examples of each to fix ideas. Of course, most production falls between these two archetypes, but the extreme contrast provided by these two examples is useful because it exposes the differences in the approaches of each to the production problem. We then examine location and trade. This we do at both an abbreviated and fairly abstract level, since the primary focus of this chapter is on "systems of production." A basic understanding of location and trade is necessary for tying issues of production to issues of development. We then turn our attention to the strengths and weaknesses of production systems within the context of global capitalism (that is to say, location and trade) for the development of the less-developed nations of the Global South. The chapter closes with a summary and conclusions.

Systems of production

Goods and services are supplied by combining capital, labor and raw materials. Capital and labor, along with the raw materials used in production, are generally referred to as the "factors of production." Obviously, capital and labor can be supplied in a variety of combinations to produce any given good or service. For any given level of technology, we refer to the various combinations of capital and labor that could be used in production as the "production frontier."

In the short run, the nature of the market determines where firms choose to operate on this production frontier. A sizable and growing market enables firms to produce standardized products in large quantities at low per-unit cost, thereby exploiting "economies of scale" (Harrison 1994: 225). In this situation, there is a tendency for production to become capital-intensive, since the highly standardized nature of the product allows the ready replacement of skilled artisans with machines. As a result, over time, productive skill or *technology* becomes embedded not in individuals, but in machines. However, the embedding of technology within special-purpose machines also means that production remains at least partially inflexible, so that capital-intensive production is extremely vulnerable to changes in demand.

In markets that are stable or growing slowly, production is primarily geared toward quality production of at least partially unique products and the major competitive focus is on novelty. In this case, firms must produce a variety of products that share a common production platform. We refer to the cost savings gleaned from the production of multiple products from a common platform as "economies of scope" (Malecki 1996: 20). Firms that compete on the basis of economies of scope must be able to switch from one commodity they produce to another very rapidly. This requires short-run flexibility in the production process. In this situation, there is a tendency for production to become labor-intensive, since the highly specialized nature of the products typically requires skilled artisans and tools or machines that are compatible with a multitude of uses. As a result, over time, productive skill or technology becomes embedded in individuals, not in machines. In what follows, we examine each of these archetypes more closely (for more on technology, see Box 5.1).

Capital-intensive production or machinofacture

As we have said, in capital-intensive production or "machinofacture," technology is vested primarily in machinery, not labor, and humans are accessories to machinery in the production process. The ability to produce unique products is therefore a function of the level of technology invested in the machinery. Not surprisingly, the history of machinofacture is the history of increasingly more sophisticated machinery producing increasingly more sophisticated goods.

Lean production is the most current form of machinofacture. The goal in lean production is to establish stable production processes that can be relied upon to produce the required quantity at the time requested with minimal waste of resources (Yingling *et al.* 2000: 232–233). Compared to earlier forms of machinofacture, lean production uses less of everything – human effort, manufacturing space, investment in tools, and engineering hours for developing new products. It requires less stockpiling of both inputs to production and finished products, results in fewer defects, and produces a greater variety of products (Hancock and Zayko 1998; Knuf 2000: 59; Lebow 1990; Yingling *et al.* 2000: 216–217).

Box 5.1 Globalization's technological revolution

Production involves the transformation of raw materials into products and services that are useful for human consumption. This transformation uses certain rules and practices, and varying amounts of capital and labor that are, taken together, termed *technology* (Malecki 1996). Maskell (1996b; see also Malecki 1996) identifies four kinds of technology: machinery, labor, intra-firm and inter-firm.

Machinery-based technology is typical of mass production. In this instance, increasing technological capability is incorporated in the machines of production. This is possible because of product standardization and the highly repetitive nature of tasks. Examples might include high-end machining centers, automated welding machines and pick-and-place robots.

Labor-based technology is typical of learning-based economies. In this instance increasing technological capability is incorporated as social capital in increasing labor skill. This occurs because the highly flexible and customized nature of production rules out the use of specialized tools. Examples here might include services that rely on professional certification, as well as the highly customized goods production common to many European luxury products from apparel to automobiles.

Intra-firm technology is typical of all forms of production whether mass-produced or customized. Intra-firm technology includes multiple forms, but two are especially salient: operations and management style. A particular form of machine-based technology – the computer – has revolutionized intra-firm operations in the last three decades. Part of this revolution has brought with it techniques such as just-in-time and pull production which, in the absence of computerization, are impossible. An equally dramatic transformation has occurred in management with the disappearance of Taylorist management principles in favor of those that derive from Deming.

Inter-firm technologies are those that speak to the articulation of production between multiple firms. These technologies are particularly central to just-in-time and pull production where the "arm's length" relationships of Fordism have been replaced by close coordination between, say, assemblers and subcontractors. Close cooperation and coordination is also typical of specialized industrial regions dominated by small firms.

The automobile industry is a prime example of lean production and is examined in the case study in Box 5.2. Under modern machinofacture, waste is eliminated by: (i) producing only what customers want, (ii) continuous production improvement, and (iii) production on demand (Harrison 1994: 200; Knuf 2000: 58). Producing what customers want involves understanding customers' needs and applying these needs to product design (Yingling *et al.* 2000: 218) so that goods that will not sell are not produced.

Box 5.2 The automobile industry and lean production

The automobile industry is often considered archetypical of machinofacture (Dicken 1992). Within the industry, lean production is most heavily associated with the Japanese, who pioneered this system of production. In the 1950s and 1960s, Japan invested heavily in new technology and is today the top automobile producer in the world (Dicken 1992).

There are three main foci to Japanese lean production: long-term relationships with suppliers, consumer demand, and lean organization. The Japanese utilize a tier system with their suppliers. The company works directly with the first-tier suppliers, who work with the second-tier suppliers, and so on (Dicken 1992). The suppliers use "just-in-time" methods, which require close geographic proximity to the automobile assemblers (Toyota, Nissan, etc.), and typically long-term relationships evolve between suppliers and assemblers. Often, first-tier suppliers become involved in the production process to increase quality and lower cost (Womack *et al.* 1990).

There is also a link between the production system and customer demand (Womack *et al.* 1990). The shorter development cycle of lean production allows lean companies to be more responsive to changes in demand. Japanese companies also involve existing customers when planning new products. They also use periodic surveys of their customers to avoid inaccurate market assessments, reduce inventory costs, help fine tune new products, and instill brand loyalty in their buyers.

Lastly, Japanese companies are lean companies (Womack *et al.* 1990). Until recently, the Japanese auto industry guaranteed lifetime employment, and pay is steeply graded by seniority rather than specific job function. They believe that guaranteeing employment in the long term enhances labor flexibility and increases a company's ability to rely on its employees' knowledge and experience. New company members are introduced to the entire range of activities involved in auto production before given a specific assignment in a department. There are teams with team leaders, and each team member can perform a variety of jobs, and suggestions and criticisms are given collectively.

Continuous improvement begins with the process of defining each step in the production process and assessing the degree to which improvements can be made in each of these steps to enhance the product's value-added (Yingling *et al.* 2000: 219). It is important that continuous improvement includes an examination of both waste within the firm and the firm and its suppliers and distributors (Yingling *et al.* 2000: 219). Not surprisingly, in a system in which a firm continually improves the production process, the relationship between that firm and its suppliers is much closer and formal business relationships are often established (Harrison 1994: 196, 241; Yingling *et al.* 2000: 219).

A third way in which waste is eliminated is through use of production on demand using one of two forms of production organization: "just-in-time production" or "pull production." Just-in-time involves producing the precise quantity of product needed at the time it is needed. In pull production the construction of another unit of product begins only when a finished unit "rolls off the line," thus products are "pulled" through the line (Yingling *et al.* 2000: 231). In both just-in-time and pull production, products should flow continuously and firms "level" production by producing products in direct proportion to the demand (Yingling *et al.* 2000: 222). Leveling and the standardization that occurs as part of leveling allows stable processes, thereby minimizing disruptions (Yingling *et al.* 2000: 223). Standardization in turn works to minimize variation due to human error, the working environment and machine malfunction (Yingling *et al.* 2000: 224–225). Leveling can be achieved only through use of flexible equipment (typically through the purchase of flexible machining centers; see Knudsen *et al.* 1994) and a flexible workforce (Hancock and Zayko 1998; Yingling *et al.* 2000: 222, 226). Flexible machining equipment allows the manufacture, with minimum changeover between products, of a variety of different, closely related products (Yingling *et al.* 2000: 229). Flexibility in work assignment allows both 100 percent labor utilization and minimal staffing of the production process (Yingling *et al.* 2000: 227, 229).

Labor-intensive or craft-based production

Labor-intensive or "craft-based production" takes place when production must be highly flexible in the short run or when it is difficult or impossible to organize large amounts of capital. In craft-based production, labor uses tools, not the reverse. Typically, high levels of human or social capital are substituted for physical or financial capital, so this form of production revolves around skilled individuals and their social organizations (Malecki 1996: 19). Chief among these social organizations are those that transfer labor-force skill and information about suppliers and markets, and those that enhance collaboration (Harrison 1994: 209; Malecki 1996: 16; Storper 1997: 45). Collaboration spreads risks and helps producers cope with the uncertainties (Harrison 1994: 209). Collaboration also may lead to localized, regional or even national production networks (Harrison 1994: 240; Malecki 1996: 25). The Danish furniture industry is a prime example of modern craft-based production and is examined in the case study in Box 5.3.

Modern craft-based production is based on the ability to produce, reproduce and exchange knowledge. Penrose (1959) makes a fundamental distinction between codified knowledge and tacit knowledge, and this distinction is crucial to understanding modern forms of craft-based production. Codified knowledge is what we normally think of as "factual information." That is, it is knowledge that is written down and transmissible through modern forms of communication (Foray and Lundvall 1997: 21; Lundvall and Johnson 1994: 27).

Tacit knowledge is learned through practice and experience (Maskell and Malmberg 1995). It is often described as "learning by doing." Tacit knowledge is not as transmissible as codified knowledge (Lundvall 1995). In an age where

Box 5.3 The Danish furniture industry

The Danish furniture industry is a prime example of craft-based production in a developed country. The Danes have remained competitive through their innovative products, their focus on quality and trust-based, long-lasting relationships between furniture companies and their suppliers (Maskell 1996). The Danish furniture companies have remained small and are in close physical proximity to one another. This has proven to be beneficial to the fast exchange of knowledge, it has reduced costs and enhanced efficiency (Maskell 1996). It also makes entry by competitors extremely difficult. The success of the industry is its annual growth rate of approximately 19 percent.

Designers Poul Henningsen, Arne Jacobsen and Verner Panton have been critical to the development of the industry and their innovative creations remain in high demand today. In 1924, Henningsen created the "Paris lamp," a multi-shade lamp that dispersed light around a room and avoided intense light in one location (Scandinavian Design 1997). There have been alterations made to this lamp over time, but essentially it is still the same lamp, created in 1924, that is popular today. Arne Jacobsen is known for his originality in chair design. He created the "Ant," model "3107" (the Number Seven Chair), the "Swan," and the "Egg" (Scandinavian Design 1997). The Number Seven Chair is believed to be the most important success in Danish furniture history because it has sold over five million copies since its introduction (Scandinavian Design 1997). Verner Panton worked with Jacobsen, but eventually broke away, and in 1960 created "the Stacking," the first single-form, injection-molded, plastic chair (Scandinavian Design 1997). He is also known for his "Panton System 1-2-3," which is a chair with six bases, three seat heights, optional armrests, and two kinds of padding (Art and Culture 2003). These are only a few of the innovative products that have made the Danish furniture industry successful.

information (codified knowledge) is both accessible and virtually costless (witness the myriad of internet sites and email posts), it is the difficulty surrounding the generation, reproduction and exchange of tacit knowledge that forms the basis of competitive advantage in craft-based production (Maskell and Malmberg 1995: 5; Maskell and Malmberg 1999; Storper 1997: 31).

Institutions play a crucial role in the production and reproduction of knowledge. These institutions can be formal (schools, etc.) or informal (groups of friends, etc.) (Edquist and Johnson 1997; Edquist and Lundvall 1992; Morgan 1997). These institutions form an infrastructure or *milieu* (Cammagni 1991) for the production and reproduction of knowledge. Furthermore, the forms these institutions take are often historically specific (Adler 1990; Crevoisier and Maillat 1991; Cooke *et al.* 1997; Garnsey 1998; Hansen 1992; Macdonald and Williams 1994; MacLeod

2000; Maillat *et al.* 1995; Malmberg 1996, 1997; Putnam 1993). It is for this reason that "(t)he process of ... economic development ... tend(s) to be highly path-dependent" (Maskell *et al.* 1998: 70). This existence of institutions for production and reproduction of knowledge, however, does not explain the exchange of knowledge.

As geographers, we know that ease of exchange is a function of spatial and cultural proximity. Spatial proximity enhances the ability of individuals to interact face-to-face by reducing the costs of exchange and by improving its efficiency (Gertler 1995; Maskell and Malmberg 1995, 1999; Morgan and Murdoch 2000). However, Garnsey (1998) is quick to point out that spatial proximity alone does not guarantee knowledge exchange. Exchange requires not only spatial proximity, but also cultural proximity. When people feel that they have similar perceptions and values, this engenders a profound level of trust that facilitates knowledge exchange. According to Maskell (1996a: 11), trust is a "remarkably efficient lubricant to economic exchange." Like knowledge production and reproduction, the exchange of knowledge can be further facilitated by cooperative effort of institutions (Cooke *et al.* 1997; Lawton Smith 1997).

Trade as location and comparative advantage

Having described the basic forms of production, we now turn our attention to location and trade. Our treatment of both is fairly abstract, yet it will serve to make our main points. With respect to location, we use Weber's theory of industrial location. While overly simplistic, it will allow us to specify the reasons for the location of industry in various places. For a theory of trade, we draw on the notion of comparative advantage and Samuelson's conditions for the movement of goods between regions or nations.

Weberian location theory

Weberian location theory specifies the location of production based on a consideration of the location of factor inputs and markets. Weberian location theory focuses on the idea of minimizing transport cost based on the weight of inputs to production versus the weight of the final product. Weber (1929) investigates three types of production processes: pure, weight-losing and weight-gaining. His elementary analysis finds that pure goods are insensitive to transport costs and therefore highly sensitive to production costs. In the production of pure goods, total transport cost is the same everywhere, thus any location is as good as any other. Production of goods involving weight loss leads to the location of industries at the input source and production of goods involving weight gain leads to location of industries at the market or point of sale.

The theory of comparative advantage, non-autarky and the direction of trade

The theory of comparative advantage is the principal theory of international trade, and thus international competitiveness. Comparative advantage explains changes in international competitiveness in terms of factor prices, aggregate demand, the rate of savings and investment, and international currency exchange rates (Hart 1992: 27). The theory of comparative advantage can be summarized as follows. If two countries engage in trade, each will have incentives to increase production and reduce consumption of goods in which it has the lower relative marginal cost prior to trade. Note that this holds regardless of absolute productivity levels (Dixit and Norman 1980: 2–3).

Two additional insights can be drawn from the basic theory. The first is the Heckscher–Olin or factor abundance hypothesis, which states that the factor that is relatively abundant will be relatively cheaper and that the goods that use this factor most intensely in production also will be relatively cheaper. Therefore we expect a country to have its comparative advantage in goods that most intensively use that factor or set of factors that are relatively abundant in supply (Dixit and Norman 1980: 4). The second states that if there are differences in relative costs before trade, then free trade should eliminate these differences, so that in the long run no country has a comparative advantage (Dixit and Norman 1980: 4).

Ruffin (1974) examines international trade under uncertainty. His results indicate that, whereas under certainty, incentives exist for nations to remain autarkic (to not engage in trade), under uncertainty a nation will never be worse off if it engages in trade. Thus, under uncertainty, there exist incentives for trade.

A principal weakness of the theory of comparative advantage is the lack of any spatial framework that would dictate specifically which regions or nations would trade with which other regions or nations. The spatial price-equilibrium model of Samuelson (1952) provides this specification succinctly. In order for trade to occur, the price of a good in importing region A must be greater than or equal to the price of the good in the exporting region B, plus the cost of moving the good from region B to region A. So while the theory of comparative advantage specifies what will be traded, Samuelson's formulation specifies who will trade.

Prospects for the developing world

Given the paucity of capital, domestic capital in particular, one would expect that developing countries would be dominated by labor-intensive production (Harrison 1994: 181, 186–187). While this is generally the case, this is not universally so and it is important to describe why capital-intensive forms of production exist in the developing world before critiquing the advantages and disadvantages of this form of production for the poorer nations.

That machinofacture can exist in developing nations can be seen from Weber's theory of industrial location. Recall that under conditions of production of what Weber calls pure goods, the cost of location is the same everywhere (since in

Weber's model only transportation costs are considered), thus only labor costs and other direct costs of production influence location. If technology is fixed at some global standard in the short run (a reasonable assumption), then competitiveness of a firm globally rests entirely on labor costs. While most textbooks illustrate this case of the Weberian model using the apparel industry, Weber's findings apply to any assembly process, whether computers, automobiles or furniture. Thus machinofacture is relatively easily attracted to the less-developed world when the principal draw is inexpensive labor.

There are a few advantages to capital-intensive growth for developing nations, at least in the short run. Principal among these is employment growth and short-run increases in GDP related to wages and taxes on those wages. However, there exist powerful disadvantages to this arrangement as well. First, firms, having invested considerable capital in production facilities, frequently insist that all or a very large proportion of profits be returned to the "home country" and the profits from production in the developing nation be tax-free. Typically, this is facilitated by Exclusive Economic Zones (EEZs) that allow free and tariff-less movement of goods into and out of "off-shore" production facilities. Second, because comparative advantage of less-developed nations hinges on a single factor, cheap labor, they are extremely vulnerable to disruptions in supply of inputs, changes in demand, and predatory behavior of both transnational corporations and other less-developed nations (Hart 1992: 6–7). Third, capital-intensive growth tends to exaggerate existing class distinctions. Fourth, capital-intensive growth tends to increase national debt and it may have deleterious effects on existing national industry (that Gandhi used a traditional spinning wheel as the symbol for the Indian independence movement is instructive). Finally, there are well-documented social costs associated with the highly repetitive and standardized work typical of machinofacture (Karasek and Theorell 1990; Lewchuck and Roberts 1996, 1997).

Successful and globally competitive craft-based production requires a craft tradition, highly educated and skilled craftsmen, and a network of formal and informal institutions that govern production and serve as efficient conveyors of information about markets. While capital inputs to production exist and are crucial to success of craft-based production, capital inputs are lower than those required for successful machinofacture since, in craft-based production, human capital is substituted for physical and financial capital (Maskell 1996b, 1998). There are several advantages to this form of production for the developing world. First and foremost is that craft-based production exists in the developing world, thus the principal issue is to be more economically successful by becoming globally competitive. A second advantage is that, since craft-based production is less capital-intensive than machinofacture, developing nations are less beholden to advanced capitalist nations and multinational corporations for capital, and this may help resolve, or at least make it less likely, that developing nations become debtor nations.

Disadvantages of craft-based production also exist. Principal among these is that craft-based production is a more realistic development strategy in the long run than in the short run. This is because a successful craft-based strategy revolves around institution-building and the formation of an international reputation or brand. Craft-based production hinges on the development of a set of national-level institutions for governing production and global export, passing market information and promoting innovation to producers, while guaranteeing product quality to global consumers. These systems of governance typically have their basis in strong cooperative movements or in formal government bodies. These same governance bodies also are important actors in the education and training of skilled workers. It is crucial this system of education match the codified knowledge requirements of craft-based production. Further, since the competitive advantage of craft-based production lies in the tacit knowledge that is accumulated on top of the codified knowledge obtained through schooling, a commitment to life-long learning is essential. This may lead to the establishment of adult-learning and industry research centers. Governance organizations also play an important role in reducing information asymmetry. In the absence of cooperative or public governance organizations, there is a tendency for production and information networks to center around a single large corporation (Harrison 1994: 220; Malecki 1996: 18, 25).

Finally, because craft-based production revolves around novelty and quality, branding of products is crucial. The development of brands and loyalty to those brands on a global scale takes astute marketing and considerable time, as does the building of reputation around a brand once it is established. However, this branding process need not be firm-specific (for example, note that the reputation held by the Danish for their furniture or the Swedes for their glass is industry-wide, not firm-specific) and recent advances in electronic media make this task much easier than in the past.

Conclusions

In this chapter we have compared the two common approaches to production, machinofacture and craft-based production, as possible "technological avenues" for the less-developed world. Each has strengths and weaknesses. Machinofacture is a capital- not labor-intensive form of production, in which governance takes place within an existing firm or inter-firm governance framework, typically that of the transnational corporation. Its principal advantage for the developing world is that, under the dictates of comparative advantage, the developing world can benefit from machinofacture in the short run without expending much effort. Machinofacture requires a low-skilled, inexpensive labor force and requires no endogenous production governance. In this way machinofacture is "off-the-shelf" development.

Machinofacture, however, incurs substantial costs in the long run. First, because machinofacture is capital-intensive, and because developing nations are cash-poor, capital moves in and out of developing countries with relatively little capture of value-added beyond wages to labor; and, despite defense of a machinofacture development strategy on the grounds of technology transfer, there is little evidence such transfers take place. Second, because machinofacture is capital- not labor-intensive, and because in the short run technology is fixed, with all other things being equal, less labor is used in imported machinofacture than would be the case in domestic production. Thus imported machinofacture is "overcapitalized." Third, since the principal draw to machinofacture is inexpensive labor, not labor skill, development via machinofacture is fleeting. Finally, since production governance in machinofacture is firm-based (typically in a transnational corporation), the governments of developing nations will find it difficult to regulate machinofacture when the objectives of firms and the nation diverge (Harrison 1994: 229). This may lead to nationalization of production facilities and the "blackballing" of that nation from future rounds of development through machinofacture.

Craft-based production is a labor- as opposed to capital-intensive production method, where governance takes place within existing or newly derived domestic institutional frameworks – including, but not restricted to, the national government. Its principal advantages for the developing world are that it builds on existing craft traditions, it promotes skill-building in the existing labor force and it leads, potentially, to a higher level of employment than does machinofacture. Craft-based production relies heavily on the development of brands, which is a long and time-consuming process. The maintenance of brand loyalty in turn depends on the maintenance of quality and the ability to continuously design and produce innovative and novel products. This, in turn depends on efficient and effective systems of production governance that coordinate knowledge dissemination to producers and guarantee quality to consumers. These same governance institutions also play a crucial role in the education of labor, the reproduction of existing skills, the organization of domestic systems of production, and the production of new skills by promoting technological advances and the possibility of productive growth (Harrison 1994: 231, 239).

In summary, the machinofacture approach to development is at best a short-run strategy to be pursued as a stop-gap measure at the same time as other, more long-term and craft-based, development strategies are initiated. In the long run, machinofacture is associated with a host of detrimental effects that potentially trap developing nations into long-term poverty. Thus capital-intensive approaches to production are clearly capitalism, but they are frequently not development. Craft-based production, while a long-term strategy, relies on the social organization of society, particularly institution-building, and less on capitalism *per se*. Nevertheless, it is craft-based, not capital-intensive, production that holds the greatest hope for "genuine" technological development. This observation is true not only for the developing world, but for the less-developed areas of the advanced capitalist nations as well.

Globalization's unruly spaces

6 Globalization of labor
Increasing complexity, more unruly

Dennis Conway

Introduction

Although relatively small in total volume in comparison to global patterns of internal rural-to-urban migration, the growing significance of international mobility of people in today's globalizing order warrants a deeper, exhaustive examination. The globalization of labor might be said to accompany the globalization of capital, but the two are not so simply tied, nor are their patterns of circulation mutually determined by each other (Daly 2003; Sassen 1988). Global capital and global labor are, however, increasingly mobile factors of production. Both have become more volatile and more unpredictable in their patterns as globalization has strengthened its hold. Their global relationships as well as their national relationships are fraught with sovereignty contradictions, cross-border complications, and conflictual situations (Linard 1998; Schindlmayr 2003). In addition, while global trade and commerce have experienced greater "freedom to move" in this post-1980s era of globalization, global migration by comparison is less free, and (somewhat counter-intuitively) less regulated (Keely 2002).

Today's global patterns are a complex mixture of moves; of varying distances and varying durations, of varying degrees of permanency, of wider-flung mixtures of ethnic and racial identity, and of deepening and widening self-perpetuating social networks; all, with varying consequences and impacts for host and source societies. The determining structural dimensions of this new geography of labor mobility (and its partner, immobility) are both biophysical and social/anthropogenic, but the ensuing complex flows both reflect the power and authority of global forces as well as resistance and avoidance – human agency and innovation. Forced mobility is as common a reality as voluntary movement, with each accompanying the other as interrelated global processes of relocation.

In comparison to internal mobility, however, international movement is fundamentally influenced, fashioned, interrupted, baulked, and possibly even facilitated by nation-states' institutional barriers and borders, and their immigration controls and policies. Accordingly, international movement in today's globalizing world is a diverse mixture of formal and informal modes, of legally sanctioned and illegally practiced entry strategies, as well as a means for diversifying the survival strategies of many of the world's poor and powerless households and communities, and for securing a higher material quality of life among others more fortunate – the international skilled, for example (Massey *et al.* 1998).

People from all walks of life participate, with the exception of those with the least resources, the infirm, the institutionalized, and those rendered immobile through age, circumstances and/or persuasion. Extreme crises and life-threatening situations have, however, prompted mass flight and refuge-seeking among even the most immobile and weak, and today's globalizing world has witnessed several humanitarian crises brought about by natural and anthropogenic disasters – environmental, economic and social (including civil war, ethnic cleansing, and other forced dislocations).

Some international migration patterns are long-standing, and precede globalization's ascendance in the last three decades. Others appear to be evolutionary, and derive their added complexity and unruliness from globalization's influences. Some others might even be regarded as direct consequences of globalization, or indirectly the result of social, economic and political upheavals and restructuring that has led to the new global order, and this "new age of migration" (Castles and Miller 1998, 2003; Stalker 2000).

One particular characteristic of this new-age, dynamic process is its "unruliness" in its avoidance, or circumvention, of border regulatory mechanisms, its informal, underground economy associations, its unregulated, or difficult to regulate, nature, and its volatility and unpredictability. Increasingly becoming a more widespread global phenomenon, "illegal migration" or "irregular" immigration is affecting nation-states the world over. Other labels have been coined to characterize this age-old practice that has, in recent times, grown substantially to be self-perpetuating and of considerable geopolitical concern. "Clandestine," "unauthorized" and "undocumented" have all been used as characterizations of this unruly and difficult-to-regulate strategy (Castles 2003b; Jandl 2004; Miller 1995; Passel 2005; Tapinos 1999; Williams 1999). Concerns for irregular immigrants' human rights, as well as border security and regulatory concerns, fuel the debates over the impacts and consequences of these volatile, unpredictable and difficult-to-estimate flows (Jandl 2004), so that in the first decade of the twenty-first century both regulated and unregulated international migration are raising complex human rights and ethical issues, that challenge national (and global) regimes (Massey *et al.* 1998; Schindlmayr 2003; Taran 2000).

Dimensions of the "new age of migration"

Over the last forty years or so, there have been relatively rapid increases in the numbers of people undertaking international migration. In 1965 the world's voluntary international migrants were estimated to number about 75 million. By 1985 their number had increased to 105 million, and by 2000 had further increased to 175 million; a volume equivalent to 2.9 percent of the world's 6 billion population. The most recent estimate for 2005 indicates there are now as many as 200 million migrants worldwide (World Migration Report 2005). And, some 48 percent of these international migrants are women (Zlotnik 2003). Although most of the world's mobile population still moves internally, approximately 75 percent of all international migrants move into a mere handful of all countries (12 percent), so the policy ramifications of this uneven pattern of redistribution are considerable (World Migration Report 2005; Martin and Widgren 2002). The temporal trends in forced migration both within and across borders, however, do not mirror these growth trends in voluntary migration. The number of world refugees in 1992 stood at 18 million, but declined to 13.3 million by 2000. The world's estimated number of "internally displaced persons" (IDPs) also stood at 18 million in 1992, but the estimate increased to over 22 million by 2000 (Nyberg-Sorensen *et al.* 2002).

Several trends characterize international migration today and global–national–local responses to global labor's mobility:

1 the unevenness and crisis-laden nature of globalization's economic, social, political and cultural effects;
2 geopolitical disruption and change in the post-Cold War era;
3 changing demographic trends and gender roles;
4 increasing transnationalism and increasing importance of temporary visitation;
5 increasing technological innovation in transport, communications and knowledge-based services;
6 growing streams of "irregular" migration from the Global South to the North, and related human rights concerns;
7 growing reliance on intermediaries, who profit from global migration – recruiters, smugglers, traffickers, lawyers;
8 growing diversity in "forced migration" flows and the emergence of a new form of slavery – the trafficking of women and children across borders;
9 global and hemispheric differences in migration policies, including asylum policies among major destinations – especially European and North American differences;
10 "politicization" of international migration as a national or "homeland" security concern in the US-led, "war on drugs/war on terrorism" discourses of post-9/11 politics.

Each is treated in turn, although there is considerable overlap in their scopes.

Crisis-laden nature of globalization's economic, social, political and cultural effects

The global economy being promoted today by client politicians, international financial organizations, neoliberal economists and the like is being fashioned for the benefit of transnational corporations, their stockholders, their CEOs and attendant managerial classes, and the aforementioned promoters: no less than a self-serving agenda for the privileged, capitalist classes of the Global North.

Following Aguilar and Cavada (2002), "ten plagues of globalization" can be identified: (i) growth in poverty and inequality; (ii) greater concentration of income; (iii) the explosion of consumption and exclusion; (iv) increase in unemployment and growth in the informal sector; (v) the loss of labor rights and the double exploitation of women; (vi) environmental deterioration; (vii) less participation of poor countries in world trade; (viii) the economic domination of transnational corporations; (ix) financial crises; and (x) decrease in international assistance and increase on foreign debt. It is scarcely surprising, therefore, that millions of people would vote with their feet and respond to their vulnerability, increasing powerlessness and declining/deteriorating circumstances by migrating. In smaller volumes, but nevertheless as significant flows, higher skilled labor has also taken advantage of globalization's increasing reach, and the concomitant increases in the international mobility of the wealthier classes for tourism, business and temporary liaisons have also added to the global volume of transnational and international movement and its direct and indirect influences on consumption, trade and tourism.

Geopolitical disruption and change

The twentieth century closed with considerable geopolitical disruption and chaos featuring as major factors in the transition. The Cold War came to an end with the disintegration of the Soviet Union and its break up into many smaller nation-states. Mass migration and considerable redistribution resulted. Eastern European countries also underwent transitions to capitalism and restructuring of their centrally planned economies – again prompting considerable internal and international movement. More dramatic and problematic, however, was Yugoslavia's disintegration and ensuing ethnic conflicts and genocide atrocities in Bosnia–Herzegovina and Kosovo.

African civil wars broke out in many locations – Angola, Congo, Rwanda–Burundi, Côte d'Ivoire, Sierra Leone, Somalia, Sudan, Eritrea, Mozambique – some initiating mass flights of refugees, others internally disrupting and destroying livelihoods. The 1980s featured Central American civil wars in Nicaragua, El Salvador and Guatemala, prompting substantial refugee flights, not only to nearby countries but also to the United States. Arab–Israel conflicts persisted from the 1960s to present, with Palestinian *intifada* movements fiercely opposed by Israeli military action and martial law. Elsewhere, increasing violence accompanied separatist movements – Ireland, Spain, Mexico, Kosovo – and Maoist guerrilla movements in places as far a field as Peru (The Shining Path) and Nepal (The People's War) contributed to the heightened state of tension and fear. The Gulf War of 1991 was not to be the sole UN-mandated incursion of global armed forces into this troubled, unstable region. Then, post-9/11 anti-terrorism conflicts in Afghanistan to depose the Taliban regime and capture Osama bin Laden, and most recently the pre-emptive war and invasion of Iraq by US and UK armed forces, have again disrupted peoples' lives in these regions, and forced many to flee for their lives.

There was, of course, some geopolitical restructuring that was negotiated rather than coerced. German unification was accomplished, for example. The European

Union grew and widened its membership. This expanded European "federation of states" coordinated many economic and social policies, and even embarked on the adoption of a common currency – to create the euro zone. Most significantly, unification and the Treaty of Rome in 1968 brought about the freedom of movement of labor within the EU, which helped distribute labor, but didn't result in uncontrollable mass migration from South to North, from Italy or Spain to Germany, etc. Indeed, guest-worker programs had their moment, with Greeks and Turks moving in, and today immigration of non-Europeans into the lower wage sectors of European labor markets is on the increase. As a consequence, there have been increased South → North and East → West flows of migrants and refugees, and this "new age of migration" has brought racially-diverse mixes of asylum seekers into European communities from Africa, Asia, the Middle East and Latin America.

Changing demographic trends and gender roles

The "demographic divide" between the Global South and North continues to be wide and problematic. The countries of the Global South have experienced a large growth of their population, and will continue to do so because of above-replacement levels of fertility. Africa remains the continental region with the highest fertility rates. Asia also has considerable overall growth potential, while in contrast the OECD countries of the North are now experiencing below-replacement fertility rates. In the Global South, the rapid growth of urban populations, the problematic excesses of labor in rural and urban markets – structural unemployment – reduced access to international aid and assistance and declining shares of global trade and capital investment, the persistence or worsening of South–North inequalities, together, make for a heady brew of demographic problems, social and political turbulence and tremendous upheavals, which prompts many to seek emigration as a solution to these overwhelming circumstances. Accelerated aging of OECD country populations adds to the demographic dilemma. In 1960, one person in 71 was aged 80 or over, but the ratio will have climbed to one in 21 by 2020; and, this is a conservative projection. In OECD Europe today (in the mid-1990s), there are 13 children under the age of 15 for every ten over 65. By contrast, Sub-Saharan Africa has 159 children for every 10 old people (65+) (Golini *et al.* 1993).

Along with these demographic changes in population growth and different aging profiles are changes in the role(s) of women in society. Women are increasingly pursuing educational opportunities and employment outside the home, they continue to be responsible for child-rearing, home-making and household management, and are at the heart of many civil society initiatives. Education and income provide women with greater autonomy and/or negotiating power, so that they are not only migrating as "tied-movers" or as "reunifying spouses," but are principal applicants for work permits and visas on their own (and their children's) behalf. Of course, in many parts of the world, women's roles are still socially constructed to restrict their autonomy, inhibit their independent movement and subordinate them. However, education is changing and challenging the social constraints that needlessly inhibit women's egalitarian rights, and today's globalizing world is being actively challenged to become a more gender-neutral environment, wherein women's work, lives and mobility options are more equal to those of their male counterparts (Martin 2001). As noted earlier, women now make up the majority in some regional immigration flows and migrant stocks – North America and Europe for example.

Increasing transnationalism and increasing importance of temporary visitation

Transnationalism and remittances

International circulation – undertaking one or more repetitive moves from home and back across borders – has been a common mobility strategy for a century or more, even though travel across oceans was difficult and sojourns in one or the other country was sequential. Partly because of the greater ease of global travel, and of the "strategic flexibility" of those involved – the migrants and their families – transnational migrants today maintain two "homes," circulating between them and living in two societies, or between "two worlds" (Conway 2000b). Indeed, transnational families may interact within multi-local transnational fields, with members keeping in touch, moving between nearby and distant places and sharing resources across boundaries (Conway and Cohen 2003). Transnational migration is commonly undertaken as a family-directed strategy in which members "cross-the-border" to search for and gain employment, to raise a target amount which is then remitted "back home," and to subsequently return home.

All signs point to the further consolidation and perpetuation of these transnational migration fields and networks, with more and more migrant and non-migrant families benefiting from this flexible strategy and its remittances (Faist 2000; Massey *et al.* 1998). It is very likely to be a growing practice elsewhere as South and Central Asian and African linkages with Europe and North America consolidate (Rogers 2000), although research on these global diasporas is in its infancy.

International migration's link to the development of the source regions and communities migrants leave behind is best reflected in the flow of remittances and "gifts in kind" that the transnational migrant donors send back. Once derided as evidence of hapless dependency, of inappropriate conspicuous consumption, of community divisiveness and the like, remittances are now viewed in a much more positive light (Connell and Conway 2000; Massey *et al.* 1998; Orozco 2002a/b). By 1990, the world total of remittances was estimated to be around US$75 billion, and it further increased to US$100 billion by 2000. One 1999 estimate of the North-to-South remit of migrants' capital arrived at the total of US$60 billion (Nyberg-Sorensen *et al.* 2002). Worldwide, India (US$11.5 billion), Mexico (US$6.5 billion), China (US$5 billion), Turkey (US$4.5 billion), the Philippines (US$4 billion) and Egypt (US$3.7 billion) were the six countries receiving the largest amounts of remittances from their migrant donors in the year 2000 (Orozco 2002b), although even these impressive flows of remitted capital into national, "home" economies should be considered as conservative estimates given the informal and family-oriented nature of the transfers (Conway and Cohen 1998, 2003).

The international skills exchange

The international recruitment of low-skilled labor as "contract workers," or as "guest-workers," is a time-honored practice. Indeed, contract labor is invariably associated with agricultural employment, and even today, agriculture is the major employer of international labor crews and families: for example, Mexican farm workers in the United States and Canada to help bring in the harvests, or Eastern Europeans working in Western Europe farms. Contract or seasonal workers are, however, also recruited in large numbers in unskilled and semi-skilled occupations – construction, services, tourism, for example. The greatest concentration of contract workers today are found in the Middle East and the Gulf States – in 1990 the contract labor force was estimated to be about 6 million, many coming from neighboring Arab States such as Egypt, Jordan, Palestine, or from Pakistan and Bangladesh (Stalker 1994).

The diversity of international skill exchange mechanisms in today's globalizing world is considerable. There are self-generated flows of "skilled transients" or professional expatriates to locations and jobs offering lucrative, short-term returns for their skills. Global service firms in health and technology sectors contract themselves and their workforces to provide contractual services worldwide, especially in infrastructure development in developing countries – the oil-rich Gulf States, for example. Global service firms, and their mobile workers, also conduct contractual work in the military, aeronautical and munitions industries – one aspect of the "privatization" of the military-industrial complex, no less. Global tourism in some of its contemporary forms – the cruise industry, enclave all-inclusive resorts, hotel personnel development, ski-resort development – also incubates and generates international migration of the skilled. Corporations seeking the highly skilled may acquire overseas businesses to expand their labor stocks, they may enter into partnerships or joint ventures, or they may utilize specialist firms' expertise in outsourcing phases of their production ensemble. Once linked within the wider corporate net, much needed expertise can be moved, seconded, hired and transferred, as befits their knowledge-base and skills.

In addition, there is the globalization of higher education, the international movement of young people for training and education, and the inevitable patterns of recruitment that spin off from the North's universities and technical institutional "ties that bind" (Findlay 1995; Gould 1988; Salt 1997). International students' global mobility has its roots in colonial ties, in Cold War geopolitical strategies, and in post-colonial traditions of metropolitan dominance, but today it has re-emerged as part of contemporary global recruitment efforts by global business and Core economies (Li *et al.* 1996). It is as much a "brain exchange" as a "brain drain," though clearly excessive losses of the highly educated and highly skilled through emigration, or overzealous recruitment, may be an acute, if temporary, problem for small countries in the Global South. The contemporary volume of international students and exchange visitors is not only relatively large, but it is an embedded and growing feature of the globalization of education systems in North countries, such as the United States (450,000 in 1993, in 2000 a million), France (140,000 in 1993), and the United Kingdom (100,000 in 1993) (Salt 1997; Jachimowicz 2003).

Increasing technological and logistical innovation

Technological innovations and logistic system developments in transportation, communications, information-processing and money transfer services have often been viewed as the essential revolutionary "tools" of globalization. Airline travel, global communication networks, integrated global logistic systems of production and service provision, new and faster information systems like the internet, wireless communication systems, satellite transmission of media, music, radio programming; all have directly and indirectly influenced peoples' lives in the Global North, one way or another, and have indirectly influenced growing proportions in the Global South. Do all these technological advances help human mobility? Many do, such as making travel cheaper and easier than ever before, making international communication easier than before, making it easier to develop and maintain transnational networks, keeping migrants in touch with their families "back home," and keeping families in touch with migrants "far away." Remittances transferred back home are facilitated by technological improvements in the logistic support systems of money – brokerage firms and transfer agencies – and of financial intermediaries – ATMs for example – and of international courier services and shipping companies.

Quite possibly, and logically, these technologies' major effect will be to increase the tendency towards more temporary international mobility, rather than facilitate more permanent dislocations, but the jury is still out on this predicted substitution. Global distance might be shrunk for these technologically dependent, but does this translate into an unconditional diminution, or removal, of the "friction of distance" for would-be migrants or circulators? In the international sphere, I don't believe so. Distance still matters in terms of cultural and social geographical realms. Communications technologies impose barriers and channels and exclude the non-literate, the non-connected, those on the other side of the "technological divide." Some technologies can be used for inclusive social purposes – the cellphone comes to mind as an example – but we are still a long way away from a world where the majority have direct access to these influential technological "crutches."

"Illegal," irregular and unauthorized migration and human rights concerns

Estimates of the world's "illegal alien" populations are not only hard to come by, they are also extremely unreliable and imprecise. Usage of terms such as illegal immigrants, illegal aliens, clandestine or undocumented migrants is often imprecise, if not pejorative. Unauthorized entrants, visa over-stayers, clandestine workers, underground workers, the illegally employed are other terms used to characterize this stigmatized group of international migrants; many being critical of the informality or non-legal nature of these migrants' situation (Miller 1995). Characterizing these immigrant non-nationals as "illegal" also implicitly places them outside the scope and protection of the rule of law, and the human rights protection the host nation's legal systems provides (Taran 2000).

A less prejudicial label, sanctioned by global institutions such as the International Labour Organization (ILO) and the International Organization for Migration (IOM), is "irregular migration." And, although the magnitude of irregular immigration can never be known, estimates suggest it may be as high as 30 million (Stalker 1994). Irregular migration is not only a Global South-to-Global North cross-border phenomenon, it is a growing global search for gainful work. It is driven, in large part, because of the limitations of domestic markets to provide sufficient, or adequate, employment opportunities. Irregular, unauthorized, clandestine migrants find employment in work characterized as "dirty, dangerous and difficult," but many are also forced into this cross-border escapade by another set of three d's: desperation, destruction and dislocation.

Irregular, unauthorized migration has become a major feature of migration systems in North America, Europe, South Asia, Southwest Asia (the Middle East), Asia–Pacific, Africa and Oceania, although the estimated flows in their respective global systems differ markedly in volumes and geographical spread. Border regulation and enforcement, and the well-established institutional barriers to unrestricted movement into beckoning and enticing labor markets, diverts many to seek unauthorized means of entry, or convinces many to enter legally and then work illegally, or overstay the visiting visa, stay after a failed asylum petition, among other strategies. Some, of course, don't intend to be "illegal," though it turns out that way. For example, young British backpackers top the list among the illegal workers in Australia, as they extend their stay a couple of months or more, because they are enjoying themselves too much, and, as one immigration official intimated, "[t]here's a legitimacy that comes with a white face" (BBC News 2005).

The United States is the country with the largest estimated number of unauthorized immigrants in 2004 – 10.3 million. This is a considerable increase from previous estimates for 1990 in the range of 4.0 to 4.5 million, and it does represent a considerable upturn in unauthorized entry during the 1990s. The Canadian situation differs from that of the US, the total of irregular migrants in that North American country being much smaller – an estimated total of 200,000 irregulars in the first decade of the twenty-first century, of which most overstayed their visas or were failed refugee claimants (Jimenez 2003).

Estimates of the amount of clandestine or irregular immigration into Europe are difficult to come by, in large part because the numbers who enter illegally, or who enter legally but work illegally, are by and large undocumented and unobservable events (Tapinos 1999). Border apprehension data has been used, however, to derive estimates for the EU-15 and EU-25 groups of countries in 2001, and the resultant estimated annual "illegal migration flows" are 650,000 for the EU-15 group, and 800,000 for the EU-25 group. Police authorities suggest that about half of all illegal migrants to the EU make use of smuggling organizations: with long-distance smuggling from sources such as Iraq, Afghanistan and China costing anywhere between 3,000 and 40,000 euros; medium-distance smuggling from sources such as Ukraine, Turkey and Georgia costing between 1,500 and 6,000 euros; and short-distance smuggling and/or the provision of basic documents costing 200 to 5,000 euros (Jandl 2003).

China, as well as several other Asia–Pacific countries, has become a global source for irregular, as well as sanctioned, managed emigration in today's globalization era, but the volume of smuggled Chinese (mainly from Fujian province) is relatively small in comparison to other trafficked nationals into Europe, North America and Japan (Skeldon 2004). That said, the potential for irregular Chinese migration to rapidly increase in the near future is an ever-present threat. Other Asia–Pacific sources, such as the Philippines and Indonesia, have long-standing and deeper-embedded migration cultures, and for decades have sent appreciably larger irregular and sanctioned migrant volumes overseas to North America as well as to Malaysia, Thailand and Singapore (Wickramasekera 2001). Southeast Asian "newcomers" in the irregular circuits are an estimated two million migrant workers from Myanmar (Burma), Cambodia and Lao PDR, who are believed to be working in Thailand's recovering economy (IOM 2005).

Irregular migration is now truly a global phenomenon, and these aforementioned regional examples highlight its unregulated character, persistence and its varied geographical reach. Crossing the nearest border, being transported across regions and through countries and arranging to cross a continent or ocean are all options today, albeit risky or dangerous options. And, as will be discussed in the next section, the global growth of irregular migration is very much related to the effectiveness of facilitating agencies to operate successfully in the "gray zones" of our world – destabilized and weak nation-states and poorly regulated regimes.

Growing reliance on intermediaries: the "commodification of migration"

Migration's facilitators

There are a host of transportation and transfer agencies, labor brokers and recruitment agencies, fraudulent document services, legal services and the like aiding and abetting migration across borders, over land-bridges, across seas and rivers, and helping migrants navigate through legal petitioning procedures. Legal practitioners and institutional organizations that help sponsor and recruit much needed workers from overseas are part of the mix of facilitators. For example, one country where such "managed migration" of health workers has been effectively promoted by public and private institutions is the Philippines (Bach 2004); but today, the international recruitment of doctors and nurses has a much wider global scope, both in terms of sources and destinations (WHO 2005), and in terms of their overall scarcity (Hamilton and Yau 2004). The global recruitment of migrants with particular (scarce) skills has a long history; but today, the commercial profitability of intermediary "facilitators" drives the system to enlarge its reach, diversify its sources and promote "brain drains" from the Global South (see Thomas-Hope 2003, for the Caribbean case).

Illegal, underground organizations and syndicates are the other part, profiting from migrant trafficking and smuggling. There are, of course, global underground economy networks, paths and transit routes – drug-smuggling routes, gun-running routes – which might use clandestine migration pathways, where migrants are recruited as mules for cocaine, opium smuggling, gem-smuggling. Migrants might be innocent, or incidental, parties to such criminal activities. Clandestine modes of entry might well be used both for goods as well as human transfers, and there is some circumstantial evidence to suggest that human-smuggling is as lucrative as drug-smuggling to organized crime (Bruggeman 2002). International cooperation to counter global human trafficking is under way, but the political and economic power of the underground syndicates involved and the "shadowy" nature of this illicit "facilitating industry" make interception and interdiction extremely difficult. As discussed in the next section, human trafficking and smuggling is benefiting from the crises and chaos at many borders and in many destabilized regions in today's globalizing world. Demonstrating this despondent reality is the following recent (2005) IOM Counter-trafficking finding that, in the destabilized region of the Balkans, victims of trafficking from the top five sending countries – Moldova, Romania, Ukraine, Belarus, Bulgaria – are predominantly found in the sex industry in Macedonia, Bosnia–Herzegovina, Kosovo and Albania (World Migration Report 2005).

Forced migration and human trafficking

Forced migration

"Forced migration" has become a suitable categorization of a range of global movements in which an element of coercion exists, including threats to life and livelihood arising from biophysical or social/anthropogenic crises – environmental disasters, chemical or nuclear disasters, famine, civil war, genocide or development-induced displacement. Indeed, several of Aguilar and Cavada's (2002) "plagues of globalization" qualify as indirect or direct determinants of forced migration flows – growth in poverty and inequality, loss of labor rights and the double exploitation of women, environmental deterioration, less participation of poor countries in global trade, economic dominance of transnational corporations and financial crises. Refugees, asylum-seekers, internally displaced persons (IDPs), development-induced displacees, environmental and disaster displacees (a majority being the rural poor and powerless in the Global South suffering from disruption, destruction and displacement) are some of the main groups forced to flee their homelands, or are seeking asylum beyond their nation's borders (Castles 2004).

Coinciding with the post-WWII "development era," in which the Global North – First and Second Worlds – competed in a Cold War contest to offer the Global

South/Third World development projects, many of the major refugee flights in the 1950s and 1960s occurred in the Global South: in Korea, Malaysia, Afghanistan, Southeast Asia, the Middle East and Central America. The mass disruptions and displacements that resulted were in large part a consequence of Cold War military interventionism, or Cold War political maneuvering, which cause internal strife, polarized societies, and hardened nation-state (dictators and governments, alike) treatments of their ethnic minorities, their indigenous peoples, their oppositions.

With the 1980s emerging from the troubled decade of the 1970s, globalization's "plague of influences" added to the mixture of warfare, violence and chaos, to jointly foster regional instability in East and West Africa, the Middle East, the former Yugoslavia, Central America and the Asia–Pacific regions. And, through the 1990s into the twenty-first century, new war theaters were added in West and East Africa, Iran and Iraq, East Timor, Kosovo and Bosnia–Herzegovina, and most recently Afghanistan and Iraq. According to UNHCR (2003) estimates, the global refugee population grew from 2.4 million in 1975, to peak at 18.2 million in 1993 after the end of the Cold War. By early 2003 the global refugee population had dropped to 10.4 million, however.

Internally displaced persons, development-induced displacements and forced resettlers are other categories of forced migration, but their relocation usually occurs within nation-state borders. When such forced displacement results in a border crossing and the establishment of refugee camps or communities immediately across the border, security tensions inevitably occur, but the refugee status might better aid the displaced in these cases, rather than the more helpless IDP situation, where the state government might very well be the perpetrator, or aider and abettor, of the dislocation. The causal forces, as well as humanitarian concerns for the human rights of these unfortunates, are similar to those affecting refugees and asylum seekers.

Asylum seekers, on the other hand, are people who move across a border in search of protection, but whose refugee status is yet to be determined. During the Cold War, political asylum petitions were most common, and judicial distinctions between economic and political migrants often made the deciding difference in petition proceedings. Since the early 1990s, however, humanitarian grounds for asylum have become the more persuasive arguments in European courts, and even in the United States a wider set of petition briefs than political asylum are now being used, including gender-discrimination.

"Environmental refugees" have emerged as a "politically correct" label for rural poor groups who have been displaced by natural disasters (floods, volcanoes, landslides, earthquakes and tsunamis) or whose livelihoods have been disrupted and severely threatened by desertification, deforestation, land degradation and groundwater pollution to such a degree that they are forced to flee (Myers and Kent 1995). According to this US-based report provided by the Climate Institute, there was estimated to be as many as 25 million environmental refugees, and the total could climb to 50 million by 2010, unless environmental degradation is curbed. Countering this claim, Black (2001) convincingly argues that environmental causes of displacement can rarely, if ever, be separated from social, political and development-related influences, as well as local and regional anthropogenic factors. Such forced displacement and subsequent migration because of extreme environmental factors is always going to be linked to social, political and ethnic/ indigenous conflicts, weak or non-existent nation-state governance and human rights abuses. It is meted out on the most powerless of the marginalized people, with women and children being the most vulnerable.

Human trafficking: new slavery

Smuggling humans across borders, and its more insidious partner, human trafficking, has grown to be a profitable business in today's globalizing world. It is estimated that, globally, there are more than 50 organized crime groups engaged in human trafficking activities, charging about $27,000 for each person. As of the year 2000, the price for Chinese passage to the United States – the highest in the world – had been raised from $30,000 a person to about $50,000. A recent reconceptualization of trafficking as capitalist enterprise also views this dehumanizing practice as a "commodification of migration," from which migration merchants are able to prey on, and profit from, people's mobility. Drawing upon evidence from Ecuador (Aznay province) and China (Fujian province), Kyle and Liang (1998) suggest the "embedded commodification" of clandestine trafficking occurs within groups bounded by ethnic or racial stratification and regional power structures, in the sense that these intermediary services are provided to insiders, not outsiders (also see Bales 2000a; Kyle and Koslowski 2001).

The growing practice among international criminal groups, syndicates and organizations to profit from migration has become a new form of slavery and coercion, praying upon young women and children by offering hope, while tricking, brutalizing and selling them into prostitution and sex-working, sweatshop labor, and similar illicit, dehumanizing and/or dangerous occupations in which they have little autonomy or basic rights and human dignities (Bales 2000a; Williams 1999). The International Labour Office has recently estimated that at least 12.3 million people work as slaves or in other forms of forced labor. In what is the first formal estimation of the magnitude of this new global industry – characterized as the "underside of globalization" – as many as 2.5 million are in forced labor as a result of cross-border trafficking, with approximately half being employed against their wills in the sex trade (ILO 2005).

The global sex trade involves the trafficking of women and children for the purposes of commercial sexual exploitation – prostitution, sex services and pornography. In this dehumanizing realm of transnational criminal activity, women and children are valued exclusively as commodities rather than human beings; as disposable "new slaves." One estimate suggests that each year more than one million children and teenagers are forced into the commercial sex industry. Global profits from trafficking total $32 billion a year, or $13,000 per trafficked worker, while profits from forced commercial sexual exploitation totaled $27.8 billion annually, or $23,000 per worker (ILO 2005).

Global and hemispheric differences in migration policies

Throughout the 1990s, there were serious attempts by many regional blocs to regularize and harmonize migration policies and cooperate on issues related to unauthorized migration, refugee flights and refugee assistance, and the humanitarian treatment of migrants and refugees. The UN encouraged such regional cooperation, recognizing that a global policy and regulatory mechanism on international labor mobility was impractical. Coordinated by the International Organization for Migration (IOM), in East and Southeast Asia, the "Manila Process" attempted to regularize regional responses to unauthorized migration and human trafficking among 17 countries. IOM also helped coordinate Asia–Pacific consultations amongst governments on a broad range of population movements within the region (Martin 2001).

With formal channels of entry into European countries very much restricted, asylum petitioning has become a common means for aspiring immigrants to use this refugee path as an entry vehicle. With the Cold War behind them, most receiving countries now base their asylum decisions on humanitarian considerations, so that decisions are made on a case by case basis, and much more rarely on the grounds of political persecution, communist/dictator oppression or politically-motivated civil strife, which were the *modus operandi* of earlier petitions in the 1960s and 1970s. One estimate suggests that approximately three-quarters of the asylum petitioners stay in the country, half receiving legal permission, the other half just staying on illegally (Widgren 1993).

Recently, and especially since 9/11, 2001, there appears to be a divergence between European and US immigration policies and growing differences between these two regions' perspectives towards legal immigration, in terms of social responsibilities and humanitarian respect for immigrants' and refugees' rights. Whereas the 1997 Amsterdam Treaty solidified the policy that the free movement of labor across national borders within the European Union would be facilitated, and visa issuance decided by national vote, 9/11 and its aftermath of insecurity and domestic fear turned a similar negotiating situation in North America around. It led to a dramatic resurgence of the anti-immigration lobby in the United States, and a general retreat by politicians in Washington on immigration harmonization and humanitarianism. National "homeland security" interests were recouched in anti-immigration terms. The INS, now within the US Department of Homeland Security, was empowered to accelerate deportations of criminal "foreigners." The discussions about amnesty programs, or guest-worker programs, between US administration officials and Mexican and Central American regimes, that had been considered in earnest in 1999 and 2000, have been abruptly shelved.

America's borders were to be made more migration-proof, and "homeland security" was to be defended on all fronts. International students' access to university entry in the US was also made more difficult, and the security of their study abroad was made more tenuous, and more prey to institutional rigidity than before. Security measures in US airports, insensitive and brusque search procedures, and a host of reactionary practices discriminating against and stereotyping Asian entrants have changed the "welcoming" atmosphere for Eastern hemisphere visitors; while singling out, and discriminating against, European Asians, Arabic minorities of European nationality, even the nation's own citizenry – Asian-Americans. Whether this xenophobic reaction by the US government, and the prolonged sense of fear and insecurity among the American populous, has long-term effects on this country's traditional "welcoming role" remains to be seen. It is quite possible that Europe, by comparison, will become a more attractive magnet. At the same time, this "new age of migration" is posing challenging racial and ethnic questions for European citizenry, with new cultural dimensions of difference emerging in the melting-pots (or salad-bowls) of their cities and countrysides.

Conclusions

Peter Stalker (2000) characterizes globalization's impact on this new age of international migration as one of "workers without borders." Globalization's economic impulses are driving an international skill exchange of labor, ideas and human and social capital, but they are also stimulating Global South-to-Global North flights of the dislocated, the discriminated and the disposable. The "commodification of migration" has its deeply troubling side, as human trafficking with its long-standing links to organized crime appears to be on the increase. This highly profitable global industry has generated new forms of slavery and unconscionable abuses of human rights, as too many "disposable" foreign women and children have been tricked and coerced into the sex industry or into dehumanizing domestic servitude.

Social, racial, ethnic and transnational diversity in the global migration streams is already a growing reality, with more diversity to be expected. Combining this transition dynamic with the increasing vulnerability and inequality experienced by more and more of the world's less privileged, we can predict that the volume of internationally mobile people will continue to increase. Furthermore, we can expect that increased multicultural diversity will occur, despite the xenophobia and racist divisions that continue to surface again and again (Castles 2000; Castles and Davidson 2000). Predictably, as well as unfortunately, forced migration is one of globalization's unruly spaces, as environmental, societal and development-induced forces of dislocation, together with warfare and breakdowns in civil order, continue to displace the weak and the powerless and force them to ever-more desperate means of survival, including flight, asylum seeking, and trafficker-inducements and broken promises – "bride-to-be" marriage recruitment and "entertainer" offers, among other syndicate tricks (Castles 2003, 2004).

Unconscionably, and also unfortunately, the human rights of too many global migrants continue to be compromised, dismissed or disrespected, regardless of their legal status. Migrants all over the world, especially "illegal" migrants, have been cast as outsiders and the root cause of criminal activity in the news media and popular discourses: migrants are portrayed as "drug-mules," as HIV/AIDS carriers, as disease transmitters (Taran 2000). Less dramatically, but still the similar age-old condemnation rings out for today's global migrants: "They are taking away jobs from the nation's poor, they come to take our welfare services, they're invading us!" Homeland security and anti-immigration agendas have coalesced to serve as formidable, reactionary institutional mechanisms to thwart the plans of the global migrant and his/her dependents; to keep "things the way they are" by "keeping *them* out!"

Despite the obstacles, the social barriers, the cultural wars (?), many international migrants will devise their own particular strategies to accomplish their goals, in large part because the institutional mechanisms attempting to monitor, regulate and control such movement across national borders will force them to be creative in their avoidance/accommodation strategies. Migration facilitators will continue to prompt irregular entry, because it garners obscene profits. Forced migration and irregular migration will continue to be "unruly sisters," accompanying managed and legal immigration, temporary contract labor, and the like; with both regulated and unregulated flows and resultant diaspora stocks stimulating and regenerating each other.

Signs also point to the growth in importance of shorter-term temporary international movement(s), as people in search of work and sustenance eschew longer duration emigration and immigration practices. In the international skill exchange, highly skilled migrants will be as prevalent as the less-skilled, the internationally educated will (re)position themselves to be responsive to global markets, and the exchanges of capital, people and information utilizing today's global technologies and logistics platforms will insure the globalization of labor is multidirectional, multidimensional and multicultural in its complexity. The continued growth of transnational strategies is also expected, and a widening of multi-local transnational networks to incorporate Europe, North America, Asia and Oceania "places" into truly global networks and diasporas is more than likely.

Globalization's transformations of production, consumption and commercial systems, the accompanying restructuring of international finance, the heightened concentrations of global capital in corporate hands, the hyper-mobility of global capital, and increasing levels of social and economic inequality, among other consequences; all have influences on the mobility of labor, and of labor's dependents. Labor, if immobile, is at a considerable disadvantage in the global conflict with capital interests, but migration, both international and internal, continues to provide opportunities for people to seek and find better lives and livelihoods (see Standing 1999 for further insights). Global labor's complex mobility responses should be expected, although unpredictable patterns and unruly processes are going to be part of the mix for some time to come.

7 Unruly spaces
Globalization and transnational criminal economies

Christian Allen

Introduction

Globalization is an uneven transition process from an international economy comprised of discrete national units to a global economy of integrated national economies. Advances in telecommunications, information management and transportation technologies facilitate this shift, as does an international political economy committed to reducing the role of the state in economic affairs. Globalization stimulates increased social, political and economic interaction of all types between places, in terms of increased flows of people, information, commodities and capital across borders. Yet globalization is also qualitatively different from earlier forms of international exchange. More important than increased "flows" is the functional integration of economic activities and "national" economies across borders (Dicken 1998). This integration includes a cross-border restructuring of production and distribution processes by business enterprises, with a concomitant emphasis on strategic alliances with other actors (Portnoy 2000: 157).

Globalization processes have increased the scale and scope of transnational exchange for legitimate and criminal enterprises alike. Where cross-border economic exchange is simplified, increased trade flows provide many opportunities to hide contraband in licit flows. State institutions are increasingly challenged by a tension between promoting free market capitalism while simultaneously restricting the flow of drugs, arms, prostitutes, "conflict" diamonds, or other undesirable commodities. Harriss-White (2002) identifies this recent growth in illicit cross-border exchanges as the "underside" of globalization, worthy of research attention, yet neglected and poorly understood. This knowledge deficit results largely from the secretive nature of illicit trade, which greatly restricts the availability of valid empirical data on the subject.

The challenge involved in gauging even basic trends in criminal economies, like total annual gross revenue, illustrates this point. The most thorough and careful estimates of the annual revenues generated by organized crime vary significantly – from $500 billion (International Monetary Fund – see Cormier 2001: 200) to $1.5 trillion (UNDP Human Development Report – see Kendall 2001: 269). When studying criminal activities at any scale and scope (e.g. the "conflict" diamond trade in Africa; or the clustering of cocaine trafficking activities in Medellin,

Colombia; or the location choices of retail drug sellers in urban, open-air drug markets), the same difficulties in acquiring valid measurements exist. For this reason, researchers have called for a qualitative and investigative approach to criminal economies (Holden-Rhodes 1997: 152).

Globalization has stimulated unruliness in a variety of places and spaces where "post-modern" security threats like organized crime, insurgency and terrorism flourish. These emerging threats predate the recent phase of globalization and were not created by it. Nonetheless, globalization has transformed them in profound ways, much as it has so many licit institutions. Crime and terrorism are now trans-sovereign problems because they occur across state boundaries in ways that individual states cannot alone control. The organizations now involved link actors in many different places through functional networks. The spatial scope of their activities has expanded greatly in recent decades as groups have engaged in successful searches for overseas partners.

Unlike most Cold War era security threats, these emerging ones are diffuse, dominated by non-state actors, and often motivated by entrepreneurial interests. State authorities tend to conflate organized crime and terrorism, seeing them as "two sides of the same coin" (Farer 1999: 286). Terrorist or other politically motivated groups may support themselves, in whole or part, through criminal enterprise of one sort or another. They may coexist with organized criminal gangs in "underground" networks, and may occasionally engage in mutually beneficial transactions. Yet they have fundamentally different goals: politically motivated groups seek to challenge the very existence of the liberal–democratic state, while commercially oriented criminal actors do not. In fact, criminal organizations benefit from the open borders and deregulated markets encouraged by most state authorities.

Studies of organized crime have traditionally focused on the motivations and personalities of individual criminals (Martin and Romaro 1992: 107). This focus has encouraged a "Mafia/Godfather" model of organized transnational crime emphasizing centrally governed and strictly hierarchical structures that seek to monopolize criminal markets. If this model were accurate, the elimination of major crime figures would have a noticeable, long-term impact on criminal economies, but they have not. The fact is that law enforcement efforts would be much easier if criminal economies were organized this way, considering that large, fixed hierarchical structures are relatively vulnerable to law enforcement efforts. Criminal markets are better understood as complex, densely interconnected networks comprising hundreds of organized enterprises and thousands more *ad hoc* associations engaged in informal and fluid relationships.

These myriad actors compose densely interlinked circuits of drugs, arms and other illicit or illicitly traded commodities and services. "Criminal" commodities include art and antiquities, stolen cars, counterfeit goods, pornography, valuable and/or endangered flora and fauna, human organs, hazardous waste, nuclear material, migrant laborers, sex workers, cigarettes, gemstones and other precious minerals, timber and oil. Criminal economies are also composed of a variety of services that facilitate the cross-border exchange of these commodities. Illicit "producer" services include the production of counterfeit documents, money-laundering, transportation and warehousing services, protection rackets, and contract killing or other "muscle."

Drugs are the primary source of income in transnational criminal economies, accounting for perhaps two-thirds of total revenues (Farer 1999: 276). Money earned in drug trafficking funds related activities like corruption, money-laundering and arms trafficking. Criminal organizations vary greatly in terms of size, functional scope, goals, duration of operation, and formal organization. The term "criminal organization" might refer to large-scale criminal syndicates, to informally connected networks of individual criminal entrepreneurs, or anything in between. "True" organized crime refers to entrepreneurial individuals and groups engaged in systematic law-breaking characterized by continuity of action, a relatively formal organizational structure, and a capacity to corrupt and co-opt state authorities (Finckenauer 2001: 168). This differs from crime that is organized, like a coordinated one-off event like the theft of valuable art and artifacts.

"True" criminal organizations play a central and coordinating role in establishing networks, determining the basic purpose, identifying functional role specializations, and brokering interactions between network actors (Williams 2002: 77–81). Their role is not exclusive, however. There are also many smaller criminal entrepreneurs operating singly or in small, impermanent groups. "Licit" actors, like corrupt officials or experts in financial security and international law, are also active in these networks. These "gray" activities link licit and illicit economies in ways that complicate the definition of clear boundaries between them.

Networks developed to smuggle humans from one place to another offer a valuable illustration. Here, criminal organizations (in many forms and sizes) are only one type of a range of actors involved. Numerous "legitimate" actors involved include travel and employment agencies, freelance recruiters or other individual entrepreneurs, transport companies, and corrupt state authorities. Such actors are neither criminal organizations themselves, nor have permanent linkages to criminal groups (Ruggiero 2001: 235).

Consider the "criminality" of two very different human smuggling activities: first, the provision of counterfeit documentation to migrant laborers along with transportation to a destination chosen by the "victim"; and second, the coerced international movement of captive women and children for purposes of sexual exploitation. These are very different activities, undertaken by different actors, filling different demands, and each deserving of unique law enforcement responses. Perhaps a "continuum of criminality" could be devised for human smuggling. At the least-criminal end would be those entrepreneurs who facilitate the unlawful cross-border movement of migrant workers, or what Van Duyne (2001: 7) terms the "criminal human mobility industry." On the opposite end are actors who smuggle desperate victims to be exploited in various forms of debt-bonded slavery. This activity is better termed human "trafficking" – smuggling when coercion, force, deception and exploitation are present (Martin and Miller 2000: 969). Links to "true" organized crime are more common on the criminal end of the human smuggling spectrum involving commercial sex work.

A network approach to criminal economies

A network approach to transnational crime reflects a growing appreciation of network organization and governance in explaining all manner of economic and social systems (Hakansson and Johanson 1993; Axelsson and Easton 1992). Castells (2000: 180) notes that "networks are the fundamental stuff of which new organizations are and will be made." It is the network, and not any individual entrepreneur, business firm or industrial sector, that is the basic unit of economic organization and therefore the appropriate unit of analysis for examining strategy and structure in economic systems (Hagstrom 2000). Networks are a series of nodes (which may be individual entrepreneurs, organizations or institutions) connected by flows of goods, services, capital and information. Such alliances provide flexibility and allow members to pursue external economies by sharing knowledge, resources and risk.

Trends toward network governance in criminal economies mirror shifts in the organization of production in licit industries. Traditional Fordist production systems were rigidly organized on the principle of vertical integration, a structure that limited the firm's capacity to respond to uncertainties associated with dynamic economic, regulatory and technological environments. The systems that have supplanted Fordist organization are characterized by their flexibility, both in the production process itself and in the management of upstream and downstream linkages with associated firms. The high degree of functional specialization in these systems is perhaps the most identifiable tendency of what Dicken (1998: 165–172) calls "after-Fordist" production.

Williams (2002: 73–75) argues that criminal enterprises actually moved more quickly than their counterparts in licit industry to adopt flexible production and network relations. Law enforcement efforts forced them to operate covertly – focusing less on rigid structures and fixed investments and more on flexible organization and cooperation with groups that have complementary skills or resources. A good example of cooperative network relationships are the alliances that Colombian cocaine trafficking organizations formed with Italian and Russian criminal groups to facilitate distribution in European markets. Not all network interactions involve this sort of long-term cooperation, however. Many involve short-term contract relationships or even one-time exchanges of specific goods or services.

Underground networks can be organized in a variety of ways. Arquilla and Ronfeldt (2001: 7–10) suggest three generic models: chain, hub-and-spoke, and all-channel. In chain networks, commodities and information flow along a line of contact, with interactions taking place through intermediate nodes. The compartmentalization and spatial diffusion of such networks serve to "distance the criminal hand from the criminal mind" (Passas 2001: 30). In hub-and-spoke systems, a core organization performs a coordinating role for a series of linked nodes connected through the hub. This central actor establishes the basic purpose of the network and manages the flow of resources, knowledge, capital and products through the network. In all-channel networks, each actor is connected to all others – a system that requires dense communications links to organize and sustain.

These are ideal types and hybrids are common. For example, a network's core actors may form an all-channel system, while its peripheral relationships are managed through chains. Because actors can be members of more than one network, and networks are themselves embedded within surrounding networks, complex combinations will incorporate a multitude of nodes into sprawling forms that Arquilla and Ronfeldt (2001) call "spider's webs." Networks integrate this diversity of nodes into associations that blur organizational and territorial boundaries, such that any attempt to delimit their extent (geographically, functionally, by product, around a "core" actor) is essentially arbitrary and based on imperfect interpretations. "Members" perceive the network only from their particular position within it. Network actors may therefore interpret a network in very different ways, even in fundamental matters such as network structure and membership (Hakansson and Johanson 1993: 43; Axelsson and Easton 1992: 19). Because network organization is so variable and flexible, they are both elusive targets for law enforcement and problematic objects of study.

The diversity of potential network forms reflects the dynamic nature of criminal economies themselves. Some market participants are eliminated while new ones are continually attracted by high profits. State regulation and the intensity with which it is enforced varies through time and space. There may be shifts in market demand, the introduction of new sources of supply, or even new products. As industry conditions change, so do appropriate business strategies. Flexible production and network organization allow criminal actors to best respond to emerging opportunities and threats.

Unruly places: "embeddedness" and transnational crime

Globalization processes are complex, contested, and difficult to identify and measure. They are simultaneously social, political and economic, dependent on local contingencies, and thus unevenly developed over space and time (Hay and Marsh 2000: 3). Specific local characteristics interact with global processes to generate distinct outcomes. All manner of organizations and enterprises, including criminal ones, are rooted in some particular "local" set of conditions and institutions that shape their opportunities, goals and means (Castells 2000: 188). Therefore, any examination should take into account their social and historical "embeddedness" in space and time.

Indeed, we can identify a number of location conditions that encourage the "embeddedness" of criminal activities in particular places. These include a widespread acceptance of violence as a means to political and economic ends (Colombia), porous borders (Russia), institutionalized corruption (Nigeria), proximity to major markets for illicit commodities (Mexico), and access to raw material inputs like drug crops (Bolivia) or exploitable natural resource commodities (Congo). The most fertile places for criminal activities to emerge and prosper feature a combination of these conditions. These "advantages" are best exploited in places where political and economic instability has diminished the state's ability to enforce legal sovereignty over its territory. Criminal groups establish operations in these weak, delegitimized and/or failed states because they can operate there with a minimum of risk.

"Failed states" are those characterized by an inability on the part of state institutions to maintain infrastructure, provide basic services, or provide for the physical security of the population. Such basic services and protections are instead provided by tribes, clans and other sub-state groups, with a corresponding transfer of loyalty from the state to these new social units (Naylor 2001: 211). Political power and control over territory is therefore fragmented among corrupt remnants of the state and various non-state actors like clan leaders, warlords and crime bosses (Willett 2002: 190).

Many cases of state collapse can be attributed to the demise of the Soviet Union and the end of the Cold War. The withdrawal of strategically motivated aid to many peripheral states exacerbated the vulnerabilities of their fragile economic and political systems (Laasko 2000: 72). In places like the former Soviet Union and Yugoslavia, Afghanistan, Angola, Liberia, Mozambique and Somalia the ruling elite was fractured and national unity dissolved, with various ethnic movements or religious fundamentalism filling the power vacuum (Amin 1997: 59–61). Conway (Chapter 6) notes considerable civil disruption and chaos contributing to state failure in Congo, Rwanda–Burundi, Sierra Leone, Sudan and Eritrea. Many other states, including Colombia, Mexico, Nigeria, Myanmar and Indonesia, have not experienced "failure" of a similar degree, but are nonetheless deeply corrupted and heavily influenced by non-state and/or criminal actors.

The emergence of internationally competitive criminal organizations from the "unruly" world periphery contrasts sharply with the absence of competitive enterprises in licit industries from those countries. Criminal enterprises should therefore be considered as successful responses to both unfavorable terms of trade in licit industries and the painful structural adjustments associated with policy prescriptions like fiscal discipline, deregulation and privatization. Bayart *et al.* (1999) argue that the still limited integration of the "South" into the global economy has occurred in large measure through the growth of all sorts of illicit cross-border transactions.

Crime and the commercialization of conflict

Globalization processes have exacerbated existing disparities in wealth and power both among and within nations (Passas 2001: 34; Harriss-White 2002: 10; Herod *et al.* 1998: 16). Inequalities arise in part because market-oriented economic reforms have reduced the economic sovereignty of weak states and diminished their capacity and willingness to provide for social welfare or address domestic political unrest (Woods 2000: 12). In this manner, globalization has contributed to growing insecurity and civil conflict throughout the periphery.

In the post-Cold War era, the insurgent and terrorist groups participating in these assorted civil conflicts have increasingly had to rely on informal sources of funding to sustain their operations. These include a wide range of criminal activities, including: kidnapping and protection rackets; theft and diversion of humanitarian relief supplies; looting local landscapes and populations; drug production and trafficking; and the exploitation of natural resource commodities like oil, timber, gems and precious metals.

Such groups may also offer protection against state authorities to entrepreneurial criminal actors in exchange for money, weapons, or business connections. Current and recent insurgencies supported primarily through criminal activities include Sendero Luminoso (Peru); FARC/ELN (Colombia); KLA (Kosovo); and separatist movements in Myanmar, Chechnya and "Kurdistan" (Farer 1999: 252; Martin and Romaro 1992: 103).

Exploitable natural resource wealth not only funds civil conflict, but also motivates it. As the economic and political opportunities of marginalized populations decline, they take to arms seeking direct control over scarce but exploitable resources like mines, forests or fields of drug crops. Such conflicts are especially likely to occur in places where resource exploitation fails to benefit local populations, generating frustration and a desire to wrest control from "outsiders." Here, natural resource commodities become the prize in territorial struggles between the ruling elite and their domestic rivals. Le Billon (2001: 573–575) provides an extensive list of countries, internal civil conflicts, and their associated resource "prizes." In each of these fragmented societies, conflicts are rooted more in the economic logic of predation than in any political or ethno-nationalist motivations (Bayart *et al.* 1999: 18).

Such conflicts are more commonly the commercial means for individuals and groups than the political ends of states. The ruling elite in many weak but resource-rich states have adjusted their economic strategies in favor of informal economies and privatized companies. A United Nations report (UN Security Council 2002) and the non-profit watchdog Global Witness (2000) describe how a number of African governments are controlled by clandestine power-brokers who use their influence to manipulate the process of deregulation and privatization advocated by international lenders to their own advantage. These hidden "elite networks" surrounding prominent elected officials are actively engaged in criminal activities, and are linked to broader transnational criminal networks through relationships with both licit multinationals and criminal organizations (Le Billon 2001: 562). These groups are the main beneficiaries of the "economy of plunder, fraud and smuggling" that characterizes much of Sub-Saharan Africa (Bayart *et al.* 1999: 23).

Another important factor contributing to the frequency, duration, savagery and criminalization of civil conflicts around the world is the super-abundance of weaponry available through licit and illicit channels. Weapons manufacturers in the United States and Soviet Union have historically produced many more weapons than their militaries needed or could absorb. This surplus weaponry was historically disposed of through transfers to loyal client states, but arms exports have become increasingly commercialized over time. There has also been an increase in production by developing countries that had not before been major producers. These countries build arms industries for the same real or perceived benefits, including foreign exchange, technological spin-offs, manufacturing jobs, and international prestige (Naylor 2001: 215–216).

Moreover, weapons are relatively durable and are commonly recycled among conflicts. Regional arms markets have emerged in conflict zones like Lebanon, the Horn of Africa and Central Asia. The importance of such conflict zones for black market arms distribution comes not simply from the volumes of military supplies poured into them, but also from the fact that, once arms are there, all trace of them is effectively lost. Naylor (2001: 219) suggests that a conflict zone does for weapons what offshore banking centers with strict secrecy laws do for money. Arms purchasers in conflict zones include rogue states, terrorists, insurgents, and criminal organizations from around the world.

State sovereignty in the globalization era

Traditional notions of state sovereignty are challenged by globalization. The options of states to manage and execute trade and fiscal policy are constrained by their participation in the global economy and its various institutions. Many states are beholden to international creditors and therefore subject to disciplining action by multilateral economic entities (Kelly 1999: 389). They sacrifice sovereignty over economic decision-making regarding debt service, exchange rate values, international credit ratings, and other development choices to transnational institutions. States also face international pressures to eliminate obstacles to trade and investment, and to minimize regulation, taxation and spending. For these reasons, the state is commonly portrayed as increasingly marginalized, or "hollowed out."

The disjuncture between globalizing markets and traditional systems of static, territorially bounded sovereign states is particularly apparent in the realm of international finance, an unruly space navigated by huge flows of "stateless" capital. Hudson (2000: 275–276) observes that globalization has stimulated an "unbundling" of sovereignty, in which states cede sovereignty in some areas, but retain it in others. For example, offshore financial centers (OFCs) retain sovereignty over various legal and regulatory mechanisms, but cede fiscal authority through relaxed tax regimes. This unbundling allows them to provide spaces with minimal regulation and taxation without undermining sovereignty in other areas.

OFCs are critical nodes in the global financial system that functions as the nexus between licit and illicit markets. The economies of these micro-states are based on business services like banking, trust management, business formation, ship registration and insurance. These services are provided in environments characterized by secrecy and minimal or no taxation or state regulation. Corporations and accounts are set up and managed by legitimate producer service professionals like lawyers and accountants. These service providers commonly do not know (or care to know) the identities of their clients. As far as they are concerned, they are conducting legitimate business.

There are dozens of OFCs, arranged in regional groupings around the world's three main financial centers in New York (Caribbean), London (Europe and Middle East), and Tokyo (Pacific). OFCs manage enormous flows of capital and are of critical importance to the global financial system used by legitimate and criminal actors alike. Even the majority of the "hot" money channeled through

OFCs is not from organized criminal enterprises, but from the legal or illegal earnings of "licit" actors involved in tax evasion, capital flight, or the laundering of bribe money (Ruggiero 2001: 233). Nonetheless, OFCs play a major part in criminal economies by acting as "black boxes" that obscure illicit transactions from law enforcement authorities (Passas 2001: 31).

Yet, the influence of globalization processes on state sovereignty is not nearly so clear-cut. While weak states have certainly experienced a notable decline in sovereignty, most core, "strong" states continue to play an active role in constructing globalization through their influence on the discourse of transnational institutions (Herod et al. 1998: 14). It was through the efforts of sovereign nation-states that such agencies were created in the first place (Kelly 1999: 389). The role of the state has changed, but not necessarily diminished. States remain the most important actors in the regulation of markets, the reconstruction of borders, and the development and enforcement of prohibition regimes. It is through these decisions that states define the "illicit spaces" of economies (Farer 1999: 251).

States are undergoing simultaneous processes of retreat and re-engagement with regard to both licit and illicit cross-border economic exchange. Globalization weakens states by making it more difficult for them to control entry into their territories. Nonetheless, they remain firmly committed to notions of national sovereignty. Increased volumes of cross-border "flows" make the delimitation and enforcement of social and territorial boundaries, especially those separating core from periphery, an ever more critical task for the state. Border enforcement efforts in Core countries have intensified as states seek to reinforce notions of territorial sovereignty (Nevins 2002: 173). For example, in the five years following enactment of the North American Free Trade Agreement (NAFTA) in 1994, US manpower and resources committed to enforcement efforts at the US–Mexico border has more than tripled (Nevins 2002: 179; McCaffery 1998: 3).

Intensified efforts to secure borders against undesirable flows are one sure sign that the sovereign state remains an important actor, despite globalization rhetoric that trumpets its disappearance. State attempts to manage migration flows suggest that globalization has brought about a selective regulatory retreat by the state. Andreas (1999, 2000) identifies an inherent tension between free trade and drug prohibition with the simultaneous promotion of both internationalization (NAFTA) and nationalization (strict border enforcement regimes targeting drugs and migrant laborers) in the US–Mexico border region. Such contradictory policies might promote globalization, but they strengthen criminal organizations and impair state control efforts. The obvious paradox suggests current US policy goals may be incompatible.

Furthermore, there is scant evidence that intensified border control efforts by Core countries are effective deterrents against migration streams from the periphery. There are, nonetheless, meaningful differences in the nature and dimensions of labor flows under globalization. One noteworthy change is that international migration has become more difficult and costly for potential migrants. Stricter border controls and asylum policies have stimulated smuggling operations. Migrants must increasingly engage the services of "professional" smugglers – such as coyotes, snakeheads – to facilitate their border crossing. Koslowski (2001: 352) argues, however, that intensified law enforcement operations against migrant smuggling operations are bound to fail without complementary efforts to reduce demand for migrant labor in destination countries. Similar criticisms have been leveled at source-country drug interdiction efforts (Lee 1999; Castells 1998: 195; Holden-Rhodes 1997: 164).

A progressive agenda to counter transnational crime

The regulatory mechanisms of globalized markets are highly fragmented, creating numerous opportunities for criminal actors to exploit a variety of structural inequalities in law, politics, culture, and economics. These asymmetries stimulate demand for illicit commodities, create incentives to engage in illegal markets, and reduce the capacity of the state to respond to such activities. As long as these "criminogenic" asymmetries remain, criminal entrepreneurs will continue to pursue transnational business strategies to take advantage of them (Passas 2001: 23).

Cross-border smuggling has been around as long as international trade, but it is only recently that transnational crime has been considered an acute security problem. The scale and scope of cross-border illicit activities have clearly expanded in recent decades, but an important question remains: just what kind of a security threat does transnational crime pose? Farer (1999: 253) argues that political leaders and security institutions in search of a post-Cold War mission have transformed crime from a national law enforcement problem into an international threat to basic national security interests. Traditional notions of security, however, have been concerned primarily with the territorial integrity of the state. In this sense, the threat posed by criminal gangs is unclear and disputable. Indeed, criminal actors seem to be more of an irritant than a serious threat. So, what is the best way to address an irritating (but not truly threatening) phenomenon, destructive on the whole, yet stimulated by demand for illicit goods and services from a growing number of consumers?

The obvious solution is to foster greater international cooperation to tighten up exploitable asymmetries, especially the widely differing levels of commitment to and capacity for enforcing the rule of law. It is worth mentioning that state authorities already cooperate with foreign counterparts more than they have ever before. The problem is that they do so within a system built on the foundations of state sovereignty. While organized crime is increasingly transnational, state responses remain essentially national. To build a consistent regime of international law, states would have to cede power to transnational actors, something they have been reluctant to do so far (Passas 2001: 43).

A related concern is that increased transnational police cooperation will contribute to institutions and practices that remain outside the democratic control of the populations of nation states (Ruggiero 2001: 237). International law enforcement institutions might act to reduce civil liberties or violate the national sovereignty of "host" countries. Strong states will increasingly seek to intervene in the domestic affairs of less powerful ones, claiming to act in the "common" interest by targeting criminal actors. Perhaps more importantly, efforts to intensify border controls against illicit flows will likely hinder legal commerce in unacceptable ways. There exists a precarious balance between security and the facilitation of licit trade. Given long-term priorities and historical trends, this balance seems likely to tip in favor of commerce (Holden-Rhodes 1997: 166).

Moreover, even successful responses to criminal activities can have unforeseen, negative consequences. The disruption of markets or organizations can cause them to re-emerge elsewhere in a different form, more diffuse, less familiar, and more difficult to counter. This location substitution strategy is popularly referred to as the "balloon effect" (referring to the displacement of contained gases when compressed). As state efforts against one source, route or market become more effective, incentives mount to increase production, trans-shipment or distribution in other, less risky, locations. Therefore, "getting tough" on transnational crime is a strategy with noteworthy limits. It implies a high cost in state resources yet quickly experiences a point of diminishing returns. But, must we simply accept transnational crime as an undesirable but unavoidable element of a globalizing economy? I rather think not!

A radically progressive response would be to implement a program of drug legalization. Such an effort would help besieged state governments cope with security threats posed by drug traffickers by removing drug money from criminal economies (Lee 1999: 34). Castells (1998: 174) asserts that drug legalization is perhaps the greatest potential threat facing drug trafficking organizations. Because drugs account for the majority of revenue in transnational criminal economies, their removal would greatly reduce opportunities for corruption and violence (Farer 1999: 276). Allowing for the free movement of labor would serve to take criminal actors out of the human mobility market in the same way.

Such an approach seems unlikely in the short to medium term. It is not clear what effects the decriminalization of illicit drugs or labor would have on drug use and abuse or migration rates or on the health of criminal economies more generally. Effective methods of implementing such a strategy deserve thoughtful and comprehensive research attention. In the meantime, stable core states concerned with trans-sovereign security threats should seek to prevent state failure; increase transparency in government, thereby reducing opportunities for corruption; and generally seek to mitigate the social, political and economic instabilities that result from globalization.

Globalization's geopolitical faces

8 Geopolitical globalization
From world systems to global city systems

Dennis Conway and Richard Wolfel

Introduction

In this chapter, the geopolitical power relations in this era of contemporary globalization are examined at several scales: the supranational, the nation-state, the urban and the regional. Today's global system of international relations between nation-states, between cores and peripheries, and between the Global North and Global South, has grown out of a long sociohistorical process of expanding and contracting commercial and geopolitical relationships in which the modern state and the developmental state have assumed sovereign power over their territories and its resources, as well as sovereign responsibility for the safety and welfare of the people within their territories (Taylor 1993). The nation-state has "come of age" in the twentieth century to become the major functioning and decision-making geopolitical unit of independent jurisdictional authority, and to be recognized as such by the United Nations. Although it was common in the 1980s to suggest that globalization forces would undermine the legitimacy and authority of the nation-state, rendering the world "borderless" and the nation-state as a "de-territorialized" borderless space, such early claims of the nation-state's demise have been found to be premature (Agnew 2003; Weiss 1998).

Hegemonic power, all along the yardstick by which the European empire-builders forced themselves on their colonial dominions, and the objective of the ideological struggle for global (military- and nuclear-power) superiority in the second half of the twentieth century between the superpowers of the West and East, the US and USSR respectively, remains as central a mission in today's global system of international relations as it was in previous world systems (Taylor 1993, 1996). Globalization – or perhaps more correctly, external and internal political–economic transformations – since World War II which led to the collapse of the Stalinist state and President Gorbachev's decisive breaking up of the USSR, at first appeared to give the United States an open field, as the world's sole remaining hegemonic nation-state and superpower. Globalization and neoliberalism have, however, brought about changes in geopolitical relationships, so that they are no longer as easily explained in terms of geostrategic and military power contests and hegemonic cycles of imperial or neo-imperial dominance. That said, geostrategic strategies and military might, as well as growth of the lucrative global market for many Global North core nation-states' military industrial consortia, still very much influence today's geopolitical complexity (Taylor 2000).

Less than twenty years later, US hegemony is under challenge, not only because of its current administration's flawed foreign policies and militaristic adventurism, but more fundamentally because its unilateral, economic dominance in the global economy is on the wane. Not only are Japan and the European Union major commercial and industrial competitors, but China and India are even more so. The world's two emergent newly industrializing countries (NICs) and demographic "heavyweights" are overhauling the United States in industrial capacity, in commerce and trade and in financial reserves. China on its own appears to be destined to become the world's largest nation-state economy within the next decade (Brown 2005a,b). US hegemony and unchallenged superpower status is also being undermined internally, by the damaging geopolitical and economic effects of an ill-conceived, neoconservative, "nationalist" agenda (Greider 2005; Golub 2005a,b). (See also Huntington 1999 for his "patriotic" plea for, and defense of, this myopic model of national conservatism.)

Beyond the nation-state scale, though scarcely global legislative bodies, supranational organizations such as the United Nations, the World Health Organization, the World Bank, IMF and WTO have emerged to serve as global forums, global regulatory bodies and global neoliberal institutions. These supranational institutions' roles and functions, their democratic accountability, and their global power are important considerations in the geopolitical struggles and hegemonic power-plays of Global North nation-states (and a small number of challengers from the Global South) in today's globalizing world (Roberts 2002). Some serve global humanitarian constituencies, some serve as regulatory institutions monitoring governments, some serve global, neoliberal capitalism, and some appear to have lost their regulatory power, or find their authority contested in other supranational arenas. None, however, serves as global "policeman" or "lawman," in large part because sovereignty principles still retain their central role in nation-state governance and authority.

Today's global systems of production, trade and commerce, of information and technology exchanges, and the geopolitical interactions, negotiations and power-brokering among nation-states are not only rendered more complex with the growth in political power and capitalist authority of supranational corporations, but the ascendancy of global city systems – established and emergent, first and second tiers and even upstart "wannabees" – is an extremely important contemporary development. The geo-economic power of these two global systems has come to challenge the geopolitical power of international relations, and the complex cross-cutting and interplay of their global linkages makes our contemporary global world much more geographically and geopolitically diverse; and quite possibly contributing to its "unruliness."

In this chapter on geopolitical globalization, global cities, functioning beyond the reach of the nation-states in which they are located, will be the second subject of our attention. Global cities' expanding and deepening geopolitical influence and "essential" geo-economic and financial significance not only makes them highly significant in geopolitical terms, but their networks of exchange, influence and power function in parallel to nation-state global systems, though not as their direct replacement (Knox and Taylor 1995). Furthermore, their internal restructuring pits capital against labor, offers opportunities to new immigrants and refugees, while at the same time promoting neoliberal modernization and global cosmopolitanism, and harboring South-to-North transnational networks which create new complexities of multicultural ethnic diversity (Sassen 2002b). In equally significant ways, the mega-cities of the Global South, metropolitan and urban populations as majority voters, nation-states' city systems and their entangled geopolitical relationships and entrepreneurial (as well as communal) spirit, are also redefining and re-strengthening their local-to-global political positions (Knox and Taylor 1995; Taylor 2004). The evolution of our contemporary global system to its current complex multi-local form, and the very real significance of urbanization's geo-economic agendas, in addition to the power and authority of our global city systems, is convincing evidence that our contemporary era is taking on a different form from previous hegemonic orders, with new global urban entrepreneurial and political activities coming to the fore.

Globalization's supranational geopolitical institutions

The earliest and still highly influential, international geopolitical organization has to be the Roman Catholic Church, which, from the fifteenth century onwards, maintained its central Papal authority on one of the world's most widespread religions. Starting with the 1494 Treaty of Tordesillas in which the Pope "divided the world" into a Spain-dominated Western Hemisphere and a Portuguese-dominated Eastern Hemisphere, Papal edicts emanating out of Vatican City have determined Catholic religious practices, supported and denounced rulers, taken strong and binding positions on social practices, and in many important ways have influenced government/regime policy-making. More recently, Papal visits around the world have come to be important geopolitical gestures, often with considerable influence, albeit remaining conservative and pragmatically in support of the status quo. So, in today's neoliberal and globalizing world (dis)order, the global power of the Roman Catholic Church is unyielding in its conservative social influence, and its global reach is politically influential and complementary to the new world order. The radical treatises of Latin American Catholic "liberation theologists," which sought to redirect the church's mission to help the poor and the needy, find little favor in Vatican City these days (Daudelin and Hewitt 1995). There may be calls within the church for resolving its differences with other global religions such as Islam, but the recent entitlement of conservative Archbishop Joseph Ratzinger to become Pope Benedict XVI as John Paul's successor scarcely positions the Roman Catholic Church among the critics of globalization's destructive consequences.

Other supranational organizations with a global agenda or global responsibilities did not exclusively come into being during the post-World War II period, although major European-based wars and the peace agreements that followed them appeared to be important catalysts for the formation of these global oversight and human rights organizations. Peace, health, treatment of war participants, disease-control, child labor exploitation and workers' rights were some of the priority areas for these early global institutions (Table 8.1).

Table 8.1 International organizations

Name	Date established	Summary of purpose	Headquarters
Roman Catholic Church	1472*	Global religion	Vatican City
International Red Cross	1859	Provide assistance to military wounded	Geneva, Switzerland
International Federation of the Red Cross	1919	Provide assistance to military (later civilian) wounded	Geneva, Switzerland
League of Nations	1919	Global forum of governments to facilitate disarmament, prevent war through collective security, settle disputes by negotiation and improve global welfare	Geneva, Switzerland
International Labour Organization	1919	Formulates international labor standards and practices through International Labour Conventions	Geneva, Switzerland
International Telecommunications Union	1932	Promotes international cooperation in telecommunications	Geneva, Switzerland
Food and Agricultural Organization	1943	Leads international efforts to defeat hunger, raise nutrition levels and increase food production	Rome, Italy
United Nations	1945	Replaced the League of Nations and inherited many of its agencies to serve as forums for global oversight of peoples' human rights and governments' sovereignty rights	New York City, USA
World Health Organization	1948	Established by the UN and inherited mandate to combat infectious diseases from the League of Nation's Health Organization	Geneva, Switzerland
World Meteorological Organization	1951	Encourages coordination of collection and dissemination of meteorological information	Geneva, Switzerland
International Atomic Energy Agency	1957	Promotes safe, secure and peaceful nuclear technologies	Vienna, Austria

Table 8.1 (Continued)

Name	Date established	Summary of purpose	Headquarters
United Nations' Agencies			
UN Educational, Scientific and Cultural Organization	1945	To promote scientific and cultural education	Paris, France
UN Children Fund	1946	Protecting and supporting the needs of children	New York City, USA
UN High Commission for Refugees	1951	Provide protection and assistance to refugees	Geneva, Switzerland
UN Development Programme	1966	To coordinate efforts to promote various aspects of development	New York City, USA
UN Environment Programme	1972	Assist countries in the protection of the environment	Nairobi, Kenya
Other supranational organizations			
The Socialist International	1951	Global IGO organization of social democratic, socialist and labor parties to help promote left-wing democratic political agendas	London, England
European Union	1993	Formally known as the European Community (EC) or European Economic Community (EEC) this regional union of 25 member states has a common currency, the euro (€), and is attempting to develop common constitutional and legal frameworks	Brussels, Belgium

Note
* 1472 represents the date when the Eastern Orthodox Church split from the Western Roman Church (Fortescue 2003)

The United Nations

The United Nations (UN) was established by the victorious "Allies" after World War II to continue the "negotiating" model on behalf of humanitarian and peace issues, revitalize the international cooperation agenda of the League of Nations and provide this new international communal forum with much more regulatory authority and international legal power. The institution's two major internal organizations are the General Assembly, where each recognized, independent country has a seat, an equal voice and one vote, and the Security Council, which is concerned with maintaining peace and security. The General Assembly was designed as a forum for all of the nations of the world to discuss their concerns and grievances. Importantly, recognition of a nation-state's independence and its sovereign authority is afforded by being admitted to the UN General Assembly by democratic vote of the members – every "recognized" independent country's formally recognized government, irrespective of their political ideology, their changed authoritarian regime, or their state of civil instability. While Global South countries are in the majority in the General Assembly, the true "power broker" in the United Nations is the Security Council, which comprises a set of ten revolving members (elected by a two-thirds majority of the General Assembly to serve two-year terms) and a set of five permanent members: the United States, United Kingdom, France, China and the Russian Federation – the victorious "Allies" of World War II (Drake 1994; Roberts 2002). These countries have an even greater concentration of power through the establishment of veto power: any of the five permanent members of the UN Security Council has the right to veto any resolution. This creates quite a disparity of power between these five Security Council members and the rest of the world. Numerous times, propositions or resolutions that have the support of a majority of the states of the world are vetoed by one or more permanent members of the Security Council, thereby rendering them "mute" and void of any substantive authority.

Beside these two global forums, there are four other major internal bodies directly answerable to the General Assembly: the Secretariat – the UN staff of international civil servants headed by the Secretariat-General (currently Kofi Annan); the Economic and Social Council – concerned with humanitarian issues, regional development issues and human rights; the International Court of Justice (or World Court) – which was established to adjudicate over disputes between nation-states; and the recently opened (in 2002) International Criminal Court in the Hague – established by the Rome Statute in 1998 as the first ever permanent, treaty based, international criminal court to put international criminals on trial for "crimes against humanity" (Roberts 2002).

The global reach of the UN deals with a range of responsibilities, including twenty-seven UN-sponsored peacekeeping assignments, the UN-sponsored monitoring of nuclear power and armaments generation (UN-IAEA), UN emergency assistance to refugees and victims of natural disasters, as well as monitoring the welfare of the world's powerless. The United Nations Children's fund (UNICEF) was established to protect and care for children throughout the world. The United Nations Educational, Scientific and Cultural Organization (UNESCO) focuses on "promoting collaboration among nations through education, science, culture and communication in order to further universal respect for justice, for the rule of law and for the human rights and fundamental freedoms which are affirmed for the peoples of the world" (UNESCO 2003). The United Nations Development Program (UNDP) was established to assist in the development (very broadly defined) of the underdeveloped countries of the world – the Global South as we know it. The United Nations High Commission for Refugees (UNHCR) was created to protect and care for refugees and also to assist in the repatriation of refugees when conditions improve. More recently, in terms of its rise to prominence in the UN's global mission, the United Nations Environment Program (UNEP) has been charged with promoting sustainability and environmental protection and has been instrumental in coordinating the signing of protocols to bring about reductions in pollution, among other environmental initiatives. The regulatory and managerial effectiveness of these many UN commissions and supranational institutions has not always been without its limitations, and calls for comprehensive revisions of UN organizations, either by particular nation-states such as the United States, or by groups of nation-states, have always dogged the institution. Yet, despite the geopolitical wrangling that seems to follow the UN, regardless of its performance, and despite the internal squabbling, internal inertia and cumbersome institutional mechanisms it works with, the UN remains a valid global forum (Drake 1994; Roberts 2002).

The post-Cold War era has represented a major challenge for the United Nations as a widening of geopolitical stances and competing geo-economic priorities among the permanent members of the Security Council have undermined the credibility of the Security Council in particular and the UN's regulatory authority in general. The impasse brought on by UN inaction to prevent ethnic cleansing and human rights violations during the break-up of Yugoslavia is one example of how the Security Council has been bypassed by a small coalition of global powers in an effort to regulate and intermediate in a regional conflict. This represents an example of Miller's (2000) "scale jumping" as a method of exercising global (military) policing and intervention. Experiencing direct opposition from China and Russia, the United States and Western Europe (led by Tony Blair's Britain) turned to NATO as an agent of legitimization for their military interventionist campaign in Serbia and Kosovo. NATO then justified the action in terms of intervention on behalf of humanitarian concerns in general, and because of widespread "ethnic cleansing" which not only led to the murder of thousands of innocent civilians but also threatened internal regional stability – hence, the use of a defensive military alliance, NATO.

A "new" regional supranational organization still under construction – the European Union of 25 and counting?

The European Union (EU) has become an important regional organization that has been a major agent in the restructuring of the global system. The EU differs from other supranational political organizations in several ways. First, the EU has a strong political focus along with plans for economic integration. The EU created a flag for the organization and maintains several political organizations. Along with this has been the creation of a free travel zone within the EU. The Schengen Agreement of 1995 eliminated the need for passports and visas and allows for relatively quick and "hassle-free" travel for citizens of the EU within the borders of the communal union.

One symbolic, and possibly the most significant, supranational "expression" of the European Union's organizational maturity has been the establishment of a common monetary unit, the euro, which entered circulation in 2002. The members of the euro zone traded their national currency for a single "European currency." This represents a major loss of sovereignty for the users of the euro, as it took away national currency fluctuations, and the ability of these countries to chart their own monetary policy. The loss of sovereignty is something that has not been forgotten by the citizens of several European countries. For example, Germany was concerned about the debts of certain potential euro-zone members, specifically Greece and Italy in the time leading up to the introduction of the euro. This concern led to the introduction of strict monetary policies. Some of the major issues under these monetary policies include: keeping deficits in countries below 3 percent in a year, and the requirement that each country submits a spending plan each year that meets the deficit requirement.

Finally, the European Union is an important source of identity for the European region. This is especially visible in the countries aspiring for membership in the EU. Eastern European countries have pushed for membership in an effort to become identified as "European" rather than as part of the old "Eastern Bloc." This demonstrates the malleability of scale and regions and the ability of agents to restructure the global system. The expansion of the EU represents a dramatic shift in regional identity and a destruction of geopolitical, territorial categories that, until recently, were seen as unbreakable. One only has to view the irony of the term Iron Curtain and how something that was seen as indestructible now has little geopolitical meaning in the modern world.

Global capital's supranational organizations

Another group of geopolitical, supranational organizations have emerged in the post-World War II era, that appear to directly challenge, or indirectly influence, the aforementioned global negotiating forums and global humanitarian, or people-centered institutions, such as the United Nations, ILO, WHO and FAO. These are global capital's (de)regulatory, or managerial, supranational institutions such as the World Bank (formerly the International Bank of Reconstruction and Development – IBRD), the International Monetary Fund (IMF), and the World Trade Organization (WTO), all of whom are involved in the regulation and development of the global economy through geopolitical and economic strategies and global regulatory authority – with the latter often self-assumed and self-aggrandized.

The emergence of these influential, neoliberal institutions and their consolidation as extremely powerful and unyielding disciplinarians over global political–economic conflicts of interest has been detailed in Chapter 2, so little more will be added here, in the interests of parsimony. Suffice to say that the crises in our runaway world, the complexity of institutional turf-battles between these two main groupings of supranational organizations (by no means working in concert), as well as the weak state of international law and the lack of a coherent code of regulatory authority for global issues, above and beyond sovereignty principles, make the supranational geography of geopolitical activity an extremely unpredictable landscape of global spaces.

Nationalism and globalization: companions or competitors?

History reminds us that the common doctrine of nationalism is a social ideology that should never be underestimated. The idea of "nation" is so embedded in our consciousness and everyday vocabulary that it is even referenced when we describe non-national scalar relations such as supranational, binational, multinational or transnational, which all assume the pre-existence of nations, or more ideally nation-states. Inter-state relations are more commonly referred to as *international relations* in geopolitical discourse, again showing how embedded the idea of nationhood is in popular and social science narratives.

Conventionally, the doctrine can be reduced to a set of maxims, defined at three scales: the global, nation-state and individual–personal. At the global scale the world consists of a mosaic of nations by no means represented by state divisions, and world order, harmony and national autonomy depend upon expressing this mosaic in a system of relatively small, free nation-state territories. At the nation-state scale, "nations" are conceived as the natural human-environment units of society; nations have an "imagined" cultural homogeneity based upon common ancestry and/or history; every nation requires its own sovereign state for the full legitimization of its existence; and, all nations (rather than nation-states) have an inalienable right to a territory or homeland. At the individual–personal scale, every individual must belong to a nation and claim a national identity. A person's primary loyalty and fealty is to his/her nation; and only through their nation and national identity can a person find their true identity (Muir 1997). Furthermore, in nationalistic discourse men are the active agents, while women are typically passive onlookers (Johnson 2002).

History also demonstrates that nationalism runs counter to liberal individualism, or international socialism, overpowering both as political ideologies. Nations have been conceptualized as "imagined communities" for people seeking communal identities. Nationalism has been the rallying cry for unification of nation-states, for secession and separation, for liberation from colonial domination, and for renewal of historic "ancient" cultures. Israel, for example, is a very distinctive case of renewal nationalism, based on a reversal of a diaspora, which in effect meant renewing and conquering its territory, as well as resettling its people. Some modern states evoked the ideology of renewal nationalism, when their establishment was associated with a radical, socialist/communist revolution. Stalin's "socialism in one country" had many of the hallmarks of a renewal of the Russian nation. China's People's Republic was similarly renewed, relatively intact. Mexico's 1917 people's revolution prompted the same nationalist call.

Clearly, nationalism has been a powerful geopolitical rallying cry in conflicts and territorial disputes in times past, taking on new meanings and new "imaginings" during the post-World War II period. And it remains so today, as globalization's de-territorializing forces broaden the geopolitical debate and a critical geopolitics has to deal with polymorphous territorialities, multiple identity formation, transnational plurality in global cities, and the rest (Ó'Tuathail 1998). We can only agree wholeheartedly with Johnson's following pronouncement:

> Whether the basis of nationalist imaginings be linguistic, historical or symbolic (or combined), the global restructuring that has taken place since the end of the Cold War appears to have raised nationalist discourse more profoundly than ever on the Global political stage.
>
> (Johnson 2002: 142)

Unpacking this assessment further, Shapiro (2003) draws upon theoretical and historical "narratives" to demonstrate that the contemporary nation-state has always involved coercive governance, and that there has always been contestation and image-making, since the initial aggregations in Europe were established by the Treaty of Westphalia in 1648. He draws attention to the interpretive and material practices through which the (misleading) nation segment of the hyphenated term – nation-state – achieves its standing. Then, he goes on to reiterate that "the historical emergence of nationalized 'statecraft,' a term for a complicated territory- and people-managing mode of governmental practice, must be understood in the context of the variety of specific, aggregating and disaggregating, material as well as symbolic conditions shaping the contemporary political entities recognized (in varying degrees) as nation-states" (Shapiro 2003: 272). Shapiro sees the military and economic/fiscal coercive practices of early nation-state formation becoming supplanted in recent times, "by a progressively, intense cultural governance, a management of the dispositions and meanings of citizen bodies, aimed at making territorial and national/cultural boundaries coextensive" (Shapiro: 272). In today's global order, internal contestation, cultural governance, multiple discourses, and the management of historical narratives as well as territorial space, are dynamic tensions challenging the sovereignty of many a nation-state and even challenging the power and legitimacy of central government authority.

Contemporary global geopolitics: old wine in new bottles?

British Empire-building geopolitics had its roots in Mackinder's *heartland theory* and its colonialist civilizing code. German geopolitics had its roots in *Geopolitik: "lebensraum"* (living-space) and was instrumental in the build up to World War II. American geopolitics, this time based on an updated version of Mackinder's geostrategic model, led up to the Cold War superpower stand-off and nuclear weapons arms race (Dalby 1990). During the post-World War II period, global geostrategic models continue to be conceptualized in military (and strategic alliance) terms, both during the Cold War (until 1990) and continuing to present.

Cohen (1994) argued that two global geostrategic regions could be differentiated: one as a "trade-dependent maritime region" dominated by the United States, and the other "the Eurasian continental world" dominated by the Soviet Union. Geostrategic maneuvering between these two worlds was conducted by nuclear arms stockpiling and the ICBM race, with the threat of outright conflict and warfare between the two diminished because of its absolute nature. Between these two major geostrategic regions there are distinctive geopolitical regions, which are characterized as shatter-belts – the Middle East, or Southwest Asia, and Southeast

Asia. Geopolitical competitive and imperialistic maneuvering in these shatter-belts is invariably conducted by powerful outside military interests (aided and abetted oftentimes by corporate interests). It is in these shatter-belts that warfare and conflicts are likely to occur, and reoccur, with global instability being the long-term result. Tragically, we see this is very much the case in the Middle East–Southwest Asia shatter-belt, where today's twenty-first century geopolitical globalization is witnessing a "war on terrorism" and a "clash of civilizations." These latter-day geopolitical clashes are pitting Judeo-Christian Western fundamentalism and neoconservatism against the Islamic East's fundamentalism, and are characterized by extremist geopolitical strategies, guerrilla warfare, state-sponsored terrorism (in the case of the Israel–Palestine conflict) as well as occupation forces' excessive use of deadly force, the resultant anti-occupation insurgencies and the death of innocent civilians (callously left uncounted by the Pentagon as inevitable "collateral damage" of pre-emptive modern warfare) in the Afghanistan and Iraq "wars." This is developed much more substantially in Miller's "Globalization of fear" (Chapter 11).

Cohen (1994) does, however, consider changing geostrategic contexts, and in his seminal article he predicts both the continuity of the major geostrategic regions, and the fluidity of their relationships within the shatter-belts and beyond (beyond Southwest Asia into the Horn of Africa, for example). Then, by analyzing the interdependence of economic, cultural, social and political processes within changing spatial milieus, Cohen's new geopolitics sheds light on what constitutes military-strategic considerations for the peripheral Third World or Global South. He claims that the Global South (Sub-Saharan Africa and Latin America) is not becoming strategically marginalized, just because the need for outside military bases has been dramatically reduced. Rather the Global South remains globally important in a variety of other geopolitical ways: as an additional source of environmental warming and pollution; as a place of origin for drugs/narcotics and certain diseases; as a world market with dynamic growth possibilities; as a source of regionally and globally disruptive migration/refugee streams; and as a locus for the massive starvation, genocidal conflicts and human rights abuses that sorely trouble the international community's consciousness. Cohen rightly concludes that the world is becoming a much more interconnected geopolitical place.

Taylor (2000) adds to this new perspective on the complex interconnectivity of geopolitical relationships, by challenging the inevitability of cyclical change in our globalizing geopolitical world. With Global North Core countries, restructured former Soviet territories and emerging NICs in the Global South's Semi-Peripheries all becoming more central to global restructuring in both political and economic roles, the nation-state's relevance in today's globalizing geopolitical landscape and its changing, if uneven, patterns is no longer under debate. Drawing upon recent opinions by "world systems theory"'s theoretical guru, Immanuel Wallerstein (1996a,b), Taylor (2000) identifies three critical contemporary societal changes underway in our globalizing era which are not so easily explained in cyclical or sociohistorical terms; either in terms of hegemonic power shifts, or as part of the latest macroeconomic, Krondratieff long-wave phase of growth and recession.

The first "different societal change" involves the challenge to the nation-state's singular geopolitical position (and social responsibility) as the main center of power and authority. From the "long sixteenth century" onwards, hegemonic cycles and geostrategic contests have dominated the world's changing commercial (and later industrial) systems, with a succession of Global North Core countries increasing their state power and spreading their imperial reach. In recent decades, the geopolitical state power of even the wealthiest of governments has been challenged in new ways, both externally and internally. Supranational, transnational forces now contest, undermine and collaborate with a web of nation-state governments, often all at the same time. Today's transnational corporations may have their original administrative base in a nation-state, but their reach is global, their economic power is immense (and growing), and their geopolitical strategizing is self-serving, rarely nationalistic, or state-serving. Where once the most powerful of state governments in the Global North would treat their private corporate sector as their subservient partner, now the dominant/subservient roles are reversed, and state governments are their clients. Global cities, often the most important financial centers of modern nation-states, now function much more independently, and webs of first- and second-tier global city systems now operate in parallel to governments' networks of international relations, commercial alliances and negotiated exchanges of knowledge, technology and information – a cross-cutting of global territorial relations by other global "spaces of flows" (Arrighi 1994; Taylor 1995). Internally, "nationalism" in various forms has come to challenge central state authority during this era of globalization; and this dimension is given particular notice later in this chapter, and returned to in Chapters 10, 11 and 14, as well.

The second "different societal change" involves the erosion of secularism – the separation of church and state – in the modern nation-state, in recent times. The rise in new religious fundamentalisms, both in the Judeo-Christian west and the Islamic-Hindu east, is an unexpected challenge to the prevailing "modernist" notion that rationalized the need for distinctions between religious and governmental/state practices. Much more than a simplistic "clash of civilizations" (Huntington 1996), the multicultural synergies of religious sociocultural expressions of faith have also cross-cut global territorial boundaries, forming much more loosely defined, intermingled global networks – spreading multi-culturalism in the sovereign hearths of nationalism. At the same time, the Roman Catholic Church is no longer the sole institutional mouthpiece of Western religious and societal practice, as these new global fundamentalist challenges widen the potential for conflicting dogmas and conflicting practices to erupt into "cultural wars."

Though certainly related to both the above distinctive features of globalization's uniqueness, the third "different societal change" also challenges one of the fundamental tenets of modernity, namely an erosion of faith in modern science and technology. The unchallenged authority and power of modern science and technology and of rational thought is being contested, as ecological and biotechnological arguments join with fundamentalist religious challenges in questions and debates on modern science's pivotal roles in charting progress for humankind. Science becomes a contested domain, also because corporate capital has seen fit to buy its own science, because R&D in the science and technology fields is also assessed in terms of its economic profitability, rather than its humanitarian contribution, and because scientific "objectivity" is more and more open to challenge by post-modernist and post-structural criticism (Ó Tuathail 1996).

What this means, in a nutshell, is that the long partnership of nation-state growth and city growth, which did so much for their mutual interest, is being reformulated, and in some cases – global cities, for instance – are being "decoupled." Or as Taylor (1995: 58) so succinctly adjoins:

> In contemporary globalization, territories can no longer preserve their distinctiveness behind political boundaries; rather, new identities ... "may be formed as a unique crossroad in the flow of people, goods and ideas." Or, in our terms: cities are replacing states in the construction of social identities ... The incredible spatial congruence that was simultaneously a power, economic, and cultural container is clearly unraveling.

If it is not already clear from the above arguments that geopolitical relationships in this latest era of globalization are no longer modernist, hegemonic or predictably cyclical, we should remind ourselves that our evolving world system has entered its post-modern phase of ecological uncertainty, rapid technological change, and a multiplicity of cross-cutting flows of information, cultural messages, knowledge exchange, at multiple scales and scopes of influential power and authority – ranging from the global to the local, from the exceptional to the ordinary, and from the elites to the bourgeoisie and working classes. Taylor (1996) draws parallels from the experiences and characteristics of earlier Dutch, British and American hegemonic cycles to chronicle this most recent transitional path from the consolidation of the world's modern geopolitical system to a new post-modern (and globalized) "world impasse" – where "all we can be sure of is that there will be many surprises for humanity" (Taylor 1996: 224).

Global cities in the "new global order"

Preferring to use the label "world cities" to characterize today's actual, recent or potential "dynamic cities" that Jane Jacobs (1984) identified, Taylor (2004: 52) correctly points out that "globalization has reasserted that cities are more than subunits of states, more than even the 'powerhouses' of 'national economies'; they are their own economic entity within transnational spaces of flows." Sassen (2002b: 2), on the other hand, prefers to conceptualize them as "global cities" playing "an increasingly important role in directly linking their national economies with global circuits.... [with] the management and servicing of much of the global economic system *taking* place in a growing network of global cities and cities that might best be described as having global city functions." To Sassen, global cities function as the command centers of a rescaled set of worldwide networks, and as essential nodes in this re-scaled global system of cross-border economic processes

– flows of capital, labor, goods, information, technology, sociocultural exchanges – that has come into its own during global restructuring.

Global cities' growing geo-economic influence and spectacular emergence in the last thirty years or so as the "homes" of the new transnational capitalist class involved in global finance management also makes them highly significant in geo-political terms, as well as major "functional nodes" in a highly integrated global network of capital management, investment and movement. Their fiscal role in today's global order is to function as a highly efficient network of regional centers to enable financial intermediaries, banks, accounting firms and the rest of the services of advanced capitalism to manage investment, capital transfers, savings accumulations and the like for owners of global capital stocks. Their "essential" functions are: centrality, authority, innovation, sociability (particularly embracing cosmopolitanism and modernity), and support of their financial sector's primary workers' lifestyles and life needs by provision of a secondary labor market of low-wage service providers – commonly, new immigrants and/or asylum-seekers, irregular migrants, and unskilled racial/ethnic minorities.

First-tier global cities such as London, New York, Tokyo, Paris, Frankfurt, Los Angeles, Chicago and Miami have the following major functional characteristics. They are sites of leading global financial markets for commodities, commodity futures, investment capital, foreign exchange, equities and bonds. They are sites of clusters of specialized, high-order (international in scope) business services, attracted to finance, accounting, advertising, property development and law. They are sites of concentrations of corporate headquarters (international, national and foreign firms), sites of many leading NGOs, IGOs and inter-government organizations, and sites of many powerful and internationally influential media organizations, news and information services, and culture industries. As leading cosmopolitan centers of global business, global cultural diversity, global innovation and entrepreneurial activity, global cities are thriving centers of international tourism and all have major airports with high levels of transport connectivity to others, to facilitate the high volumes of visitation of Robinson and Harris' (2000) transnational capitalist class (TCC), or Beaverstock's (2001) transnational business elites, as well as globe-trotting tourists.

This group, especially the first two – London and New York – stand at the top of the hierarchy as *the* dominant command-centers of this world/global system of cities. Together with Tokyo these three Global North core centers control their own continental sub-systems – West European, Asia–Pacific and American, respectively. The concentration of international financial power in these three world-city command-centers (plus Hong Kong, as a unique Global South "London-outlier") which came about in the 1990s is nothing short of spectacular.

Sassen (2002b), focusing on the production of financial and service products and the particular technological innovations that have enabled such global restructuring, characterizes them as a "new type of city" – to wit, the first "global city service centers" in urban history. The four share the largest proportion of global financial transactions. The four, plus Frankfurt, account for a major share of international banking. The first three command over 58 percent of the foreign exchange market, and with Singapore, Zurich, Geneva, Frankfurt and Paris they account for 85 percent of this foreign exchange market (Sassen 2002). There is truly a consolidation of international financial activity and services in these few command-centers, despite the deregulatory impulses that swept through the sector in the 1980s and 1990s, which saw the opening of secondary global capital markets in the Global South – Buenos Aires, São Paulo, Mexico City, Taipei, Moscow, Shanghai, Beirut, Johannesburg, Bangkok and Sydney. What these secondary markets did achieve, however, was a deeper and more widespread global reach of financial capital's authority and dominance, and a consolidation of global networks and linkages within this global system of "global city service centers" favoring neoliberal capitalism's geo-economic goals – accelerated economic growth, market integration, privatization, supranational autonomy, and wealth accumulation among the transnational capitalist classes.

What is clear is that the networks of communication and information transfer among these cities and across the global networks have social, economic, political and technological dimensions; and the transactions that occur within this ever-expanding global network continue to grow in volume, intensity and complexity (Sassen 2002b). These cosmopolitan cities constitute a new "face of globalization" – a new system of geo-economic and geopolitical power-sharing and power-contesting, and a system which favors and facilitates the capitalist objectives of multinational and transnational corporations. Because of their global authority, however, the cities function as independent and competitive institutional authorities, answerable to – but not subservient to – the geopolitical interests of their national territories, and answerable to – but not subservient to – the geo-economic prerogatives of their corporate "stakeholders."

On the other hand, neither the global cities of the Global South, nor the more peripheral global "wannabees," have seen their urban internal structure transformed to mirror the cosmopolitan urban landscape of neoliberal modernism and postmodernism. Despite their "world-city-ness," they don't have formally integrated modern central business districts, complete with their Western, "international/global" pot pourri of retailing and commercial services, integrated transportation and communication systems, effective police security, public services, health and welfare provisions. Much more common is the presence of a nucleated, modernized "district" or set of districts, selective improvements in transportation systems and communication infrastructure, and the emergence of privileged "spaces" of affluence, modernization and post-modern design, where the world city functions and functionaries operate.

Elsewhere, in Latin American, Asia–Pacific, African, Central and Southwest Asian cities of today's global era, the informal sector continues to thrive, spatial segregation remains acute, and the sectoral expansion of business and residential enclaves – including "gated communities," shopping malls and exclusive spaces for the internal and transnational elites – continues apace. The cosmopolitan consumer "spaces" and metropolitan "spaces" in these hybrid cities intersect as globalizing and culturally divergent representations of urban living spaces in which the former are prized for their globalized "homogeneous" character and

Western/Americanized-style "sense of place," while the latter are rooted in historical continuity and national identities (Machimura 1998; Olds 1997; Roberts 2005; Yeoh 1999). The informal, illegal cities in the Global South (Fernandes and Varley 1998), therefore, invariably make up the major part of the urbanized landscape, coexisting with the modern enclaves and districts in an uneasy social environment in which the inequality gap between the minority "haves" and the majority "have nots" is a constant source of tension, suspicion and distrust/fear. "Policing the streets," "securing neighborhoods," "enforcing the laws," become the political mandates for local authorities; and where urban heritage tourism and international business conventioneering is added to the mix, "making our streets safe for visitors and guests of our country" becomes the effective rationale for urban enforcement.

Contemporary geopolitics and the global impasse: are geo-economic competition or sustainability the only alternative choices?

The scale at which geopolitical actions occur is essential for understanding the development and restructuring of the global capitalist system. In this chapter we have examined how "agency" and structural processes interact at supranational, nation-state, urban and local scales, both geopolitically and, more recently, geo-economically. One major objective has been to chart the evolution of the world's global system of international relationships, from a system of interacting nation-states and their formal supranational alliances and global forums to a new more complex system of interacting cross-currents of global flows in which global city systems, supranational institutions and forum, transnational networks and informal and irregular systems of social and economic exchange have become influential restructuring forces. The contemporary globalized world of today is now geopolitically and geo-economically different from any previous capitalist epoch. The hegemonic power relations are more complex and no longer defined solely in terms of military might and nuclear armament capabilities. Geo-economic contests now rival geopolitical parlaying, and macroeconomic robustness and resource stocks are now the significant "competitive advantage" in today's global neoliberal marketplace. The formal regulatory environments have given way to deregulated and more volatile geo-economic circumstances, and social divisions within this new world order are more multifaceted, and more uncertain and unpredictable in geopolitical terms than in previous orders.

While reflecting on the ahistorical conditions and unprecedented geopolitical relationships that are abroad in our globalizing world, Taylor (1996) expands upon Wallerstein's new social trends and characterizes the resultant global impasse as a tension between "eco-fascism" and "deep green" political economics. His focus on the "unsustainability" of the global capitalist system in its latest neoliberal guise – dependence upon mass consumerism, unfettered free trade, deregulated financial management, greater concentrations of wealth and power in corporate hands, the cultural "imperialism" of Americanization, and other such political–economic processes of modernity and post-modernity – is echoed here. We prefer to widen the notion to argue for a geopolitical future in which "sustainable systems" of our life-world are re-conceptualized with humanitarian goals of equity, social justice and social–democratic ideals blended with ecological goals for our socio-environmental support systems. Sustainable urbanism must be the way forward, and from global cities in both the Global North and Global South all the way down national hierarchies to the most modest-sized towns, "green managerialism" must be embraced. Sustainable transportation systems support this achievable goal, and sustainable energy solutions clearly need to be found, globally, nationally, regionally and locally.

As will be further demonstrated in the final chapters of this collection, grassroots globalization from below, local urban green networks, local empowerment of stakeholders, local participatory planning, are some of the enduring and powerful democratic movements of the twenty-first century, and such leadership "from below" can refocus geopolitical action, and take back "the people's country" – revitalizing social–democratic principles and goals and pursuing a sustainable future for their children and their children's children. Environmental sustainability is the overarching goal, and this can be best pursued geopolitically within a global regulatory regime, where the United Nations and an international legal system built around humanitarian principles and principles of communalism, environmentalism and social justice preside. There should be no place for a unilateral military superpower, or for another nuclear arms race, or for a clash of civilizations, and there certainly needs to be a reasoned, peaceful solution to combat the rise in state-sponsored and ideologically driven terrorism, instead of the current military option to conflict resolution still, unfortunately, in favor.

Such wishful thinking, however, must be offered with a strong dose of caution – a reality check, no less. As O'Loughlin (2005: 104) ruefully observes: "Though the number of wars is down slightly from a year ago, the constellation of US unilateralism, resource greed, local tyrants and hegemonic competition does not augur a more peaceful world." Today's post-Fordist, post-Cold War world is firmly in the embrace of a geo-economic political construct of globalization and neoliberalism that dismisses any responsibilities to the "losers" and their welfare and instead is designed to reward the "winners" – often excessively so. Our geo-economic world is Darwinian in that entrepreneurial governance is privileged and state government and private sector partnerships are horizontally and vertically networked for their mutual survival and continuing/expanding authority. The "hollowed out" state may be the democratic unit of responsibility, but the elected government's wider responsibilities overpower the citizen-to-representative links the democratic process implies (Sparke and Lawson 2003).

The infusion of ideas on economic liberalization into democratic discourse, helped by the 1980s' and 1990s' ideological swings to the center-right in major Global North Core countries, not only had the effect of marginalizing and rolling back social democratic principles and responsibilities, but it also established the tenor (and geo-economic language) of the political–economic narrative, and effectively reduced the realm in which political alternatives were to be offered.

Center-left, center-right and right-wing platforms became the only "realistic choices" and geoeconomic entrepreneurial governance the choice of nation-states, regional economic alliances, metropolitan and urban mayors and their governments, and rural/provincial authorities. However, Sparke and Lawson (2003: 330) are right to remind us:

> Just as scholars of globalization have taught us not to treat the patterns of accelerated global interdependency as anonymous unstoppable forces, so too is it important to see geoeconomic tendencies as profoundly political and thus inherently resistible and transformable.

We concur.

9 Globalization has a home address
The geopolitics of globalization

John Agnew

Introduction

Globalization is one of the premier buzzwords of the early twenty-first century. In its most general usage it refers to the idea of a world increasingly stretched, shrunk, connected, interwoven, integrated, interdependent, or less territorially divided economically and culturally among national states. It is most frequently seen as an economic–technological process of time–space compression (Harvey 1989), a social modernization previously national in character scaled up to the world as a whole (Robertson 1992), or as shorthand for the practices of economic liberalism spontaneously adopted by governments the world over (Overbeek 1993; Desai 2002). Rather than questioning any of these perspectives, I prefer to put geopolitical globalization in its historical context and argue that the world economy has only recently become more globalized under largely American auspices (Agnew 2005).

As a new "master concept," globalization is often seen as replacing geopolitics (e.g. Blouet 2001). Globalization as we know it today did not just come out of geographical thin air and it has definite geopolitical roots and biases. I begin the chapter, therefore, by examining the geopolitical origins of globalization in American policies and practices during the Cold War but that have older roots in American history, particularly the experience and ideology of the "frontier." This will then *politicize* the topic, in direct opposition to the tendency to *naturalize* it, as if it were an entirely technological, sociological or ideological phenomenon. This is important because it suggests that the form that recent globalization has taken is the result of political choices that can be reversed or redirected.

Globalization, it is argued, represents a stark break with the geopolitics of the Cold War (and previous epochs). This is anything but the case. Contemporary globalization emerged out of the practices and ideas that were its foundations in the period from the 1940s to the 1970s. In the second part of the chapter, therefore, I identify those features of the "embedded liberalism" of the postwar period that helped lay the foundations for the post-1970s acceleration.

The third section depicts how this system began to erode in the 1960s and, during the Nixon presidential administration, was replaced by the beginnings of a new "market-access regime" in which the roles of such international organizations as the IMF, World Bank and GATT (later WTO) were "revolutionized" by converting them to enforcement of a much more radical economic liberalism that served American economic interests. From these beginnings, a new global economic geography has emerged in which there is a tension between continued state regulation of economic activities, on the one hand, and a world economy increasingly organized with reference to flows of capital and goods between sites in widely scattered locations. At the same time large parts of the world are increasingly left out of global economic development.

This recent transformation introduces the question of the meaning of the "geographical" in relation to the globalization of the world economy and the long-term tension between *territorial* and *interactional* (flow-based) modes for organizing capitalism. The main point is that it is not the global that is "new" in globalization, but, rather, its combination of global networks and localized territorial fragmentation. Under the "previous" regime, the world economy was structured largely (but never entirely) around territorial entities such as states, colonial empires and geopolitical spheres of influence. The main novelty today is the increasing role in economic prosperity and underdevelopment of fast-paced *cross-border flows* in relation to national states and to networks linking cities with one another and their hinterlands and the *increased differentiation* between localities and regions as a result of the spatial biases built into flow-networks. Rather than the "end" of geography, therefore, globalization entails its reformulation away from an economic mapping of the world in terms of state territories towards a more complex mosaic of states, regions, global city-regions, and localities differentially integrated into the global economy.

The nature of US hegemony

For many years, the division of the world into trading blocs and territorial empires limited US economic and political influence. Powerful strains in US public opinion were also opposed to American involvement in foreign economic and political affairs. After World War II, however, an intensely internationalist American agenda, sponsoring free trade, currency convertibility and international investment, was advanced in explicit counterpoint to the autarkic dogmas of Soviet communism and as a response to the competitive trading blocs that were seen as partly responsible for the depression of the 1930s. The effort to design a "free world" order in the immediate postwar years laid the groundwork for the internationalization of economic activities in the 1960s that brought tremendous expansion in US firms' investment overseas and the increased importance of trade for the US territorial economy (Agnew and Corbridge 1995).

The basis to American hegemony and the creation of the world economy as we know it today lie in two features of the US historical experience. First, America's own colonial past made territorial colonialism in the European style an ideologically difficult enterprise; US institutions claimed their origins in colonial revolt rather than dynastic or national continuity. This is why, straight-facedly, American leaders can claim innocence about apparent designs on controlling other places.

Second, after the Civil War, an integrated national economy emerged that was increasingly dominated by large firms; and, as they developed overseas interests, these firms were able to shape the American international agenda. I examine each of these points in turn.

America's past

From the outset of colonial settlement on the Eastern seaboard of North America, "America" has been seen by the makers of American public culture – political leaders, writers and educators – as the space where European settlers met an alien environment and by taming and absorbing it created the most powerful polity and plentiful cornucopia yet known to humanity. They created an American space out of what they saw as a pristine wilderness. From school textbooks to Western movies and political speeches, American identity is closely associated with wresting political–economic success out of a difficult environment and imprinting the values of the founders of the United States as the frontier moved westwards. Yet, "America" has also represented a set of universal ideas about political–economic and cultural organization. For example, the geography evoked by the American Declaration of Independence is neither continental nor hemispheric but universal. It is directed to "the earth," the "Laws of Nature and of Nature's God," and to all of "mankind." In this vision, "America" is seen as a model for humanity; a perfect model for any space. So, though exceptional in its own geographical experience, America has also been seen by many Americans as a role model for the rest of the world.

Spatial orientations are of particular importance to understanding America, whether this is with respect to foreign policy or to national identity. It could be argued that a geographical imagination is central to all national political cultures. However, if all nations are imagined communities, then America is the imagined community par excellence (Campbell 1992). The space of "America" was already created in the imaginations of the first European settlers en route to the "New World" as a space of openness and possibility. It was not constructed and corrupted by centuries of history and power struggles, as was Europe. Even now, America is a country that is easily seen as both "nowhere" and "past-less," constructed as totally modern and democratic against a European (or some other) "Other" mired in a despotic history and stratified by the tyranny of aristocracy. The ideology of the American Dream, an ideology which stresses that anyone can be successful given hard work, luck and un-intrusive government, marks out the American historical experience as unique or exceptional. Narratives of the history of America as a country of migrants successfully seeking a better way of life provide practical evidence for this imagination. The enslaved Africans and conquered Indians who made constructing the New World possible are not surprisingly largely absent from this vision except as incidental characters or as barriers to be overcome.

The mindset of limitless possibility was reinforced by the frontier experience of individual social mobility, of the energy of a youthful country in contrast to the social stagnation and economic inequality of "old" Europe. Americans were free to set themselves up in the vast expanse of "empty" land available on the frontier, discounting the presence of natives whose self-evident technological and religious "backwardness" justified the expropriation of their land. All settlers were equal on the frontier, so the myth goes, and those who were successful succeeded due to their own hard work, not through any advantage of birth. Clearly there are historiographical problems with this national myth, not least the violent erasure of other people and their pasts that occurred as part of this geographical movement (Shapiro 1997). However, the myth has long remained as a powerful aspect of American culture. Importantly, the frontier story is not simply an elite construction told to the population at large but one retold and recycled through a variety of cultural forms – most obviously through mass education, but more importantly through the media and in popular culture (e.g. Slotkin 1992).

The "frontier" character of the American economy – expanding markets for goods and opportunities for individuals beyond previous limits – figures strongly in the American stimulus to uncritically embrace contemporary economic, or neoliberal, globalization. This is itself tied to a particular cultural image: the ethos of the consumer-citizen (Cross 2000). The American position in the Cold War of defending and promulgating this model ran up against the competing Soviet model of the worker-state. The resultant geopolitical order was thus intimately bound up with the expression of American identity. This was spread through ideas of "development," first in such acts as the Marshall Plan to aid the reconstruction of Europe immediately after World War II, and then in the modernization of the "Third World" following the elements of a model of American society pushed most strongly during the short presidency of John Kennedy (1961–2).

The creation of a global economy under American auspices reflects the dominant ideology about the founding of the country and the essence of its national identity and character. Twentieth-century economic globalization has been linked to two important political–economic principles that have been closely associated with the American frontier ethos and its realization first in continental expansion and later in global power (Williams 1969; Agnew 1999). First was the view of the expansion of the marketplace as necessary to national political and social well-being. Second was the idea that economic liberty or independence is by definition the foundation for freedom per se. The American Constitution and early interpretations of it combined these two principles to create a uniquely American version of democratic capitalism. On the one hand the federal government underwrote expansion into the continental interior and stimulated interest in foreign markets for American products; but, on the other hand, the federal sub-units (the states) and the division of power between the branches of the federal government (the Congress, the presidency and the Supreme Court) limited the power of government to regulate private economic activity. The Constitution is open to contrary interpretations on the relative powers of both federal branches and tiers of government. Through the years, however, the federal level has expanded its powers much more than any of the Founders, including its greatest advocate, Alexander Hamilton, could have foreseen.

The American international agenda

The emerging national economy of the late nineteenth century was based in large part on the growth of the first capitalist consumer economy. American businesses pioneered in advertising and salesmanship as ways of bringing the population into mass markets for manufactured goods and processed foodstuffs. Relative to the rest of the world, American growth in manufacturing output was incredible. By 1913 the United States was to account for fully one-third of the world's total industrial production. From the 1870s on, much of this growth was managed by large industrial firms and investment banks, whose American markets generated less and less profit at ever greater expense. It was in the period 1896–1905, however, that the US saw the greatest spate of mergers and business consolidation in its history, such that by 1905 around two-thirds of the manufacturing capital of the United States was controlled by 300 corporations with an aggregate capital worth of $7 billion (in 1992 dollars). That the 1890s also saw the peak of a major economic depression with high unemployment and increasing political unrest meant that there was added incentive to look for markets beyond the territorial limits of the United States itself.

The American economic expansion after the 1890s was only intermittently territorial, and, with the exception of the Spanish–American War of 1898–1900, largely in its immediate vicinity, in the Caribbean and Central America. Otherwise it was resolutely *interactional*, focused on the possibilities of and proceeds from foreign capital investment. Unlike business in the other industrial capitalist countries, American business favored direct rather than portfolio investment and conventional trade. Economic advantages previously specific to the United States in terms of economic concentration and mass markets – such as the cost-effectiveness of large factories and economies of process, product and market integration – were exported abroad as American firms invested in their subsidiaries. A new pattern of foreign direct investment designed to gain access to foreign markets for large firms was coming into existence under American auspices. American leaders could preach against European territorial colonialism as American businesses created a whole new phenomenon of internationalized production. Unknowingly, these businesses were laying the groundwork for the globalization of production of which American governments later became the main sponsors.

The expansion beyond American shores was never simply economic in motivation. There was a mission, contentious but unmistakable, to spread American values. Pushing American ways of economic and political organization was more than simply a mechanism for increasing consumption of American products. But the mission to spread American values did often lead to the consumption of American products, later epitomized in the global audiences for MTV, the near-universal popularity of Coca-Cola, and global consumption of McDonald's hamburgers. The products represented America to the world at large (Twitchell 1999). The reach into the global arena continued throughout the twentieth century – with the exception of the Depression of the 1930s which encouraged a flurry of economic protectionism.

The "free world" economy

In 1945, the completeness of the "Allied" victory over Nazi Germany and Imperial Japan had two immediate consequences. First, Soviet influence extended over Eastern Europe and into Germany. When the war ended Soviet armies were as far west as the River Elbe. This encouraged both a continuing American military presence in Europe and a direct confrontation with the Soviet Union as a military competitor and sponsor of an alternative image of world order. This quickly found its expression in the geopolitical doctrine of "containment," whereby through alliances and military presence the US government committed itself to maintaining the political status quo established in 1945. The American development of nuclear weapons and a demonstrated willingness to use them meant that the security of the United States itself was beyond doubt (Art 1991). Indeed, the relative geographical isolation of the United States from most of its historic adversaries has always been an American advantage; if one discounts threats from nuclear armed terrorists or states that reject the "norms" of inter-state behavior. What was in doubt in 1945–7 was the allegiance of other countries to the United States and its political–economic model.

Second, in economic and political terms the United States was without any serious competition in imposing its vision of world order on both its vanquished foes and most of its recent allies. Unlike after World War I, when the United States turned its back on hegemony, this time there seemed to be no alternative. Europe and Japan were devastated. Reassessments of the origins of the Great Depression and World War II by the Roosevelt and Truman administrations suggested that the continued health of the American economy and the stability of its internal politics depended upon *increasing* rather than decreasing international trade and investment (Wachtel 1986). Europe and Japan had to be restored economically, both to deny them to the Soviet Union and to further American prosperity.

This is not to say that such an "internationalist" position went unopposed. Indeed, the Republican majorities in the US Congress in the immediate postwar years were generally as skeptical of the projection of the US's "New Deal" experience of government overseas economic intervention as they were of its application at home. Only after 1947, with the growing fear of the Soviet Union as both foreign enemy and domestic subversive, did an internationalist consensus begin to emerge.

The period from 1945 to 1970 was one in which this consensus played itself out. The US government set out in 1945–7 to sponsor a liberal international order in which its military expenditures would provide a protective apparatus for increased trade (and, if less so, investment) across international boundaries. These would, in turn, rebound to domestic American advantage. There was a presumed transcendental identity between the American and world economies, with the expansion of one being good for the other. Achieving this involved projecting at a global scale those institutions and practices that had already developed in the United States, such as: Fordist mass-production/consumption industrial organization; electoral democracy; limited state welfare policies; and government economic policies directed towards stimulating private economic activities (Maier 1978; Rupert 1990). Ruggie (1983) calls the normative content of these policies "embedded liberalism" because they were institutionalized in such entities as the IMF, the World Bank, the GATT and the Bretton Woods Agreement.

Three features of the American economy were particularly important in underpinning the internationalism of American policy. The first was economic concentration. Continuing an intermittent trend from the 1880s, in almost every American industry control over the market came to be exercised by fewer, larger firms. Expanding concentration was accompanied and encouraged by the growth of government, especially at the federal level. Much of this was related to military expenditures designed to meet the long-term threat from the Soviet Union. These trends were reinforced by what became the main challenge to the perpetuation of the model within the United States: the direct investment of US corporations overseas. Much of this was in other industrialized countries. The axis of capital accumulation now ran through the core rather than between core and periphery.

In the short run, this arrangement benefited the American economy. But by the late 1960s, as domestic technology and management followed capital abroad, traditional exports were replaced by foreign production of US affiliates to the detriment of employment in the United States. American mass consumption was no longer fully supported by the relatively high wages of its workers in mass production. This has come to define the crisis or impasse facing the American model in the United States (Agnew 1987). What Arrighi (1990: 403) calls a Free Enterprise System – "free, that is, from ... vassalage to state power" – has come into existence to challenge the inter-state system as the singular locus of power in the international political economy.

It is little exaggeration to claim that in the five decades after 1945, American dominion was at the center of a remarkable explosion in "interactional" capitalism. Based initially on the expansion of mass consumption within the most industrialized countries, it later involved the reorganization of the world economy around a massive increase in trade in manufactured goods and foreign direct investment. But this was not a recapitulation of the previous world economy. Abandoning territorial imperialism, "Western capitalism ... resolved the old problem of overproduction, thus removing what Lenin believed was the major incentive for imperialism and war" (Calleo 1987: 147). The major driving force behind this was the growth of mass consumption in North America, Western Europe and Japan. Indicative of a major transformation in the logic of capitalism, the role of mass consumption needs emphasizing (Mitchell and Rosati, Chapter 10). Thereafter, production and sale of consumer goods, not of capital goods, became the motor of the world economy. The products of such industries as real estate, household and electrical goods, automobiles, food processing and mass entertainment were all consumed within (and, increasingly, between) the producing countries.

The Keynesian welfare state helped sustain demand through the redistribution of incomes and purchasing power. If before World War II the prosperity of industrial countries depended on favorable terms of trade with the underdeveloped world, now demand was stimulated at home. Moreover, until the 1970s the terms of trade of most raw materials and foodstuffs tended to decline. This trend had negative effects on the economies of the Global South/Third World as a whole, but it stimulated some countries to engage in new models of industrialization which later paid off as they found lucrative export markets for their manufactured goods. The globalization of production through the growth of these newly industrializing countries (also aided by US Cold War military expenditures in the case of countries such as South Korea and Taiwan) and the increased flow of trade and foreign direct investment between already industrialized countries finally undermined the geographical production/consumption nexus (often referred to as "central Fordism") that was the leitmotif of the early postwar decades.

A vital element in allowing the US to have such a dominant presence within the world economy was the persisting yet historically episodic political–military conflict with the Soviet Union. This served both to tie Germany and Japan firmly into alliance with the US and to define two geographical spheres of influence at a global scale. For a long time this imposed an overall stability on world politics, since the US and the Soviet Union were the two major nuclear powers, even as it promoted numerous "limited wars" in the Third World of former colonies where each of the superpowers armed surrogates or intervened themselves to prevent the other from achieving a successful "conversion" (O'Loughlin 1989). For all their weakness, however, Third World and other small countries could not be treated as passive objects of imperialist competition. They had to be wooed and often they resisted. The boundaries and integrity of existing states were protected by the military impasse between the superpowers. Any disturbance of the status quo threatened the hegemony of each within its respective sphere of influence.

In the end, the Cold War geopolitical order came undone with the collapse of the Soviet Union. But this was not the only sign of an old order in demise; the free-world economy was also in disarray as mounting stagflation, indebtedness and balance-of-payments disequilibria clearly and successively indicated. Indeed, US hegemony had been in trouble since around 1960 when the London gold crisis showed the potential weakness of the gold–dollar exchange mechanism at the heart of the Bretton Woods system (Triffin 1960; Cafruny 1990). By 1971, when the Nixon administration abrogated the Bretton Woods Agreement, the US faced a declining rate of economic growth and needed recourse to a competitive devaluation of the dollar. Thus, and ironically, the explosion of globalization that followed has been based on the explicit pursuit of US national economic interest without much multilateral negotiation with other states. US governments since 1971 have been increasingly unilateral, combining an economic focus on using the strength of the dollar to export the costs of US fiscal policies (in particular, the twin balance-of-payments and federal deficits) and a geopolitical focus on coercing recalcitrant states that are seen as threatening to either or both globalization and US hegemony. In other words, market-based globalization has been increasingly underwritten by US neo-imperialism, with US governments disciplining others fiscally and monetarily even when profligate themselves and threatening military intervention here, there and everywhere in pursuit of security threats to the US and its economy.

The "market-access" regime

Wide acknowledgement that the world economy has undergone a fundamental reorganization since the 1970s has not meant that there is agreement as to how and why this has happened. Agreement is confined only to the sense that the world economy has entered a phase of flexible production and accumulation in which business operations around the world are increasingly taking the form of core firms (often transnational in scope) connected by formal and informal alliances to networks of other organizations, both firms, governments and communities (also sometimes known as "disorganized capitalism"). The paradox of this trend is that, while networking allows for an increased spanning of political boundaries by concentrated business organizations, it also opens up the possibility of more decentralized production to sites with competitive advantages. At the same time, networks take on different forms with different sectors and in different places.

One account of the source of this shift in the world economy from big, vertically integrated firms organized largely with reference to national economies to globe-spanning networks of production and finance emphasizes the declining rates of productivity and profits of major corporations in the years between 1965 and 1980. Profit rates, averaged across the seven largest national industrial economies and defined as net operating surplus divided by net capital stock at current prices, declined in these years in the manufacturing sector from 25 percent to 12 percent. Across all sectors, the average rate of profit fell from 17 to 11 percent (Glyn *et al.* 1989: 53). What appears to have happened is that the period from 1960 to the early 1970s was one of generally rising profit rates. Thereafter, but at different rates of decline and following different trajectories, rates of profit began to decline (Figure 9.1). These seem tied more to declining rates of productivity (efficiency in the use of equipment and resources) than to increasing labor costs. Although there has been a recovery of rates of profit in some economies (such as the US) since the mid-1980s, this seems fueled in part by suppressing wages and other labor benefits more than by returns to new technologies (such as computers) or new investment (Webber and Rigby 1996: 325).

A revisionist "market-access" regime

Globalization is partly about firms attempting to cash in on the comparative advantage enjoyed in production by other countries and localities and gain unimpeded access to their consumer markets. But it is also about governments wanting to attract capital and expertise from beyond their boundaries so as to increase employment, learn from foreign partners, and generally improve the global competitive position of "their" firms. The combination of the two has given rise to a "market-access" regime of world trade and investment (Cowhey and Aronson 1993). This has eroded the free-trade regime that had increasingly predominated in trade between the main industrial capitalist countries in the post-World War II period. In its place is a regime in which acceptable rules governing trade and investment have spread from the relatively narrow realm of trade to cover a wide range of areas of firm organization and performance.

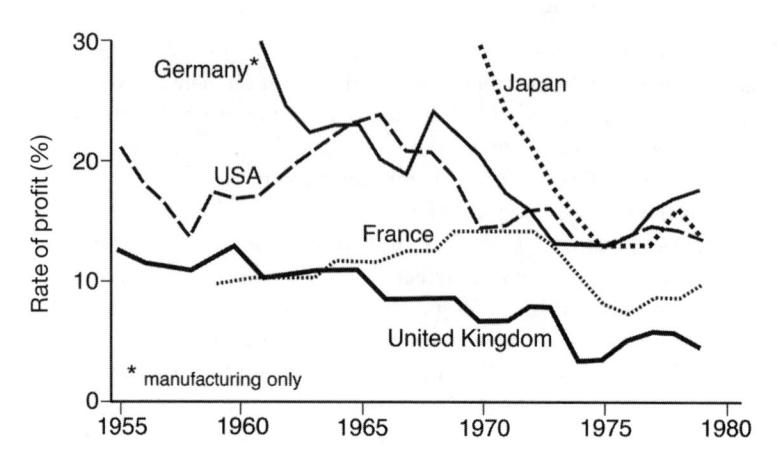

Figure 9.1 Twenty-five years of declining rates of profit for firms in major industrialized countries, 1955–1990

Six "pillars" of this system can be identified. The first is a move away from the dominance of the American model of industrial organization in international negotiations towards a hybrid model in which there is less emphasis on keeping governments and industries "at arm's length" and commitment to encouraging inter-firm collaboration and alliances across as well as within national boundaries. In this new model foreign firms are allowed to contest most segments of national markets, except in cases where clearly demarcated sectors are left for local firms.

A second pillar involves the increased cooperation and acceptance of common rules concerning trade, investment and money by national bureaucracies with an increasingly powerful role also played by supranational organizations (such as the European Commission for the EU and the World Trade Organization). Two consequences are the blurring of lines of regulation between "issue areas" (such as trade and foreign direct investment, which increasingly can substitute for one another) and the penetration of "global norms" into the practices of national bureaucracies.

The third pillar is the increasing trade in services beyond national boundaries and the concomitant increased importance of "producer services" (banking, insurance, transportation, legal, advertising) in the world economy. One reason for this is that high-tech products (computers, commercial aircraft, etc.) contain high levels of service inputs. Another is that producers are demanding services that are of high quality and competitively priced. They can turn to foreign suppliers if appropriate ones are not available locally. Banking and telephone industries are two that have experienced a dramatic increase in internationalization as producers have turned to foreign and "off-shore" suppliers.

Fourth, international negotiations about trade and investment are now organized much more along sectoral and issue-specific lines than was the case in the past. One rule no longer fits all. But many of the new rules are essentially *ad hoc*, rather than formal. This has opened up the possibilities of bilateral and minilateral (more than two parties, but not everybody) negotiations but at the expense of the greater transparency that would come from a consistent multilateral focus.

The final two pillars concern the content of the rules of the market-access regime. One is equivalence today between trade and investment, due largely to the activities of transnational corporations in expanding the level of foreign direct investment to astronomical highs. Local content rules about how much of a finished product must be made locally (within a particular country) and worries about the competitive fairness of firm alliances, however, also led to new efforts by governments in industrialized countries to regulate the flows of foreign investment. "Leveling the playing field," to use the American parlance, has meant pressure and counter-pressure between governments to insure at least a degree of similarity in regulation (in, for example, cases of presumed monopoly or anti-trust violations).

The final pillar involves the shift on the part of firms from a concern with national comparative advantage to a concern with establishing global or world-regional *competitive advantages* internal to firms and their networks. This reflects the overwhelming attractiveness of "multinationality" to many businesses as a way of diversifying assets, increasing market access, and enjoying the firm economies of scale that come from supplying larger markets. At the same time plant economies of scale (reductions in unit costs attributable to an increased volume of output) have tended to decease across a wide range of sectors, as noted first by Bain (1959) (Figure 9.2). This means that large firms can enjoy firm economies of scale and are not restricted by the lure of high average plant economies to a few production locations. Production facilities can be located to take advantage of other benefits that come from operating in multiple locations, particularly those offered by foreign sites, with "competitively low" wage regimes.

The new transnational order has four important consequences that set it apart from earlier geopolitical epochs, such as the Cold War. First, the ties that bind industrialized economies together are those of global capital investment rather than trade linkages. In the 1980s and early 1990s, the rate of growth of foreign direct

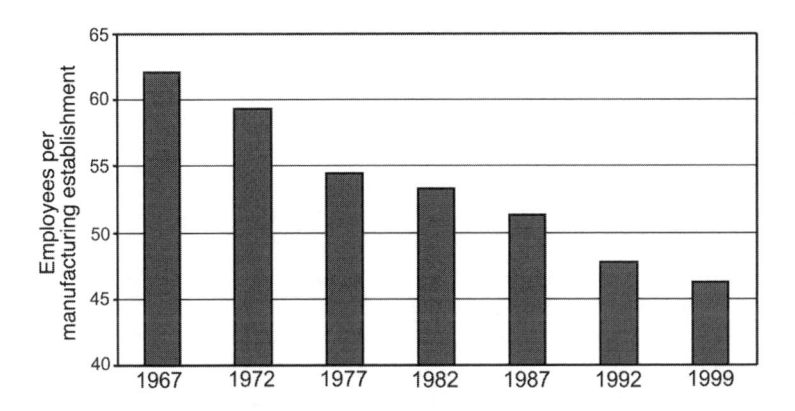

Figure 9.2 How average plant size in the United States has shrunk, 1967–1999

investment in the world economy has been three times that of the growth of world exports of goods and services (Dicken 2002).

Second, national trade accounts can be misleading guides to the complex patterns of trade and investment that characterize the new global economy. Perhaps 50 percent of total world trade between countries as of 2000 was trade within firms. Further, more than half of all trade between the major industrial countries is trade between firms and their foreign affiliates. A third of US exports go to American-owned firms abroad; another third goes from foreign firms in America to their home countries. And, because the new global trading networks involve the exchange of services as much as the movement of components and finished goods, many products no longer have distinctive national identities (Reich 1991b).

Third, as the US territorial economy loses manufacturing jobs and shares of world production to other places, the global shares of its firms are maintained or enhanced. As the US share of world manufactured exports went from 17.5 percent in 1966 to 14.0 percent in 1984, American firms and their affiliates increased their shares from 17.7 percent to 18.1 percent (Lipsey and Kravis 1987). This leads to the question "Who is US?" in relation to government policies that can favor US firms rather than the US economy (Reich 1991a). From this point of view, helping "foreign" firms locate in the United States benefits the US territorial economy more than helping "American" firms, which may be owned by Americans or be headquartered in the United States but have most of their facilities and employees located overseas. As long as the American economy is growing, through increased employment and productivity, these paradoxes will exact little political price. But under recession and as US governments reconstruct the tax code to benefit (nominally) US businesses at the expense of the median taxpayer (as with the George W. Bush administration) they can be expected to receive more attention.

Fourth, the US government remains as the "enforcer" of last resort to keep the entire market-access regime in place; but often in a more clearly neo-imperial capacity in relation to purported allies than during the Cold War. This role can take on several different forms that have varied across administrations and in response to different situations from the 1970s to the present. One is in the form of military intervention to either impose political stability or remove recalcitrant governments. A second is to oversee and underwrite financial bailouts for countries facing either bankruptcy or serious monetary crisis. A third is to publicize and recruit elite supporters around the world for present globalization (in the shape of the market-access regime) as both inevitable and positive. Whether or not US governments can afford to continue policing globalization when its benefits do not proportionately trickle back to the US territorial economy, and whether or not the rest of the world will continue to indulge US attempts at using globalization for US ends, are probably the major questions facing the long-term sustainability of the market-access regime (Wade 1998–9; Soros 1998–9; Brenner 2002; Kupchan 2002). A time may be approaching, however, when, even if the US role is much reduced, the institutionalization of globalization in various global forums might augur its continuation without domination by US governments (compare Agnew and Corbridge 1995, Chapters 7 and 8, with Hardt and Negri 2000).

The geography of globalization

The Cold War era laid the groundwork for what we see around us in the early twenty-first century. In particular, existing territorial states have become less and less "full societies." At one and the same time they are both too large and too small. They are too large for full social identities and many real economic interests. But they are also too small for many economic purposes. They are increasingly "market sectors" within an intensely competitive, integrated yet unstable world economy. This is the paradox of fragmentation in the context of globalization that many geographers have noted about the world since the "slow end" of the Cold War in the 1980s. Though frequently seen as separate processes they are in fact related aspects of a geopolitical order that has been slowly emerging. In this context, therefore, inter-state boundaries begin to take on a different significance and meaning from previously.

Globalization

British hegemony in the nineteenth century made trade more free and independent. American hegemony during the Cold War went a step further in promoting the transnational movement of all of the mobile factors of production: capital, labor and technology. Free trade could always be limited when production was organized entirely on a national basis. But today production as well as trade moves relatively easily across national boundaries. People are also moving in large numbers but face much greater barriers to movement than capital and trade (Figure 9.3).

The evidence for this qualitative shift in the character of the world economy and the diminution in the economic importance of existing territorial states as the basic units of account is of various types. First of all, since the 1950s but at a rapidly expanding pace in the 1980s and 90s, world trade has expanded at a rate well in excess of that of earlier periods (e.g. Rogowski 1989: 88). Most of this growth in trade has occurred in the already industrialized regions of the world. It owes much to the declining importance of transportation costs and to institutional innovations such as the GATT (now the World Trade Organization) and the European Union. In a world of large-scale trade there is a premium placed upon maintaining openness and balance rather than territorial expansion and military superiority (Rosecrance 1986).

Second, transnational firms are major agents in stimulating a more open world economy. For example, as I mentioned previously, even as the US territorial economy's total share of world exports shrank by one-quarter between 1966 and 1984, US-based firms still accounted for the same proportion of world exports because of their worldwide operations (Lipsey and Kravis 1987).

Third, even the relatively protectionist Japanese economy, the second largest in the world after the US, is increasingly internationalized and subject to stresses generated abroad (Higashi and Lauter 1987). For example, the "meltdown" of various Asian economies in 1997–8 had negative effects on Japan because of heavy Japanese involvement in that region through exports, investment and production.

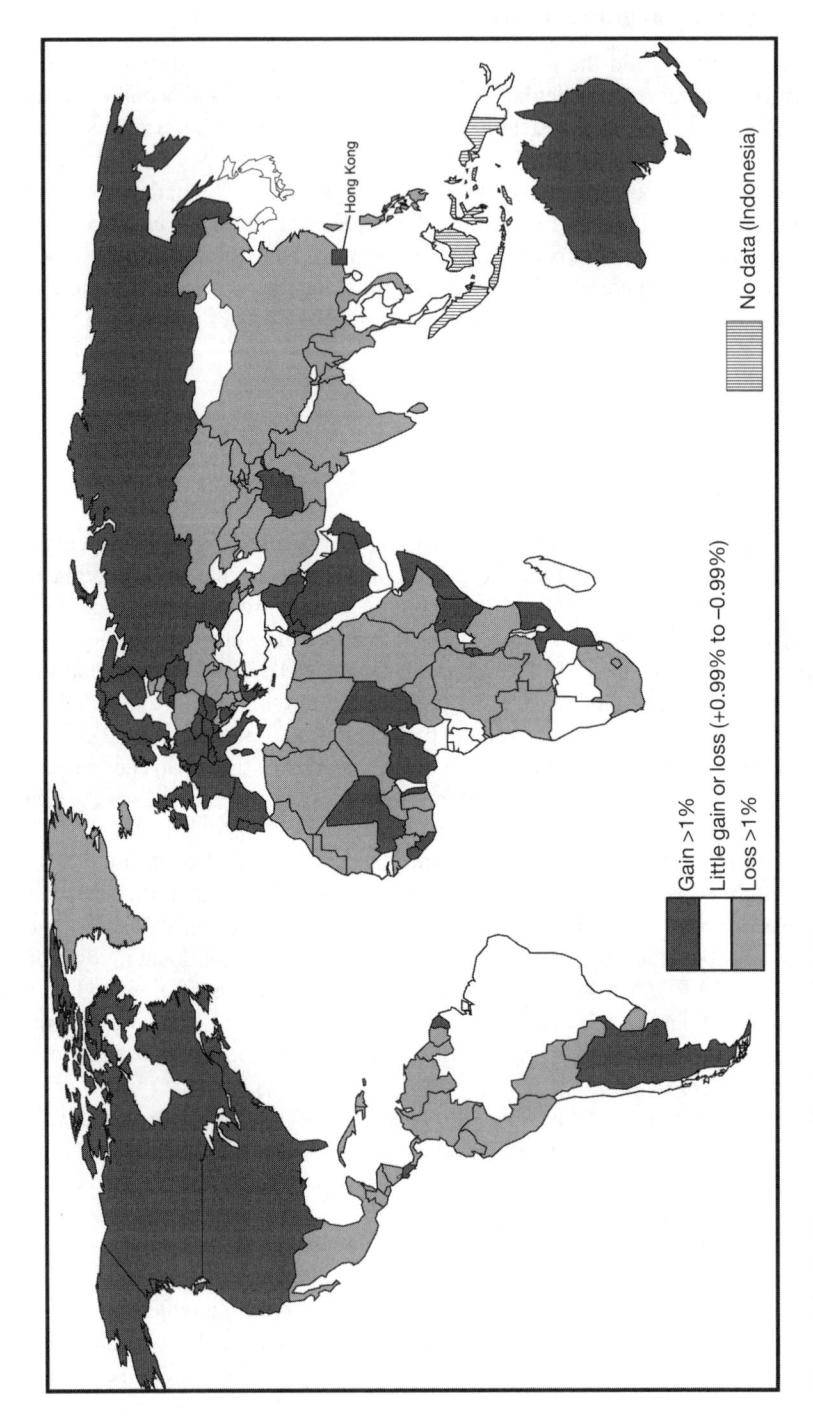

Figure 9.3 World net migration by country, 2000

Fourth, the world financial system is increasingly globalized. The demands of institutional investors, such as pension funds and insurance companies, for more diversified portfolios, the deregulation of national stock markets and the floating of currency exchange rates, have led to a transnationalization of finance. To serve their worldwide clienteles, many financial markets now operate around the clock and without the close government supervision that was once the case.

Fifth, various institutions and new social groupings have emerged as agents of the globalization of production and exchange. The IMF and the World Bank, for example, have become both more powerful and more autonomous of their member states than was intended when they were founded in the 1940s. Private organizations such as the Trilateral Commission and the World Economic Forum attempt to build an internationalist consensus among leading businessmen, journalists and academics from the United States, Europe and Japan (Gill 1990). Some commentators see the progressive growth of an international "bourgeoisie" or class of the managerial employees of transnational firms whose loyalties are to those firms more than to the states from which they come (Sklar 1976).

Sixth, and finally, boundaries between states are either slowly dissolving for a range of flows, as in the case of states within the European Union, becoming opportunities for cross-border collaboration, as with the so-called "Euregios" between adjacent European countries and the various forums on the Irish border emanating from the Good Friday Agreement of 1998, or shifting their effective locus from the edges of states to the airports and port cities where most migrants, refugees and asylum seekers attempt entry. For most people, however, interstate boundaries retain a general significance with access to citizenship rights and political identity that they have begun to lose for businesses (e.g. Newman 1998; Anderson and Bort 1999). Indeed, this is a major source of conflict in many relatively wealthy countries such as the United States, France and Britain as immigrants from poor countries become the target of political movements anxious to reinstate border controls to re-establish national cultural homogeneity. One consequence of the terror attacks of 11 September 2001 in the United States has been a "re-bordering" of the country even as the economy still depends on massive inflows of capital and goods from outside. But imposing a simple "inside/outside" set of boundaries on the country in the face of the imperatives of globalization will be no easy task.

This new world economy is neither inherently stable nor irreversible. In particular, total levels of world trade and flows of foreign direct investment could be limited by the growth of world–regional trading blocs, such as the European Union and NAFTA, which divert trade and investment into more protected circuits and reduce the global flows that have expanded most in recent years, by the failure of many parts of the world to achieve benefits from globalization, and by the difficulty of reforming international institutions (from the UN system to the IMF and the World Bank) to make them more open and democratic (James 2001).

Fragmentation

Paralleling economic globalization has been growth of within-state sectionalism, localism, regionalism and ethnic separatism. This growing fragmentation seems to have two aspects to it. One is the redefinition of economic interest from national to regional, local and ethnic-group scales. The other is the questioning of political identity as an exclusive phenomenon of existing nation-states. The first of these is the direct result of the breakdown of the national economy as the basic building-block of the world economy (Scott 1998). Economic restructuring has involved a collapse of regional–sectoral economic specialization in established industries (cars in Detroit, steel in Pittsburgh, etc.) and the decentralization of production to multiple locations, including many in other states. At the same time, markets are less and less organized on purely national grounds. One important political consequence has been a geographical redefinition of economic interests. Local areas are now tied directly into global markets where they must compete for investment with other localities and regions (e.g. Le Galès and Lequesne 1998). Meanwhile, the economically stimulative and regulative activities of national governments have both weakened and become less effective. Geared towards a national economy that has fragmented into regional and sectoral parts, government policies can no longer shield local communities or ethnic groups from the impacts of competition or readily redistribute resources to declining or poorer areas. The net result has been a substantial upswing in income inequalities between and within countries, even in a context of overall rising incomes at a world scale (accounted for particularly by the spectacular economic growth of China and, to a lesser extent, India). If anything, the trend of increasing within-country inequalities (across income categories) has been even greater than that between countries. In other words, relatively more of total global income inequality is now accounted for *within* countries than between them, although between-country differences have also increased between the world's poorest countries as a set (e.g. Pritchett 1997; Galbraith 2002; Agnew 2005, Chapter 7).

The other aspect of fragmentation has been encouraged by the crumbling of national economies, but relates more to the emergence of new political identities often based on old but revitalized ethnic divisions (e.g. Herb and Kaplan 1999). The past 20 years have seen the proliferation of "nationalistic" political movements with secessionist or autonomist objectives. In Western Europe this trend can be related to the growing redundancy of national governments and increasing levels of relative deprivation between regions and ethnic groups. In Eastern Europe and the former Soviet Union the assertion of ethnic identities has more to do with the demise of strong national governments, the exhaustion of state socialism as an ideology that incorporated ethnic elites, and the settling of old political scores from the distant past. In Africa, after the immediate euphoria of independence and the stasis imposed by the Cold War, economic development and nation-building have succumbed to ethnic and regional interests seeking their own futures in a world in which state powers, weak as they were, are increasingly co-opted by international institutions such as the IMF and the World Bank, and can no longer guarantee a return on investment in state legitimacy. Boundaries between regions and localities within countries are increasingly challenging the boundaries that appear on the world political map as the more meaningful ones from the perspective of everyday social life for many people. In the Sudan, for example, the north–south divide is more important politically than that between Sudan and neighboring states. In Ireland, while the border between north and south maintains its symbolic political importance, effectively it is the borders between neighborhoods in cities such as Belfast and the economic gap between Dublin and the rural far west of Ireland that are more important in people's daily lives.

Conclusion

Contemporary globalization is not simply the result of technological change, the spread of modernity, or the attraction of neoliberal economics. What was also required was a particular geographical logic traceable to the dominant influence exerted on the world economy by a succession of US governments putting into practice on a world scale an ideological disposition and a set of policies initially developed within the United States itself.

This "American project" has gone through two principal phases since World War II, when the United States emerged as one of the main victors. In the first, Bretton Woods phase, the US government served as the global "lender-of-last-resort," instituted a number of international economic and political organizations for multilateral management of the world economy, and integrated a free world economy through organizing alliances against its major superpower adversary, the Soviet Union. By the 1960s, the first part of this system was in serious trouble from an American perspective. Under the Bretton Woods system, US governments could not devalue the US dollar to stimulate US national exports and national economic growth. Ironically, therefore, the more open, free-wheeling world economy that came into existence beginning in the 1970s had its origins in the self-serving actions of a US government. The market-access regime for trade and foreign direct investment that replaced the old Bretton Woods system has relied on speeding up the world financial system, breaking up national economies into distinctive geographical parts, using the Bretton Woods institutions (particularly the IMF and the World Bank) to discipline states following non-conforming economic policies, and having the US as enforcer of global norms of political and economic conduct even if the fiscal consequences for the US territorial economy are grave indeed. Whether the geopolitics of current globalization is sustainable, therefore, is very much open to question.

10 The globalization of culture
Geography and the industrial production of culture

Don Mitchell and Clayton Rosati

> The tendency to create the *world market* is directly given in the concept of capital itself. Every limit appears as a barrier to be overcome.
>
> Marx, *Grundrisse* (1973: 408)

Introduction: September 11 and the globalization of culture

It is perhaps only a small exaggeration to say that the globalization of culture began on September 11 ... 1973. On that day, with American backing, Chile's democratically elected socialist government was overthrown in a military coup. President Allende was killed in the coup;[1] hundreds of government officials were murdered and jailed; and over the years, thousands of Chilean citizens were simply "disappeared." The problem was that Allende and his government represented a limit, a barrier to capital that had to be overcome. The coup ushered in a new era for capital in Latin America and for the United States. Chile became the model for a new regime of capitalist development; it became the model for the neoliberalism that we now all live in the midst of, and that is the basis of what we have come to call "globalization" (Ffrench-Davis 2002; Valdés 1995). The American sponsorship of the coup showed just how closely what we now see as universalizing globalization is always underpinned, as John Agnew (Chapter 9) shows in this volume, by specific geopolitical acts, particular historical circumstances.

But as much as the coup ushered in a new geopolitics of capital – a new era of capitalism – at the same time it ushered out a certain kind of culture, replacing it with one much more amenable to the world market. In the few years of the Allende government, a radical popular and populist culture had flourished. Indeed, what defined the Chile of the Allende years was a vital and invigorating political culture marked by a radical transformation of civil society that separated the fulfillment of needs from processes of commodification and made the former part of democratic culture itself. (In a typical poor neighborhood the people "had new homes, a community clinic, a cooperative dining room, vast popular organizations [that] took care of food distribution, child care, and education" [Cooper 2001: 59].) This radical transformation of civil society was accompanied by an equally radical efflorescence of song, theater, dance, film, storytelling and nightlife that was integral to the success of the revolution.

Popular culture was, during Allende's time, less something to be consumed, and more something to be produced, transformed and operationalized; audiences for cultural productions in Chile were less audiences and more active participants in a rising radical culture. This is not to say that mass-produced culture (Hollywood movies, global literature, schlocky TV) was absent; rather, it meant that mass-produced, highly commodified culture was only one part of the mix, and not necessarily the dominant part, either.

And to say the coup "ushered out" this activist culture is somewhat misleading. The Pinochet regime that came to power in the coup *killed* this activist culture, and *reorganized* the audience into a passive consuming one. For the coup, this was a necessary murder, since it was not just the nationalization of industry that presented a barrier to capital, but also this participatory, less-commodified culture. Therefore, among the political activists rounded up during and after the coup were countless musicians, poets and writers. For example, Victor Jara, one of the founders of Chile's "new song" movement that helped pave the way for Allende's and the socialists' electoral victories, was one of the first arrested. He was held for four days in the boxing stadium in Santiago, where he was tortured and maimed before being machine-gunned to death (see BBC News 1998). Similarly, the Pinochet regime outlawed popular civic organizers (and jailed, killed or disappeared their leaders), closed theaters, and instituted a long-lasting curfew that eliminated nightlife. Within two years of the coup, cooperative dining rooms had been replaced by soup kitchens, health clinics padlocked shut, and across Chile more than a hundred cinemas went out of business or were forcibly closed (Cooper 2001: 59, 61). Censorship of films was rigid, and soon little more than "Italian Westerns, Spanish musicals, and Hollywood disaster films" could be seen (Cooper 2001: 61).

Not that most Chileans had money for entertainment. Sponsored by the CIA, the coup had provided an opportunity for an early experiment in American-led economic "shock therapy" (Valdés 1995). Chile became perhaps the earliest test case for implementing what we now recognize as the neoliberal model of capitalist development, a model that depends on the almost total eradication of alternative means of livelihood, civic life and culture, and its replacement with a highly commodified, market-driven way of living in the world and relating to culture. The "social market economy" implemented in Chile (under the advice of consulting economists from the University of Chicago) demanded the rapid withdrawal of the state from the economy, except, as Marc Cooper (2001: 62) succinctly puts it, "for limiting wages, smashing unions, and jailing their leaders." The very fabric of social welfare was quickly unraveled in Chile, even as essential services like garbage collection, water and sewage, healthcare and pensions were privatized. Together, the violence of the regime, and the discipline of the economic "shock therapy," broke the back of social democratic culture in Chile, priming the country for externally driven, market-led development. Chile's economic landscape was prepared to become a fertile ground for globally footloose capital seeking shelter from declining rates of profit, environmental regulation, and the remnants of social security in the north.

The transformation was stark. By the end of the 1980s, Chile was being hailed as an economic miracle, with the *New York Times* crowing that Pinochet's "coup began Chile's transformation from a backward banana republic to the economic star of Latin America." Never mind that the evidence does not support either the claim that Chile was a "banana republic" (such states do not typically produce Nobel Laureates in literature at quite the rate Chile did), or the claim that Chile was an economic star (while growth in GDP was high in the late 1980s, the economy was stagnant between the coup and 1986, real salaries declined throughout the post-coup period, and the poverty rate exceeds 25 percent) (Cooper 2001: 87). It *is* true that a new, globalized economy and culture has been born in Chile:

> A stroll through downtown Santiago provides a reminder of how mesmerizing and paralyzing mass culture is when newborn. ... Imagine the *frisson* the average Chilean feels today when he or she walks the Alameda, the main downtown thoroughfare, and sees all the world's baubles offered up for sale and on easy credit. At the entrance to every department store, every shoe store, every pharmacy, there is the ubiquitous girl manning a podium offering instant credit. Air Nikes? Cash price 29,000 *pesos*. Or twelve payments of 2,900 *pesos*. A bottle of Shalimar? Cash price 16,000 *pesos*. Or ten payments of 2,200 *pesos*. That is ten monthly payments of five dollars each.
> (Cooper 2001: 102)[2]

Or imagine the *frisson* experienced by consulting University of Chicago economists when surveying the economic landscape of contemporary Chile, knowing, as the Chilean sociologist Tomás Moulin notes, that "the Chilean model anticipates Reagan and Thatcher. Owing to the neoliberal intellectual sway over the military, Chile started out early on the road everybody is now on. In this sense the Chilean terror was rational" (quoted in Cooper 2001: 103).

Moulin goes on to note that it was dictatorship, not democracy, that made possible this "miracle" of neoliberalism, and that what has replaced the dictatorship is really only a "simulated democracy" in which "the work force is too fragmented to recover and the population is distracted by consumerism and disciplined by credit obligations." Chilean culture, that is, has been completely reoriented and massively depoliticized. What was once a culture "produced" is now a culture "consumed." And it is exactly this transformation that the global media (a primary producer of this consumer's culture), many in academia, and most of us in our everyday lives, have come to call "the globalization of culture."

What is culture?

Following the coup, Pinochet's regime seized the geography of culture – and transformed its means of production. To understand how this is not just symbolic of, but even more a critical foundation for, the globalization of culture requires first that we think more clearly about what that amazingly capricious term *culture* means.

Culture as ways of life

"Culture" is as complex a concept as it is an important one (Williams 1983). Deriving originally from a Latin term signifying the husbandry of plants, "culture" implies a tending to the conditions of life in such a way that something more than and different from "nature" is produced (Eagleton 2000). For human societies, "culture" signals specific *ways of life*: specific languages, specific modes of getting a living and specific styles of dress, manners, cuisine, mating and marriage, inheritance, religion, and even dying. "Culture as ways of life" is the everyday habits and practices of living, together with the institutions that make these habits and practices possible. It is the cooperative dining rooms of pre-Pinochet Chile and the TV-dinners of pre-Nixon America. In this sense, culture consists of the material practices of everyday life (Jackson 1989; Williams 1977, 1980).

Such material practices are, of course, structured (they are not random), and they are socially produced (they are not completely voluntary at the individual level). Culture as a way of life in any location is also never singular. What is important, then, is how *dominant* ways of life come to be (and come to be reinforced), how *resistant* or *emergent* ways of life develop to contest the dominant, and how *residual*, even archaic, ways of life remain powerful as ideological – and often institutional – challenges to the dominant (Williams 1977). Culture as a way of life entails a politics of hegemony – something that both Allende's revolutionary support for grassroots culture, and Pinochet's murder of it, made abundantly clear.

Though "ways of life" are often associated with "a people" or an identity (the Welsh, the Yoruba, Okinawans), or with a sub-group (workers, gays, punks), they are never entirely local. Instead they are constructed through the intersection of local needs and desires and larger-scale processes – through trade, interaction, migration and imitation (Appadurai 1996; Shurmer-Smith and Hannam 1994). Whether dominant, resistant or emergent, and whether of a people or a sub-group, culture as a way of life is never unitary because "culture" necessarily abstracts away from difference, often strategically (Mitchell 1995), implying that commonalities of identity are more important than differences. In this sense, culture defined as ways of life *defines* ways of life and therefore shades into a second, more restrictive (but every bit as important) meaning of culture: culture as systems of meaning.

Culture as systems of meaning

If the bloody lockdown of everyday life in Chile represented the coercive arm of what would become the new corporate globalization and the authoritarian transformation of the material conditions under which life was to be lived, the Pinochet regime's assassination of the arts bespeaks a slightly less tangible (but equally important) ideological dimension. Just as dangerous to the American planned expansion of its national industrial markets and its claims on Chilean resources as Allende's political nationalization of US-owned Chilean copper mines, was Socialist Chile's alternative ways of imagining the world. If culture is the organized (and contested) everyday interaction of people with a set of material, social and political circumstances – a way of life – then it is also a way of making sense of those circumstances and the surrounding world (and hence the nature of conflict). This organization of thought and knowledge, of beliefs, beauty and imaginations, is a central part of the coherence and the legitimacy of particular ways of life.

Culture, in Stuart Hall's famous phrase, is a "map of meaning" (Jackson 1989: 2). It is a means of organizing ideas into coherent unities and rational differences. And despite popular romanticism of the timelessness of traditional values and the like, such *ways of seeing* (Berger 1972) or *structures of feeling* (Williams 1977) are never natural or timeless, or otherwise "god-given." Rather, they are projects, struggled over and made to appear contiguous, whole, ordinary, and above all unquestionable. Once in control of the sites of Chilean cultural production, globalizing corporate actors, in cooperation with the Pinochet regime, possessed the power to define new standards of beauty, national identity, popular slang, and even political ideology. The project of defining and organizing social knowledge – of defining culture – is a critical moment in the exercise of power. In this sense, culture as systems of meaning is ideology. "Culture ... [is] a sort of premature utopia, abolishing struggle at an imaginary level so that [it] need not resolve it at a political one" (Eagleton 2000: 7).

Cultural productions

Culture as "systems of meaning" is concerned with the organization of knowledge, with defining ways of thinking and ways of understanding one's place in the world. To the degree that culture seeks to "abolish struggle," it pivots on a related notion that culture is "a kind of pedagogy which will fit us for [a certain kind of] political citizenship..." (Eagleton 2000: 7). This is a way of culture closely associated with the nineteenth-century British critic, Matthew Arnold. Arnold (1993: 73) defined culture as "the *best* thought and knowledge of the time." Explicitly elitist and normative, this definition of culture points to the *things* – the worlds of art and literature, music and drama – that result from and give form to the practices and meanings indicated in the earlier definitions of culture. In this sense, culture is *art*, and especially it is artistic *productions*. It is, precisely *not* "everyday" ways of life, but rather something beyond the everyday that can illuminate, enhance and even transform life (as only transcendent music, drama or literature can).

In the years since Arnold, this sense of culture has been significantly democratized to include not just high culture (symphonies, drama, great literature), but also the popular (pop music, TV and the movies, romance novels, celebrity magazines). Cultural productions are not something *only* to be consumed (like a TV dinner); they are also things around which audiences can be organized and mobilized. This is why critics of the industrialization of cultural production are so vehement in their condemnation of the debasement that they see such industrialization entailing (e.g. Horkheimer and Adorno 1994).

Culture and the geography of social reproduction

Whether such a critique is justified or not, it is in fact insufficient, for it missed how struggles over cultural production intersect with struggles over culture in the other senses, to define a field of *social reproduction*. Societies – like Chile or like America on September 11 – do not just exist, they have been (re)produced: having been built and sustained, struggled over and transformed. "Social reproduction" is a concept that refers to the institutions and ideologies, practices and productions; in short, the "culture" that makes life possible (Katz 2001). In organizing reproduction, people inevitably change themselves: a grown woman or man is not the same as the child she/he was. But, reproduction entails both persistence and transformation. The same is true of the social institutions that define life. Yet in both individual life and society, the processes, practices and institutions of social life *can be* (and sometimes *are*) revolutionized. Chile under Allende sought to transform the institutions of social reproduction to create what Che Guevera called a "new man," who stood for "solidarity [and] the fight for justice and equality" (Valdés 1995: 8). Similarly, Pinochet's coup reoriented the system of social reproduction towards a different "new man" – this one formed through "the cult of rationality and individual liberty [and] the quest for equal opportunities to compete in a free market" (ibid.).

In Chile, both the rise of socialism and the subsequent coup entailed massive reorientations of the systems of meaning, ways of life, and modes of cultural production that defined everyday life. But the coup did something more. The long wave of post-World War II expansion in the global economy had crested in about 1968 and by 1973 the crisis was severe (Gilmore 1998). The crisis was particularly severe in the United States, Britain, Germany and other highly industrialized countries (with more or less socialized institutions of reproduction). The opening of Chile to surplus foreign capital, its neoliberal privatization of social reproduction, and the success it had in thoroughly disciplining labor and other factions of radical Chilean society thus served as a step towards a solution to the then-current *global* crisis.[3] Post-coup Chile became a new model for economic development in the Global South and *therefore* marked the birth of a new kind of globalization of culture: the full-scale reorientation of ways of life; the implementation of (often repressive) new systems of meaning; and crucially, the invention of new means for the circulation of cultural productions (like Italian westerns and Hollywood disaster movies). Among other things, post-coup Chile provided a model for transforming the *scale* at which culture – in all its senses, and as the foundation of social reproduction – was produced. To understand why, however, it is important to turn to more general issues related to the workings of the capitalist political economy.

Crisis, the world market, and the industrial production of culture

Crisis and the world market

Crisis is intrinsic to industrial capitalism. The drive to *accumulate capital* requires the production of new stuff (Harvey 1982). Simply meeting social needs is not a feasible option within capitalism (which requires continued growth merely to survive): new needs must be imagined and produced, and new demands created. New markets must be found; or more accurately they must be *made*, because effective demand for new stuff is never assured. The threat of surplus – the inability to dispose of all that new stuff – is the root of crisis.

Surplus is inherent in the logic of capital itself. The only reason to deploy money as capital is to get more money: a surplus. The surplus value this "more money" represents results from the fact that labor power, like any commodity, has a certain value (the cost of what, in any society, at any moment, is necessary to produce the commodity labor power) which is lower than the value of the new commodities that labor power can produce over the course of a day. Surplus value, in other words, is the difference between the value of labor power and the values produced by labor power. Given that, it is (usually) in the interest of any single boss to reduce the direct cost of labor power to as little as possible.

But in this seeming rationality lurks a massive contradiction: commodities must be sold if the surplus value encapsulated within them is to be realized and returned to capital, and the market for many of those commodities are the living laborers whose labor power is constantly being devalued. To the degree that capitalists as a class are successful in driving down the cost of labor power, then they simultaneously wipe out their market. Additionally, markets can become saturated. A firm can produce, for example, wrist watches from now until the end of time, but if everyone who needs or can afford one already has one, then neither the capital expended in the production process, nor the surplus value thereby produced, will ever be realized. In this sense surplus (too many watches) is not just inherent in capitalism, but eternally a problem to be solved. The specter of crisis perpetually haunts the factory floor.

One possible solution to the perennial crisis of overproduction is expanding markets: this is one reason why the progressive reproduction of capital requires the expansion of the number of wage workers. New areas – and their populations – are opened up to wage work, and new wage workers become the markets for the expanding universe of commodities (new Nikes, a bottle of Shalimar). Consequently, the tendency towards a world market is given in the very social relations that are capitalism.

A second possible solution is to not just expand the market, but to differentiate it. This can be done by convincing watch-wearers that their current model isn't good enough; that they would be a more unique identity, a "new man," if they switched brands. Such market differentiation opens up the various dimensions of culture as a field of accumulation and requires a new division of labor in which armies of workers are deployed in defining new ways of life and new systems of meaning that can only be lived through the further (often credit-driven) purchase of *new stuff*.

Imperialism and the industrial production of culture

In other words, culture as product and as ways of life must now be industrially produced. What we have come to consider as culture – ideology, styles of clothing, food, speech and artistic works (in short, whole ways of life) – is more and more produced in a manner little differentiated from light-bulbs, cars or tin cans. And it is sold in exactly the same manner.

But culture works in additional ways as well. Companies and the capitalist system as a whole have a need to avert or overcome market saturation, and to make new markets accessible and accepting of new products. While the opening of new markets is often achieved through the raw exercise of power – through military conquest, the sponsoring of coups, and outright colonization – it is also accomplished through "softer" means of legal coercion and cultural reorientation.[4] Such softer means (which obviously can work in concert with the more direct exercise of power) require that capitalists engage in a strategic dialectic of invasion and dependency with new social spaces and practices, incorporating them into the current system of production, exchange and accumulation. In this sense, the logic of capitalism is the logic of *imperialism* (Lenin 1963; Harvey 2003). It is an expansion of the scale of dominant capitalist social relations, and implies a commensurate web of reciprocal dependencies – including a growing dependency of the capitalist center on labor power either residing, or reproduced, in the capitalist periphery. The economic (consumerist) stability of the core is a function of colonized (cheap) labor.

What is now clear, however, is that capitalist imperialism need not necessarily be "absolute," seizing markets and production in regions, countries or territories that are not yet "capitalist," as such.[5] Imperialism can also be "relative," colonizing – or otherwise negotiating the *surrender* of – new practices or aspects of social life, not yet commodified or reliant upon commodification. As Cleaver (2000: 83) argues, "Capital's power to impose the commodity-form is the power to maintain the system itself." Therefore, the production of new use-values, which constructs an object, practice or idea's advantage in satisfying human needs (very often constructing such "needs" simultaneously), links the logistics of capitalist production to local systems of meaning and social reproduction (Harvey 1982; Katz 2001).

While it might be the case that cultural exchange and hybridization have always been global processes, the current era of cultural globalization differs because it revolves around the industrialization of cultural production itself. This "production of culture" represents a revolutionary reordering of social life around both the needs and limits of the expansion of capital. Realms of social life, of social reproduction, that were formally cultivated by workers, their communities or the state, are now more and more caught up in the circulation of capital. Entertainment, styles of food, education, patterns of clothing, medical care – all are now structured through global systems of commodity production and sold at home and abroad (in the cores and the peripheries) by legions of copy-writers, credit brokers and media moguls, who teach us what commodities mean and why we need them (Zukin 1995).

Communication technologies have become central in this project of "commodity imperialism." After the early 1970s, communications and the global media have reworked the various boundaries of cultural difference. If, historically, the media (from newspapers to television) have been central to the project of national identity formation (Anderson 1991; Morley and Robins 1995), new neoliberal regulations introduced as a solution to the crises of the 1970s initiated a shift in the media from this civic function to a more directly entrepreneurial interest defined almost exclusively by the logic of profit and competition. Mass media and the standardization of commercial knowledge production thus liberate cultural works from their historical and geographical contexts, only to subjugate them to a system of exchange, private property, and competition-driven profit-seeking.

Culture and uneven development

But the industrial production of culture involves not only the production of exchangeable commodities (and identities); it necessarily involves the production of difference, too. In particular, difference is critical to the production of surplus value. Marx (1987 ed.: 299) argued that surplus value can take two forms: absolute and relative. Absolute surplus value is created by making the working day longer – that is by increasing the difference between the time it takes to produce enough commodities to pay for the labor power expended over the course of the day (the "necessary labor time"), and the length of the working day itself. Relative surplus value, by contrast, arises from shortening the necessary labor time. This can be accomplished by increasing the efficiency of labor, by improving its quality, or by shrinking the market basket of goods necessary to reproduce labor power. The social conditions that determine absolute and relative surplus value obviously vary geographically, across continents, throughout regions and between neighborhoods. Difference matters. Individual firms can capture a greater amount of the total surplus value to the degree that they can exploit differences between peoples and across space, and capitalism as a system can expand only by productively incorporating and deepening these kinds of differences (Smith 1990). Divisions of labor require workers of different qualities, possessing different capacities, and differentially valued.

In addition, social and spatial differences, built up historically in places – the locally valuable systems of reproduction that define particular communities – represent to capital an important *value* that can be expropriated and exploited for the production of relative surplus values. Or to put the matter in slightly different terms, "culture" is now not only an output of capitalist production; it is also a crucial input. Different social values, different ways of life, different modes of knowing, different levels of education, and so forth, all determine how commodities are produced and valued. In capitalism, in other words, difference – uneven development – lives inside sameness: the differences of culture remain a vital aspect of the global integration of the wage relationship. *This*, as the people of Chile know only too well, is the globalization of culture.

The globalization of culture

The globalization of culture is best defined as the globalization of the conditions and contradictions that define capitalism. The industrial production of culture, as both an input and an outcome of capitalist value production, now defines social life across the globe. As output, capitalism produces globalized (if still differentiated) culture in the form of three kinds of commodities: the *everyday things* through which we define our identities, reproduce our labor power and give our lives form and substance; the *extraordinary things* that transcend everyday life and give it new meaning; and *media things*, which seem to exist more as images than tangible goods, but are so central to defining contemporary "systems of meaning." In turn, life redefined through these everyday, extraordinary and media things becomes the input for new rounds of capitalist production.

Everyday things

There is probably not a corner of the globe where it is impossible to find a Coke or a can of Pringles. Extended distribution networks of brand franchising (and hence distributed production) mean that people across the world can satisfy their thirst and hunger with the same drinks and same junk food. Clothing circles the globe looking for a market and we all end up wearing T-shirts branded by little alligators or polo players (or knock-off imitations of them). In mid-winter in snowy New York State, the supermarkets offer fresh (Chilean) grapes; South African avocados make it possible for Scots to eat reasonable facsimiles of Tex-Mex fajitas in February; and everywhere lunch is now catered by McDonalds or Pizza Hut.

But, does the proliferation of global brands and products "mean that local cultures will become homogenized and sanitized?" No, "new forms of local culture are being produced, along with new meanings of what counts as 'local'" (Thrift 2000: 109). Left unsaid is this most important point: that the provision of everyday things is more and more accomplished through the circuits of globalized commodity production. It makes a world of difference, as Debord (1994: 42) wrote a generation ago, that "it is not just that the relationship to commodities is now plain to see – commodities are now *all* that there are to see." Everyday life is the life defined by everyday commodities: Pringles change how we eat, and they change why and how food is produced.

Since that is the case, the critical issue is not that culture is the culture of commodities, but rather about who controls the means, and determines the relations, of commodity production. Moreover, it is about what to do with those residual archaic cultural practices that have not yet been brought under the great skirts of commodity production and the neoliberal regulatory regimes that now make such production possible (Williams 1989). The answer for capitalism, unsurprisingly, is to commodify *them*. All over Asia, you can pay a fee and visit "folk villages" that show what life before industrialization was like; in Costa Rica or Botswana you can go and live for a time among the natives; in Pennsylvania you can watch workers pretend to make steel; in New Lanark, Scotland or Oneida, New York, you can wander the halls and workshops of cooperative colonies and buy some knowledge about how the production of everyday things – the constituents of social reproduction – used to be possible on a completely different basis. Afterwards, it will not be hard to find another can of Pringles, or another Coke.

Pringles and Coke are universally available because they are – presumably –

what "everybody" wants. Yet what everybody wants is premised on a generalized authoritarianism that directs commodity consumption. One of the central jobs in commodity production, after all, is *marketing*, and marketing works through the exploitation of conscious and unconscious desires, but also through social averaging, to assure consumers that what appears in the market is what they want. The spectacle of commodity consumption is thus "the omnipresent celebration of a choice *already made* in the sphere of production, and the consummate result of that choice" (Debord 1994: 6).

For many, however, having the production of their everyday lives determined by such authoritarianism is not enough: they struggle to redefine themselves and to shape their relationship to culture by breaking away from the mass and focusing their desires not on the everyday, but on the extraordinary. For them, a whole different branch of the culture industry has arisen.

Extraordinary things

If cultural differences are on the one hand also necessary to the production of surplus value, they are on the other hand necessary, to the *realization* of surplus value: to the buying and selling of the commodities produced. Different cultural identities, tastes and other resistant or emergent systems of meaning ultimately pose a quandary for industrial production as they represent another "soft" barrier to expansive consumption. But like other potential barriers to capitalism, "difference" is less a limit than an opportunity to be exploited – even deepened. Niche marketing and the further diversification of consumption have become key innovations for the expansion of industrial cultural products. Uneven development, in this sense, not only advances the production of relative surplus value; it also creates geographically differentiated markets. In the process, unique dimensions of culture come to be defined by the estheticism and stylization of their properties, the better to make these properties *exchangeable* on the market.

But this is no easy or straightforward process. Cultural artifacts and works of art – the putative uniqueness of culture – pose a problem for capitalism's necessarily expansive distribution and consumption. Once the production of such artifacts or works becomes industrialized, they lose the exceptional, extraordinary qualities that separate them from (and provide them with a rather different social significance than) Coke or Pringles. As Harvey (2001: 396) explains: "the contradiction here is that the more easily marketable such [extraordinary] items become, the less unique and special they appear."

Despite the contradictions of their industrial production, certain cultural works still retain – and enhance – social expectations of uniqueness. This expectation of uniqueness is retained because the consumption of extraordinary things functions as a mark of what Bourdieu (1984) calls "distinction." We make our identities, including our class position, distinctive through the consumption of, and therefore knowledge about, extraordinary cultural products: consumption of, and knowledge about, the opera *Aida* or the band Blackalicious tells not only ourselves, but as importantly others, *who we are*.

Media things

Some cultural things, however, are not ends in themselves, but rather platforms for selling more things. Mass media are such commodities. It should be no surprise in this sense that across the United States, from backwoods towns like Culpepper, Virginia, to global cities like New York, media conglomerates like Viacom and Clear Channel are purchasing and branding billboard sites. And in many ways, for industrial capitalism, television too is a billboard. Because of the complete reliance on advertising in this sense, TV, magazines and radio in particular – though other media like film and the internet are increasingly being brought into the fold – are not ends in themselves; they are only economically valuable insofar as they can attract a critical mass of attention for a sustained period, and in the process create new needs.

The popular, international, youth culture network MTV, for instance, serves an important role in the industrial production of culture as such a hub for a variety of other corporate interests. Jack Banks explains:

> Cultural producers like Hollywood film studios and major record labels that seek to develop global markets for their wares increasingly use MTV to coordinate and organize their marketing campaigns on a global basis. Both the studios and the labels want to move toward releasing and distributing new products simultaneously around the world, eliminating the traditional lag between a debut in the USA and other countries.
>
> (Banks 1997: 51)

To be effective, media must engage in the kind of expansion commensurate with the needs of capital. If capital requires the opening of markets, the access to and acceptance of consumers, media must work to create consumers of the *right kind*. This is only possible through – and in fact part of – the sort of geographic equalization or imperialism, endemic to capitalism generally, as Schiller (1999: 39) makes concrete:

> During the 1950s at least 50 countries inaugurated television broadcasting systems; there existed around 176 million sets, worldwide by 1965. Household access throughout the poor world remained strictly limited. By 1980, in contrast, there were 561 million sets in use (126 per 1000), and by 1995, 1.16 billion (204 per 1000).

More than 300 million television sets were sold in Brazil between 1994 and 1998, which increased "household penetration" to 85 percent. Mexico (15 million TVs), South Korea (10.4 million), India (50 million) and China (300 million) are other examples of this global equalization. Media things are "expanding things," and their value is directly proportional to their geographic standardization, to the magnitude of their empire of cultural space.

The production of media, as the Super Bowl and surrounding spectacles make clear, is a cooperative venture for different corporations and industries, a class strategy, demanding in the first place the extensive (and where possible, intensive) deployment of telecommunications infrastructure. Without the imperial transformation of new social geographies through the deployment of communications infrastructure, such a strategy would not be possible. Media, then, via networking with hardware delivery companies, use their image commodities to become a manager of the relation between global accumulation and social reproduction (through consumption) at the scales of body, home and community.

Media are on one hand relentlessly imperial, seizing and transforming social spaces to create a more predictable, globally uniform, and productive organization of social time at an expanding scale. On the other hand, the media's greatest windfall is not necessarily in legal or coercive conquest, but rather in being welcomed into our homes as an authority of cultural production. In this way, media are both *everyday* and *extraordinary* things: accepted as meaningful dimensions of day-to-day social practices, knowledge and identities, but just as much, only producible by a small (and concentrating) authority. Furthermore, they are extraordinary things – or better *spectacular* things – because of the extraordinary amount of capital invested in their production; it is only through the advanced accumulation of capital that it is possible to communally envision the leveling of whole cities in *Independence Day* or the gory sinking of the *Titanic* (cf. Debord 1994). Like traditional works of art and other extraordinary things, media productions attract monopoly rent. But, media maintain the potency of their monopoly rents by distributing simulations as widely as possible but at the same time keeping their production as concentrated as possible: *their elitism is their appeal*.

Since Elvis and The Beatles, perhaps, it is impossible to imagine popular culture without also imagining a screaming mass of fans struggling to touch what they have only been able to see in simulation. Popular – and replicating – shows like NBC's *Today Show* or MTV's *Total Request Live* demonstrate and reinforce their social power through such images of "the masses" scrapping (and a few succeeding, necessarily) to momentarily occupy the dominant spaces of contemporary cultural expression. In the process, entertainment, and the deployment of systems of meaning, is made *productive*. Horkheimer and Adorno (1994: 137) elaborate this argument dramatically:

> Amusement under late capitalism is the prolongation of work. It is sought after as an escape from the mechanized work process, and to recruit strength in order to be able to cope with it again. But at the same time mechanization has such power over man's leisure and happiness, and so profoundly determines the manufacture of amusement goods, that his experiences are inevitably after-images of the work process itself. The ostensible content is merely a faded foreground; what sinks in is the automatic succession of standardized operations. What happens at work, in the factory, or in the office can only be escaped from by approximation to it in one's leisure time. All amusement suffers from this incurable malady.

It is troubling (but no coincidence) that, as the global media conglomerates tighten their oligopoly on cultural production, it is possible to witness the development of an international circulation of television shows based on humiliation and the surrender of social dignity (as is required at work) now in the name of entertainment and relatively meager parting gifts. While so-called "reality shows" like *Fear Factor*, *I Bet You Will*, *The Bachelor*, and *Temptation Island* reveal at first glance a democratization of the space of media representation, this death of elitism is really a feigned suicide. It is a feigned suicide because as television increasingly opens up the spaces of mass cultural production to its throngs of consumers, it seemingly destroys that which gives it the most value: its elitism. Yet the spaces of production remain just as concentrated; and further, all participants, including live audiences, are now cast by producers and "audience coordinators" to fit the planned look and "energy" of the show. What appears as the end of elitism is simply elitism by another, and perhaps more powerful, name.

Moreover such images naturalize the denigrating authoritarian geography of capitalist production and the humiliation (or debasement) of the individual to laws of exchange and social averages. Such degradation is part of a crucial historical agenda in media, as shows like *Survivor* present life frivolously outside of industrial incubation as a veritable political cartoon for the supremacy of contemporary capitalist accumulation. TV's images of the West's and the global "North's" de-developed others (and historical past) is both poignant and racist not only because of their overt comparison of "our" technology and "our" lives with such "primitive" ways of life, but also because in the end none of it really matters, as long as someone gets the prizes, and the fame. And, of course, in the process, advertising space is sold. This *humiliation for accumulation's sake* is a foundational (and globalized) structure of feeling and map of meaning for industrial capitalism: it defines the globalization of the industrial production of culture.

And, crucially, it defines not just how, but especially *why*, "systems of meaning" are globalized, and how culture, across the globe, and in every living room, is put on a new footing. The globalization of culture, through the globalization of "media things," transforms the humiliation that is necessarily attendant upon the exploitation and alienation at the heart of capitalism, not just into something that seems natural, but something that is positively to be desired.

Conclusion: September 11 and the industrial production of culture

If the foundations for the current round of globalization were laid in the coup of September 11, 1973, then in the wake of the terrorist attacks of September 11, 2001, a new cultural superstructure is being formulated. In the immediate aftermath of those attacks, however, it was not entirely clear what that superstructure would look like. When the World Trade Center came tumbling down, and the Pentagon went up in flames, instructors in the global media told us that we (in the United States) had now seen the ultimate reality. There was no longer the time, the need or the desire for the fantasy of "reality shows." Yet such shows have continued to proliferate, with each country, each market, developing a slight variation on the theme to appeal to local residual cultures. Why?

Perhaps September 11, 2001, marks a key point on a continuum of unfolding history more than a rupture. As horrific as the thousands of deaths were, as immediately *material* as the destruction was, as clear as was the economic and geopolitical damage done, perhaps "9/11" was more than the ultimate reality. Perhaps our *vision* of the attacks was (re)constituted as the ultimate reality show? Is it possible for US viewers to understand post-9/11 life outside the circumscribed melodrama of television shows?

For President George W. Bush and his neoconservative strategists, the images (run and re-run) of the collapse of the Twin Towers were not ends in themselves, but rather audio-visual platforms for escalating American military intervention in order to implement a new geopolitical order. This is a geopolitical order in which the industrial, global production of culture is a central component. Controlled by class-interested actors, the industrial production of culture, particularly through media things, becomes a critical method for *selling war*. This is a cooperative production, spanning every network, called *The War on Terror*.

Indeed, like the show *American Idol*, the networks and research firms polled the nation to determine the appeal of further episodes of the ultimate reality broadcast – *Should We Attack Afghanistan?* With the American public still galvanized by rage from watching the towers collapse, polls seemed to suggest that invading Afghanistan would be reviewed favorably. *Then Iraq?* No, not at first. Yet, the polls revealed that the opposite would be true, should troops – American sons and daughters – be deployed. CNN, Fox and the networks, coordinated through the Pentagon and its plans to "embed" reporters, went to work. And the networks dutifully echoed and broadcast the Bush administration's deceits and falsehoods, as well as its dissembling, when asked to name its reasons for going to war. Even abroad – like a Pentagon-sponsored Arab pop radio station – this would turn the militarized conquest and obliteration of human lives into a media event which aimed to sell a particular way of life, regardless of its costs and consequences.[6] This great event would even have spin-offs like the *Jessica Lynch Story*, detailing her heroic liberation from Iraqi imprisonment. Before it was divulged that this "prisoner of war" was well cared for in her Iraqi hospital and that her American "liberators" met no resistance, several media networks had already contacted the Lynch family about rights to the TV movie.[7]

From this, the question must be asked: who was really supposed to feel the "shock and awe" of the US military campaign in Iraq – Iraqis, those watching the war on television, or both? This is a globally integrated production where death and injury don't just have *effects* (pain, misery, the extinguishing of lives), but *meaning*. But this latest version of the industrial production of culture is not just a justification for the sort of violence inherent in capitalist imperialism; it is also geopolitical distraction. Jobs continue to disappear, social services are cut, infrastructures crumble, and national and personal debts rise; neoliberal policies bring American states to their worst fiscal crises since the 1930s; yet reality programming – of both the frivolous, *American Idol*, and the deadly, *War on Terror*, kinds – also offers an escape from the very real political and economic contradictions of Bush's international implementation of "freedom" through violence.

By looking through the "reality" of reality TV, it is possible to glimpse the inevitable logic of the industrial production of culture at work: the incorporation of social activity, time and meaning – *culture* – into the mechanisms of production and the circulation of capital. Indeed, the Bush administration is uncomfortably "transparent" that its goal is total – even totalitarian – control over global ways of life. What the Chilean coup put into practice and helped to shape (the neoliberal reorganization of social and economic life), the Bush administration has now made explicit policy in its *National Security Strategy* (http://usinfo.state.gov/topical/pol/terror/sectrat.htm). There is "a single model for national success," President Bush declares in his introduction to the *Strategy*: "freedom, democracy, and free enterprise." Published on the anniversary of the September 11 attacks, the *Strategy* commits the United States to "dissuad[ing] future military competition," at the same time assuring that other governments "follow responsible economic policies, and enable entrepreneurship," and enact "pro-growth legal and regulatory practices ... tax policies ... [and] financial systems." The language of neoliberalism is rife: "Nations that seek international aid must govern themselves wisely so that aid is well spent. For freedom to thrive, accountability must be expected and required." But what this language means was perhaps made clearest 30 years earlier in the run-up to the Chilean coup by then Secretary of State Henry Kissinger:

> I don't see why we need to stand by and watch a country go communist due to the irresponsibility of its people. The issues are much too important for the Chilean voters to be left to decide for themselves.

The *National Security Strategy* might be more subtle, but the message is the same:

> All governments are responsible for creating their own economic policies and responding to their own economic challenges. We will use our economic engagement with other countries to underscore the benefits of policies that generate higher productivity and sustained economic growth.

For which read: all countries can determine their own economy (and culture and society); there is only one sustainable model for national success; the United States will use its might to assure this model prevails.

The contradiction that seems to be at the heart of this policy is no contradiction at all to its authors and beneficiaries. If prevailing means sponsoring coups and completely reorienting social life; if it means invading countries and rapidly privatizing its infrastructure; if it means so dominating global institutions that a single legal and property regime triumphs and the industrial production of culture – and politics – spreads then so be it. The *National Security Strategy* is the means to this end of total cultural globalization; its technique is the globalization of American empire; its result will be not just reality shows and tubes of Pringles, but whole governments "mass produced and of varying quality" operating at "previously determined and indexed level[s]." *That* is what is meant by capital's tendency to create a "world market." *That* is the globalization of culture, capitalist style. And *that* is why it must be resisted.

Notes

1 Allende killed himself as the Presidential palace was overrun. It is impossible to see this death as voluntary.
2 In Chile, over a third of the population currently lives on less than $30 a month. Salaries are 18 percent below where they were before the coup.
3 In this regard, as Agnew indicates in his chapter, *geo-economic* crises are also always simultaneously *geopolitical* crises (and vice versa).
4 Once again, Agnew's chapter in this volume presents a useful analysis of these dual means towards cultural, political and economic hegemony.
5 Though this remains important. See Harvey (2003a/b, Chapter 4).
6 The script for this show, as well as the ways of life it seeks to implement as the new reality, can be read at www.newamericancentury.org
7 Since this time, and despite reports of the "miss-telling" of the event in the press (by Lynch herself), NBC has struck a deal with the Pentagon to go forward with movie plans. To secure military support for making the movie, NBC has allowed the Pentagon to "correct" the script, "making sure it was as militarily and historically accurate as possible" (Rosenberg 2003). NBC is owned by General Electric. GE is a primary manufacturer of military armaments, including Patriot missiles. It has been argued on many other occasions that NBC's substandard and often grossly biased coverage of American military actions is due to this conflict of interest between its role as both war journalist and war profiteer (Kellner 1992).

11 The globalization of fear

Fear as a technology of governance

Byron Miller

fear 1. noun: "The instinctive emotion aroused by impending or seeming danger, pain or evil"

(*The New Lexicon Webster's Dictionary*)

There is America, hit by God in one of its softest spots. Its greatest buildings were destroyed. Thank God for that. There is America, full of fear from its north to its south, from its west to its east. Thank God for that. What America is tasting now is something insignificant compared to what we have tasted for scores of years. Our nation (the Islamic world) has been tasting this humiliation and this degradation for more than 80 years. Its sons are killed, its blood is shed, its sanctuaries are attacked, and no one hears and no one heeds ... Millions of innocent children are being killed as I speak. They are being killed in Iraq without committing any sins and we don't hear condemnation ... In these days, Israeli tanks infest Palestine ... and other places in the land of Islam, and we don't hear anyone raising his voice or moving a limb ... [Osama bin Laden (translation 7 October 2001)]

(www.guardian.co.uk/waronterror/story/0,1361,565069,00.html)

Americans are asking, why do they hate us? They hate what we see right here in this chamber – a democratically elected government. Their leaders are self-appointed. They hate our freedoms – our freedom of religion, our freedom of speech, our freedom to vote and assemble and disagree with each other ... After all that has passed – all the lives taken, and all the possibilities and hopes that died with them – it is natural to wonder if America's future is one of fear. Some speak of an age of terror ... But this country will define our times, not be defined by them. As long as the United States of America is determined and strong, this will not be an age of terror; this will be an age of liberty, here and across the world ... in our grief and anger we found our mission and our moment. Freedom and fear are at war. [George W. Bush, 20 September 2001]

(www.whitehouse.gov/news/releases/2001/09/print/20010920-8.html)

A stunning feature of this terrorism is its global reach.

(Chua 2003: 255)

Introduction

While George W. Bush and Osama bin Laden have very different views on the causes of the global upsurge in anti-Americanism, they do agree on one thing: these are fearful times. Fear is increasingly the centerpiece of state and non-state geopolitical strategy, from the terrifying strike on the World Trade Center, to the "shock and awe" campaign of the US military in Iraq. Because distant and amorphous threats of violence are difficult to detect and defend against, they instill great fear. But the instillation of such fear is not random or irrational. Rather, strategic and instrumental objectives frequently lie behind it. Fear can be a powerful technology of governance (Rose 1999).

The steady upsurge in non-state acts of violence, generally known as "terrorism," represents the leading edge of the globalization of fear. The number of terrorist acts across the world increased from 28 in the 1980s, to 97 in the 1990s, to 54 in the first three years of the 2000s; the number of terrorism-related deaths rose even more rapidly, from 659 to 1196 to 3431, respectively (Pape 2003: 348). In almost all cases terrorists have explicitly targeted the populations of democratic countries. While terrorists' immediate objectives have been the creation of widespread fear, their ultimate objectives have been the expulsion of what they consider to be foreign occupying powers from national or sacred territory (Pape 2003).

The most spectacular of recent terrorist acts, with the clearest global implications, was the September 11, 2001, al-Qaeda attack on the United States. Al-Qaeda has a clear geopolitical objective – to drive the United States and other Western powers from the Islamic world (Rashid 2001; Bergen 2002). Al-Qaeda's geostrategy is to terrorize the United States and its democratic allies to the point that their governments will change policy and withdraw from the Middle East.[1] While the grievances of al-Qaeda have been consistently misrepresented by the Bush administration and much of the mainstream Western media, al-Qaeda has succeeded in creating a level of fear in the West not seen since the height of the nuclear arms race. It has done so from a great distance and its actions have affected several regions of the globe.

This globalization of fear is difficult to conceive apart from more commonly acknowledged globalization processes. Globalization is, above all, a change in global "geometries of power" (Massey 1994). While regions of the world have been intertwined in relationships of asymmetric power for centuries (Wallerstein 1979; Said 1979; Blaut 1993), under conditions of contemporary globalization many geometries of power have shifted and deepened. In the global economy, transnational processes of investment, disinvestment and trade have accelerated and become more globally integrated (Dicken *et al.* 1997). Oil and gas have become the resource "life blood" of modern industrial economies, making secure access to oil and gas resources (particularly in the Middle East and Central Asia) a primary geopolitical concern of the United States, its industrialized allies and emerging industrial giants such as China (Yergin 1992; Klare 2001; Rashid 2001, 2002). Political institutions have undergone major transformations as nation-states have been "hollowed-out," with their regulatory capacity reassigned to democratically unaccountable global institutions such as the World Trade Organization (WTO), International Monetary Fund (IMF), and World Bank, and to relatively weak local/national governments (Jessop 1994; Peck and Tickell 1994; Stiglitz 2002). Global cultural flows of images, ideas, commodities and people have accelerated at a dizzying pace (Appadurai 1996; Hannerz 1996; M. P. Smith 2000).

Not to be overlooked is the globalization of advanced technology. Virtually all forms of advanced technology, from computers to pharmaceuticals to weapons of mass destruction, are available – at a cost – around the world (Dodds 2000; Dicken 2003). This easier access to advanced technology creates considerable potential for human advancement. At the same time, increasingly uneven patterns of development, extreme asymmetries in military and political power, and cultural clashes that are often difficult to reconcile create an "unlimited potential for ... destruction" (Lanoszka 2003: A15). This contradictory combination of transformative globalizations, with their innate disparities in power and well-being, is a potent recipe for the globalization of fear.

Fear and the spaces of modernity

The modern world was not supposed to be a world of fear. The modern world, according to eighteenth-century Enlightenment philosophers and twentieth-century modernization theorists, was supposed to bring a steady march of human progress. Breaking free from pre-modern superstition, authoritarianism, intolerance and oppression, the progressive rationalization of science, economics, politics and religion would – it was believed – bring about a common secular world view and continuous improvement in the human condition. Rational and efficient economic, political and social organization would replace the irrationality and inefficiency that led to poverty, violence, war and terror. And in fact, the expansion of rational scientific knowledge did produce dramatic advances in medicine, communications, transportation, and a wide range of activities affecting human well-being and comfort, albeit unevenly. In the realms of politics and culture, the expansion of communicative rationality – that is, the discursive examination of previously taken-for-granted lifeworld values – resulted in advances for "racial" and ethnic minorities, women, gays and lesbians, and other groups who traditionally have suffered discrimination on the basis of unquestioned cultural norms.

But at the same time as these rationalization processes produced real human progress, they also produced some of the worst suffering in human history. Modern instrumental science enabled the rationalization of human labor (producing efficient but impersonal and alienated forms of work in Taylorism and Fordism), social control (making colonialism and neocolonialism possible through advances in techniques of bureaucratic organization), environmental exploitation (through advanced resource extraction and industrial production technologies, with the natural environment treated as a dumping ground for myriad forms of waste), military domination (with ever-more lethal and efficient battlefield weapons, culminating in weapons of mass destruction), and in the extreme, genocide (making mass murder an impersonal technical process through the marriage of organizational and technological power).

Our globalizing modern world is undoubtedly a constellation of contradictory processes. As McCarthy (1984: xxxvii) summarizes Habermas, the problems of the modern world are not due to rationalization processes themselves, but to:

> the failure to develop and institutionalize all the different dimensions of reason in a balanced way. Owing to the absence of institutions that could protect the private and public spheres from the reifying dynamics of the economic and administrative subsystems, communicatively structured interaction has been increasingly pushed to the margin; due to the lack of feedback relations between a differentiated modern culture and an impoverished everyday practice, the lifeworld has become increasingly desolate.

In the Global North – its Western core and Asia–Pacific "allies" – rationalization and lifeworld colonization has been advanced by a variety of corporate and state actors, encountering varying degrees of acceptance and resistance by different sectors of society. Rationalization and lifeworld colonization has not by any means been a smooth, continuous or uncontested process in any part of the world. The instability, uncertainty and fear that modernization processes provoke give rise to a variety of responses: social movement mobilization, individualistic resistance, or social withdrawal.

So-called "new social movements" are an especially important development of the contemporary modern world. Rather than emphasizing wealth redistribution, they strive to reclaim lost and threatened cultural traditions or claim new space for democratic decision-making and cultural autonomy (most address redistribution issues as well). The best known new social movements are progressive movements such as the global justice movement, the human rights movement, the civil rights movement, the women's movement, and the environmental movement. These movements strive, in the first instance, to create new realms of democratic decision-making and expand the realm of human freedom. And increasingly, they work cooperatively on a global basis, using advanced communications and transportation technologies to link oppressed groups and work for their mutual empowerment (Miller 2004).

But reactionary "new social movements" exist as well, including a host of fundamentalist religious, racist and nationalist movements around the world. In their extreme form these reactionary movements are overtly violent, such as the Ku Klux Klan, the Aryan Nations, and racist skinheads in North America, and Wahhabism, the Taliban, and al-Qaeda in central Asia and beyond. What these reactionary new social movements share is a common desire to turn the clock back on rationalization processes (both systemic and lifeworld) and return to an imagined golden era of stable and traditional – if repressive for many groups – social relations.

In the early twenty-first century, the rise of Islamism has given rise to new levels of fear and anxiety in the West. While Islamic resistance to Western influence and domination has a long history, the recent wave of fundamentalist Islam can, in part, be traced to the efforts of the United States, Saudi Arabia and Pakistan in the early 1980s to recruit, train and arm tens of thousands of Islamic radicals to fight Soviet troops occupying Afghanistan. Eventually more than 100,000 Muslims from 43 countries trained in camps along the Afghanistan/Pakistan border, camps that "became virtual universities for future Islamic radicalism" (Rashid 2001: 130). Thus the rise of fundamentalist Islam so feared in the West today was unintentionally facilitated by the United States and its allies, who mobilized and supplied resources to Islamic radicals. But this is only part of the story.

Resource mobilization can be effective only in the context of clear and deeply felt grievances, and in the Islamic world there are plenty: the colonization and partition of the Middle East by the British and French; the United Nations' partition of Palestine; the American and British overthrow of the Mossadegh government in Iran; the Soviet occupation and religious repression in Central Asia; the extraction of hundreds of billions of dollars of oil resources with minimal royalty payments by Dutch, British, French and American oil corporations; the support given by British, French and American governments to dictatorial, corrupt and repressive regimes in Egypt, Saudi Arabia, Iran, Iraq and elsewhere in order to maintain secure access to oil resources and shipping routes; the massing of US and "allied" forces in Saudi Arabia in the lead-up to the first Gulf War, coupled with their continued stationing on the Arabian peninsula after the war;[2] and, most recently, the invasion and occupation of Iraq (Yergin 1992; Rashid 2001, 2002; Klare 2001, 2004; Kepel 2002; Chua 2003). It is in this context of growing instability, inequality, corruption, cultural affronts and humiliation that fundamentalist Islam gained a following in the Islamic world. Islamism offers its followers an alternative to the contemporary global order; its radical violent offshoots offer a potential means, however repugnant, for achieving that alternative. It must be stressed that most devout Muslims subscribe to neither the radical Islamist agenda nor violence.

In a world of increasing global interconnection, it is exceedingly clear that modernization processes are not autarkic. Rather, they entail the rationalization of economic, state and cultural processes in the core, and the projection of expanded instrumental power to the periphery in service of the core interests of capital accumulation and resource control (Harvey 2003b). As Taylor (1999) observes, "modernity [arrives] through coercion" (p. 41) in the periphery, while in the core "the popular positive image of being modern does not seem to have room for victims" (p. 6). This global division of experience and awareness situates the turn toward desperate measures in the periphery and the inability to comprehend "why they hate us" in the core. Fear pervades both the core and the periphery of the modern world system, but for different reasons. In "globalization's heartland," the attacks of September 11 brought a terrifying form of violence to American citizens on American soil and shattered a long-standing sense of invulnerability. The possibility that a seemingly irrational and incomprehensible enemy may strike at any time, in any place, from anywhere, has now become a pervasive fear. In the periphery, fears of imposed austerity measures, economic misery, cultural imperialism and war – should leaders choose policies that threaten imperial interests – have a long history. Some fears, in other words, have a basis in global systemic violence. The reality of acts of violence notwithstanding, real threats and dangers must always be perceived and interpreted, and perceptions and interpretations are always open to manipulation. The manipulation of fear can be a powerful technology of social and political control; that is, of governance.

Fear as a technology of governance: global terrorism

Since the Cold War, geopolitical actors have explicitly sought to instill fear in their foreign adversaries, as well as in domestic populations, as a means of affecting policy and manipulating behavior. Fear, in essence, has become a technology of governance. Rose (1999: 52) defines a technology of governance as:

> an assemblage of forms of practical knowledge, with modes of perception, practices of calculation, vocabularies, types of authority, forms of judgment, architectural forms, human capacities, non-human objects and devices, inscription techniques and so forth, traversed and transected by aspirations to achieve certain outcomes in terms of the conduct of the governed (which also requires certain forms of conduct on the part of those who would govern).

Technologies of governance are employed to shape "conduct in the hope of producing certain desired effects and averting certain undesired events" (Rose 1999: 52). The quotation from Osama bin Laden that opens this chapter leaves little doubt that he and the September 11 hijackers intended to create widespread fear and terror in the United States as a means of changing US conduct in the Islamic world. Indeed, as Ahmad (2001: 17) points out, one dictionary definition of terrorism is "the use of terrorizing methods of governing or resisting a government."

In comparison with the nation-states of the core, terrorist organizations have relatively little power; they have few followers, little money, few weapons. The ability to instill terror is the terrorists' chief source of power. It allows them to turn the power of the powerful against the powerful. By shattering the sense of security of the well-to-do and powerful, terrorists attempt to use fear to change their policies and actions. As Barber (2003: 21) explains: "fear is terrorism's only weapon, but fear is a far more potent weapon against those who live in hope and prosperity than those who live in despair with nothing to lose."

Terrorists maximize their enemies' fear not only through the barbarity and death toll of terrorist attacks, but through symbolic violence. The September 11 attacks could conceivably have been far more deadly had the hijackers crashed the hijacked airplanes into nuclear power plants, nuclear weapons facilities or chemical factories. But the selected targets, as well as the means of attack, had special symbolic significance. The destruction of the World Trade Center, the primary symbol not only of New York City but of American global capitalism, exposed the vulnerability of the entire economic system upon which American prosperity rests.

The damage to the Pentagon, the command and control center of the American military, showed that even the world's most powerful military machine is vulnerable. And the use of passenger airplanes as weapons showed that a generally safe and widely used mode of transportation could become a horrifying tool of death at any instant. From the standpoint of spreading fear and insecurity, the attacks were extremely effective because they greatly elevated both Americans' perception of risk (any airplane can be hijacked anywhere at any time and turned into a human-piloted missile) and Americans' level of emotional distress (the primary symbol of American prosperity was destroyed and the primary symbol of American military security damaged). As Steinert (2003: 654) observes:

> Terrorist acts have a strong "symbolic" dimension, they "send a message." But to kill 3,000 and devastate two of the world's tallest buildings and an important area of a world city and center of the world economy is a barbaric kind of "symbolism." It adds another dimension to the game: it demonstrates the warriors' ingenuity and courage through the infliction of grave harm, making the enemy tremble and live in fear ... This audacious, if horrific, crime served the same function as a spectacular Mafia shooting: to convince others that they should do business with this gang when approached.

Although Steinert's "Mafia shooting" analogy may be sound with respect to terror as a means of governance, it breaks down with respect to geography. Mafia shootings typically take place within the home territory of Mafia organizations. What distinguishes global terrorism from Mafia shootings is its global reach. One of the primary distinguishing characteristics of global terrorism is that its perpetrators attempt to *govern their adversaries from a distance*. Global terrorist organizations clearly recognize the interdependence of their home territory and their adversaries' territory. And they recognize that, while they control none of the traditional networks of power that connect such disparate territories, they do have the ability to affect distant audiences through the mass media. Al-Qaeda, the best known global terrorist organization, does not attempt to command formal institutional resources or authority within the United States; it does not attempt to occupy US territory. Rather, its technology of governance relies on spectacular attacks and mass media coverage to instill fear at a distance.

Given the spectacular and barbaric nature of the September 11 attacks, their planners and operatives could certainly expect widespread media coverage. But they could not be certain how the US government would respond to the attacks or how, specifically, the media would cover them. As it turned out, the mass media would be extremely cooperative in the months and years following:

> American news anchors spread their own fear to a nation of fearful viewers (scare the opinion makers and they will scare everyone else for you). And so it [went]: American troops rehearsing for war in Iraq on television wearing scary space-age anti-gas and anti-bacterial gear they would never actually be required to wear, and being immunized against smallpox and other toxic

agents to which they were never exposed in an exercise which ... could only exacerbate rather than assuage their fears; government escalating the "terror level" from yellow to orange a few weeks prior to the assault on Iraq, then back to yellow with the war over, then up and back again, giving Americans no specific information but provoking quasi-hysterical behavior, including people wrapping their suburban homes in plastic sheeting, a run on duct tape (to seal off windows) and bottled water, and mothers purchasing gas masks for their two year olds. How such measures [did] anything other than catalyze the very fears terrorists wish to inspire is unclear. What is clear is that men who are otherwise powerless can manipulate the governments and mass media of their powerful enemies so that their adversaries do the greater part of their work for them.

(Barber 2003: 31)

Fear as a technology of governance in US domestic policies

While debate over the appropriate response to the September 11 attacks will likely never be resolved, it is clear that the Bush administration actively interpreted and framed the attacks in specific ways that not only heightened the climate of fear, but also enhanced the legitimacy of the administration.

The problematic nature of establishing political legitimacy in a democratic society has long been recognized (e.g. Habermas 1973). Even more so than most US administrations, Bush's suffered from severe legitimacy problems upon taking office. George W. Bush became President in January 2001 after a highly contentious election in which the Democratic candidate, Al Gore, won the plurality of the national vote. Without a clear election victory or mandate, the Bush administration suffered from widespread perceptions of illegitimacy, with some of its less restrained critics openly referring to it as a "junta" (e.g. Vidal 2002).

In contemporary democratic societies legitimacy issues are frequently resolved, over the medium to long run, through the demonstration of sound macroeconomic management that improves the standard of living for the general population. But legitimacy may also be established by a government "protect[ing] its citizens from predators; 'protection' obviously can include waging war" (Tiryakian 1999: 479). As Tiryakian, drawing on Simmel and Coser, observes:

> [C]onflict against an external foe serves (functions) to strengthen, or rebuild, group solidarity. Wars, especially "little wars" fought by a state against another one, help to legitimate the rule of the incumbent government. People of different political persuasions tend to "rally around the flag," even if, before the war breaks out, the majority or a significant portion of the citizenry had dissatisfaction with the rulers or ruling party. In the West during the past two decades, we have had "little wars" by big powers against smaller states that have taken place at times when the head of the big power was having domestic difficulty, whether getting a budget approved or some other [problem]: Grenada, the Malvinas/Falkland Islands war and Chechnia all come readily to

mind ... one might posit that a latent function of modern war is to mobilize flagging support for an incumbent regime.

(Tiryakian 1999: 479)

Without suggesting that the Bush administration allowed terrorist attacks to occur, or that it necessarily framed the attacks with particular political objectives in mind, it is nonetheless clear that the framing of the attacks as acts of war, and the amplification of fear through a variety of means, allowed the Bush administration to assume the role of protector of a vulnerable American citizenry, establishing its legitimacy.

Undoubtedly, the attacks could have been framed in other ways and other courses of action could have been adopted. Rather than drawing analogies between the September 11 attacks and the Japanese attack on Pearl Harbor (even though the 9/11 attacks were not perpetrated by a nation-state), different analogies stressing global networks and non-state threats could have been drawn. Rather than defining the attacks as acts of war justifying American wars against Afghanistan and Iraq (even though the latter country had no connection to 9/11), the attacks could have been defined as crimes against humanity requiring a massive global police action and trials of suspects at an International Criminal Court. And rather than pursuing a course of action that left America virtually alone in the world (substantial support for the American war effort came only from the UK), the Bush administration could have acknowledged America's interdependence in a globalizing world and pursued justice through multilateral institutions. But none of the alternative frames and courses of action would have allowed the George W. Bush administration (and its neoconservative strategists) to appear as protective and heroic.

In short, Barber's (2003) contention that terrorists manipulate the governments and mass media of their victims is only partially correct. Governments and mass media also play a direct role in the shaping of perceptions, emotions and fears. The use of fear as a technology of governance is not the exclusive province of terrorists. Rather, terrorists, governments and mass media often manipulate fear symbiotically, despite their fundamentally different objectives.

Numerous analysts have identified ways in which the Bush administration's analyses and language have served to heighten levels of fear. Edward Luttwak, a senior fellow at the Center for Strategic and International Studies, has publicly questioned the purpose of the administration's use of color-coded "threat levels" and suggested that "maybe Washington has an investment in alarm ... so long as the economy remains weak, [the Bush administration's] reelection strategy must stress the President's leadership in war and in confronting terrorism – whose importance cannot therefore be diminished" (Luttwak 2003: A15).

Indeed, members of the Bush administration's foreign policy team recognized, even before taking office, that only a major unifying national tragedy would insure the level of public support needed to achieve their ambitious foreign policy and military goals. In September 2000 members of the Project for the New American Century (PNAC) issued a report, *Rebuilding America's Defenses: Strategy, Forces and Resources for a New Century*, that called for a massive peacetime military build-up, the militarization of space, the control of cyberspace, and an aggressive policy of "shap[ing] a new century favorable to American principles and interests" (PNAC 2000: preface). Other reports and opinion pieces followed, and PNAC members were soon positioned in many of the Bush administration's "seats of power."

Former Treasury Secretary Paul O'Neill's notes suggest another reason for fostering a climate of fear: the Bush National Security Council decided to invade Iraq only ten days after the inauguration of George W. Bush in 2001 (Suskind 2003). While no conceivable justification for war existed at that time, the administration eventually justified war against Iraq based on the assertion that Saddam Hussein possessed or was trying to possess weapons of mass destruction (WMDs) that he might use against the United States. As the evidence supporting such assertions became less and less convincing, the administration did not reverse its position. Rather, it broadened the definition of WMDs to include not only thermonuclear weapons, but also biological and chemical weapons; evidence of these also proved to be lacking.[3]

O'Neill's account of the early decision to go to war in Iraq is perhaps the best known, but certainly not the only, reliable high-level account. Major General Anthony Zinni, head of the US Central Command from 1997 to 2000 and former special envoy to the Israeli–Palestinian peace negotiations for George W. Bush, has said that the Bush decision to invade Iraq reminded him of Vietnam:

> Here we have some strategic thinkers who have long wanted to invade Iraq. They saw an opportunity, and they used the imminence of the threat and the association with terrorism and the 9/11 emotions as a catalyst and justification. It's another Gulf of Tonkin.
>
> (cited in Alterman 2003b: 10)

General Zinni's position is echoed by retired four-star General Wesley Clark, who has charged that "Iraq posed no imminent threat to the United States and that the President used fear to sell Americans on the need to invade" (Alberts 2003: A11).

The September 11 attacks provided the catalyzing event the Bush administration needed to impliment its plans for a massive military build up and invasion of Iraq. For a host of reasons relating to "petro-imperialism" and the need to ensure a global *pax Americana* (PNAC 2000; Klare 2001, 2004; Falk 2003; Harvey 2003), neoconservative geopolitical strategists in the Bush administration set the United States on a path to radically remake the global geopolitical map. Because their "millennialist program" would find little public support in ordinary times, fear has been employed as a technology of governance – shaping public perceptions, calculations and actions to garner support and silence dissent.

Fear as a technology of governance in US foreign policy

The United States was the primary driving force behind the establishment of most of the institutions of multinational and global governance and security in the post-World War II era. The United Nations, the General Agreement on Tariffs and

Trade, the World Trade Organization, the International Monetary Fund, the World Bank, the North Atlantic Treaty Organization, the North American Free Trade Agreement, and even the Kyoto climate change accord and the International Criminal Court were all established and promoted with the active support of the United States. But a sea-change in policy toward the institutions of cooperative global governance occurred under the administration of George W. Bush. Under the Bush administration the United States has become aggressively (some would charge, arrogantly) unilateralist. It has withdrawn its support for both the Kyoto accord and the International Criminal Court, bypassed the United Nations to form a "coalition of the willing" to wage a pre-emptive war on Iraq, and told nations around the world that they are either with the US or against it.

That a radical change in US foreign policy was coming was signaled in George Bush's *National Security Strategy of the United States*, released in September 2002, which ratified the intent of earlier PNAC documents, declaring "Our forces will be strong enough to dissuade potential adversaries from pursuing a military build-up in hopes of surpassing, or equaling, the power of the United States" (White House 2002: 1). The theme of US domination – through overwhelming military might – of a uni-polar world runs through these documents. But how this policy of military domination would affect established mechanisms of international governance – flawed though they may be – is not clearly specified. Citing international relations analyst John Ikenberry, Chomsky summarizes its implications:

> The declared "approach renders international norms of self-defense – enshrined by Article 51 of the UN Charter – almost meaningless." More generally, the doctrine dismisses international law and institutions as of "little value." Ikenberry [2002] continues: "The new imperial grand strategy presents the United States [as] a revisionist state seeking to parlay its momentary advantages into a world order in which it runs the show," prompting others to find ways to "work around, undermine, contain and retaliate against U.S. power." The strategy threatens to "leave the world more dangerous and divided – and the United States less secure," a view widely shared within the foreign policy elite.
>
> (Chomsky 2003: 11–12)

That the Bush administration has been able to begin implementing its military and foreign policy agenda is largely a function of the administration's fear-induced popular support. But fear plays another important role in the new US foreign policy. Rather than attempt to influence world events and processes through ongoing dialogue and negotiation at world–regional and global institutions, the United States has adopted a go-it-alone, unilateralist approach that rests on the ability to induce fear in adversaries around the world. As Barber argues:

> [In] its approach to confronting terrorism, whether prosecuting wars abroad or pursuing security at home, America has conjured the very fear that is terrorism's principal weapon. Its leaders pursue a reckless militancy aimed at

establishing an American empire of fear more awesome than any the terrorists can conceive. Promising to disarm every adversary, to deploy "the mother of all bombs" and remove the taboo against the tactical use of nuclear weapons, to shock and awe enemies and friends alike into global submission, the beacon of democracy the world once admired has abruptly become the maker of war the world most fears. ... Machiavelli taught the Prince it was better to be feared than loved. America may have drawn from 9/11 the same lesson. But is fear America's best ally? ... Not in an era of interdependence. Not when going it alone invites failure. Not when terrorism has exposed the frailty of sovereignty and the obsolescence of once proud declarations of independence. If 9/11 teaches a lesson about fear's potency, it also tells a story of the insufficiencies of military power.

(Barber 2003: 15–16)

Nonetheless, the United States has adopted a foreign policy of projecting force and inducing fear. Nowhere is this clearer than in the Bush administration's "preventive war" doctrine. As historian Arthur Schlesinger observes:

The president has adopted a policy of "anticipatory self-defense" that is alarmingly similar to the policy that imperial Japan employed at Pearl Harbor ... [As a result] the global wave of sympathy that engulfed the United States after 9/11 has given way to a global wave of hatred of American arrogance and militarism ...

(Schlesinger 2003: A22)

Indeed, global surveys conducted in 2002 and 2003 by the Pew Research Center for the People and the Press show high levels of dissatisfaction with US foreign policy, the US war on terrorism and with the actions of the United States generally. Disapproval of US policy and conduct is especially high among citizens of the Global South and, in particular, Islamic nations.

As Table 11.1 demonstrates, most citizens of the Global South do not think US foreign policy sufficiently takes the well-being of other countries into account. In Jordan, Lebanon, Egypt, Turkey and Argentina especially, high numbers (in excess of 65 per cent) think the United States has a unilateralist foreign policy. There is a similar pattern of opposition to the US-led war on terrorism, with pluralities opposing the anti-terror war in Jordan, Pakistan, Lebanon, Egypt, Turkey and Argentina. The highest levels of disagreement with US foreign and anti-terrorism policy are found in Islamic countries – the countries most likely to be directly affected by military action in the current geopolitical climate. Rather than build stronger and better relations with the citizens of these countries, current US policy is building resentment in the very places where resentment may breed terrorism.

The US is viewed negatively not only with regard to its foreign and anti-terrorism policy, but also with regard to (a) the effort it puts forth to solve world problems and (b) its impact on the widening divide between rich and poor. As the authors of the 2002 Pew survey conclude:

there is a strong sense among most of the countries surveyed that US policies serve to increase the formidable gap between rich and poor countries. Moreover, sizable minorities feel the United States does too little to help solve the world's problems.

(Pew Research Center 2002: 61)

It should be added that clear majorities in all of the Middle Eastern countries believe the US does too little to solve world problems (or interferes too much), a statistic that undoubtedly reflects frustration with the ongoing Israeli–Palestinian conflict and US support for undemocratic, authoritarian governments in the Middle East.

American ideas about, and promotion of, "democracy" receive less than universal approval (see Table 11.2). This American view of "democracy" receive mixed reviews around the world – including in Western Europe – but the "greatest antipathy toward American ideas about democracy" are found in Middle Eastern countries (Pew Research Center 2002: 64). The Pew survey does not allow a precise determination of the reasons why so many people around the world are troubled by American concepts of democracy, however. Nevertheless, likely reasons include a preference for Keynesian-style social democracy, the association of American democracy with the imposition of neoliberal economic policies, and the association of American democracy with American culture, which is viewed negatively in most countries surveyed. Opinions of the United States are also particularly unfavorable in the Middle East (see Table 11.2).

It should be stressed, however, that dislike of American concepts of democracy is not to be equated with an aversion to democracy per se. In Islamic countries, with the sole exception of Indonesia, clear and often overwhelming majorities support

Table 11.1 US foreign policy and the war on terror: countries of the Global South (2002)

	US foreign policy considers others		US-led war on terrorism	
	Yes (%)	No (%)	Favor (%)	Oppose (%)
Argentina	16	76	25	67
Bolivia	45	48	64	32
Brazil	37	55	57	35
Egypt	17	66	5	79
Guatemala	57	39	77	17
Honduras	61	33	86	10
Jordan	28	71	13	85
Lebanon	20	77	38	56
Mexico	42	52	52	37
Pakistan	23	36	20	45
Peru	52	41	81	12
Turkey	16	74	30	58
Uzbekistan	56	38	91	6
Venezuela	79	19	79	20

Source: Pew Global Attitudes Project (2002)

Table 11.2 Middle East/Asia Minor opinions on the United States

Countries of the Middle East/Asia Minor	On American ideas about democracy		Opinions of the United States	
	Like (%)	Dislike (%)	Favorable (%)	Unfavorable (%)
Egypt	–	–	6	69
Jordan	29	69	25	75
Lebanon	49	45	35	59
Pakistan	9	60	10	69
Turkey	33	50	30	55
Uzbekistan	65	22	85	11

Source: Pew Global Attitudes Project (2002)

the proposition that social democracy can work in their country (Table 11.3). One of the significant differences between Islamic and American ideas of democracy concerns the separation of church and state which is codified in the US constitution, although blurred in practice. As the Pew Research Center (2003: 36) points out:

> Muslims around the world would like to see more religion in politics, [but] this view does not contradict widespread support for democratic ideals among these publics. In fact, in a number of countries, Muslims who support a greater role for Islam in politics place the highest regard on freedom of speech, freedom of the press and the importance of free and contested elections.

In short, large majorities in Islamic societies desire modern, open, democratic political institutions, but not ones modeled on the United States. To be viewed as legitimate, political and cultural rationalization processes must emerge from domestic social and cultural relations; they cannot be imposed from outside. A foreign policy based on the forceful imposition of a US-centric world order can only heighten resentment, tension and conflict. As the Pew Research Center summarizes:

> [The] U.S.'s perceived unilateral approach to international problems and the U.S. war on terror play large roles in shaping opinion toward the U.S. Those who think the U.S. does not take their country's interests into account when making international policy and those who oppose the U.S.-led war on terror are much more likely than others to have an unfavorable opinion of the U.S. This is particularly true in the Middle East/Conflict Area, Eastern Europe and Latin America.
>
> (Pew Research Center 2002: 69)

Above all, the Pew survey results show that around the world, citizens desire peace, self-determination, and the capacity to democratically shape political institutions in accord with their own cultural and religious traditions. That the United States is now attempting to govern distant strategic regions of the globe through the

Table 11.3 Muslims' views of democracy (2003 and 2002)

	Democracy would not work here (%)	Democracy can work here (%)
2003 survey		
Indonesia	53	41
Jordan	25	68
Kuwait	16	83
Lebanon	29	68
Morocco	27	64
Nigeria	20	75
Pakistan	26	58
Palestinian Authority	38	53
Turkey	–	–
2002 survey		
Bangladesh	12	57
Ghana	12	83
Ivory Coast	16	82
Mali	21	76
Senegal	9	87
Tanzania	12	64
Uganda	18	77
Uzbekistan	12	83

Source: Pew Global Attitudes Project (2003)

projection of military might and fear bodes very poorly for a peaceful resolution to the "war on terror." If anything, the present war footing of US foreign and military policy, and US efforts to impose US institutions on countries like Iraq, is likely to heighten the already high levels of anger and resentment against the US found in several regions of the periphery. Rather than preserving a *pax Americana*, we may well see a downward spiral of humiliation, conflict and desperation. Those who feel oppressed and disempowered will continue to attempt to strike back, leading to more, rather than less, terrorism. As playwright and actor Peter Ustinov has darkly observed, "terrorism is the war of the poor, and war is the terrorism of the rich" (cited in Berger 2003: 34).

Conclusion: toward a globalization of hope

There is little doubt that we live in a world of interdependence. Still very much open to debate is what the basis of that interdependence should be. Since September 11, 2001, the United States has come to rely on the projection of massive military force and a concomitant instillation of fear. But governance through fear relies on the exercise of instrumental and strategic reason, exactly what produces militant fundamentalism. Fear can be a powerful technology of governance, effective at a great distance. As the United States has withdrawn from meaningful engagement with the institutions of global governance, it has forgone discussions and negotiations that might include, and give voice to the world's less privileged and produce courses of action based on shared, multilateral understandings. Instead, the US has pursued a techno-military strategy that combines force with the imposition of US political and economic models, e.g. privatization without representation in Iraq (Shorrock 2003). This approach cannot work precisely because it exacerbates the conditions that gave rise to terrorism in the first place.

There are, however, other options. Modernization is not defined by the expansion of instrumental and strategic reason alone. Another major component of modernization is the expansion of communicative reason – the capacity for human beings to discuss and debate issues, give representation to those who have not been represented, and arrive at shared understandings and consensual courses of action. What this other dimension of modernization implies, in practical terms, is the expansion of democracy. As Barber (2003) has recently argued, the United States and the world need to pursue a strategy not of preventive war, but of "preventive democracy." People around the world not only long for meaningful democratic institutions, but ones that reflect their social and cultural traditions. A program of preventive democratization would not only entail democratization of presently undemocratic countries, it would encourage the development of culturally compatible democratic forms at the national scale, and just as importantly, the meaningful democratization of institutions of multinational and global governance. Giving voice to those who have been voiceless and power to those who have been powerless is a necessity if levels of fear, suffering and conflict are to be lowered.

Ultimately, we cannot conquer our fear and terror with more fear and terror. Fear and terror can be conquered only with democratic self-governance, empowerment and hope for a better future. As Lieutenant General Romeo Dallaire, the former commander for United Nations Assistance for Rwanda, concludes:

> [M]any signs point to the fact that the youth of the Third World will no longer tolerate living in circumstances that give them no hope for the future. From the young boys I met in the demobilization camps in Sierra Leone to the suicide bombers of Palestine and Chechnya, to the young terrorists who fly planes into the World Trade Center and the Pentagon, we can no longer afford to ignore them. We have to take concrete steps to remove the causes of their rage, or we have to be prepared to suffer the consequences ... Human beings who have no rights, no security, no future, no hope and no means to survive are a desperate group who will do desperate things to take what they believe they need and deserve.
>
> The only conclusion I can reach is that we are in desperate need of a transfusion of humanity. If we believe that all humans are human, then how are we going to prove it? It can only be proven through our actions: through the dollars we are prepared to expend to improve conditions in the Third World, through the time and energy we devote to solving devastating problems. We have lived through centuries of enlightenment, reason, revolution, industrialization and globalization. No matter how idealistic the aim sounds, this new century must become the Century of Humanity, when we as human beings rise above race, creed, colour, religion and national self-interest and put

the good of humanity above our own tribe. For the sake of the children and of our future – *Peux ce que veux. Allons-y.*

(Dallaire 2003: 521–522)

Notes

1 Of course, it goes without saying that no grievance can ever justify the barbarity of al-Qaeda's actions.
2 In 1993 Osama bin Laden accused the United States of "occupying the lands of Islam in the holiest of its territories, Arabia, plundering its riches, overwhelming its rulers, humiliating its people, threatening its neighbors, and using its peninsula as a spearhead to fight neighboring Islamic peoples" (Ajami 2001: 2).
3 Not surprisingly, the American Dialect Society chose "weapons of mass destruction" as its 2002 "word of the year," calling it a "long winded phrase whose meaning reflects a nation's worry about war with Iraq" (*USA Today*, cited in Barber 2003: 29). Paul Wolfowitz dropped the phrase, using "weapons of mass terror" instead (Barber 2003: 27) – a phrase that more clearly specifies the intended effect of WMD discourse.

Part III
Alternative visions
Constructive, democratic and hopeful

12 The neoliberalization of the global environment

Nik Heynen and Jeremia Njeru

> The first premise of all human history is, of course, the existence of living human individuals. Thus the first fact to be established is the physical organisation of these individuals and their consequent relationship to the rest of nature ... All historical writing must set out from these natural bases and their modification in the course of history through the action of men [sic].
>
> Marx and Engels (1845/1998: 37)

> The need of a constantly expanding market for its products chases the bourgeoisie over the whole surface of the globe. It must nestle everywhere, settle everywhere, establish connections everywhere.
>
> Marx and Engels (1848/1998: 54)

Introduction: the neoliberalization of nature?

These opening quotes by Marx, when linked together, help elucidate the complex and interrelated driving forces that mediate global economic, political, cultural and environmental relations. From the onset, we award full recognition to Marx's suggestion that there can be no human history without the environment, since human history has been made possible only through the metabolization of the environment *via* human labor power. This notion encapsulates what follows and helps us recognize the fundamental material relations between global societal processes and the environment at a multitude of spatial scales.

There has been a recent burst of scholarship that is helping to better elucidate the complexities, and specificities, inherent in the neoliberalization of both global and local environments. In an attempt to both theorize, and empirically ground, the interdependent and interrelated dimensions of neoliberal capitalism's stranglehold on global/local ecologies, geographers have looked particularly at issues of privatization, marketization, deregulation and re-regulation, among other processes, through varied environmental contexts (Baker 2003; Heynen and Robbins 2005; McCarthy 2004; Prudham 2004; Swyngedouw 2005; Young and Keil 2005). While the wide-ranging environmental issues investigated within this growing literature seem to be extremely valuable at first glance, Castree (2005) has recently suggested that perhaps these processes are more dissimilar than similar, and has raised critical, and thoughtful, questions about the utility of the very idea of neoliberalism as a generalizable ontological category. One of Castree's salient points is that the extant literature, because it focuses on diverse processes such as privatization, marketization, deregulation, etc., and examines them in even more diverse environmental contexts, it is too diffuse to be especially useful. Furthermore, among other issues, there is a lack of "transition rules" between resources and processes within this literature that makes it difficult to construct logical epistemological and ontological connections between these processes as if all are occurring under the banner of neoliberalism.

Some of Castree's frustration seemingly comes from the lack of theoretical specificity that has resulted from the more broadly ongoing "fetishization" of neoliberalism as a monolithic thing unto itself, as opposed to an embedded set of interrelated and interdependent processes occurring within this particular – most recent – historical phase of capitalism. We argue that it is only through rigorous empirical research (some of which is cited above) can we collectively reach a better understanding of how contemporary processes of capitalism are producing an increasingly uneven global environment. More to the point, if other scholars are going to refer to privatization, marketization, deregulation, re-regulation, etc., as all comprising the most important processes inherent in a broader system of neoliberal capitalism (Brenner and Theodore 2002a; Harvey 2005; Peck 2004), then not considering contemporary environment trends under this same theoretical perspective will only serve to impede our understanding of contemporary society/environment interactions more generally.

We are convinced of the need to consider contemporary capitalist relations that are undoubtedly affecting nature through an explicit historical–geographical material lens in order to better grasp the myriad and interrelated specificities. Accordingly, we begin this chapter with a Marxist political ecology explanation of society's impact on the environment. Continuing further, we then illuminate the contemporary social and spatial processes that have led to greater environmental inequality under neoliberal capitalism: to wit, the root causes of global environmental change. Sharpening the focus even more, we examine a series of issues that are contemporarily relevant and highly charged, in political economic–ecological terms; namely, global economy vs. local production and consumption, the international politics of environmental conservation and the political ecology of grassroots resistance movements.

Our Marxist conceptual lens

One fundamental way to think about environmental discourse relates to how explicitly it seeks to politicize contemporary environmental issues. Through this lens, it becomes clear that most historical models for understanding environmental issues, such as ecoscarcity and modernization arguments, were largely apolitical and characterized nature/society interactions in overly simplistic ways (Malthus [1793] 1992; Ehrlich 1968; Meadows *et al.* 1972). The emergence of political ecology has been a response to these apolitical approaches to the environment. As Robbins (2004: 12) suggests:

> As critique, political ecology seeks to expose flaws in dominant approaches to the environment favored by corporate, state, and international authorities, working to demonstrate the undesirable impacts of policies and market conditions, especially from the point of view of local people, marginal groups, and vulnerable populations.

While related in many ways to these same general goals, Marxist political ecology is a more specific perspective/mode of critique through which to recognize and excavate the interrelated processes of economy, polity and culture that lead to the uneven social production of the global (and local) environment(s) as explicitly related to social relations and the inherent materiality of nature (Eagleton 2000). This approach, in turn, helps to elucidate some of the all-too-often ignored processes, flows and technologies that contribute to global environmental change under neoliberal capitalism (Benton 1996; Castree 1995; Grundman 1991; Harvey 1996; Hughes 2000; Smith 1990).

Much of the recent attention toward the global environment has focused on issues of "global environmental change." To be sure, the global environment is changing. Through the lens of Marxist political ecology, however, as well as other similarly informed lenses, it is apparent that the global environment has always been in a state of change.

Although from necessity a historical–geographic project, the processes of global environmental change will not be examined from time immemorial within this chapter, but will rather focus on the last several decades. It has been argued, quite rightly so in our opinion, that the agricultural revolution led to the most profound human impacts on the global environment (Mannion 1995). Nor would we argue with the profoundness of anthropogenic processes of environmental change that accompanied the industrial revolution and the onset of industrial capitalism and primitive accumulation, and the succeeding eras of capitalist expansion and restructuring. Instead, we sharpen our focus to deal specifically with the most recent era of neoliberal capitalist expansion; that is, since the 1970s.

For the last 30 years, and following the "onset" of globalization (see Conway and Heynen, Chapters 1 and 2 in this volume), the global environment has experienced many extraordinary changes – often as not destructive and exploitative – as a result of political economic processes that have squeezed the planet's resources in order to increase profit for national economic coffers and transnational corporations alike. While decimating the Earth's resources, industrial capitalism's triumphal march and its latest offspring, neoliberal capitalism, have contributed to a state of the world that is now suffering from the hyper-proliferation of global toxic waste, effluence and general contamination (World Watch Institute 1990, 1993, 2003). These waste streams have not only negatively affected the environment at both local and global scales, they have accumulated unevenly at unstable hybrid scales (combinations of national, regional, urban/rural, etc., depending on issue) around the planet to disproportionately affect those locales less/least able to fend off the "global garbage truck" – Third World peripheries, heavily indebted countries, nation-states in crisis.

When attempting to recognize the dialectic processes at the core of global environmental change, it is helpful to use a perspective which recognizes that the appropriation, maintenance and transformation of the environment produces historically specific socio-natures that are imbued with numerous social power relationships (Swyngedouw 1996). According to Haraway (1991, 1997), humans – and other social beings for that matter – inevitably produce environments. As such, environments become a sociophysical process permeated by political power and cultural meaning. In addition, the transformation of nature is embedded in a series of economic, political and cultural (read all as social) relations that are tied together in a nested articulation of important, but inherently unstable, geographical scales (Swyngedouw and Heynen 2003).

Despite their significance, society–environment relations have only recently become a pressing topic of academic interest, and have taken longer to be of policy interest (Haughton and Hunter 1994). As Engels (1940: 45) discusses, nature itself is extremely complex, which might explain why these relations have taken so long to reach the forefront of inquiry:

> When we consider and reflect upon nature at large ... at first we see the picture of an endless entanglement of relations and reactions, permutations and combinations, in which nothing remains what, where, and as it was, but everything moves, changes, comes into being and passes away.

Our understanding of the complexities inherent to society–environment relations is far from complete, yet is needed now more than ever. Unfettered, unregulated and thoughtless human exploitation of the natural environment results in unsafe and undesirable environments for humans and other living things (Marsh 1965; Wisner 1978). Thus, we must move forward to complicate, not simplify, our understanding of political ecology, so that we may unearth and better understand the biophysical and anthropogenic–social processes that lead to the production (and commodification) of the global environment. Even without the wealth of scientific information available today, Dudley Sears (1956: 473) was able to give voice to the importance of this mission at the first conference on *Man's Role in Changing the Face of the Earth*:

> There are many interesting approaches to the problem of man [sic] and his environment, and all, save perhaps the technological, seem to lead to the same conclusions. With this possible exception, these various approaches indicate that humanity should strive toward a condition of equilibrium with its environment. This is the verdict of ethics, aesthetics, and natural science. And, despite the prevalence of the idea of a continually expanding economy, it is probably the verdict of that branch of economic analysis known as accounting.

Within the last two decades, theorization and modeling of society–environment relations has made substantial progress. Critical to this progress is the realization that the forced bifurcation between humanity and the environment that first became prominent during the seventeenth century (Gold 1984) has only served to impede understanding of environmental issues. Despite progress in realizing the holistic nature of society–environment relations in the academy and grassroots alike, there is still a greater need to recognize the structural processes and power relations that lead to the social production of uneven environments and of environmental crises under neoliberal capitalism.

Scalar consequences of global environmental change

Just as defining the society–environment relations is problematic and complex, so too is fully comprehending the scalar ramifications of global environmental change. The socio-natural consequences of environmental change are multifaceted and multidimensional. The consequences are best considered in terms of a hierarchically nested set of interdependent scales (global, regional, local, corporal, etc.) as well as within the context of myriad social–demographic power relations (ethnicity, age, class, gender, etc.). As should be expected from a historical–geographical materialist perspective, socio-natural consequences of global environmental change are spatially and temporally variant in relation to the power relations that produce them throughout the world. And, social power relations play out differently in rural/urban contexts, as well as global, national and local "spaces."

In order to excavate the social (and spatiotemporal) processes and relations that demonstrate the scalar contradictions of neoliberal capitalism, and the ways these processes contributed to environmental change, we must widen our lens beyond the limited characterization of global cities and their contribution to both global and local environmental change. There is a hierarchy of global cities, each commanding particular proportions of the global totality of capital, resources and power (Sassen 2001). As discussed in some detail in Chapter 8, seated atop this "global city hierarchy" are London, New York and Tokyo – well known as global cities with a "big g." Luke (2003) suggests that more attention must be paid to smaller and mid-sized cities and towns across the planet, because while not as large in population, extent or impact as "big g" global cities, "small g" cities collectively have superior populations and collective impact. "Small g" global cities are global precisely because they are home to the majority of the planet's human population. Their diffusion and continued spatial evolution is saturated by, and in turn affect, the power and purposes of capitalist expansion across the planet and the resulting uneven development that occurs (Smith 1984). Essential to the relations between "big g" and "small g" global cities are a set of contradictory scalar relations that have been augmented through the proliferation of neoliberal capitalism (Heynen and Perkins 2005).

It is becoming increasingly apparent that fewer and fewer cities, towns and villages across the planet can resist the caustic processes inherent in neoliberal capitalism. It has spread like a plague to urban areas once less susceptible to its effects. While the gears of urbanization have always been typified by a set of interconnected processes considered social, physical and "imagined," cities are becoming increasingly interconnected because of capital's need to annihilate space with time. As urban networks increase in size, extent and "reach," the facilitation of capital's never-ending quest for the expansion of value is awarded, renewed and made all the more powerful, as well as contradictory.

The infectious spread of markets should not be examined or accepted as an innate or natural process, but rather articulated as the continuance and proliferation of Western imperialism under the guise of neoliberal capitalism. As free-market-eering and the privatization of property and resources spread via the incantation of the neoliberal politics of inevitability, urban ecological crises increase in destructive and spatial/scalar extent – ultimately and simultaneously linking urban and global ecologies. Here, the link between strategies of global capital and ecological disasters ensuing from the exploitation of economically lesser-developed urban (and hinterland) areas becomes most apparent.

As will be discussed in more detail later, one of the political complications impeding the implementation of the Kyoto protocol is that the already industrialized countries produce more greenhouse gases in their cities than do less-developed countries (LDCs). Physical scientists believe that increases in global warming will push food production further northward in parts of Russia, Japan and Canada, while increasing the heat and water stress and heat waves and substantially lowering cropland nearer the equator (Meyer and Tuner 1995). Incidentally, this is the part of the Earth where the ability to mitigate the consequences of global environmental change is the most inadequate. As such, the swirling society–environment processes at the heart of global warming create immense ethical contradictions, because countries, cities and people that produce the least amount of greenhouse gases will bear the most painful burdens from global climate change.

The regionalized consequences of global warming cannot just be considered through an environmental lens, but rather must be understood as explicitly spatial, scalar and socio-naturally complex. For example, within Central America, grain production has sharply decreased as a whole, particularly within Costa Rica and Guatemala, both of which have experienced increases in non-traditional exports. At the same time, staple-food production in this region has declined, forcing countries (and citizens) to purchase them on the world market, thereby subjecting the citizenry to the vagaries of market forces that are decidedly unfriendly. While these shifts have not necessarily occurred as a result of global warming, they foreshadow the market consequences of localized economies in the face of potential environmental change.

As "glocal" (global/local; see Swyngedouw 1997) forms of capitalism have become more embedded in all forms of social life, they have only added weight to the ongoing and formidable inclinations in society to continue to externalize nature and exploit it. All the while, the intricate and ultimately vulnerable dependence of capital accumulation on nature (and its socio-natural resource bases) expands and amplifies continuously. It is on the terrain of the urban that this metabolic change of nature becomes most noticeable, both in its physical form and its socio-natural consequences.

At urban scales, the consequences of environmental change on rapidly growing populations, which are class-differentiated by social–economic and demographic characteristics, are obvious. Within such hierarchical scales, the unequal distribution of the burden of environmental change among the population becomes apparent. The poor and the "new poor" take the brunt of the impact(s). Then, and further complicating the urban ecological crisis, scores of rural poor in LDCs, who find themselves landless or their land degraded as result of environmental change, end up migrating to urban areas. This results in greater stress on urban environmental resources, because it is in urban areas where the drivers for environmental change originate and return.

While most cases of "environmental (in)justice" are focused around environmental problems – particularly those related to technological origins, such as landfills and operation problems connected with toxic releases – environmental problems resulting from global climatic changes also impact urban communities unequally. Social structures underlying the observed ethnic and class differences in terms of environmental exposure and environmental health effects appear to determine (and bias) the distribution of effects of global environmental change in urban areas. The 1995 Chicago heatwave that killed slightly over 700 people is an example. While most of the victims (73 percent) were elderly, the deaths were concentrated in the low-income, African American communities (Klinenberg 2002). An additional interesting point in this regard is that men turned out to be more vulnerable than women, suggesting gender differences likely feature in environmental health emergencies and crises.

Nature and capitalism "in a cup of coffee"

In the Marxist tradition of considering the environment, markets and global power structures dialectically, we need look no further than the cup of morning coffee, bowl of corn flakes or donut to excavate, or unravel, the global power relations embodied within everyday commodities used by most of us in the advanced capitalist world. All we have to do is start by asking the simple question: "Where did our coffee [or any other commodity] come from?" However, as ignorance is truly bliss, those who would ask such simple and mundane questions must be prepared to go down Wonderland's rabbit hole. And, like Alice, it is entirely possible that returning to the world you previously knew will be entirely impossible. The answer/trip is a transnational journey/enlightenment best made possible through neocolonial (and post-colonial) power relations, uneven hybridized socio-natural networks and *our* consumption habits.

So, where does my coffee come from? Because coffee beans grow only in tropical climate regions, countries such as Colombia, Guatemala and Kenya have had their old growth forests cleared to make room for coffee plantations. While convenient for coffee drinkers, it is leading to endangerment of cloud forest ecosystems. In order to grow the coffee trees, insecticides from Europe or the United States are sprayed on the trees; but while protecting the trees from "pests" some of the chemicals are likely to be inhaled by the workers maintaining the trees (and getting paid pennies to do so). Beyond leading to potentially terminal health problems for many of these workers, the chemical residues will be washed down the mountainside and will pollute the land and eventually whatever body of water they flow into.

There is a good chance the beans, after being harvested, will be shipped to New Orleans, Louisiana, in a freighter produced in Japan from Korean steel made from ores mined in Papua New Guinea. The extraction of the iron ore has a good chance of being mined from tribal lands, where the local people receive little or no monetary compensation for the environmental damage that will be imposed through the mining of such extractive resources. In New Orleans, the coffee beans will be roasted and packaged in foil and three layers of plastic that were made from oil shipped from Saudi Arabia. The plastic was likely manufactured in an industrial corridor in Louisiana, which is infamously referred to as "cancer alley" because of the disproportionately high rates of cancer within the African-American population that lives and works within the area. The aluminum foil layer of the bags that the beans will be packaged in is primarily made from bauxite ore mined in Australia. Similar to the situation with mining ores in Papua New Guinea, the power relations inherent to obtaining bauxite in Australia have also led to the displacement of aboriginal peoples from their ancestral lands. The bauxite was refined in the US's Pacific Northwest with energy from a hydroelectric dam on the Colombia River that drastically changed the complete ecosystem around the river. The cultural ramifications of the dam prevented Native American groups from fishing for salmon, which has historically constituted their livelihood. (See During and Ayers [1994] for the original history of "your cup of coffee.")

Thus the production of the coffee that you might have sipped this morning had to go through a complicated socio-natural process; at each step there are additional environmental spillover effects that are not considered when we drink our morning "cup of joe." Resources are extracted from the less-developed countries of the Global South at a devastatingly lower price than resources will bring on the global market. The value added to the coffee beans may have occurred within the advanced capitalist country where it is consumed, but the complete story is that all facets of the process are permeated by environmental degradation, human suffering and exploitation.

This aforementioned deconstruction of the processes whereby coffee is commodified is but one useful way to unpack the fetishization of nature's commodities as they are produced, marketed and reproduced within global capitalism. The hyper-expansion of trade, and the frenetic production and marketing of commodities under the guise of neoliberalism, is the most recent, and arguably most destructive, form of global capitalism. And it is all done at the behest and benefit of *our* consumption (World Watch Institute 2004).

Foundations of global environmental change

While it useful to consider everyday patterns of consumption for getting a sense of the pulse of neoliberal capitalism, being able to appreciate the history of our morning coffee hinges upon recognizing the powerful structural processes that facilitate socio-natural relations under neoliberal capitalism. In order to investigate the political economic causes of global environment change, we need to begin by discussing how the idea of economic growth shaped through capitalist voracity and self-indulgence has permeated the economic discourse of the LDCs. Neoliberal capitalism is premised on the idea that, when countries remove trade barriers, competition is enhanced leading to creation of jobs, lower consumer prices, increased consumer choice, increased economic growth, and generally benefiting almost everyone. In essence, economic globalization is about spreading capitalism from the MDCs to the LDCs in an attempt to increase and maintain maximum profits (see Conway and Heynen, Chapters 1 and 2, this volume). Unsurprisingly, the spread of capitalism has been devastating to environmental health (broadly defined) at all scales. Capitalism sustains itself through exploiting the biophysical environment. Destroying the environment upon which it depends sets in motion an inherently contradictory process that will drive capitalism to its eventual demise (M. O'Connor 1994; J. O'Connor 1998).

In the hope of gaining similar economic development to that enjoyed by MDCs, many LDCs have embraced the capitalistic economic system, or at least government officials who see short-term personnel benefits have embraced free markets. The hoped-for benefits of this process, however, have not materialized. To the contrary, LDCs have been dragged along their path-dependent, neocolonial trajectories and have thus only fueled the growth of global neoliberal capitalism, while continuing as the "martyrs" in the global economy (Amin and Graham 1997). In an attempt to become more competitive within the global marketplace and attract capital investment, many LDCs have fallen back to comparative advantage opportunities, which have further deepened their dependence on global economic interests.

Too often, sustained economic growth, which is calculated in destructively simplistic measures like gross national product (GNP), is proposed as the path to "human progress." Ironically, reliance on such callous aggregate measures amplifies environmental destruction and produces (and reproduces) inequality (Yapa 1992, 1999). The notion of a sustained economic growth presupposes a finite availability of natural resources. However, from its onset this capitalist presupposition is inherently contradictory given that nature's systems, upon which economy is dependent, are finite. As such, sustained economic growth is a myth that this most contemporary version – neoliberal capitalism – can continue to believe in, because of the subsidization via exploitation of resources and labor from countries within its talons (Seis 2001).

The inherent contradiction to this way of viewing the environment is that it presupposes that nature is not socially produced, but produced via capitalism, thereby expecting nature to exist as a disposable, or marketable, commodity. The failure to recognize that nature is not already commodified, but rather becomes commodified through human labor power, leads to the utilization of nature in a crisis-laden manner. According to O'Connor (1998), we should focus on the way that the combined power of free-market capitalist production relations and productive forces self-destruct by impairing or destroying rather than reproducing their own conditions. Of course, "their own conditions" are both socially discursive and materially based (Eagleton 2000).

This perspective, then, stresses the process of exploitation of labor and self-expanding capital, state regulation of the provision or regulation of production conditions and social struggles organized around capital's use and abuse of these conditions. The results of these contradictions have been evident for some time, as Goldsmith (1997: 242) observes:

> Everywhere our forests are over logged, our agricultural lands over cropped, our grassland over grazed, our wetlands over drained, our groundwater over tapped, our seas over fished and just about the whole terrestrial and marine environment over polluted with chemical and radioactive poisons. Worse still, if that is possible, our atmospheric environment is becoming ever less capable of absorbing either the ozone-depleting gases or greenhouses generated by our economic activities without creating new climatic conditions to which we cannot indefinitely adapt.

Given the above conditions, the only way to ensure our planet's sustainable habitability is by taking methodical steps to effectively diminish or abate neoliberal capitalism's impact(s). This is, of course, easier said than done. Under the neoliberal "magic spell," it appears to be the overriding goal of almost every country in the world to maximize their global trade and commercial dealings as part of the global economy. As we have learned elsewhere in this volume, this "myth of the global market place" was institutionalized with signing of the 1994 Uruguay round of the General Agreement on Tariffs and Trade (GATT) and the emergence of the World Trade Organization (WTO) (Sachs 1999). Hence, we are now witnessing a new era of unprecedented corporate power that is not only affecting the economic and legal structures of both MDCs and LDCs, but is also plundering everyone's environmental systems and resource stocks. This new "predatory era" of corporate capitalism (Falk 1999) is an attempt to restructure national legal environments through international trade agreements signed by countries but heavily influenced by transnational corporations (TNCs) (Tokar 1997). By their very nature, organization and mandate, TNCs are strongly goal-oriented and principally concerned with corporate performance efficiencies (i.e. profit maximization). We wholeheartedly agree with Chomsky's (1999) critical response to, and forcible rejection of, such a maxim which preaches "profit over people."

In essence, profit maximization translates to increased economic activities at the expense of the environment. Furthermore, a clean environment is simply an antithetical goal to many TNCs that need to pollute the air, water and land in order to produce their commodities (Keil *et al.* 1998). Under the current tendencies of neoliberal capitalism, there is little hope to ameliorate the health of the planet. This is more so, because neoliberal capitalism by its very nature must be controlled by these increasingly multinational and stateless, unaccountable, and unregulated TNCs. In turn, these TNCs are aided by the WTO, which by its supervisory charter has made it virtually impossible to adopt controls that would increase their costs and thereby reduce their competitiveness (Nader and Wallach 1996). Interestingly, as the free-market assault on our environment continues, the more our understanding of its impact grows, and the more determined we must be to remedy the situation before it is too late.

Global economy versus local production

With the creation of a global economy, world nations have competed for their share of the world market. In line with principles of economic globalization and free trade, countries have specialized in producing and exporting select commodities that they produce particularly well and import almost everything else from other countries. Production is thus not limited by local demand but by world demand – and hence a massive increase in production for export. In an attempt to harness world markets, most LDCs have expanded export-oriented production. These countries now produce non-traditional commodities for export such as fruits, as opposed to traditional ones such as coffee, tea and sugar cane, which of course were themselves once planted for export by colonial powers in most cases. Environmental problems associated with large-scale production of export-oriented commodities have drastically escalated. In Malaysia, for example, more than half of the trees felled for timber are exported. The Malaysian peninsular, which was 70–80 percent forested fifty years ago, is now largely deforested mainly for export. Consequently, soil erosion has escalated, as has annual increases in drought and floods.

Similarly, export-oriented "high-tech" fishing industries, with 38 percent of fish caught worldwide being exported as global commodities in the privileged markets of Asia, Europe and North America, are causing untold damage to the Earth's seas. It has been noted recently that nine of the world's 17 major fishing grounds are in decline and four are already "over-fished." The cod, of British "fish and chips" fame, has vanished from the Newfoundland Banks; the anchovy has gone from Chilean waters (as Americans' cat food); the herring has gone from the North Sea (with fresh-smoked kippers becoming a reminiscence of the past). The list of this modern industry's victims appears endless – including turtles, dolphins and swordfish. With fish stocks being depleted in MDCs, fleets are converging on oceanic realms of LDCs where fish for export has already increased four times since the 1960s. Modern industrial trawling and long-line fleets are plundering the oceanic waters off West Africa, to such an extent that locals have turned to wild animal poaching for their protein, having been increasingly denied access to, or forced to leave, their fishing grounds. Europe's fish markets, therefore, might be being replenished, but Africa's forest reserves are indirectly suffering predation.

Another interrelated consequence of expansion of the fishing industry is the destruction of the world's mangrove forests. Mangroves have been cleared to pave the way for intensive prawn farming. With world demand for prawns growing – now worth 6.6 billion dollars annually – the future prospects for mangroves are in the balance. As we have seen, export-oriented industries present a whole range of adverse consequences to local environments (Goldsmith 1997).

Global economy versus local consumption

Creating a global economy means seeking to generalize the destructive process of economic globalization, which in turn means transforming the vast number of still largely self-sufficient people living in the rural areas of LDCs into consumers of capital and services largely produced by TNCs (Sachs 1993). In the same context, people living in MDCs have been transformed into consumers of "exotic" products mainly produced in the LDCs by TNCs. Let us take, as an example, the case of supplying tropical fruits to MDCs. Mendis and van Bers (1999: 18) observe that Canadians take for granted the fact that they can walk into the nearest supermarket in the middle of winter and find an excess of imported fruits such as bananas, melons, citrus, pineapples and grapes. While "tropical" fruits are generally affordable for Canadians, the human and environmental costs of their production are high.

The proliferation of global economic flows has made the availability of exotic fruits to consumers in MDCs more convenient, cheaper and responsible for increased inequality and degradation. Unsurprisingly, most of the fruit producers are TNCs such as Dole, Chiquita and Standard Fruit Company, whose activities have led to wanton environment problems. Vast areas of rainforest have been cleared in countries such as Costa Rica, Nicaragua and Guatemala to make way for fruit plantations. This corporate rape of the environment is causing untold loss of biodiversity in the tropics. The long-term contradictions of this become more visible every day as ecologists continuously recognize how little they know about biodiversity, and how important it is likely to be. Furthermore, the imperial histories that allowed TNCs from advanced capitalist nations to secure the means of, for example, banana production in Guatemala speaks to the very worst of humanity but represents the very best that can be hoped for the US economic actors, in economic terms (Schlesinger and Kinzer 1982).

Still on the subject of consumption and its wider implications for environmental health, let us look at how lifestyles are being transformed in LDCs to meet the supply of corporate goods. Goldsmith (1997: 250) fittingly articulates how the transformation of LDCs' consumption tastes is made possible: "[The] cultural patterns [of] most Third World people, at least in rural areas ..., must of course be ruthlessly destroyed by American television and western advertising companies and supplanted by culture and values of western mass consumer society."

Simply stated, the biosphere would be incapable of sustaining the impacts on it if the increased economic activities required to sustain that kind of lifestyle were to be realized. It is argued that if all nations of the world were to live like people in the

MDCs, five or six planets would be needed to serve as "sources" for the inputs and "sinks" for the waste of economic growth. Furthermore, it is estimated that it would require 4 percent growth a year for all LDCs to reach the consumption of the United States by 2060. Another way to look at environmental implications of *our* lifestyle is to compare the four to six hectares of land required to sustain one average person in MDCs to the 1.7 hectares per capita of ecologically productive land available on the planet. It has been calculated, for example, that one US child does twice the ecological damage of a Swedish child, three times of an Italian child, thirteen times of a Brazilian child, 35 times of an Indian child and 280 times of a Chadian or Haitian child (Goldsmith 1997). Thus, globalizing our consumption to meet the supply of the global economy is a sure way to hasten the death of our planet, or destroy its capabilities to support the Earth's people and their "ecological partners," the socio-natural systems.

Environments of hope: politics of ecology, grassroots resistance and new beginnings

Administrations and governments of Global North and South states have been accused of doing little in the realm of environmental regulation, and seem more content to sign protocols and global accords than actually implement environmental regulations and controls to conserve the environment. Economic considerations have more often than not overruled ecological considerations, and governments have been reluctant to adopt "green" policies, unless politically challenged and threatened by "green" activism.

Indeed, the global environmental movement and growth of "green" politics has been in large part motivated by the reluctance of liberal democratic governments to pursue environmental conservation and preservation against the wishes of business interests. The influence of corporate lobbying and political party monetary support by corporate donors might have very well helped neutralize environmental agendas. But, it also mobilized opposition and outrage among a citizenry growing more and more aware of the environmental limits of today's runaway industrialization processes – greenhouse gas increases, global warming, ozone-layer depletion, glacier retreat, coral reef damage because of ocean temperature increases, and their short- and long-term effects on the general public's health and welfare.

Environmental non-governmental organizations took up the causes of conservation and preservation, of biodiversity, the extinction of endangered species and wetlands renovation, at first promoting domestic agendas, then broadening their interests and membership to global issues. NGOs such as the World Wildlife Fund (WWF), Greenpeace and Friends of the Earth International have grown to be global IGOs, actively championing "green" agendas, fighting legal battles and securing protective legislation at the nation-state level; all in the cause of global environmental conservation. Others such as the Sierra Club, the Environmental Defense Fund and National Resources Defense Council have remained concerned with domestic environmental conservation agendas.

Today, the agendas of environmental and activist NGOs and IGOs are being reformulated as new global dangers appear. Some new topics of concern are genetically modified foods or genetically modified organisms (GMOs), which agro-business is promoting as the new "Green Revolution" in food production (this topic is taken up again in Chapter 14). Others are the corporate or First World's bio-piracy of indigenous foods or knowledge under the WTO's TRIPs agreements, and the industrial control of agriculture at large, which threatens the total demise of the small farmer and his/her annihilation. Global IGOs/NGOs have taken up the challenge of these threats to environmental security and sustainability, but the monetary power and influence of the controlling corporate institutions in state affairs is still considerable enough to promote and secure the industries' high-technology (and highly profitable) agenda. State and government alliances with such business interests are at their highest level in the neoliberal capitalist phase of globalization the world is currently experiencing. The "Washington consensus" is anything but down and out!

Given there is merit to the notion that the global environment is socially produced as a result of interrelated processes inherent to both global and local political economies, so too must the solutions to enduring environmental destruction necessarily be socially created. Much discussion has been orientated toward notions of "sustainable development" in this regard. However, the lack of serious consideration regarding the structural processes that contribute to global environmental change impede any likely success in "sustaining" the environment through *any* kind of development.

The struggle against environmental degradation at all scales has substantially strengthened through resistance ranging from the Indian *Chipko* movement (original tree huggers) to the ambitious saga of Julia "Butterfly" Hill's two-year residency in a California Redwood named Luna. These and other cases of resistance to neoliberal environmental devastation have brought much needed attention to struggles to preserve environments in the face of the increasingly destructive contradictions of capitalism. Much of the mobilization that has occurred around environmental issues has happened precisely because of the evolution of the *idea* of the environment. The preservation movement initiated by American pioneer John Muir did little for inner-city children suffering from lead poisoning, just as the environmental justice movement has done little to quell deforestation of the Amazonian rainforest. However, as the processes inherent to neoliberal capitalism become more visible and their destruction more eminent, theory and activism are together synthetically forming a new environmental praxis that continues to become more substantial, less binary and more hopeful.

It is also with regard to the formation of defiant forms of environmental praxis that we should revisit Castree's (2005) critical discussion of the utility of *the neoliberalization of nature* as an epistemological and ontological construct. For even if Castree is right that the myriad processes that comprise neoliberal capitalism are too disparate to provide insight into contemporary society–environment relations from a theoretical perspective – a point of view we disagree with, by the way – *the neoliberalization of nature* has provided a discursive "bull's-eye," which in turn has helped galvanize grassroots environmental resistance to a level without precedent. Thus, the political utility, if not the theoretical function, is worth embracing and valuing, since we would rather "rage against" the destructive power of this most recent form of capitalism, than intellectually quarrel over what to call it, or how best to characterize it.

Dare we offer the utopian vision of recognizing the intrinsic value in nature, while at the same time dialectically recognizing the social production of nature? If not with an eye to the intrinsic value, at least dare we suggest that the failed logic of neoliberal capitalism, with its insatiable appetite for privatizing nature, reducing the importance of national sovereignty and generally reducing the quality of *most* life on Earth, is in need of replacement? We think both are appropriate and necessary responses to the eminent ecological catastrophe that becomes more likely with every privatized forest and over-fished ocean. We need utopian forms of environmental praxis to help us imagine alternative future possibilities. Without daring to recognize alternative futures to that likely to be created by neoliberal capitalism, we are destined to consume ourselves into an environmental situation that mirrors the harsh, destructive processes that created it.

13 Globalization's cultural challenges
Homogenization, hybridization and heightened identity

Nanda R. Shrestha and Dennis Conway

The simple reality ... is that while western ideas and best (and worst) practices have found their way into the minds of all men (and women), the hearts and souls of other civilisations remain intact. There are deep reservoirs of spiritual and cultural strengths which have not been affected by the western veneer that has been spread over many other societies ... Only someone who has lived outside the west – as I have – can see both how powerful the impact of the west has been upon the rest of the world and at the same time how limited its impact has been on the souls of other peoples. The real paradox, contrary to John Roberts (author of *The Triumph of the West*), is not that western culture has taken over the hearts and minds of all men – the real paradox is that western ideas and technology will over time enable other societies to accumulate enough affluence and luxury to discover their real cultural roots ... from which they have been effectively cut off for centuries.

(Kishore Mahbubani 2000: 9–10; parenthetical words added)

In time, culture comes to be associated, often aggressively, with the nation or the state; this differentiates "us" from "them," almost always with some degree of xenophobia. Culture in this sense is a source of identity, and a rather combative one at that, as we see in recent "returns" to culture and tradition. These "returns" accompany rigorous codes of intellectual and moral behavior that are opposed to the permissiveness associated with such liberal philosophies as multiculturalism and hybridity. In the formerly colonized world, these "returns" have produced varieties of religious and nationalist fundamentalism ... [C]ulture is a sort of theater where various political and ideological causes engage one another. Far from being a placid realm of Apollonian gentility, culture can even be a battleground on which causes expose themselves to the light of day and contend with one another, making it apparent that, for instance, American, French, or Indian students who are taught to read *their* national classics before they read others are expected to appreciate and belong loyally, often uncritically, to their nations and traditions while denigrating or fighting against others ... Now, the trouble with this idea of culture is that it entails not only venerating one's own culture but also thinking of it as somehow divorced from ... the everyday world. Most professional humanists (and others, including the general populace) as a result are unable to make the connection between the prolonged and sordid cruelty of practices such as slavery, colonialist and racial oppression, and imperial subjection on the one hand, and poetry, fiction, philosophy of the society that engages these practices on the other.

(Edward W. Said 1993: xiii–xiv; parenthetical words added)

Introduction

Beyond these quotes from two "non-Western" intellectuals, it is what their messengers represent in the cultural realm of globalization, both historically and in terms of personal experiences and observations, that is significant. Simply expressed, the *message* cannot be separated from the *messengers*, as their lives offer a microcosmic window into the contradictory "duality" of Western culture and its impact on non-Western humanity. This duality is a result of Western-modernization's global diffusion and imperial "reach," which began with the onset of colonialism; itself, a decisive phase in the long history of global imperial adventurism (Chanda 2003; Memmi 1965; Fanon 1963; Rodney 1974; Shrestha 1995; Wallerstein 2000). In other words, not only do their lives reflect the multi-faceted manifestation of Western-promoted, globalizing processes – political-economic, social, cultural, technological and ideological – they also experience the *hegemonic* as well as *liberating* power of western modernization and cultural diffusion and, hence, pose a cultural paradox in the challenges to contemporary globalization's influences, today.

Educated in Western tradition, Mahbubani, Said and countless other non-Western intellectuals and activists from the colonized world were both subjected to, and benefited from, its hegemonic allure. To apply a biblical metaphor, Western education was like the mythical apple from the fabled "Tree of Knowledge of Good and Evil" in the Garden of Eden. Once they ate the apple, they shed their native innocence and identity but gained a keen sight, the knowledge of good and evil – in this case, the *good* and *evil* of the Western cultural tradition. In other words, the West and "the Rest" (the colonizer and the colonized) were culturally bound. As these "non-Western" elites found themselves caught up in Western culture's embrace, they struggled with this contradictory duality. Emerging from their romance with the Western culture was not only cultural adoption, adaptation and hybridization, but also an eye-opening experience, a form of revelation, as exemplified by one of the present authors' painful account of his own colonial odyssey (Shrestha 1995).

The story does not end there. Underlying this "revelation" was "a wrenching tug of war" between their *personal* life and *public-professional* life; one in which the personal closely reflected their adoption of Western values (a native replica of the West) and the public revealed a semblance of identity crisis where they decried Western hegemonic policies, using the very language and critical discourse that they had acquired and sharpened through the course of their Western education. It is a tug of war that continues to haunt non-Western intellectuals and activists to this day. More specifically, it was/is a tug-of-war between their measure of material achievement (e.g. education, social status and economic benefits) and their experience of emotional emptiness; that is, between the *materiality* of what their body and mind desired versus the (national) *native identity* that their heart and soul longed for and sought to preserve in the face of its gradual erosion or outright denigration under the constant assaults of Western modernization. The deeper the sense of loss of identity, the greater was their level of internal tension. Not surprisingly, therefore, countless non-Western intellectuals and activists "found" an empowering (vocal and literary) means to forcefully express their views. Western education and its "enlightenment traditions" equipped them with an intellectual "camera" and courage to confront and expose the cultural dualism (contradiction) and moral hypocrisy they endured. So, as its own unique blend of liberal/liberating traditions and with its own tarnished history, Western cultural diffusion is an imperialistic paradox; a paradox that engenders hope and fear, promise and peril.

The historical roots to the paradox

There is little dispute that we live in an age of globalization. Although the term itself is quite new, global processes are not, because, in one form or another, they have been under way for centuries (Chanda 2003; Wallerstein 2000). Global power relations, global imperialism and contemporary globalization have many common roots and ramifications and they have emerged, ascended and declined in many shapes and forms.

One example from the past, an early wave of globalization which led to a significant degree of cultural homogenization, was Buddhism. This Eastern religion brought various territorial entities and countries under one cultural roof or worldview in terms of common religious principles and practices. One of its first apostles and certainly the most powerful was Emperor Ashok from northern India. In the third century BC he was instrumental in spreading the gospel of Buddhism across a vast territory, stretching from Afghanistan to East and Southeast Asia, thus creating a world governed by one religious system – or some may call it the world's first theocratic empire dominated by the Buddhist dogma. Such a universalizing process was later followed and extended by Islam and Christianity, with the latter pair colliding and clashing with established cultural norms and values as well as religious worldviews in many parts of the world. Southeast Asia where we see distinctly concentrated patterns of Buddhism (Cambodia, Laos, Myanmar, Singapore, Thailand and Vietnam), Christianity (the Philippines), Islam (Brunei, Indonesia, Malaysia and southern Philippines), and some patches of Hinduism (Bali in Indonesia, Singapore) offer a good example of such religious collision, conflict and coexistence (although at times tenuous).

Western "modernization" and colonial "cultural homogenization"

What is notable about the present configuration of globalization – its neoliberal pedigree being one of its most distinctive features (see Chapters 1 and 2 in this volume; also Rankin 2004) – is that it is markedly different from one of its main global predecessors, colonialism, in which European colonizers exercised total control over all aspects of life and society in their respective colonies. With the colonies' linkages closely confined to their respective colonizers, for example, India and Nigeria to Great Britain, Indochina and a large portion of West Africa to France, and Indonesia to the Netherlands, external competition within the colony was kept at bay. But, to the extent that the world economy was "globalized," it functioned as a set of competing European colonial orbits. Today it is a different story; of cross-cutting spatial social, economic and cultural networks and global commodity chains transcending all colonial ties and boundaries. Although the past colonial ties remain visible and intact to some extent, cultures and capital are no longer bound to the nexus of the colonizer and the colonized. They roam the world quite freely as footloose multinationals hop around the world, from one frontier of globalization to another, and US military bases and outposts dot the world map to facilitate their march (Editors 2002).

The world has certainly witnessed *cultural homogenization*, especially in the area of material cultural values. Ali Mazrui – a Kenyan intellectual whose life parallels that of Mahbubani and Said – points out that as a consequence of globalization the world is getting to be more and more alike, decade by decade. This is occurring because of what Mazrui (2000: 3–4) terms "hegemonization – the paradoxical concentration of power in a particular country or in a particular civilization ... the emergence and consolidation of the hegemonic centre," meaning the West.

Consequently, an isomorphic landscape occurs across the globe of what we may term *hegemonic cultural homogenization* and *adaptive hybridization*. Nowhere is this more noticeable than in the public domain of popular and material culture. For instance, when Palestinian youngsters in Gaza deploy American rap music to protest against Israeli occupation and suppression (NPR 2005), when recently elected President Mahinda Rajapakse of Sri Lanka flashes a "V" sign to signal his victory in a half-way Nixonian fashion, or when communist activists/party members wear baseball caps (perhaps one of the unique and popular symbols of American capitalism); these are telling signs of how widely Western culture has diffused and is adopted, adapted and hybridized.

During the colonial phase of globalization, Europeans not only established total economic and territorial control over the colonies, they also implanted their cultural values and educational systems, thus leaving hegemonic imprints everywhere within their imperial reach. They created heathens and barbarians out of the natives, thus claiming a higher cultural position for themselves and, subsequently, justifying their colonial conquests and savagery as civilizing missions. They wrote histories and invented anthropologies to reinforce their imperial preconceptions and civilizing plans. They practiced colonial cartography, drawing boundary lines that showed little regard for existing ethnic and cultural realities of the lands they colonized; all in the imperial cause of territorial expansion (*Economist* 1984; Edney 1997; Shrestha 1997: 37–42). They routinely equated the natives to the polarized image of a dog – docile and obedient when tamed and wild and dangerous if untamed (Fyfe 1992). They brought the Holy Bible to salvage the heathen and bayonets to tame those "dogs" who defied the colonial order and refused to be "tamed" to march to the drumbeats of imperialism; countless were, of course, readily maimed and mutilated (Stevenson 1992). They also brought along their medicines, perhaps to demonstrate their "Christian heart and kindness" – either to symbolize European paternalism, or to keep the natives healthy enough to dig the mines and work on the plantations. Whatever the rationale, their medicines (including immunization vaccines) seemed to do wonders in terms of curing the sick and reducing death rates. Also added to the colonizer's arsenal were a host of production technologies that were transferred, or introduced, to better exploit the colony's natural resources and utilize local labor for the greater good of the imperium: the mother country (Davidson 1992). In short, what Europeans achieved with their cultural wars, coupled with their colonial rules, was dehumanization of the natives in one form or another (Blaut 1993; Shrestha 1997).

Caught in the vortex of their own vested interests and imperial designs, the native elite classes in one colony after another ardently pursued and embraced Western education, some at home and others in the home country of their colonizer; emulating almost everything Western that projected imperial power, prominence and presence. What is more, on the domestic front, many of those elites not only adopted and promoted many Western values and practices, they actually used their "westernized" status, education and consumption of Western goods to reinforce their class position and power among the natives (Liechty 1997). As a consequence of their single-mindedness and pursuit of every mannerism and means to embrace Western cultural adaptation and the enthusiastic adoption of "all-things western," hegemonic cultural homogenization seemed not only justified, but all too prevalent (Shrestha 1997). As Fanon (1963: 236–237) aptly depicts:

> Colonial domination, because it is total and tends to oversimplify, very soon manages to disrupt in spectacular fashion the cultural life of a conquered people. Every effort is made to bring the colonized person to admit the inferiority of his culture which has been transformed into instinctive patterns of behavior, to recognize the unreality of his "nation," and, in the last extreme, the confused and imperfect character of his own biological structure.... [The] intellectual throws himself in frenzied fashion into the frantic acquisition of the culture of the occupying power and takes every opportunity of unfavorably criticizing his own national culture.

Hegemonic cultural homogenization

Of course, European colonialism's age of imperialism is over. But this seems to have done little to mitigate the long shadow that it cast over the formerly colonized world. "Westerners may have physically left their old colonies in Africa and Asia, but they retained them not only as markets but also as locales on the ideological map over which they continued to rule morally and intellectually" (Said 1993: 25). Hegemonic homogenization, in other words, remains "culturally alive" as the Global North's "westerners" continue to dominate the process of globalization and its cultural, economic and technological spheres, along with their mass media methods and global information flows. But the centrifugal radiation of Western cultural hegemony no longer emanates from Western Europe hearths. Its axial center shifted to the United States following the end of World War II when global territorial restructuring entered its post-colonial phase.

With this shift of the hegemonic axis from Western Europe to the US has come a new cultural epicenter with its own politico-economic configuration and "reach." Following Stuart Hall (1997a: 27), contemporary globalization "is American" and in cultural terms it represents "global mass culture," in that it goes well beyond the narrow confines of colonial societies' socioeconomic elites and primate cities and transcends both class lines and spatial parameters. As this new globalization becomes omnipresent with its influence radiating from every city to every hinterland, it influences an ever-increasing mass of people. As (former) Queen Noor of Jordan (2000: 2) remarks:

> [W]hat separates the current phase (of globalization) from the previous waves of international interaction that have washed across the map over the past several millennia is the increased role that individuals, and local businesses, organizations and communities (not just the nation-states and their elites) ... play in the process. The innovation of the new technology is its lightning speed and its limitless interactivity – the routes of communication are no longer top-down. [parenthetical words added]

So contemporary globalization – or "American globalization" to apply Hall's (1997) logic – is much more globally expansive and integrated, but no less imperial and contradictory than its colonial predecessor with respect to its cultural challenges. (This "Americanization" is convincingly argued both in Agnew's Chapter 9, and Mitchell and Rosati's Chapter 10.)

Contemporary globalization's cultural challenges

Having established Western modernization's *global* hegemonic reach, its pedigree and colonial roots, we now undertake an exploration of contemporary globalization's cultural challenges by focusing on the issues of homogenization, hybridization and heightened identity. Specific questions are as follows. How are cultural homogenization and hybridization playing out under American globalization? What are the implications of hegemonic cultural homogenization and hybridization with respect to globalization's core cultural challenge – *cultural identity* – which is increasingly becoming a terrain of clashes and contestations, instead of becoming blurred or disappearing in the face of global homogenization as some envisioned (Huntington 1993; Inglehart and Baker 2000; Queen Noor 2000)? In other words, where are the sites of cultural convergence (homogenization or hybridization) and cultural conflicts (heightened sense and assertion of identity)?

Exploring these questions, the first part is largely conceptual with the focus set on the core issue of cultural identity which, we argue, rests on two fundamental pillars: *material* and *territorial* (defined in the next section). Because these two pillars often tend to pull in opposite directions, there is normally tension within every culture; a tension between the forces of change favoring material progress and the forces of continuity bent on territorial entrenchment. It logically follows that cultural conflict is thrown into high relief, so we examine its theoretical dimensions next. The concluding part deals with the experiential domain in which we focus on the future, offering our ideas on the reconfiguration of cultural power relationships as globalization's influences on hybridization, cultural identity strengthening bring about significant changes in the global geopolitical and geo-economic landscapes of tomorrow. "Continuity and change" are going to be the pillars of cultural restructuring and of global social power relationships.

On cultural identity

By definition, every culture is *material* and *territorial*. It is material because its civilizational advancement through time and space is contingent on its ability to advance its technological and material bases as represented by, for example, its arts and artifacts, mode of living, and amenities of life. No culture, in other words, can thrive in the absence of continued material growth and expansion which depends on technological advancements as related to the means and methods of production. In addition, to apply Mitchell and Rosati's logic (in Chapter 10), material growth and expansion may occur – and take on a different cultural (symbolic) meaning – as the materiality of cultural identity is increasingly commodified and globalized (i.e., producing and propagating the culture of consumerism). They argue that "capitalism produces globalized culture in the form of ... *everyday things* through which we fashion and define our identities ... and give our lives form and substance." In other words, from a cultural perspective, capitalism itself can be characterized as a circuit of commodity production, "the means and materials out of which new cultures are formulated and radically changed. ... The cultures we produce are the cultures of commodity. Everyday life is the life defined by everyday commodities."

Let us carry the argument a little further. Regardless of how we define and determine everyday life, the materiality of cultural identity is real. It is not merely a matter of economic security; it is, in public eyes, imbued with a sociocultural meaning, for it stands as a source of power and as a powerful symbol of not just whether one is materially endowed but also whether s/he is "divinely blessed." One materially based cultural dichotomy universally common to almost all cultures is between the "*fortunate* rich" (blessed) and the "*unfortunate* poor" (not blessed or condemned). (So, "count your blessings," as the cultural cliché goes!) In short, materiality is embedded in virtually every culture, at least in terms of everyday cultural perception and practices. Take Hinduism, for example. Although often seen by many as a non-material religion, Hinduism has its own venerable goddess of fortune, Laxmi, whom the Hindus worship for wealth and prosperity. There is even a special day dedicated to her worship, *Laxmi puja*; a day that is an integral part of one of the liveliest Hindu festivals, variably called *Tihar*, *Dipawali* or *Diwali*. Given her designated status, one could readily claim that Laxmi is the goddess of merchants and material culture in Hindu societies. The Buddhists in East and Southeast Asia have invented a Buddha of money and wealth, the one with a stocky posture and fat and protruding belly that most Asians see as a symbol of material prosperity. (A fat belly is literally regarded as a sign of sufficient or even excessive food consumption which is invariably equated with wealth; a cursory observation does indeed suggest that as Asians become wealthier, their food intake increases, physical activity decreases, and, consequently, bellies get bigger.) Similar patterns can be detected in Christianity and other institutional religions as well. In essence, success itself, however defined and determined, is invariably equated with cultural materiality and associated with divine blessings.

Although conceptually cultures are considered to be merely different, neither superior nor inferior, all cultures are, in reality, separated by their levels of economic and technological development. Not surprisingly, hierarchical divisions and divides are erected along cultural lines, both locally and globally, as cultures (countries) that are more advanced economically consider themselves culturally superior and usually look down upon those that stand lower on the economic ladder. As a cultural class and as a privileged elite class in general, the rich find means to distance themselves from the poor and downtrodden. Social exclusion, socio-spatial separation, social "distancing" via a host of distinguishing and differentiating methods follow the dictates of the privileged and the socially powerful. So, in more practical terms, the *material* is more than simply a source of sustenance or survival imperative; it is a matter of social status and class identity, because it comes to symbolize the level of economic achievement and advancement and, hence, "cultured" and sophisticated. Since a person's material cultural identity is often equated with his/her socioeconomic class identity, material accumulation and advancement turns into a social system with its own meaning. And this is what the body desires, apparently, the materiality of cultural identity and life. Furthermore, what the body desires materially seems globally insatiable, thus closely reflecting one of the most fundamental of economic (capitalist) assumptions that "wants are unlimited." It is this desire to elevate material cultural identity that tempts and drives many in what was once the colonized world to identify and affiliate with Western cultural values, whose material and technological achievements are currently standing at the highest point of what may be referred to as the modernization trajectory. Symbolically seen as the material "Mecca," the West is "it" – the material cultural norm that the "Rest" seeks to imitate and emulate. Not surprisingly, therefore, we would expect to see globalization leading to cultural changes and convergence in the material arena and, consequently, facilitating cultural homogenization (and Western-dominant hybridization).

On the other hand, cultural identity takes on a different meaning when it comes to its territorial dimension. All cultures are *territorial* because they are boundary forming. Such a spatial boundary separates cultures from each other to affirm their distinct territorial domains within which they nurture and nourish certain practices, values and worldviews for generations to follow and uphold. Not only does a culture tend to have a geographically defined core with definable coordinates that indicate its place of origin or where it has established its home base (Jordan-Bychkov and Domosh 2003), it is also territorial, in that it is often exclusive or selectively inclusive. More specifically, cultural identity is about differences between one cultural group and another, and such differences may be based on, for instance, nationality, race/ethnicity, religion, gender, social class or economic status, or some other differentiating criteria and categories (Shrestha *et al.* 2005).

Irrespective of which particular criterion is applied as a basis for differentiation, they all signify boundaries and, hence, help determine the territoriality of cultural identity. But territorial cultural identity is more than a matter of simply having a territorial base, origin or affiliation. It is about having a profound sense of group belonging and security, a sense of self-respect, dignity and pride. So the territorial "image" (or "imagined") is an integral part of a person's emotional needs; it is what the heart requires and often fights to protect and preserve. It is because of this emotional dimension of territoriality that cultural identity is *heightened*. And, such a heightened cultural affinity to a person's "place in the world" turns societies into terrains of contestations and conflicts when a cultural group encounters a perceived or real threat to its cultural identity or territorial integrity. What often transpires under such circumstances is that cultural identity forms a powerful fault line, a basis for the politics of culture (identity politics) and, hence, cultural conflicts, at internal, intraregional, national and international levels. As argued in the following section, such "nationalistic" cultural conflicts reside at the heart of globalization's cultural challenges, though the pursuit of resolutions to such conflict does not necessarily require armed conflict and military struggle.

Globalization's cultural divide

In their volume on cultural economy, Amin and Thrift (2004: xii) note that "there has been an explosion of interest across academe in matters cultural." Clearly, culture is back in favor as a globalization dimension. Whether culture is actually back or it never went away is not as interesting an issue as the fact that culture is central to many things surrounding human enterprise. While we do not subscribe to the notion of cultural determinism, we could, however, posit that the whole modernization theory of development which was pushed heavily after World War II was fundamentally rooted in culture both as an economic behavioral outcome and determinant. As the argument went, economic and technological development would lead to a transformation in people's "traditional" behavior which would, in return, engender their modern outlook and orientation, thereby reinforcing the march of modernization (Inglehart and Baker 2000). Conversely, if non-Western people remained "tradition-bound" instead of adopting Western values and ways of life consistent with the so-called notion of *economic rationality* (and *economic man/woman*), then society would stagnate as it failed to modernize. By implication, then, the whole modernization project was no less focused on molding newly independent countries' cultures and their citizens' outlooks and orientations than on their economic transformation in the image of Western cultural values; all at the behest of global capital. It was, in this sense, a project oriented toward creating a consumerist society, that is, producing a *new man* – and a *new woman* – with a *new cultural way of life*; one in which the cultural meaning of life is more attached to material fulfillment than anything else.

The whole modernization project promoted by the West in general, and specifically by the United States during the post-colonial phase of globalization, turns out to be a systematic attempt to play up the materiality of cultural identity in order to break down the inward-oriented "traditional" cultural and nationalist barriers to the worldwide penetration of global capital. Having been successful in fending off the rising tide of communism, or diverting others from socialist paths or non-capitalist paths of development, today's new "global project" seeks a path in which the new wave of globalization and neoliberal capitalism is unencumbered and untarnished by the fetters of traditionalism and colonialism. Cultural survival is yesterday's goal, today's and tomorrow's cultural futures are to be global, "western," "hybridized" and "synergistic."

That said, in this exploration of globalization's cultural challenges, we go beyond this often-used dichotomy between "traditional" culture/behavior versus the culture of modernization with its umbilical cord tied to Western values. We do so for two main reasons, both rooted in the premise that modernization is globalization, and globalization, in its current form, is primarily Western as it acts as a purveyor of Western cultural values and global capital wherever it penetrates. First, some of the principal values associated with modernization, such as emphasis on economic development, science and technology, have become fairly universal in the form of local/national development plans and projects (Shrestha 1997). Second, to further extend the logic of modernization, it was, by initial definition and proclamation, a project intended to generate economic growth and development, to spread the consumerist version of material culture everywhere, or simply to enable people to enjoy a "good life," a life that is progressively better than the previous generation's from a materialistic perspective. We now know better that development's underlying mission, to repeat an earlier assertion, was to create a world where cultural barriers and the rising tides of anti-imperial nationalism would subside and where capital would freely roam and rule as a universal cultural and economic system. We were led to believe, by Fukuyama (1992) and other like minds, that there would be one world under global capital, following the triumph of the capitalist internationale led by the United States as opposed to communist international championed by the former Soviet Union. What was required to achieve this was to dislodge "traditional" culture, since it was fundamentally anti-materialistic and, hence, antithetical to progress and prosperity, to the culture of consumerism, now globalized, or simply to global capital.

Such a faulty logic defies not only the material imperative and impulses of life, but more importantly the history of civilization, the showcase of a culture's collective material achievements as defined in terms of economic and technological advancements, along with social and institutional development to govern society in an orderly fashion. But, the cultural and economic dominance exercised by the West is a double-edged sword. Specifically, every dominant force produces a counter force. In other words, for those who have been historically relegated to the margins of cultural integrity and denied national sovereignty (independence) with their voices silenced and humanity diminished, material success, no matter how sumptuous, does not by itself fully satisfy or meet the full emotional aspects of identity self-sufficiency. Burning underneath is the eternal thirst for respect for one's cultural identity and humanity, irrespective of times and space, so that s/he is no longer viewed and treated as the perpetual "other" or simply as inferior, deserving little respect and dignity. So, the more Western cultural dominance emasculates their cultures, sovereignty and humanity, the greater the assertion of their national/local cultural identity and hardening expressions of their resentment. Consequently, the cultural fault lines are drawn leading to a heightening of cultural resiliency, the partial or total rejection of Western culture and outright cultural conflicts if territorial schisms mount and cultural territoriality is violently threatened. Such is the paradox of Western culture's hegemonic pursuit: its achievement of dominance is also its greatest weakness and a widespread cause of resentment and resistance against it. It is no wonder, therefore, that the outcome of globalization led by the West is invariably contradictory, simultaneously producing two polarized currents. This is the fundamental cultural challenge *of* globalization, and the challenge *to* globalization.

Material cultural convergence and territorial cultural contestation

The antipodal relations of West-dominated globalization and its cultural challenges – namely, *cultural convergence* on the material front and *cultural contestations* and conflicts on the territorial front – are ever present in today's globalizing world. One obvious common denominator underlying these contradictory and/or antagonistic relationships is global capital's imperialistic reach (Harvey 1982), which has not only linked different parts of the globe into transactional networks and nexuses, but has also brought different peoples and cultures face to face (Shrestha *et al.* 2005). But the question that goes to the heart of our examination of the cultural challenges facing globalization's transformative and destructive reach is: How does this interface generally play out in the multicultural arenas of everyday living?

Although economic urges and imperatives generally form the core of globalization drive, its economic reach cannot be isolated from its cultural and political dimensions and outcomes. As they are combined into a dominant and dominating force called the "politics of culture" or "identity politics," they plow furrows for open cultural contestations and clashes. Accordingly, it is vitally important to pay attention to the multifaceted cultural dynamics of international power relations embedded in the process of globalization.

First, although globalization is characterized as an interdependent process, because of the imbalance in power relations, it often operates as a central command and control system with its rudder commandeered by Western navigators. History reminds us that as the latest variation of the world system of commercial and geopolitical relationships (Wallerstein 2000; Shrestha 1985) globalization's manifestation and mode of operation can be dichotomized into center and periphery "spaces." In this spatio-temporal dynamic system of international relations and commercial networks, the center invariably dictates the macroeconomic processes and their directional patterns, while the periphery is generally subjected to the center's dictates. In a worst-case scenario, peripheral states, regions and localities can be relegated to such a marginal status that they are effectively a *non-global entity* almost in every respect: economically, politically and culturally (Amin 2002; Hall 1997a,b).

Second, in societies where power relations are ominously obvious and severely imbalanced, conflicts arise between what we may call the culture of external hegemonic domination (that subverts, subordinates or negates the culture of the dominated) and the culture of internal resistance (that fights back against the former to protect and preserve local/national cultural identity). But, where is the site of this cultural interplay of social power?

Usually left out of cultural discussions as related to heightened identity and cultural conflicts between the West and "the Rest" is the public domain and site of resistance, where the *territoriality of cultural identity* assumes center stage. This is the space occupied by the people, the general populace, who are often subordinated and treated with indignity by both the national government and the dominant power. It is in the public domain where heightened identity and cultural conflicts play out in a volatile space of cultural contestations. This is where certain segments of the population see the territoriality of their cultural identity under attack from the hegemonic power, leading to its visible as well as perceived erosion. This is where they experience and suffer their national humiliation and cultural denigration brought on by the dominant power; especially when the Western hegemon openly/ arrogantly behaves like a global dictator. In short, the public domain is both the theater of everyday cultural commodification and convergence and an ever-volatile and fluid terrain of cultural contestations and conflicts. So, when cultural conflicts subside, take a back seat or when they erupt, largely depends on how the United States as the West's hegemonic powerbroker conducts itself on the international stage of geopolitics and cultural relations. Having made this point, we conclude this section by exposing contemporary trends in heightened identity and cultural contestations.

Heightened identity and cultural contestations

The contemporary trend does not seem to bode well for globalization's relentless advance (Shrestha *et al.* 2005). Despite ongoing cultural homogenization and cultural hybridization as related to everyday commodities or in the material arena, heightened senses of cultural identity and resultant cultural conflicts seem to be on the rise, especially in Asia. Again, this rise is mostly attributed to the public reaction and response to the cultural relations of dominance and dependence, not so much to the government policy and cultural behavior of the co-opted ruling classes (vis-à-vis the West).

Take, for example, what has transpired in Indonesia in response to what was seen by the public as the "belligerent" American foreign policy, following 9/11. Its government was openly supportive of the US position on terrorism. Yet, the public reaction in Indonesia was just the opposite as the middle-class youth, along with other demographic segments, were generally hostile to American policy and its pronouncements. In their eyes, America was a bully with little respect for them and their cultural values and the George W. Bush administration's war on terrorism merely a pretext to demonize Islam and dominate the world (DeFleur and DeFleur 2002; see also Hersh 2005). The generally uncomfortable position that US foreign policy has created for America and American businesses was summed up by Mr. Kevin Roberts, of Saatchi & Saatchi, when he reportedly told the *Financial Times* that "... consumers in Europe and Asia are becoming increasingly resistant to having 'brand America' rammed down their throats" (Lobe 2004).

The cultural fault lines vis-à-vis the US/West's imperialist drive reside not with the national government except for a few rare cases of aberration, but in the general public domain, at the street level. Indeed, anecdotal observations suggest that the more their countries and their rulers are perceived to have been "sold out," the deeper the people's sense of cultural subordination and threat to their territorial cultural identity. As a result, they resist and react with emotional resentment and reprisals against the US/West on the territorial cultural identity grounds, while at the same time remaining attached to Western material values. They evoke nationalism, cultural pride, or the unfair geopolitical and economic policies of the US/West as their rallying "battle cries." Their resentment deepens further as globalization appears to be widening the socioeconomic gap between the rich and poor (*Business Week* 2000: 74–75; Soros 1997). Frustrated and resentful, the people fight back against the West and oppose the continued subordination and subversion of indigenous and native/national cultures by mobilizing support and by appealing to cultural identity (e.g., religion). Rarely is this activism militaristic, however, but the antagonism can lead to adversarial public reactions to global business, mainly American. For example, "Across the Middle East, America's war on terror and its threats to Iraq have inspired consumers to boycott American brands from Pampers nappies to Heinz ketchup" (*Economist* 2002: 65). Where economics and politics fail, people and their pride, religion and culture fill the void, venting their anger on the United States and its allies, including their own governments (Huntington 1993).

It does not have to be this way, however. Cultural divisions however hardened are not immutable, implacable and irreversible. The world's interconnectedness and its growing multicultural character is not destined to revert to isolationism, greater social separation, and a re-territorialization of people's life worlds. Rather, the interconnectedness and, yes, the fragmentation of nation-states into culturally distinctive locales, of cities into ethnic and culturally distinct neighborhoods, and of our remaining rural communities into indigenous and mixed-race entities, will continue. But change will be happening at the same time, as hybridization and syncretization become self-perpetuating cultural expressions, cultural practices, and "senses of place" change with the movements and circulations of people, ideas, knowledge and power. (In Conway's Chapter 14, "transnationalism" is detailed as one such significant globalizing force of multiculturalism.)

Conclusion: new cultural identities and hybridization "level the playing field"

In this conclusion we wish to focus on the future. Although we have been highly critical of the iniquitous power of Western colonialism and modernization, and of globalization's ascendancy with its dominating and domineering neoliberal global capital, we envisage there will be further dramatic changes in the cultural compositions of societies West and East that will significantly challenge global homogenization pressures. Rather than stop at the high point of our critique, we would rather offer our (more hopeful) ideas on the reconfiguration of cultural power relationships as globalization's influences on hybridization, cultural identity strengthening bring about significant changes in the global geopolitical and geo-economic landscapes of tomorrow. "Continuity and change" are going to be the pillars of cultural restructuring and of global social power relationships. Cultural territoriality is a strong and, we would argue, progressive dimension, if contradictory as well. The heightened identity that comes with the hybridization of cultural messages and expressions not only challenges colonial and post-colonial legacies, it undergoes transformation and supplants the antagonistic relationships that have long divided the privileged "modern" from the underdeveloped "traditional," rather than mixed and diversified and built-up former colonized peoples' self-reliance and cultural strength. That said, we must concur with Mitchell and Rosati (in Chapter 10) who have convincingly uncovered the dehumanizing effects of the commodification of material cultural expressions in "western," or "American," messages, transmissions and diffusions. We also acknowledge the cultural fissures and conflictual pressures that are ever-present in contemporary international relationships.

However, when "west meets east" there will not be the clash of civilizations, nor the ineluctable dominance of the former over the latter, because hybridization "out-scores" homogenization, transnational cross-cutting enhances cultural diversity, and multicultural interactions do not inevitably result in social conflict, or crises in the everyday lives of people, on the streets, in public places, and in our globalizing, urban life-world "spaces." We reject outright Huntington's (1996) and Barber's (1995) polarization thesis that globalization's cultural consequences will lead to a clash of civilizations, or a clash between Jihad fundamentalism and "McWorld." Such an extremist and bipolar cultural hypothesis is territorially limited (if not naive), because the "geography of globalization" is no longer a hemispheric division. It is no longer a dichotomous cultural divide of core–periphery relationships, and the latter peripheral societies are no longer an undifferentiated colonialized and post-colonialized world in which modernization and traditional cultural impulses simply "clash" and accordingly remain in conflict. On the other hand, we do agree that the past is still very much with us and Occident/Orient cultural distinctiveness is still with us, so Said's (1978) original argument that the West's subordination of "things Eastern" is a colonialist, or post-colonialist, denigration of the cultural faces of the "Others" continues to have merit as an insightful depiction of the continuity of social power relationships at the global scale.

How, then, might we better conceptualize the cultural challenges our globalizing world face? Following one of John Friedmann's (1978) early perspectives into the *ying* and the *yang* of the "cosmic unity of opposites" between city and countryside, we can synthesize some of Mao's philosophical thoughts to good effect in this global cultural context; starting with: (1) "Contradictions are everywhere in this world. Without contradictions there would be no world," and (2) "Contradictions and struggle are universal and absolute, but the methods of resolving contradictions, that is the forms of struggle, differ according to the differences in the nature of the contradictions" (Mao 1990: 14). Friedmann (1978: 7) reconceptualizes the contradictory nature of peoples' territorial interactions by utilizing "contradiction to refer primarily to a *standing in mutual opposition of two social forces which, through interpenetrating and clashing, are complementary to one another, composing a unity, a whole*," and by distinguishing between contradiction's "several moments" – non-antagonistic, antagonistic, historical and cosmic. The resultant nested set of contradictions positions these four moments as follows:

> Every *historical* contradiction expresses certain *cosmic* contradictions which, even though they are in one sense supra-historical, are manifest only in history. Similarly, all *non-antagonistic* contradictions arise exclusively within as framework of *antagonistic* contradictions. It is the latter which are the truly generative force in history, disrupting and recreating structural unities in an unceasing variety of pattern and relation. This concatenation of contradictions renders historical analysis contingent on human aim and purpose. It is for this reason that the verification of historically-contingent truth occurs only in practice.
>
> (Friedmann 1978: 10)

Accordingly, Mao's two bases of social integration, functional and territorial, constitute a *cosmic* contradiction, with the former set of social linkages being organized into hierarchical networks on the basis of self interest and the latter referring to those ties in history and collective sociocultural experiences that bind communities together. Such a *cosmic* contradiction binds both social forces in a mutual relationship, in which neither one can render the other inoperative without destroying itself, so that territorial power and territorial cultural resistance will always contest social power, regardless of the functional scales of the interacting system – and whether in global, regional, urban–rural or core–periphery relationships. Cultural resistance is, therefore, an expected response to, and outcome of, cultural imperialism. Indigenous cultural practices of the traditional past may be threatened, subordinated and even replaced, but hybridized cultural practices take their place. Cross-cultural synergies will be both functionally driven as well as territorially grounded, and the resultant new "unity of opposites," of the *ying* and *yang* cosmic contradictions, will insure that today's global exchanges – unequal though they may be – will realize "continuity and change," rather than the linear paths towards a homogenization of cultural worlds.

What we envisage is an empowering of people through multicultural hybridization and synergization, as the world's ex-colonial and post-colonial societies join their colonizers as equals who are no longer culturally subordinated, and as fledgling social democracies with cultural integrity and diversity not as dependencies with post-colonial mentalities and class schisms. Modernization and "Enlightenment" principles have brought universal education, improved health, urbanization and technology as well as "cultural challenges"; but the growing acknowledgment that multicultural diversity, cultural heterogeneity and strong territorial ties can coexist and not undermine sovereignty helps us look forward to a more promising future, beyond post-colonialism and its divisive cultural messages.

So, as a final rejoinder, let us end with the promising message that "cultural diversity belongs to us all." This slogan appeared to be the welcome consensus of nearly all member states of the United Nations who, soon after 9/11, adopted a Universal Declaration on Cultural Diversity. In November 2001, all member states were keen to oppose "inward-looking fundamentalism," make cultural diversity part of humanity's common heritage, and "uphold lofty principles," lauding the plurality of difference "capable of humanizing globalisation" (Mattelart 2005: 12). In the end, such geopolitical negotiations, and progressive (and humanizing) consensus-building, will prevail, especially when the pursuit of fairness and democratically supported "diversity initiatives" drives the political will of representative governmental regimes. Cultural resistance was almost always about political and economic power struggles and the reconstitution of social power relations. But, cultural hybridization is likely to smooth the political pathways in times to come; in large part, because such cross-cutting patterns of mutual exchanges and sharing of cultural knowledge bring about new, multicultural practices and experiences.

We started this chapter with quotations from Edward Said and Kishore Mahbubani. So it is fitting that we conclude with a quotation from one of their twenty-first century peers, Arundati Roy. Addressing the rhetorical question "What can we do?" at the 2003 World Social Forum in Porto Alegre, Brazil, she made the following visionary appeal:

> We can hone our memory, we can learn from our history. We can continue to build public opinion until it becomes a deafening roar.... Our strategy should be not only to confront empire, but to lay siege to it. To deprive it of oxygen. To shame it. To mock it. With our art, our music, our literature, our stubbornness, our joy, our brilliance, our sheer relentlessness – and our ability to tell our own stories. Stories that are different from the ones we're being brainwashed to believe. ... Remember this: We be many and they be few. They need us more than we need them.
> [...]
> *Another world is not only possible, she is on her way. On a quiet day, I can hear her breathing.*
>
> (Roy 2003)

14 Globalization from below

Coordinating global resistance, alternative social forums, civil society and grassroots networks

Dennis Conway

> Resistance means saying no. No to contempt, arrogance and economic bullying. No to the new masters of the world: high finance, the countries of the G-8, the Washington consensus, the dictatorship of the market and unchecked free trade. No to the quartet of the World Bank, International Monetary Fund, World Trade Organization and the Organisation for Economic Co-operation and Development. No to hyper-production, to genetically modified crops, to permanent privatizations, to the relentless spread of the private sector. No to exclusion, no to sexism, no to social regression, poverty, inequality and the dismantling of the welfare state.
>
> Resistance also means saying yes. Yes to solidarity between the six million inhabitants of this planet. Yes to the rights of women. Yes to a renewed United Nations. Yes to a new Marshall plan to help Africa. Yes to the total elimination of illiteracy. Yes to a campaign against a technology gap. Yes to an international moratorium that will preserve drinking water. Yes also to generic medicines for all, to decisive action against AIDS, to the preservation of minority cultures, and to the rights of indigenous peoples.
>
> Yes to social and economic justice, and a less market-dominated Europe. Yes to the Porto Alegre Consensus. Yes to a Tobin tax that will benefit citizens. Yes to taxing arms sales. Yes to writing off the debt of poor nations. Yes to banning tax havens.
>
> To resist is to dream that another world is possible, and to help build it.
>
> (Ramonet 2004: 1)

Introduction

This chapter explicitly focuses upon the set of human responses – societal, communal, familial and individual – which can be classified as "resistance" to the dehumanizing and iniquitous effects of globalization's dominance by disenfranchised, disadvantaged and dislocated peoples; those harmed, threatened and downtrodden by globalization's privileging of elites and corporations; to wit, the "vulgarly wealthy." In similar vein, people's collective resistance to environmental destruction, to nuclear arms proliferation, to pre-emptive warmongering, and on behalf of "world peace," animal rights, environmental conservation, endangered species, among others, can also take the form of activist demonstrations, of popular political movements, pamphleteering, popular broadsheets and underground literature. These grassroots movements have, of course, a longer history than contemporary globalization's, but the progress made by such democratic activism, their successful demonstrations of peaceful resistance, and the authority and power of people's collective action, certainly reinforces today's "globalization from below" initiatives. Many of these popular opposition movements, indeed, continue through today, and add their weight to the anti-globalization platforms, if not reinforce many of them; the environmental "green" movement, for example, with pro-peace/anti-war coalitions being another example.

"Globalization from below," therefore, is not one monolithic, unified global resistance movement that has blossomed among the world's poor and oppressed to counter the power and authority of "globalization from above" in the first decade of the twenty-first century. Rather, it is a collectivity of "globalization from below" resistances, some highly activist, and globally organized, others highly activist but nationally or regionally/locally organized, while others are not publicly activist, but more restrained, not at all confrontational, but more familial or communal in scale and scope – in short, not so much a revolution as an avoidance, or self expression of autonomy, independence, self-identity and pride.

Building on a discussion of the collective power of global resistance movements, the chapter first focuses on environmental activism, and the parallel emergence of a "globalization from below" movement among NGOs and IGOs to accompany formal inter-governmental action (and inaction) at the supranational level of global consensus-building. The chapter's "globalization from below" theme is then extended to include a wider collectivity of resistance movements, some with cultural consequences, some within ethnic contexts, and some occurring as new immigrant group dynamics.

Many of these latter less-confrontational social movements and societal expressions occur within national or urban contexts; some widespread in the Global North and Global South because of global coordination by NGOs, IGOs and the internet, while others are much more geographically limited responses to local conflicts arising from globalization's external penetration, foreign (corporate) interference, exploitation, and indifference to local human rights and dignities. The range of civil disobedience is considerable, with social activism opposing injustice, inequality and governmental inadequacies with everything from peaceful, non-violent demonstrations, to much more activist and confrontational street political action, and disobedience. Anarchy, and anarchist action, is not absent, and excesses in violence can erupt, because of the challenges such popular activism might pose to central authorities. Accordingly, the authoritarian responses by police, the military, or even by the private mercenary armies and bodyguards contracted to defend and secure corporate property, are always going to be part of the "confrontational equation" and be the counter-foil to the people's mass protests, their activism, and their collective appropriation of spaces to demonstrate on behalf of their rights and the rights of their cause(s).

A convergence of activist agendas

Globalization's ascendancy and "extended honeymoon" in the 1980s appeared to continue well into the 1990s without much critical reflection and very little public counter-commentary (except in the left-wing fringes and among the few relic socialist journals that were still read by their faithful, but declining readership). By the late 1990s, however, emerging concerns in several theaters of civil conflict and societal breakdowns were translated into widespread activism in the late 1990s and early twenty-first century. The resultant confluence of grassroots, national and regional movements promoted a global coalition of opposition – a "globalization from below" – which is mobilizing itself to counter the immensely powerful, yet selfish agendas of global capitalism's "establishment" – the Washington Consensus, the WTO, the G-8, the World Economic Forum (Brecher and Costello 1998).

Despite the seeming hopelessness and continued marginalization that continues to impact millions within globalization's clutches, an ever-growing, "grassroots" opposition has been mobilized. Though rooted in local communities and people's communal interactions and mobilization, the global reach of these local messages of resistance, and the building of a common pool of global solidarity, suggests that capital's continuing supremacy in this new era of globalization may not be inevitable. Women's rights organizations, grassroots coalitions promoting environmental, humanitarian and justice agendas, local popular movements and indigenous communal resistance movements are all "resistances from below," as they react and mobilize opposition to authoritarian, corporate, managerial, bureaucratic dictates "from above." Union solidarity, though considerably undermined in the United States, has not been silent in this struggle, and global strikes against corporate injustice have had their successes elsewhere. Social justice movements in Europe, such as the Jubilee 2000 campaign, have found common cause with others, and global coalitions of extremely varied constituencies have often found common ground in activist demonstrations: WTO meeting confrontations, World Bank and IMF gatherings, G-8 meetings, to name a few.

The momentum of the "globalization from below" movement appears to rise in direct response to, and in large part because of, the ideological hard-line rhetoric and actions of the altogether selfish and self-serving neoconservatives and unilateralists; in short, the privileged minority who appear to be the major beneficiaries of globalization from above – the corporate elite, their political elite clients, the extremely wealthy and their entourages, and their clienteles. One (seemingly deserving) label for this cabal in the US is "the predator class" (Falk 1999; Meyer 2003). Disgust, dismay, outrage and popular opposition to these global predators' excesses did not express itself as a unified movement, as it got under way, however. Activist groups, both in the Global North and Global South, had specific agendas – human rights, women's rights, workers' rights, animal rights, endangered species, global warming, global justice, global poverty alleviation, global health and HIV/AIDSs assistance, anti-sweatshop causes, anti-tobacco corporations, anti-agribusiness, anti-GMOs, anti-nuclear war, anti-free trade, anti-NAFTA, anti-globalization. But, the 1999 Battle for Seattle signaled the convergence of these interests, and the growing strength of cooperative activism (Shiva 1999). The convergence was always strongly anti-establishment, anti-corporatist, anti-capitalist, anti-elitist, anti-neoconservative. On the other hand there was also a growing progressive confluence around common values of social democracy (as a replacement for economic democracy), environmental conservation and societal sustainability, global justice, equality, and world-wide solidarity (Brecher *et al.* 2002). It is this consensual global movement that can be considered an enduring globalization from below, that is not so much anti-globalization as a positive advocacy of "alternative globalization" (International Forum on Globalization 2002), and of "fair globalization" (ILO 2004). More on these future manifestos will appear in the concluding chapter.

This upsurge of "anti-globalization" activism that has challenged, and sometimes effectively undermined, the neoliberal and globalizing agenda of corporate capital is not occurring only at the global level. It is manifesting itself through the rise of national social movements in Latin America, and other countries of the Global South. Pliant, center-right governments that have embraced neoliberalism and collaborated with, or become clients to, external corporate forces have been challenged by urban uprisings in Bolivia, rural uprisings in Mexico and Brazil, and indigenous people's and women's rights "grassroots activism."

"Street activism" has, of course, always played a role in political wrangling in the mature democracies of the Global North, but the authority of central government in these mature advanced capitalist societies is rarely directly challengeable, or effectively undermined by such extraneous "popular disturbances." The tried-and-tested rules and regulations of governmental power and authority in the mature democracies of the world have been so crafted to insure anarchy and rebellion do not disturb the institutional integrity of formally elected, democratic governments, and do not undermine or bring down the hierarchical power structure of governance. The fragile democracies of the Global South are another matter, however.

Alternative "spaces of resistance"

This chapter now moves on to deal with global environmental politics and NGO/IGO activism, and then focuses on the growth in geopolitical strength of alternative globalization events and well-publicized (globally shared) visions for a more sustainable future. Specifically, the World Social Forum is highlighted as an example of a global peoples' collective (and alternative) platform and "global gathering" which is presented as a "counter-challenge from below" to corporate globalization's World Economic Forum. Though visionary in its inception, and inclusive in its logistical organization, the World Social Forum has experienced its internal conflicts, and has not been without its dissenters and critics.

The third and fourth sections change the scale of interrelational "spaces of resistance," first dealing with national and local social movements and then moving down to the family- and community-level within globalizing cities. This last section brings to the fore transnational community politicization and transnational enterprise as informal and largely unseen *urban/metropolitan* dimensions of "globalization from below." These intra-urban progressive movements are not, of course, as confrontational and activist as others, but nevertheless are empowering and progressive for those involved – the immigrant under-classes, urban ethnic minorities, asylum-seekers, and irregular migrants in general. With transnational urbanism as the prevailing societal and political context, local activism in support of human rights, immigrants' rights, and women's rights among multicultural communities in many of the world's metropoli, is now a common feature of "globalization from below" initiatives in today's cosmopolitan cities.

Supranational institutions and "alternative" global forums

Environmental insecurity, natural resource depletion, deforestation, "global warming" and environmental degradation have become as much political and economic problems as they are environmental in today's world. Concern over environmental degradation and the possible impacts of climate change, rising sea levels, global warming and the like have been the focus of global debates in which planetary sustainability, militarism, global governance and regulation have been viewed as interrelated global responsibilities.

The UN-sponsored "Environmental Summit" which took place in Rio de Janeiro in 1992 was supposed to heighten global awareness of the environmental crisis the Earth was rushing towards, but the more strident critics and environmentalists at the accompanying NGO Forum claimed the UN Summit and its Agenda 21 favored the Global North in terms of its emphases, while marginalizing the wider agenda of the Global South. Globalization critics and Third World activists are at pains to stress that environmental issues cannot be ignored when considering policies and plans to alleviate some of the world's most pressing problems – poverty, land and resource scarcity, development, consumption, production and North–South/First–Third World relations.

Environmental NGOs: today's global monitors "from below"

Administrations and governments of both Global North and Global South states have been accused of doing little in the realm of environmental regulation, and seem more content to sign protocols and global accords than actually implement environmental regulations and controls to conserve the environment. Economic considerations have more often than not overruled ecological considerations, and governments have been reluctant to adopt "green" policies, unless politically challenged and threatened by "green" activism.

Indeed, the global environmental movement and growth of "green politics" has been in large part motivated by the reluctance of neoliberal democratic governments to pursue environmental conservation and preservation against the wishes of business interests. One of its dimensions, "green politics" and the growth of the Green Party in European countries such as Germany, however, was not a global movement at its inception. Initially, it was an underground movement among students and youthful environmentalists. In Germany, its underground beginnings and erstwhile anarchic effectiveness would become transformed and incorporated into a formal political party organization, so that in the end more centrist governments, both of the center-right and the center-left, began to embrace "green" programs and "green" policies as their own (Bomberg 1998).

Elsewhere in Europe, this national movement's success in Germany has been repeated so that today there is an active European Federation of Green Parties, and environmental ministries and green portfolios have become cabinet-level responsibilities in every social democratic government in the wider European region. The informal grassroots movement has been transformed into a formal, institutionalized responsibility of state government, and environmental agendas commonly feature in the democratic debates, and many wide-sweeping environmental regulatory policies have been enacted through formal parliamentary channels (Burchell 2002). At the same time, it is only fair to admit that few environmental ministries hold the same power as economic and fiscal ministries, and environmental legislation and regulatory authority will not be enacted and enforced if it hinders economic expansion and privatization initiatives of the ruling governments. Today's "Third Way" social democratic regimes or more overtly conservative and neoconservative governments are intensively lobbied and co-opted by corporate interests, by business alliances, media moguls, and even private wealthy donors, conservative foundations, and the like, so that the environmental conservation and "green" agendas of local and grassroots organizations compete with these powerful groups' interests in environmental management, environmental resource extraction, environmental protection, and environmental risks and natural disasters.

Environmental NGOs and IGOs in many instances have had to become expert in legal matters, and sophisticated in environmental legal petitions and in launching formal legal actions and litigation proceedings. The influence of corporate lobbying and political party monetary support by corporate donors might have very well helped neutralize environmental agendas, but it also mobilized opposition and outrage among citizenry. Environmental non-governmental organizations (NGOs) have taken up the causes of conservation and preservation, of biodiversity, the extinction of endangered species and wetlands renovation, at first promoting domestic agendas, then broadening their interests and membership to global issues. NGOs such as the World Wildlife Fund (WWF), Greenpeace and Friends of the Earth International have grown to be global IGOs, actively championing "green" agendas, fighting legal battles and securing protective legislation at the state level; all in the cause of global environmental conservation. Other NGOs in the United States, such as the Sierra Club, the Environmental Defense Fund and the National Resources Defense Council, have remained concerned with domestic environmental conservation agendas.

Environmental activism, however, in similar fashion to the collective strategies of other grassroots campaigns – peace movements and anti-war movements, anti-nuclear campaigns, anti-corporate crime, and pro-labor movements, being notable examples – found strength in joining with other activist causes, and found common cause in campaigning against the same perfidious opponents who were bent on power wielding, and on exploitation, domination and destruction while they pursued their capitalist goals of accumulation for accumulation's sake. Anti-globalization messages appeared to unify this popular opposition "from below" and served the common purpose.

Forums debating the social injustices heaped upon the world's most powerless and disadvantaged, as a consequence of global capitalism's excesses and imperialistic tendencies, could handily set wide agendas stretching from environmental concerns to extreme poverty, from anti-war, anti-nuclear armament proliferation, and landmine and cluster bomb global ban campaigns to human rights, from global concerns for indigenous people's "intellectual property rights," landless movements, and literacy campaigns to concerns over genocide, women's reproductive rights, and a whole range of desperate public health dilemmas and crises. One such global project is the World Social Forum; the organization is scrutinized in the following section.

The World Social Forum

The World Social Forum was conceived as an international forum against neoliberal policies, financial and corporate globalization, built around the goal that "*another world is possible.*" It sought to provide a space for discussing alternatives, for exchanging experiences and for strengthening alliances between social movements, unions of the working people and NGOs. The first WSF was held in January 2001, in the city of Porto Alegre, Brazil. It was timed to coincide with the holding of the World Economic Forum in Davos, Switzerland. Every year since 1971, an exclusive club of chief executives of the world's largest and most influential transnational corporations meets with academics and political leaders in the Swiss resort town of Davos, to chart the global economic agenda. WEF is sponsored by a Swiss organization that is financed by more than one thousand corporations and serves as an economic consultant to G-8 governments and to the United Nations. The WSF was thus also seen as a counterweight to the options proposed by the World Economic Forum (Fisher and Ponniah 2003).

The decision to hold the Forum in Porto Alegre, Brazil, was not without its locational significance. On the one hand, Brazil is a country that has been greatly affected by neoliberal policies. On the other hand, the richness of Brazilian grassroots organizations – the Amazonian landless movement, Porto Alegre's progressive and democratic popular government model, workers' struggles and the like – represented a source of inspiration for the development of the World Social Forum.

The World Social Forum is an:

> ... open meeting place for reflective thinking, democratic debate of ideas, formulation of proposals, free exchange of experiences and inter-linking for effective action, by groups and movements of civil society that are opposed to neo-liberalism and to domination of the world by capital and any form of

imperialism, and are committed to building a planetary society centred on the human person.

(From the WSF's *Charter of Principles*)

The WSF does not adhere to a common (left-leaning) political manifesto on which all those who participate have to agree. The basic idea is the creation of a space, or "global stage" for everyone to come together with a *respect* for that space. The WSF constituency is critical but at the same time inclusive and welcomes multiple interests and multiple perspectives. There are those, for example, who say that reforming the WTO and the Bretton Woods institutions (World Bank and IMF) is possible, and there are those who believe that reforming them is impossible and that a more fundamental and systemic change is necessary. There are those who propose dialogue and negotiation, and others who believe only in confrontation (Cooper 2002).

After the two successful global forums in Porto Alegre, the International Committee of the World Social Forum and the Brazil Organizing Committee then decided that, from 2003 onwards, the annual global WSF meeting would be accompanied by regional, continental and/or thematic forums across the globe. While the main WSF event was held in January 2003 in Porto Alegre again, in 2004 the World Social Forum moved out of the western hemisphere and activists moved to the eastern hemisphere, holding their meeting in Mumbai (formerly Bombay), India.

The way the Indian WSF was conceived, the process of organising events and activities across the country was as important as the final event itself. These events and activities were not to be seen as merely an exercise to mobilize for the final event, but as important contributions to the output of the WSF process. These processes, in the spirit of the WSF, would be open, inclusive and flexible and designed to build capabilities of local groups and movements. Moreover the process was designed to seek and draw out local peoples' perceptions regarding the impact of neoliberal economic policies and imperialism on their daily lives. The language of dissent and resistance towards these policies was to be specifically informed by local idioms and forms. "East" was to meet "West," progressives in the Global North were to seek common cause with their compatriots in the Global South, and a forward-looking agenda, even if not a global consensus, was expected to emerge.

At Mumbai there were, however, signs of internal disagreement concerning how WSF would continue to function. Some wanted the Forum to be made more inclusive, as criticisms of its white, western, male predominance surfaced. Others sought to make the Forum more project-oriented and presented their ideas on how it might be more aggressive and confrontational/activist in its programmatic pressures. West–East tensions became more apparent in Mumbai, as Porto Alegre's visionary initiation of the Forum's wide-reaching, multi-program agenda was felt to have run its course. The World Social Forum was compared to the Non-Aligned Movement as one of the most significant civil and political initiatives to emerge in its challenge to global imperialism and the hegemony of "so many empires" (Hardt and Negri 2002; Sen *et al.* 2004).

On the other hand, it remains for us to be reminded that the World Social Forum started at the turn of the millennium as an "anti-globalization" movement, but in just a few years has grown and diversified its perspective to also opposing communalism (religious sectarianism and fundamentalism), casteism (oppression, exclusion and discrimination based upon descent and work), racism, and patriarchy. For a much more comprehensive account of these internal tensions and debates within WSF, see Sen *et al.* (2004).

Forcing the World Economic Forum's hand

The Mumbai WSF achieved its purposes, and not surprisingly, by 2004 the World Economic Forum appeared to be more willing to embrace issues of inequality and poverty alleviation than in times past with its presentation of the Global Governance Initiative (WEF 2004). The progressive and socially critical messages of the WSF process of engagement and discourse were in contrast to the austerity recipes of neoliberalism and the economist discourse of WEF and G-8 policy-making. Being pilloried as the "summit of the privileged" had apparently hit home, even among the bankers and corporate executives and other WEF clients and regulars. The World Economic Forum would still be held in closely guarded, secure locations to avoid disruption and pressure from activist opposition, but henceforth the WEF's privileged global elites would at least have to pay more than lip service to global problems of poverty alleviation, disease eradication, and related social crises afflicting the poorer masses of the world. Some, if not all, of the UN's Millennium Goals (2005) – of extreme poverty and hunger eradication, achievement of universal primary education, gender equality and women empowerment goals, infant mortality reduction, maternal health improvement, combating HIV/AIDS, malaria and other infectious diseases, insuring environmental sustainability and developing global partnerships for sustainable development – would have to find their place on the WEF agenda.

National and local social movements, as "glocalization from below"

Resistance movements "from below" are not only occurring at the global level, or as local-to-global, IGO-networked campaigns, or as IT-facilitated local and regional responses to globalization's excesses. A growing number are manifesting themselves as national and local social movements in Latin America, and other countries of the Global South, where client, center-right governments have embraced neoliberalism and collaborated with external corporate forces. Although ostensibly democratic, most Latin American centrist governments of the 1980s and 1990s have been too ready to side with the policies and promises of the Washington Consensus – the IMF, the Inter-American Development Bank, USAID. They have been too ready to open their borders to corporate exploration and penetration, to promote privatization initiatives and reduce food subsidies, to decrease the public payroll – in effect, slavishly following the neoliberal dictates of SAPs, as did the "internal colonialists" of earlier times.

Indigenous peoples' resistance movements: "solidarity" from local to global networks

Latin American countries may no longer be European nations' colonial holdings, but the colonial mentality that has guided their system of governance since their independence in the nineteenth century remains a twenty-first century reality among the region's elite classes. Most states' populations are still divided into a socioeconomic hierarchy where fairer-skinned Western/modernized elites rule in their own interests, allied – yet still subordinate – to the rapacious designs of global capitalism. The most (dis)affected by this mentality and the rapacious policies that it favors are the same groups of people who were most affected by "The Encounter" over 400 years ago, the self-identified "indigenous" populations: the Zapatistas in Chiapas, Mexico, the Aymara and Quechua in Bolivia, and the Quichua and Shuar in Ecuador, for example.

The unabashed, external exploitation and appropriation of many of these peoples' territorial resources – old growth hardwoods, mineral wealth, forested tracts, river and lake fish stocks, even their indigenous knowledge and intellectual property rights – are being practiced by transnational corporations and condoned by client national governments, with added "help" and arm-twisting from the neoliberal, economic development policies imposed on their national governments by the like of the WTO, the World Bank, US bilateral aid and development agreements.

Is it surprising, then, that "street activism" and even outright civil revolution against the excesses of "globalization from above" has again become the indigenous peoples' "last stand" – their own version of a "glocalization from below" resistance movement in which their local mobilization gains media exposure and international support by effectively linking to global networks of anti-globalization, global human rights organizations, cultural survival compatriots, and global indigenous networks of information sharing, exchanging and organizing.

Such has been the harshness of these urban-biased neoliberal policies that they have been challenged by urban uprisings in Bolivia and Ecuador, by rural uprisings in Mexico and Brazil, and indigenous peoples' and women's rights "grassroots activism" throughout Central and South America (NACLA 2005). Recently, however, there has been a dramatic shift to the left in the political climate of several Latin American democracies, reflecting the growing "formal" power of these grassroots initiatives and popular "anti-globalization" and "anti-neoliberalism" movements. For the first time (in December 2005), an indigenous leader, Evo Morales, has won election to the presidency of a Latin American country, Bolivia. Surely this is evidence of a sea-change in that region, and of indigenous peoples' growing geopolitical power.

These struggles of Latin America's indigenous communities in the early years of the twenty-first century are against social inequity, extreme poverty, harsh political repression and the privatization of utility companies. They are for the defense of land and territories against oil drilling and mining, and timber transnationals, that are destroying indigenous peoples' traditional ways of life, threatening their ancestral lands, and in many cases displacing them from their homes in the name of capitalist expansion and economic growth.

We should admire the determination of the region's indigenous communities to reassert their voice and continue to press for their full (and genuine) involvement in a truly democratic and participatory government. The resurgence of indigenous identity and mass mobilizations can be said to be evidence of the manifestation of the centuries-old *tupaj katari* prophecy (literally "balanced upheaval"): "I may die alone, but I will return and I will be millions" (NACLA 2004: 14). Neoliberal economic policies that protect transnational corporation's extractive agendas and which destroy land and appropriate indigenous community's territories must be opposed, not only by the indigenous, but also by the wider body of Latin American citizenry. Events in Bolivia appear to be in the right direction, it seems.

Transnational connections as a "globalization from below"

The "globalization" discourse focuses upon social processes and structure–agency relations in a "space of flows" (Castells 2004), which differs in scope, scale and "reach" from "transnationalism." Transnational processes depict transnational social relations, both "anchored in" and "in-between" nation-states, where the significance of borders (and border-crossing), of state policies and of multiple, national identities continues to be important determining and consequential factors. Family- and kin-networks are very much at the fulcrum of transnational connections, and transnational communities, both "home" and "away from home," form bi- or multi-local worlds in which a growing number of people are participating.

Four contemporary social processes appear to be contributing to the proliferation of transnational networks today. They are:

1 the discursive repositioning of localities in relation to nation-states and globalizing forces;
2 the emergence of cross-national, political and institutional networks that deploy the discourses of decolonization, human rights, global justice and other universalistic tropes to advance the interests of heretofore marginalized groups;
3 the facilitation of transnational social ties by new technological developments that have widened access to the means of transnational travel, communication and information-exchange;
4 spatial reconfigurations of social networks and transnational "spaces" that facilitate more temporary movements, the reproduction of migration, transnational entrepreneurialism, cultural exchanges of beliefs, practices, cross-over foods, musical genres and heightened political agency from "below" and transnationally "in-between" (Smith 2003).

Transnationality is expressing itself in people's mobility behaviors, in family network support structures, in transnational community self-help both at home and away from home, and in the international transfer of people, goods, ideas, knowledge and skills. It is only rarely one of globalization's "activist" momentums, however. Transnational political mobilization occurs, of course, and it can be a very effective "new" form of electronic telecommunications networking of transnational solidarities "from below," as Law's (2003) examination of the informally organized Migrant Forum in Asia (MFA) shows. Among Caribbean transnational communities in the United States, such as the Dominicans, Salvadorans and Hondurans, transnational political campaigning has also grown to become an effective cross-border mobilization of émigré resources (Cordero-Guzmán *et al.* 2001; Smith and Guarnizo 1998). Transnational migrant remittances sent back to home communities might also influence local political campaigns, but these wealth transfers mainly occur within family networks; between transnational donors and their dependent families and communities (Conway and Cohen 1998, 2003), so their direct use is rarely activist, and certainly not an anti-globalization resistance strategy.

Transnationalism is a global or international strategy of many people and their families, not directed, or promoted, by institutions and agencies of global capitalism, or the structural forces of neoliberalism and corporate capital. On the other hand, this new form of international mobility has *accompanied* contemporary globalization, and has come to be practiced by more and more people as social networks have deepened, overlapped and become more socially, economically, racially and ethnically complex in terms of their interconnectivity and in their multiple fields of social practice (Smith 2005). Decidedly urban in context and growing more global in its spatial and social diversity and complexity, Smith (2001) perceptively directed us to reconceptualize and "situate" the process at the appropriate scale of "transnational urbanism." Transnational urbanism, therefore, offers a view from below – from inner city neighborhoods, enclaves in suburbs, multi-ethnic communities, minority spaces and places – in which transnational migrants and their cross-border networks both "forge the *translocal* connections and create the translocalities that increasingly sustain new modes of being-in-the-world" (Smith 2005: 237).

Transnational networks are peoples' constructions for sustenance and survival, or their creative solutions to the limitations of their immediate environmental and societal situations. These latter may have been directly impacted by the global forces of neoliberal capitalism, so transnational strategies can be viewed as peoples' grassroots alternatives to the strictures of global disciplines, the ravages of corporate penetration, and the destruction/disruption of local economies brought about by "free trade" policies. The widespread and embedded nature of Mexican transnationalism is surely one example of this relationship (Conway and Cohen 2003; Massey *et al.* 1998).

All transnational networks of migrants, or mobile internationalists, are not merely sustenance social webs of the poor, the destitute and irregular. Transnational business elites, oft-times beneficiaries of globalization and neoliberalism, also are spatially and socially situated in translocal geographies of interaction, connection and the everyday material practices of people living, working and socializing. As Conradson and Latham (2005: 228) remark:

> Even the most hyper-mobile transnational elites are ordinary: they eat, they sleep, they have families who must be raised, educated and taught a set of values. They have friends to keep up with and relatives to honor. While such lives may be stressful and involve significant levels of dislocation, for those in the midst of these patterns of activity, this effort is arguably simply part of the taken-for-granted texture of daily existence.

In between this "global class divide" – the transnational business elites and the developing world's desperate transmigrants – there are middle-class transnational migrants who also form global networks, such as professional health workers, nurses, English-as-a-second-language teachers, civil and electrical engineers, IT specialists, artists and performers. Following professional careers in which short-term contract-assignments abroad can be a welcome broadening of experience and a highly profitable remunerative return for the relatively young, and relatively independent (unmarried, and unencumbered with children), these modern-day transnational globe-trotters diversify the transnationally mobile categories even more. "Middling" forms of transnationalism is how these middle-class cohorts have been labeled, to express their character and their translocal situations in which: "In terms of the societies they come from and those they are traveling to, they are very much in the middle" (Conradson and Latham 2005: 229).

We can conclude, then, that transnationalism is a growing everyday practice among the world's mobile sectors, in which global communications networks, informal social networks, urban multi-ethnic and multicultural milieus, transnational entrepreneurism and international, cross-border exchanges of knowledge, people, ideas, capital and political power and authority form the complicated and highly diverse nexus of interconnected social–spatial structures and agency interactions. Transnationalism can be a "resistance" to globalization's pressures, it can be facilitated by globalization's reach and its technological and logistical systems of communication, transference and exchange, or it can occur as an accompaniment to globalization's societal transformations – even as an incidental passenger. Globalization has certainly encouraged new forms of mobility, new forms of social intercommunication, and helped rather than hindered cross-border transfers and cross-border exchanges. Globalization, indirectly, has provided the global contexts – global cities, second-tier cities, global-to-local connectivities, and the like – which have fostered the growth and deepening strength of multi-local, transnational networks, and stimulated multiculturalism, cosmopolitanism and cross-cultural synergies in transnational communities, and extended family systems. The global mobilization of transnational community political energies is perhaps the most obvious "globalization from below" institutional agency. There is a possibility, however, that the majority among transnational networks are not political agents, do not have anti-globalization agendas, or do not perceive themselves as members of a resistance movement. In comparison to the grassroots social activists and the local confrontational "peoples' politics" in Latin America who we visited earlier in this chapter, transnational urbanism is by no means revolutionary, though it is transformative in societal terms.

Conclusions

Since globalizing tendencies began to rear their ugly head there has been opposition, primarily generated by leftist groups and other concerned citizens, much of which has gone unnoticed, or unmentioned by popular media in North America. In Europe, there is a wider political spectrum among the formal media – newspapers, TV channels, popular journals and the like. In metropolitan Asia, modernization's penetration and North American consumerism are embraced by a growing middle-class, so that wealth accumulation becomes the singular path to upward social mobility, and class activism is muted in favor of individualism – "getting on, and getting rich." Social activism persists among intellectuals, and in some progressive regions in Asia, but the powerless and disenfranchised no longer receive the social and communal support previous social orders offered. Equally unfortunate, the centralizing tendencies of global communication empires, like Rupert Murdoch's Fox News empire, and the oligopoly control the three/four major US TV networks have over their media messages, insured that conservative and status quo positions are revered, and globally distributed. This insures that any activist/progressive messages that might be aired are subsequently minor irritants, or at best marginalized and localized (Alterman 2003).

On the other hand, advances in grassroots mobilization via the internet – email, websites, weblogs and other online communications – promise the kind of global intercommunication and information-sharing necessary for large-scale opposition and popular activism to be well-prepared, well-organized and transnationally influential. The enormous amount of information shared over the internet, the growth and sophistication of website information bases, and the *openness* of this medium of exchange and information-sharing, means that global coalitions of opposition, activism and of all kinds of anti-globalization, anti-poverty, anti-war coalitions and peoples' forums can be effectively mobilized. No longer will the media or our governments – if they seek to in the name of national security, or homeland security – be able to totally control and suppress information. The internet provides a global window to "whistle-blowing," official leaks, and anonymous sources of "insider information," so that the long-practiced art of formal institutions to censor and suppress information is compromised, if not completely undermined. Together, with "on the ground," face-to-face local mobilization, this global community of civil society representatives has a very real potential to fight, and counter, the destructive and damaging effects of "globalization from above."

15 Towards "fair globalization"

Opposing neoliberal destruction, relying on democratic institutions and local empowerment, and sustaining human development

Dennis Conway and Nik Heynen

Introduction

The main objective of this volume has been to critically interrogate the many interrelated processes that together comprise *globalization*. Too often in past research authorities have stressed the singular importance of one or two globalizing forces – information technology, financial capital, for example. Rarely has the range and scope of *all* the important dimensions of this global "project" been scrutinized. Rarely has an examination of globalization and neoliberal capitalism's ascendancy and growing structural dominance been accompanied by in-depth exposés of the varied, yet interwoven, "spaces" and "faces" of globalization. This comprehensive and critical assessment of the many dimensions of globalization has, however, put all of them under the microscope: from the deeply structural, to the unruly and unpredictable; from the profoundly destructive and disciplinary to the activist and progressive.

This concluding chapter has three sections; each a logical follower of its predecessor. First, we revisit the assessments our contributors have made, and provide our summary of globalization's contradictory economic, political, cultural and social tendencies since its consolidation in the 1980s to our crisis-laden present; in short, its complex geographies, unevenness, unruliness and volatile trajectories. Following this synthesis, we then focus in on our critical findings of globalization's destructive tendencies, the disciplinary might of its macroeconomic institutions, the geopolitical momentum of an increasingly multipolar world order, rife with conflict, tension and schism, and last but by no means least, globalization's "alter ego"; its opposition, its seamy underside, its hidden worlds. Then, looking ahead to a more enlightened time that is long overdue, we seek a future that will be kinder, more humane and more socially just. Building on recent calls for a fair globalization (ILO 2004; New Economics Foundation 2002; Saith 2004), for alternatives to the neoliberal diet of corporate capitalism and G-8, OECD, WTO, IMF and World Bank global directives (Henderson 1999; International Forum on Globalization 2002; Stiglitz 2002), and for a more truly democratic future (Fabian Global Forum 2003a,b; Simms *et al.* 2004), we conclude with a more positive and hopeful message. But first, let us revisit and summarize our collection's insights on the restructured new international (dis)order that we have come to know as globalization and its neoliberal capitalist orthodoxy.

How contradictory is globalization, anyway?

Capitalism is inherently contradictory, crisis-laden and subject to booms and busts of its own making, so we should not be surprised, nor feel we are surprising anyone, when we assert that neoliberal capitalism has continued the genre's contradictory impacts and unevenness in transformative effects. Neoliberal capitalism's particular feat since its emergence in the 1980s has been to increase social divisions, widen the economic gap between the very rich and the very poor, centralize authority for the management of corporate and financial capital, elevate "soft capitalism" to a position of unassailable influence in global financial affairs, give monopolistic/oligopolistic privileges to smaller and smaller groups of highly influential power-brokers, and, as a consequence, encourage insider-trading, corrupt practices of accounting, tax-evasion and bribery of officialdom, avoidance of regulatory oversight, and the use of technological fixes to further hide the actual economic health of corporate enterprises. Of course globalization is contradictory, in no small part because neoliberalism is contradictory.

Globalization and neoliberalism's championing of free trade, privatization, deregulation, and the opening of protected markets was born on the promise of unfettered national economic expansion for those countries of the Global North and South with "competitive advantages," if only they unharnessed their entrepreneurial energies. Global returns for everyone were promised – for everyone who successfully transformed their political economic agendas, that is. Unfortunately, such excessive promises failed to materialize for the majority of countries and governments who embraced neoliberalism, and the majority of their citizens, who have suffered from the predatory forces of corporate capital, from unexpected capital flights, widespread bankruptcies, the "downsizing" of labor forces, the withdrawal of public support for welfare services, and the one-size-fits-all formulas of the structural adjustment programs of the World Bank and the IMF, and the business-friendly plans of the World Economic Forum. The WTO was in its ascendancy adjudicating the free-trade message throughout the 1980s and 1990s, but since 1999 and the "Battle for Seattle" this seemingly impregnable, neoliberal institution has ceased to function as the global watchdog of "free trade," as US versus EU trade disputes dominate their schedule, and internal dissention both among the privileged members of the Global North and between the G-7/G-8 and the G-22 (previous outsiders) has just about rendered it impotent, and incapable of decisiveness, or even consensus-building. As the latest round of WTO talks in Hong Kong attest, contradictions abound, with the loudest proponents of "free trade" and the opening of developing countries and emerging markets to outside capital ventures – the USA, member countries of the EU such as Britain and France – continuing to defend their own protectionist policies and government subsidization programs.

Beyond the contradictions within financial and commodity production systems of global exchange, the geopolitical transformations underway in our globalizing world are also contradictory in that they are geographically uneven in their concentration, subject to volatility in the rapidity of events, and subject to disruption by the unpredictable occurrence of natural disasters and environmental calamities. At the same time, geopolitical agendas "have geographical addresses." Geo-economic transformations are occurring in newly emerging industrial markets, and the BRICs (Brazil, Russia, India and China, with their impressive reserves of resources) and more and more global cities (second-tier and third-tier "wannabees") are providing their own entrepreneurial challenges to their more elderly forerunners – the "Old World's" first tier.

Global contradictions are geographically explicit, with different nation-states, cities, regions, locales and communities experiencing extremely different, often opposite, returns from globalization's influences, be they financial, economic, geo-economic, technological, cultural, and unruly, or combinations of such influences. What may appear to be China's gain in geo-economic and geopolitical arenas is not Indonesia's experience. Brazil may be an emerging industrial giant potentially, and Russia might appear to be likewise endowed with valuable energy resource reserves, but oligarchic unruliness in the latter's case, and geoeconomic unevenness in the former case, compromise these BRICs' path to become major global powers in the near future.

The plight of labor, as opposed to the continued excesses in accumulation of capital by a privileged minority of corporate leaders and their elitist minority of stockholders, money managers and accountancy partners, may be global in extent, but widely divergent in its local and regional manifestations. The erosion of the working wage in advanced capitalist, industrialized and post-industrialized Core nation-states, and neoliberalism's assault on entitlement programs, social welfare nets, and the pension and retirement packages of organized labor, is unevenly experienced across the global landscape, with the most advanced depredations occurring in the United States, while labor's position in many European countries appears to be more resilient, and better protected.

In the global periphery and countries of the Global South, however, labor's plight vis-à-vis global capital's accumulation record is couched in very different terms. Oppressive, dehumanizing and extremely dangerous working conditions, and job insecurity, are at the forefront. Regulatory institutions are non-existent, and outside capital interests have used their geo-economic and geopolitical clout to impose their will, or bribe their way, to acquire a pliant government's collusion in their commercial exploitation of local labor. Different degrees of social resistance to these penetrations in the Global South are to be expected. Different alliances of interest groups, NGOs, IGOs and local grassroots movements bring changes to internal power-relationships that can counter, or compromise, elite control and authority, and globalization's transformative influences are not always in the elite classes' favor. Accordingly, the contradictions in the outcomes of global influences on capital–labor relationships and levels of empowerment of the underclasses, the laboring classes, working women and men, will be different in Bolivia and

Argentina than in Chile, for example, and different in Pakistan and Bangladesh than in Malaysia, or different in the Philippines than in Thailand.

Culturally, global homogenization has certainly become a trademark of globalization's increasing reach in consumer markets, media markets, music and entertainment, information dissemination, cross-over foods, and technology diffusions. All the while, cultural contradictions become the rule rather than the exception, as class, cultural identity, wealth and conspicuous consumption "mix the pot," and the growth and diversity of material culture's offerings in many globalizing societies, global cities and transnational urban domains mirror the cosmopolitan and multicultural social mosaics of these global and transnational locales. The unabashed commodification of "all things cultural" imposes capitalism's rules of the marketplace on cultural expression, cultural practices and cultural values, so that cultural survival can become an end product of its marketability, its market price or "exchange value" rather than its intrinsic "use value." Contradictions abound in the local-to-global and global-to-local exchanges of cultural practices and cultural commodities, and again geographical diversity and differentiation characterize not only the globalized "consumerscapes" of today's global cities and transnational urban centers, but of many smaller less-integrated cities and towns further down the urban hierarchy in both the Global North and South – though this might be more prevalent and pervasive in the more highly urbanized societies of the Global North, and less the general case in the rural-and-small town interiors of countries in the Global South.

Globalization's transformations of the architecture of financial institutions – the easing of restrictions on international capital transfers, thereby increasing the volume of foreign direct investment (FDI) flows, speeding up FDI investments into and out of national economic accounts, capitalist ventures, and generally helping owners of capital realize profits unheard of in previous capitalist eras – has not been accompanied by the easing of restrictions on the reallocations of labor. Put another way, global labor has not enjoyed the same "freedom to move." Although international migration has registered considerable increases in volume during the last 30 years, these increases have not been facilitated by government policy-making, or geopolitical decision-making, but rather by default. Formal immigration policies continue to be administered at the nation-state level, and are designed in terms of national interest, national security considerations, domestic labor supply, and so on. Perhaps only among the members of the European Union has that collective group of countries' Schengen agreement begun to ease labor movement across national borders, and attempted to deal with labor transfer problems within the EU.

Emerging as a counter, or resistance, to globalization's privileging of capital, and responding to many nation-states' defensive concerns to control and secure their borders, irregular migrants have responded to deprived or disrupted conditions at home by illegally crossing borders to seek employment and better opportunities. Globalization's transformations of the business environment, the internationalization of commodity chains and the drive for productive efficiencies and labor cost-cutting, encourage recruitment of irregular labor for its greater efficiencies, its lower cost, temporariness and its disposability. There is, therefore, the contradictory situation where irregular labor is preferred to local labor, where disposable temporary workforces can be hired and fired with impunity, and where the human rights of irregular/illegal workers in the informal economy are too easily subject to abuse.

Other contradictory tendencies and uncertainties in the new global order are further exposed in the following section, where the destructive and disciplinary tendencies collide, combine and coalesce in unpredictable, volatile and often extremely dangerous ways, or in an extremely iniquitous and unsustainable manner.

Destructive and disruptive tendencies of globalization and neoliberalism

Globalization's perpetuation of underdevelopment, of unequal development and mass impoverishment, and the widening social divide at all scales

For the world's rural and urban poor classes, globalization and neoliberalism have been "assault vehicles" with the dual aims of undermining democracy and increasing wealth for the elite minority at the expense of the poor majorities (Martin and Schumann 1997). The social contract of mutual responsibility has been replaced by the social divide in which it is "every (wo)man for her/himself, and the winner takes all!" This latest era of rampant neoliberal capitalism has shown its ugliest face, its meanest side, its corrupt (and corrupting) character, its dehumanizing consequences, and its scant regard for peoples' human rights and social livelihoods.

In recent times, globalization and neoliberalism, as the latest version of dominance of the Global South by the Global North, have fostered a "new imperialism" in which the United States, Japan and the European Union compete for global penetration, commercial dominance and privileged access to energy resource stocks, in partnership with their transnational corporate conglomerates (Harvey 2003). Everywhere, it seems, rich and poor communities, rich and poor families, extremely rich and extremely impoverished people are locked in an uneven conflict over living space, sustenance space, survival space, and unruly, competitive spaces, even armed and increasingly militarized spaces.

It is instrumental to be reminded that the UN's Millennium Development Goals for the year 2015 are prompted and urged by this depressing global picture: the eradication of extreme poverty and hunger; achievement of universal primary education; promotion of gender equality and empowerment of women; reduction of child mortality rates; improved maternal health and reduced danger of maternal mortality to the point of elimination; combating HIV/AIDS, malaria and other pandemic diseases; insuring environmental sustainability; and developing a global partnership for sustainable development (Millennium Goals 2005). This global agenda was particularly crafted to redress the insidious iniquities that had become more desperate and in need of immediate amelioration under "globalization's watch," yet would be achievable if the political will of the global community could be galvanized to address these problems, and if/whether the economic support could be garnered through multilateral global partnerships, rather than by neoliberalism's mechanisms, which favor unilateralism and free-market solutions. These millennium goals, at the very least, identified some of the most pressing and urgent concerns for the sustenance of humankind, and were a telling indictment of neoliberalism's failings.

The crisis in development thinking and the bankruptcy of "modernization theory"

Modernization theory, which was so fundamental to the thinking behind efforts to promote post-colonial development in the Third World periphery, has been exposed as a totally misleading model. Development was never about "modernization," though it was embraced as such. "Development from above" was a vehicle for continuing Core dominance over the Periphery, for maintaining dependent relations, and for co-opting the Third World's elite classes to promote the modernization project (Stohr 1981). But, it hasn't.

Unfortunately, The World Bank's pursuit of solutions for the "developing world" have always been discipline-bound with neoclassical economic orthodoxy the narrative, "modernization" and "industrialization" the goal, and self-serving (often corrupt) appropriations of wealth and prestige the practice (Hancock 1989). Other development agencies, such as USAID or CIDA, and World Bank look-alikes such as the Asian Development Bank, also appear to be uncritically married to the same doubtful promotions of neoliberalism. There is, indeed, a crisis in these global institutes' development thinking, as well as in their development praxis (Hancock 1989).

The developmental state undermined by the globalization project

The "Westphalian" principles of state authority and responsibilities which supported the growth of the democratic nation-state are being undermined by global penetration and global mechanisms (Fine 1997; Fine and Stoneman 1996). Keynesian economic principles, which underscored the state's role in capitalist economies, are being supplanted by neoliberalism, with its policy messages of privatization, market efficiencies and competitive struggles. There is an emerging "soft capitalism" which sets stock-market portfolios, brokerage firms and business consultancies as influential driving forces of corporate investment, disinvestment, and reinvestment strategies (Thrift 1998) which further empowers capital and capitalist interests at the expense of the state. Apologists for the failure of the international aid community to deal with the Third World's woes have, more than once, criticized post-colonial governments' ineptitudes, attributing lack of progress to "deficiencies in institutional capacity," or more bluntly to corruption and mismanagement. Indeed, the increased presence and ascendance to prominence of

NGOs in the development arena is a *de facto* recognition of many a national or local government's inadequacy and inability to successfully manage "top-down" development projects (McAfee 1991). The global reliance on NGO activism and involvement in local development initiatives may have moved the projects along, but at the same time resorting to such models of "private philanthropy" poses a diversionary threat to the potential for a truly participatory system of representative social democracy to eventually flourish.

The ideologically driven replacement of foreign aid packages with foreign direct investment, by the Thatcher and Reagan administrations in the early 1980s, and their substitution of Core countries' public responsibilities to their post-colonial, modernization projects in favor of private-sector capitalist ventures, changed the international aid landscape, fundamentally. Not only did this ideological turn strengthen the bargaining position of corporate capital, it also weakened, or undermined, their states' role as "development provider," or as a humanitarian agency responsive to United Nations ethical positions on human development, global justice, poverty alleviation, and the rest (Burnell 2002). United Nations programs were not to be consensually supported; rather the reins of supranational authority (and guidance) were to be passed, more and more, to neoliberal capitalism's global institutions (Hancock 1989). Third World, post-colonial problems were no longer the responsibility of the colonial and neo-colonial "mother countries." Globalization was going to "deliver the goods."

Neoliberal structural adjustment programs (SAPs) still imposed on the indebted Global South

Global institutions' responses to the plight of the indebted countries of the South have been paltry. IMF/World Bank SAPs still promote the neoliberal agenda, still insist on debt repayment, still insist that macroeconomic policies of debtor states must be judged by their economic accountability in the global marketplace, their export-oriented initiatives, and openness to external competition. Public-sector management of social and welfare service sectors must be scaled back and replaced by "privatization initiatives."

And, although the Jubilee 2000 movement appeared to have convinced some European politicians that they should help alleviate the debt burdens of the most highly indebted Third World countries (Jubilee 2000), the IMF's response has been paltry to date. Debt alleviation, apparently, has to be tied to structural readjustment, even for the most impoverished states and those in the "highly indebted" categories, such as Haiti. Despite the "comfy" rhetoric at meetings of the World Economic Forum, where the global business elites and their G-8 client administrations – "engaging its corporate members on global citizenship" – offer platitudes and briefs on the necessity for poverty alleviation, accelerated job creation, reduction of the digital divide, improving "competitiveness," and the like (World Economic Forum 2004), neoliberal solutions to economic restructuring and engagement with the global economy remain the disciplinary "faith."

Transnational corporate power more centralized than ever

Transnational corporations have continued to grow, consolidate and become multinational in structure, function and identity, especially the core–origin transnational corporations (see Susan M. Walcott's Chapter 4). More recently, 1998–9 heralded the onset of a period, now considered the "years of mega-mergers," with oligopolies coming to dominate whole sectors of the global economy and the corporate merging of smaller companies continuing at a spanking pace, to this day (New Economics Foundation 2002–4).

As mentioned earlier, European and US governments have come to act as client-protectors of corporate interests. The GATT trade talks and WTO's "free-trade" mission have always been "negotiated" on behalf of G-8 and transnational corporate commercial interests – aided and abetted by client Core states' administrations.

The turmoil and debate over global trade as directed by the WTO rulebook, first actively demonstrated in the "Battle of Seattle" in 1999, then continued until the impasse in Cancun in 2003, through to the latest talks in Hong Kong in 2005, has resulted in irreconcilable divisions in Core versus Periphery positions and an almost complete breakdown in its global authority. Other areas of contention between the Third World (or Group of 77) and the First World and its corporate plunderers (Mokhiber 2002) are in the biotechnology industry, where the TRIPs agreement and the rapacious activities of US corporate patent-seekers have been aptly labeled as "bio-piracy," because of their blatant disregard for indigenous peoples' and farmers' property rights and their attempts to monopolize and privatize food and genetic substances, many of which are generally regarded as public goods, for example basmati rice (ActionAid 1999b, 2000).

Hyper-mobility of capital

Since the 1980s, there has been a rapid takeover of supremacy of international financial capital over domestic (national) capital management, with "fictitious capital" decoupled from productive capital (Arrighi 1994). Nation-states' central bank power over currency management has weakened, as global currency trading has ascended to its dominant position. The late 1990s' US stock-market "bubble" replicated the 1923–9 crisis. Market volatility was pronounced as investors responded to subjective, suggestive signals, and corporate management behavior, in large part, behaved in response to stock-market signals – downsizing, new technology, IPOs, merger-mania, monthly and bimonthly reports of earnings and profits (Thrift and Leyshon 1994).

The Asian "melt-down" of 1998 was an unexpected demonstration of the volatility of global capital, and of the fallibility of the much-acclaimed "Asian Tiger" export-oriented development model. Foreign direct investment, which had supplanted foreign aid as the essential external input to capitalize productive enterprise and development, proved it could be withdrawn even faster than local financial regulators and central banks could stop the hemorrhaging.

Predictably, there were the development establishment's post-hoc rationalizations that "fingered" the dysfunctional Thai economy as the culprit for the ensuing collapse of the more robust neighboring Asian economies of Malaysia, Indonesia and Korea, and the unwelcome accumulation of "bad debt" by Japanese financial institutions which had invested heavily in the region. Not so predictably, the ensuing financial crises in Brazil, Argentina and Russia, as the world passed uncertainly into the twenty-first century, were not so easily rationalized and excused. The volatility of the international financial markets, and the continuing hyper-mobility of capital, remain unpredictable global forces at magnitudes of potential impact(s), never before imagined or experienced (see Adam Tickell's Chapter 3).

The globalizing underground economy: international narcotics and armaments trade profiteering

The highly profitable narco-trade is destabilizing Caribbean, Central and Southern American societies, yet the "war on drugs" in the United States is not directed at limiting the power and dominance of organized crime syndicates distributing narcotics to the client public. Rather, it focuses on interdiction and interruption of trade routes (e.g. Ship-rider Agreement), and on eradication of crops at source (in South America and the Caribbean), or high-profile arrests of cartel members.

Though less in the spotlight of scrutiny as an international commodity, and more often viewed as an alarming aspect of urban crime and homicide, small-arms manufacturing and the commercial exporting of such sophisticated weaponry are mutual growth industries with considerable global impacts – many highly destructive. In the 1990s' "resource wars" of Sub-Saharan Africa, diamonds and valuable minerals like gold, tin and oil may have been the resources that prompted desperate conflicts, civil wars and destruction, but small-arms smuggling and the resultant wholesale arming of warring people has brought on the disastrous consequences (*Small Arms Survey 2003*).

Commercial networks handling this lethal association of "drugs and small arms" are invariably controlled by the underground economy, and there is in the world today a wider spectrum of ethnic identities to mafia networks of protection, money-laundering and enforcement, operating in both the supply and marketing domains. Not surprisingly, the trans-shipment of this lethal pair is perhaps the most threatening and destabilizing influence that Caribbean and Central American societies face as a consequence of their unfortunate geographical location in between the South American suppliers and the North American consumers of heroin and cocaine. The growth in gun violence in societies previously not known for such armed confrontations, and frontier-style "rough" justice, is not an unrelated residual of the globalizing penetration of such underground, highly profitable commerce.

International trafficking of children and women, and exploitation of refugees: the new slavery

A new slavery is violating vulnerable people's rights, and it is an unsavory, deregulated industry. "Human trafficking" among international criminal groups, syndicates and organizations has become a new form of slavery and coercion, preying upon young women and children by offering hope, while tricking, brutalizing and selling them into prostitution and sex-working, sweat-shop labor, and similar illicit, dehumanizing and/or dangerous occupations in which they have little autonomy or basic rights and human dignities (Bales 1999, 2000; Williams 1999).

In this dehumanizing realm of transnational criminal activity, women and children are valued exclusively as commodities and disposable assets, rather than as human beings. A related "trafficking" phenomenon, though not perceived in the same light as the illicit sex industry, is equally dehumanizing and threatening to the world's most vulnerable children. Some 16 percent of the world's children are caught up in child labor, and around one in eight children are engaged in either hazardous work or the very worst abusive and coercive forms of child labor. Persistent poverty, inadequate education, economic shocks and natural and human disasters and crises precipitate many of these children into coercive work environments, which can not only maim and scar them, but can have long-term debilitating effects on their growth and maturation. Ending child exploitation is one more challenge for the globalizing world, in which neoliberal and deregulatory economic environments favor the employer, not the employed, and favor the intermediary "facilitator," recruiter and smuggler, not the disadvantaged, disposable child (UNICEF UK 2004).

Globalization and the environment: two steps forward, one step back?

The important population–environment relationship: over-consumption

While the advanced capitalist societies of the Global North promote, yet suffer from, thoughtless over-consumption of the world's environmental resources, the Global South's poor practice conservation and survival with the most modest amount of resources at their disposal. Not inconsequentially, there are wide technological gaps that parallel this situation, with high-technology accompanying and aiding and abetting the consumption of resources, while low-technology labor-intensive methods of production feature prominently in the poor's survival strategies. Advocates of intermediate, or alternative, technologies as environmentally friendly and appropriate replacements for capital-intensive technological solutions find common cause with grassroots activists who welcome the mobilization of local people to find communal solutions for their everyday problems of resource scarcity and political ecological limits (Price 1999).

Global eco-politics

Such is the state of environmental insecurity in today's world that some writers fear that international environmental relations will be influenced by power relations and military interventions as states view their access to resources in terms of national security, and wars are fought over oil, water, energy sources and forest depletions, among other environmental issues (Mofson 1999). In recent decades, environmental and developmental issues have assumed a higher political profile. Supranational debates and protocol signings may be an integral part of the geopolitical discourse on the environment, but a global consensus is still a long way off. Environmental degradation and the possible impacts of climate change, rising sea levels, global warming and the like have been the focus of global debates in which planetary sustainability, militarism, global governance and regulation have been viewed as interrelated processes, but there is still a distinct lack of global regulatory authority in this essential arena (Dodds 2000; Speth 2003).

Is a fair, alternative globalization possible?

Proponents hail globalization as a societal transformation that has brought more democratic regimes into being, has realized huge efficiency gains in production, capitalist competition and exchange, enhanced consumer satisfaction (at least, among those able to purchase commodities), increased environmental consciousness, enabled greater intercultural communication and brought an end to the Cold War, East–West arms race. We critics, on the other hand, fault globalization for deepening social inequality, impeding social democracy, imposing a post-colonial imperialism, suppressing vulnerable nationalities and cultures, undermining every fabric of community, assaulting human rights of the most vulnerable, contributing to environmental and ecological degradation and deterioration, and compromising every claim to knowledge – by allowing it to be privately appropriated for profit (Scholte 2000).

In terms of resistance and opposition to the "globalization from above" that has precipitated us into the current stage of crises and disruptions, "globalization from below" is responding with experiments in alternative forms of social democracy and popular political institutions, alternative kinds of local and regional economic restructuring, alternative modes of identity politics, alternative approaches to ecology and alternative constructions of knowledge. These *alternative globalizations* are viewed as empowering and emancipatory reactions to the disastrous consequences of the globalization wolf in its neoliberal sheep's clothing (Scholte 2000).

We wholeheartedly believe that the world desperately needs a *fair globalization* – an alternative path, more sustainable, more socially just and accountable, more democratic. Being anti-globalization isn't sufficient, though it is an essential starting line. If we are to craft a path for a sustainable future, then it is crucial to liberate the full complement of assets that current and future generations need for humankind to progress. These assets are: *human capital* – the skills, knowledge and education embodied in human beings; *natural capital* – the stock of biophysical resources and the waste-handling capacity of natural environmental systems; *human-made capital* – machines, infrastructure, production and logistics systems; *social capital* – the social "webs of common interest" that bind families, interest groups and communities together, which build self-reliance, empower people, and increase local democratic participation; and *technological change* – the process by which these human assets' utilities are maximized, and the per-capita levels of these assets are raised so that the poor and future generations can have a better quality of life (Pearce 2002).

It's democracy, stupid! The need for global democracy institution-building

In a powerful and critical assessment of the state of our global world, the New Economics Foundation (Simms *et al.* 2000) answered the question about "what's the big issue with globalization" using a succinct paraphrasing of Bill Clinton's "It's democracy, stupid." Their summation was that the most powerful multilateral institutions currently directing and disciplining (and some of us would add, destroying and distorting) the global economy – the International Monetary Fund (IMF), World Bank and GATT's stepchild, the World Trade Organization (WTO) – are also among the least democratic and inclusive. Many of the financial sector's oversight commissions, though national rather than international regulatory bodies, are similarly undemocratic and exclusive, and unaccountable to the public good.

To make matters worse, the United Nations may be (in theory) a truly representative forum in the international system, but its supranational effectiveness has been continually undermined. It has either been crippled by superpower political wrangling and the glaring anachronism of the imbalance of members of the UN Security Council, or its anti-war and peaceful coexistence principles have been compromised by the most powerful nation-states' military expeditions and national defense alliances, by rogue-state unilateralism, and by illegal globalization's "criminal capitalism" – drug and human trafficking, arms-smuggling, bribery and corruption. The Non-Aligned Movement, today's G-77 Group, among other political alliances of the disadvantaged peripheral states, may find voice in the General Assembly, and in UN Commissions, forums and conferences; but the geopolitical power within the body is nakedly demonstrated by G-8 members. Especially in recent years, the United States – as the world's only remaining military superpower – has wielded unilateral, hegemonic authority, by "negotiating" (?) bilateral agreements, and only rarely has embraced multilateral agendas, or sought to ally itself with consensus-builders and humanitarian agencies within the UN. Instead, the business-friendly "Washington consensus" was to be fostered.

An agenda for progressive globalization

Developing a progressive social democratic future will require coalition-building, global forums and international dialogues across cultures – from East to West, North and South – among progressive groups with a common purpose to guide humanity towards a sustainable future; including, but not restricted to, social–democratic parties aspiring to government, labor and trade union movements, landless and peoples' popular movements, indigenous peoples' movements, NGOs and civil society. These must be developed globally, within Europe, between

Europe and the realms of the developing world or South, and South–South dialogues, including an American hemisphere not dominated (and dictated to) by US-led imperialism and US-promoted neoliberalism (i.e. NAFTA, FTAA, Plan Colombia).

Social democrats take a non-neoclassical approach to economic progress, and make a crucial distinction between individual markets and market forces, which are the collective outcomes of those markets. Left to themselves – or worse, monopolized by capital for accumulation's sake – market forces generate many problems damaging to the public good. Because market forces are unaccountable, they are essentially beyond democratic regulation and management. Social democracy, therefore, seeks to use the democratic state to manage capitalism to avoid these problematic effects of market forces. In turn, individual markets (for labor, capital, goods and services) are regulated for the dual protection of capital *and labor, consumers and the environment*, and institutional mechanisms are established at the supranational and national levels to control instability, redistribute resources to the disadvantaged, impoverished and destitute, as well as provide a plethora of social goods – healthcare, education, welfare. In a nutshell, "social democracy presents itself as a moral force, aiming to create a decent human society; and as the ultimate guarantor of capitalist wealth creation" (Fabian Global Forum 2003a).

Such a social–democratic approach to the management of globalization requires discussion and consensus-building over many areas of policy, and in many different spheres of society. Fuller coverage of just such an agenda is discussed elsewhere (Fabian Global Forum 2003b), but what follows here is a skeleton of the brief.

1. Political issues: governance, security and culture

- Democratic governance – building national democracies with protection for human rights, and increasing the democratic legitimacy of international institutions by making them an accountable and coherent system of supranational governance; i.e. answerable to citizens and civil society.
- Security and conflict mediation – building a new global security system and strengthening international law, global legal frameworks and protocols.
- Culture – protecting cultural diversity and indigenous cultures and allowing autonomous nation-building within states.

2. Trade and exchange

- Social and environmental minimums and rights, including the relationship of minimum standards to trade agreements, international property rights, and the regulation of transnational corporate power.
- Fair-trade frameworks and rules fashioned both for autonomous national development (including protectionist measures) as well as for multilateral efficiencies.

- Provision of basic social goods (health, education, water) by public and public–private capital investment portfolios.
- Financial architecture, including debt reduction and forgiveness – a new "Bretton Woods" settlement of international financial regulatory mechanisms.

3. Global redistribution

- Development aid and global taxation – the use of non-discretionary mechanisms for raising funds for sustainable development according to national or private abilities to pay.
- Migration – developing just and workable frameworks for peoples' mobility in the search for "decent work" (Fabian Global Forum 2003b).

Fair globalization: a socially just manifesto

The International Labour Organization's (ILO's) pursuit of "labor-friendly" notions to counter neoliberalism's favoritism of capital interests began in the 1990s, when it fashioned an important conceptual argument and associated policy agenda concerning the ideas of *social protection* and *decent work* as essential development goals. "Social protection" is cast in the framework of a development-rights based approach, where the security of life, livelihood and citizenship needs is taken as a basic right of all individuals in all societies. "Decent work" is somewhat beyond the ILO's traditional mandate – work conditions, technical cooperation, child labor protection and the like. It is a more emancipatory concept and challenges neoliberal globalization's cosseting of capital interests. As an interventionist concept, highlighting the status, rights and role of labor, this call for social protection of the excluded, the unemployed, unskilled and vulnerable, and their basic right to decent work, opens up a countervailing strategic space to that promoted and expounded by capital and its protagonists. "It potentially reclaims visibility and voice for silenced and subordinated labour" (Saith 2004: 4).

The World Commission on the Social Dimension of Globalization recently (February 24, 2004) presented their report to the ILO, in which they urged the building of a *fair* and *inclusive* globalization as a worldwide priority. Focusing upon globalization's social dimension, the World Commission addressed many domains of policy-making and institutional organization – such as trade and capital market liberalization, international standards for labor, the environment, corporate behavior, agreements on intellectual property rights, migration and other integrationist policies pursued at both the national and international levels. Specifically, the impacts of globalization on the life and work of people, on their families and societies were scrutinized and concerns were raised about the impact of globalization on employment, working conditions, income inequalities and social protection. The social dimension should include also "social protection" issues beyond the world of work; importantly, security, culture and identity, inclusion and/or exclusion and the cohesiveness of families and communities.

The World Commission's "vision" was that a better world was "do-able" but that it would take a major commitment for a sustainable future to be achieved. Notably, the strategies that were advocated built upon social democratic precepts, not those of the Washington Consensus. Several themes underpinned the report's recommendations, the most important being: "Beginning at home" in local and national arenas; "Fair rules and equitable policies" in the governance of global markets; "Reinforcing the UN multilateral system" by improving the quality of global governance, and democratizing parallel governing institutions; "Buy-in of multiple stakeholders" to increase accountability and citizenry participation; and "Utilizing the value and power of dialogue" as an instrument for change at local, national, regional and global levels (ILO 2004).

Return to scale: localization is the alternative scale

The year 2003 marked the thirtieth anniversary of Fritz Schumacher's (1973) classic *Small is Beautiful*, in which he called for "a study of economics as if people mattered." Scale matters, local scale matters, people's immediate environments are those which matter the most. Global matters, by contrast, are remote, beyond control, beyond accountability. Local is the antithesis of global in terms of human–environment interactions, although global-to-local linkages and interactions have come to fruition in today's globalizing world. "Glocalization" is a term coined to represent such forms of global entanglement, which influence, often in disparate ways, the paths of local development and empowerment (Bebbington 2000; Swyngedouw 1997).

Swyngedouw (1997) appears to have it right when he identifies different spatial scales – global, national and local – as arenas and (space–time) moments that are socially produced, where global, national and local power relations intersect – are contested – and where conflicts and compromises are negotiated. Spatial scales are not, however, fixed in an immutable hierarchy in which structural influences flow down from top to bottom through scalar levels, from the global to the local. More contingently, peoples' territorial and environmental envelopes, in which activities, livelihoods and behaviors occur, are systemic products of changing technologies, modes of human organization and geopolitical negotiation and struggle (Harvey 2000).

Utopian though they may seem, progressive ideas on localization's appropriateness as the scale at which a "people-centered, ecologically sustainable development" can be achieved point the way to a twenty-first century in which new lifestyles, new technologies, new enterprises, new approaches to governance, to business management and to welfare service delivery, promise a more equitable future for all (Robertson 1998). Daly and Cobb's (1990) *For the Common Good*, Ekins and Max-Neef's (1992) *Real-Life Economics*, and the New Economics Foundation's (2003a) *Return to Scale* all present convincing arguments that localization is an essential alternative to neoliberal globalization and the "unsustainable" advanced capitalism it promulgates.

While we too are sympathetic to these alternative visions and their sustainable goals, a nostalgic yearning for a simpler, less volatile, more manageable and secure life – *and attaining it* – is unlikely to be a realistic solution for the world's six billion, the majority of whom are trying to survive under a capitalist system that has scarcely lost its momentum, and certainly has not lost its power. Local/global relationships are deepening, local communities can no longer behave as self-reliant autonomous entities, and the local–national–global scalar system has tied "most everyone" together, even if such hierarchical ties are not evenly developed, and the many of the world's remoter localities remain marginal and beyond the scope of "global reach" (Barnet 1974; Bebbington 2000).

The nation-state, particularly one in which social democracy flourishes, representative government is accountable to all its citizenry, and the regional and local institutional structures are well developed, and well integrated into peoples' affective social relations, can play an essential intermediary role in muting the local/global nexus of interrelationships to the benefit of locales and their people. Struggles for decent work, for social protection, for environmental justice, will need to be fought (or negotiated) at national and "supranational" global levels. Conflicts over resource access, over sovereignty issues, and class conflicts and fundamental disputes between capital and labor will all be part of the crucible, and will be instrumental in determining whether a forward (or backward) path is taken.

Our choice is simple: democratic global governance or global dictatorship?

Neoliberal capitalism and neoliberal modernization have not only forced disciplinary punishments on the unfortunate and impoverished, but they have been as destructive as they have been transformative, contradictory as they have privileged the already privileged, and unruly and volatile in their geographies. Yet, they have also empowered resistance, consolidated grassroots movements and mobilized progressive forces, and convinced us that the world needs a different path, a different and sustainable model of fair globalization. George Monbiot (2004) in his *Manifesto for a New World Order* has called for drastic action in global governance, such as the replacement of the World Bank and the IMF – neoliberalism's disciplinarian institutions – by a "Keynesian" International Clearing Union. His progressive arguments, as well as Herman Daly's, Hazel Henderson's and Ray Kiely's, are all worth digesting in full.

Finally, as George Monbiot (2003) reminds us, we must not forget that global governance takes place whether or not "we the people" participate in it. His call for a new world order is an appropriate concluding reminder to this anthology:

> Now is the time to turn our campaigns against the war-mongering, wealth-concentrating, planet-consuming world order, into a concerted campaign for global democracy. We must become the Chartists and Suffragettes of the 21st Century. They understood that to change the world you must propose as well as oppose. They democratised the nation; now we must seek to democratise the world. Our task is not to overthrow globalization, but to capture it, and use it as a vehicle for humanity's first global democratic revolution.
>
> (Monbiot 2003: 4)

References

Abrams, E. *et al.* 1997. "Statement of Principles." www.newamericancentury.org/statement ofprinciples.htm

ActionAid 1999a. "Astrazeneca and its Genetic Research: Feeding the World or Fueling Hunger?" www.actionaid.org/

—— 1999b. "Crops and Robbers: Biopiracy and the Patenting of Staple Food Crops." www.actionaid.org/

—— 2000. "Trade Related Intellectual Property Rights (TRIPs) and Farmers' Rights." www.actionaid.org/

Adams, N. 1994. "The UN's Neglected Brief," in E. Childers (ed.) *Challenges to the United Nations: Building a Safer World*. London: Catholic Institution for International Relations (CIIR).

Adams, P. 1999. "The Debts of Corruption," Jubilee 2000 Features. www.jubilee2000uk.org/

Adler, P. S. 1990. "Shared Learning," *Management Science* 36(8): 938–957.

Agnew, J. 1987. *The United States in the World Economy: A Regional Geography*. Cambridge: Cambridge University Press.

—— 1999. "North America and the Wider World," in F. W. Boal and S. A. Royle (eds) *North America: A Geographical Mosaic*. London: Arnold.

—— 2003. "A World that Knows No Boundaries? The Geopolitics of Globalization and the Myth of the Borderless World," Centre for International Borders Research, Queens University Belfast, CIBR Working Paper in Border Studies, CIBR/WP03-2: www.qub/ac/uk/cibr/WPpdffiles/CIBRwp2-3_2.pdf

—— 2005. *Hegemony: The New Shape of Global Power*. Philadelphia, PA: Temple University Press.

—— and S. Corbridge 1995. *Mastering Space: Hegemony, Territory, and International Political Economy*. London: Routledge.

Aguilar, J. V. and M. Cavada 2002. *Ten Plagues of Globalization*. Washington, DC: EPICA (transl. K. Ogle).

Ahmad, E. 2001. *Terrorism: Theirs and Ours*. New York: Seven Stories Press.

Ajami, F. 2001. "The Sentry's Solitude," *Foreign Affairs* 80(6): 2–16.

Alberts, S. 2003. "Outspoken Bush Critic to Join Democratic Fray," *Calgary Herald*, September 17, A11.

Allen, C. 2005. *An Industrial Geography of Cocaine*. London: Routledge.

Alterman, E. 2003a. *What Liberal Media? The Truth about Bias and the News*. New York: Basic Books.

—— 2003b. "Why Chickenhawks Matter," *The Nation*, December 1, 10.

American Red Cross 2003. "American Red Cross – History Timeline." www.redcross.org/museum/briefarc.html

Amin, A. 2002. "Spatialities of Globalization," *Environment and Planning A* 34(3): 385–399.

—— and S. Graham 1997. "The Ordinary City," *Transactions, Institute of British Geographers* 22(4): 411–429.

—— and N. Thrift 2004. *Cultural Economy Reader*. Oxford: Blackwell.

Amin, S. 1997. *Capitalism in the Age of Globalization*. London: Zed Books.

—— 2002. "Africa: Living on the Fringe," *Monthly Review* 53(10): 41–50.

—— 2003. The Alternative to the Neoliberal System of Globalization and Militarism: Imperialism Today and the Hegemonic Offensive of the United States. Contra informació en red, NODO50.org. www.nodo50.org/cubasiglioXXI/congreso/amin_25feb03.pdf

Anderson, B. 1991. *Imagined Communities: Reflections on the Origins and Spread of Nationalism* (rev. edn). London: Verso.

Anderson, M. and E. Bort 1999. *The Irish Border: History, Politics, Culture*. Liverpool: University of Liverpool Press.

Anderson, S. 2000. *Views from the South: The Effects of Globalization and the WTO on the Third World*. Oakland, CA: FoodFirst Books.

—— and J. Cavanagh 2000. *Top 200: The Rise of Global Corporate Power*. Global Policy Forum, Corporate Watch 2000, www.globalpolicy.org/socecon/tncs/top200.htm

——, J. Cavanagh and T. Lee 2000. *Field Guide to the Global Economy*. New York: New Press and W.W. Norton.

Andreas, P. 1999. "When Policies Collide: Market Reform, Market Prohibition, and the Narcotization of the Mexican Economy," in R. H. Friman and P. Andreas (eds) *The Illicit Global Economy and State Power*. Boulder, CO: Rowman & Littlefield, pp. 125–141.

—— 2000. *Border Games: Policing the US–Mexico Divide*. Ithaca, NY: Cornell University Press.

Appadurai, A. 1996. *Modernity at Large: Cultural Dimensions of Globalization*. Minneapolis, MN: University of Minnesota Press.

Arnold, M. 1993. *Culture and Anarchy and Other Writings*. Cambridge: Cambridge University Press.

Arrighi, G. 1990. "The Three Hegemonies of Historical Capitalism," *Review* 13, 365–408.

—— 1994. *The Long Twentieth Century: Money, Power, and the Origins of Our Times*. London: Verso.

—— and B. J. Silver 1999. *Chaos and Governance in the Modern World System*. Minneapolis, MN: University of Minnesota Press.

Arquilla, J. and D. Ronfeldt 2001. *Networks and Netwars*, National Defense Research Institute.

Art and Culture 2003. Verner Panton. www.artandculture.com/arts/artist

Art, R. J. 1991. "A Defensible Defense: America's Grand Strategy after the Cold War," *International Security* 15, 5–53.

Aulakh, P. S. and M. G. Schechter 2000. *Rethinking Globalization(s): From Corporate Transnationalism to Local Interventions*. New York: St Martin's and Macmillan Presses.

Axelsson, B. and G. Easton 1992. *Industrial Networks: A New View of Reality*. London: Routledge.

Babich, P. [host of radio interview] 2000. "A Popular Uprising: A Look at Ecuador's Coup." www.radioproject.org/archive/2000/0020.html

Bach, S. 2004. "Migration Patterns of Physicians and Nurses: Still the Same Story?" *Bulletin of the World Health Organization* 82(8): 624–625.

Bain, J. S. 1959. *Industrial Organization*. New York: John Wiley.
Baker, K. 2003. *An Uncooperative Commodity*. Oxford: Oxford University Press.
Bales, K. 2000a. *Disposable People: New Slavery in the Global Economy*. Berkeley, CA: University of California Press.
—— 2000b. *New Slavery: A Reference Handbook*. Santa Barbara, CA: ABC-Clio.
Ballvé, T. 2005. "Bolivia's Separatist Movement," in *Social Movements: Building from the Ground Up*, Special Issue, NACLA Report of the Americas, March/April, 38(5): 16–17.
Bamyeh, M. A. 2000. *The Ends of Globalization*. Minneapolis, MN: University of Minneapolis Press.
Bangkok Declaration 1999. *The Bangkok Declaration on Irregular Migration*. www.thaiembdc.org/info/bdin.html
Banks, J. 1997. "MTV and the Globalization of Popular Culture," *Gazette* 59(1): 43–60.
Barber, B. 1996. *Jihad vs. McWorld: How Globalism and Tribalism are Reshaping the World*. New York: Ballantine.
—— 2002. "Democracy and Terror in the Era of Jihad vs. McWorld," in Ken Booth and Tim Dunne (eds) *Worlds in Collision: Terror and the Future of the Global Order*. New York: Palgrave Macmillan, pp. 245–262.
—— 2003. *Fear's Empire: War, Terrorism, and Democracy*. New York: W. W. Norton.
Barff, R. 1995. "Multinational Corporations and the New International Division of Labor," in R. J. Johnston *et al.* (eds) *Geographies of Global Change: Remapping the World in the Late Twentieth Century*. Oxford: Blackwell, pp. 50–62.
Barnet, R. J. 1974. *Global Reach: The Power of Multinational Corporations*. New York: Simon & Schuster.
—— and J. Cavanagh 1994. *Global Dreams: Imperial Corporations and the New World Order*. New York: Simon & Schuster.
Barnum, B. 2004. "What It Means to Know: Reflections on a Visit to Chiapas," Common Dreams NewsCenter, 22 April: www.commondreams.org/views04/0421-09.htm
Bayart, J.-F., S. Ellis and B. Hibou 1999. *The Criminalization of the State in Africa*. Bloomington, IN: Indiana University Press.
BBC News 1998. "World Americas: 'They Couldn't Kill His Songs'." BBC Online Network (http://news.bbc.co.uk/2/hi/americas/165363.stm), 5 September.
—— 2005a. "Al Qaeda Shadow Looms over London." http://news.bbc.co.uk/1/hi/uk/4661273.stm
—— 2005b. "The British Illegal Immigrants," BBC News Magazine, 2 February. http://news.bbc.co.uk/2/hi/uk_news/magazine/4226949.stm
Beaverstock, J. V. 2001. "Transnational Elite Communities in Global Cities: Connectivities, Flows and Networks," GAWC Research Bulletin 63, Globalization and World Cities Study Group and Network, Loughborough University, UK. www.mi.vt.edu/Research/Files/Transnationalelite.pdf
Bebbington, A. 2000. "Globalized Andes? Livelihoods, Landscapes and Development," *Ecumene* 8(4): 414–436.
Bello, W. 2002. *Deglobalization: Ideas for a New World Economy*. London: Zed Books.
Bennett, B. 2005. "The Perils of Defending a Tyrant," *Time*, 28 November.
Bennett, C. J. 1991. "What is Policy Convergence and What Causes It?" *British Journal of Political Science* 21, 215–253.
Benton, T. 1996. *The Greening of Marxism*. New York: Guilford Press.
Berberoglu, B. 2004. *Nationalism and Ethnic Conflict: Class, State, and Nation in the Age of Globalization*. Lanham, MD: Rowman & Littlefield.

Bergen, P. 2002. *Holy War, Inc.: Inside the Secret World of Osama bin Laden.* New York: Free Press.
Berger, J. 1972. *Ways of Seeing.* London: Penguin.
—— 2003. "Fear Eats the Soul," *The Nation*, 12 May, 33–35.
Berger, P. L. and S. P. Huntington 2002. *Many Globalizations: Cultural Diversity in the Contemporary World.* Oxford: Oxford University Press.
BIS (Bank for International Settlements) 1997. *Compendium of Documents Produced by the Basle Committee on Banking Supervision. Vol. 1: Basic Supervisory Methods.* Basle: BIS.
—— 1999. *69th Annual Report.* Basle: BIS.
—— 2001. *The New Basle Capital Accord.* Basle: BIS.
—— and IOSCO (International Organisation of Securities Commissions) 1995. *Framework for Supervisory Information about the Derivatives Activities of Banks and Securities Firms.* Basle: BIS.
Black, R. 2001. "Environmental Refugees: Myth or Reality? New Issues in Refugee Research," Working Paper 34, UNHCR. www.jha.ac/articles/u034.pdf
Blaut, J. 1993. *The Colonizers' Model of the World.* New York: Guilford Press.
Blouet, B. W. 2001. *Geopolitics and Globalization in the Twentieth Century.* London: Reaktion Books.
Board of Banking Supervision 1995. *The Report of the Board of Banking Supervision into the Circumstances of the Collapse of Barings.* London: HMSO, HC673.
Bogusz, B., R. Cholewinski, A. Cygan and E. S. Zyszcak 2004. *Irregular Migration and Human Rights: Theoretical, European and International Perspectives.* Leiden: Martinus Nijhoff.
Bomberg, E. E. 1998. *Green Parties and Politics in the European Union.* London: Routledge.
Bootle, R. 1996. *The Death of Inflation.* London: Nicholas Brearly.
Borosage, R. 1999. "The Battle in Seattle," *The Nation*, 6 December.
Bourdieu, P. 1984. *Distinction: A Social Critique of the Judgment of Taste.* Cambridge, MA: Harvard University Press (transl. R. Nice).
—— 1998. "The Essence of Neoliberalism," *Le Monde diplomatique*, December.
Bowden, M. 2001. *Killing Pablo.* New York: Atlantic Monthly Press.
Boyle, P., K. Halfacree and V. Robinson 1998. *Exploring Contemporary Migration.* Harlow: Pearson Education.
Bray, J. 1998. "Web Wars: NGOs, Companies and Governments in an Internet-connected Age," *Greener Management International* 24: 115–130.
Brecher, J. and T. Costello 1998. *Global Village to Global Pillage: Economic Reconstruction from the Bottom Up*, 2nd edn. Cambridge, MA: South End Press.
——, T. Costello and B. Smith 2000. *Globalization from Below: The Power of Solidarity.* Cambridge, MA: South End Press.
Brenner, N. and N. Theodore 2002a. *Spaces of Neoliberalism: Urban Restructuring in North America and Western Europe.* Oxford: Blackwell.
—— 2002b. "Cities and the Geographies of 'Actually Existing Neoliberalism'," *Antipode* 34(3): 356–380.
Brenner, R. 2002. *The Boom and the Bubble: The US in the World Economy.* London: Verso.
Briguglio, L. 1995. "Small Island Developing States and their Economic Vulnerabilities," *World Development* 23(9): 1615–1632.
Brown, L. R. 2005a. "China Replacing the United States as World's Leading Consumer," Earth Policy Institute, *Eco-Economy Updates*, 16 February 2005, 1.

References

—— 2005b. "Learning from China: Why the Western Economic Model will not Work for the World," Earth Policy Institute, *Eco-Economy Updates*, 9 March 2005, 2.
Brown, P. and R. McNaughton 2002. "Global Competitiveness and Local Networks: A Review of the Literature," in R. McNaughton and M. Green (eds) *Global Competition and Local Networks*. Aldershot: Ashgate, pp. 3–37.
Bruggeman, W. 2002. "Illegal Immigration and Trafficking in Human Beings Seen as a Security Problem for Europe," paper presented at the STOP II European Conference, Brussels, Belgium, September. www.belgium.iom.int/STOPConference/Conference%20Papers/20%20Bruggeman%20Brussels%20IOM.19.09.02.pdf
Bruno, K. and J. Karliner 2002. *Earthsummit.biz: The Corporate Takeover of Sustainable Development*. Oakland, CA: FoodFirst Books.
Bryan, L. and D. Farrell 1996. *Market Unbound*. New York: John Wiley.
BTS 2002. *US International Travel and Transportation Trends*. Washington, DC: Department of Transportation, Bureau of Transportation Statistics, BTS02-03.
Burbach, R., O. Nunez and B. Kagarlitsky. 1997. *Globalization and its Discontents: The Rise of Postmodern Socialisms*. London: Pluto Press.
Burchell, J. 2002. *The Evolution of Green Politics: Development and Change within European Green Parties*. London: Earthscan.
Burnell, P. 2002. "Foreign Aid in a Changing World," in V. Desai and R. B. Potter (eds) *The Companion to Development Studies*. New York: Oxford University Press, pp. 473–476.
Business Week 2000. "Special Report. Global Capitalism: Can It Be Made to Work Better?" 6 November, pp. 72–100.
Cafruny, A. W. 1990. "A Gramscian Concept of Declining Hegemony: Stages of US Power and the Evolution of International Economic Relations," in D. Rapkin (ed.) *World Leadership and Hegemony*. Boulder, CO: Lynne Rienner.
Calleo, D. P. 1987. *Beyond American Hegemony: The Future of the Western Alliance*. New York: Basic Books.
Camdessus, M. 1998. "Toward a New Architecture for a Globalised World," address at the Royal Institute for International Affairs, 8 May. Available from the International Monetary Fund, 700 19th Street, N.W., Washington, DC 20431 (www.imf.org).
Cammagni, R. 1991. *Innovation Networks: Spatial Perspectives*. London: Belhaven Press.
Campbell, D. 1992. *Writing Security: United States Foreign Policy and the Politics of Identity*. Minneapolis, MN: University of Minnesota Press.
Carling, J. 2005. "Gender Dimensions of International Migration," *Global Migration Perspectives* 35. Geneva: Global Commission on International Migration.
Carlsen, L. 2002. "Indigenous Communities in Latin America: Fighting for Control of Natural Resources in a Globalized Age," *A Self-Determination Commentary: Foreign Policy in Focus*, July. www.fpif.org/
Cassen, B. 2005. "Romance Speakers Unite," *Le Monde diplomatique*, March.
Castells, M. 1989. *The Informational City: Information Technology, Economic Restructuring and the Urban–Regional Process*. Oxford: Blackwell.
—— 1996. *The Rise of the Network Society*. Oxford: Blackwell.
—— 1998. "The Perverse Connection: The Global Criminal Economy," in *End of Millennium*. Oxford: Blackwell.
—— 2000. *The Rise of Network Society*. Oxford: Blackwell.
—— 2004. *The Power of Identity*, 2nd edn. Malden, MA: Blackwell.
Castles, S. 1995. "Contract Labour Migration," in R. Cohen (ed.) *The Cambridge Survey of World Migration*. Cambridge: Cambridge University Press, pp. 510–514.

—— 2000. *Ethnicity and Globalization: From Migrant Worker to Transnational Citizen.* London: Sage.
—— 2003a. "Towards a Sociology of Forced Migration and Social Transformation," *Sociology* 37(1): 13–34.
—— 2003b. "The International Politics of Forced Migration," *Development* 46(3): 11–20.
—— 2004. *Confronting the Fundamentals of Forced Migration*, Migration Information Source, Washington, DC: Migration Policy Institute. www.migrationinformation.org/Profiles/display.cfm?ID=2722
—— and A. Davidson 2000. *Citizenship and Migration: Globalization and the Politics of Belonging.* Basingstoke: Palgrave.
—— and M. J. Miller 1998. *The Age of Migration*, 2nd edn. New York: Guilford Press.
—— and M. J. Miller 2003. *The Age of Migration: International Population Movements in the Modern World*, 3rd edn. Basingstoke: Palgrave Macmillan.
Castree, N. 1995. "The Nature of Produced Nature: Materiality and Knowledge Construction in Marxism," *Antipode* 27: 12–48.
—— 2005. "The Epistemology of Particulars: Human Geography, Case Studies and 'Context'," *Geoforum* 36: 541–544.
Catchpole, B. 1982. *A Map History of China.* London: Heinemann Educational.
Cerny, P. G. 1997. "The New Governance: Governing Without Governance," *Political Studies* 45, 1–2.
—— 1998a. "Capital Ungoverned: Liberalising Finance in Interventionist States," *Millennium-Journal of International Studies* 27: 353–361.
—— 1998b. "Governments, Banks and Global Capital: Securities Markets in Global Politics," *Millennium-Journal of International Studies* 27: 353–361.
Chanda, N. 2003. *What Is Globalization?* http://yaleglobal.yale.edu (accessed 17 July 2005).
Chin, J. K. 2003. "Reducing Irregular Migration from China," *International Migration* 41(3): 49–70.
Chomsky, N. 1999. *Profit over People: Neoliberalism and Global Order.* New York: Seven Stories Press.
—— 2003. *Hegemony or Survival: America's Quest for Global Dominance.* New York: Metropolitan Books.
Chossudovsky, M. 1997. *The Globalisation of Poverty: Impacts of IMF and World Bank Reforms.* Penang, Malaysia: Third World Network.
Choudry, A. 2003. "The Twin Terrors: Neoliberal Globalization and the War against Humanity," Montreal: Centre for Research on Globalization. http://globalresearch.ca/articles/AZ1309A.html
Christian Aid 1999. *Selling Suicide: Farming, False Promises and Genetic Engineering in Developing Countries.* www.christian-aid.org.uk/reports/suicide/index.htm
Chua, A. 2003. *World on Fire: How Exporting Free Market Democracy Breeds Ethnic Hatred and Global Instability.* New York: Doubleday.
Clark, G. L. 2000. *Pension Fund Capitalism.* Oxford: Oxford University Press.
Clark, G. L., D. Mansfield and A. Tickell 2001. "Emergent Frameworks in Global Finance," *Economic Geography* 77: 250–271.
—— 2002. "Global Finance and the German Model: German Corporations, Market Incentives, and the Management of Employer-sponsored Pension Institutions," *Transactions, Institute of British Geographers, NS* 27(1): 91–110.
Clawson, D. L. 2000. *Latin America and the Caribbean: Lands and People.* Boston, MA: McGraw-Hill.

Cleaver, H. 2000. *Reading Capital Politically*. San Francisco, CA: AK Press.
COHA (Council on Hemispheric Affairs) 2003. Research Memorandum (cited 9 October 2003). www.theamericas.org/whitehouse_in_latinamerica.htm
Cohen, S. B. 1994. "Geopolitics in the New World Era: A New Perspective on an Old Discipline," in G. J. Demko and W. B. Woods (eds) *Reordering the World: Geopolitical Perspectives on the Twenty-first Century*. Boulder, CO: Westview Press, pp. 15–48.
Collier, G. A. 2000. "Zapatismo Resurgent: Land and Autonomy in the Chiapas," *NACLA Report on the Americas* 33(5): 20–25.
—— and E. L. Quaratiello 1999. *Basta! Land and the Zapatista Rebellion in Chiapas*. Oakland, CA: FoodFirst Books.
Collins, J. 2000. "A Sense of Possibility," *NACLA Report on the Americas*, March/April, 33(5): 40–49.
Collinson, H. 1996. *Green Guerrillas: Environmental Conflicts and Initiatives in Latin America and the Caribbean*. London: Latin American Bureau.
Collyer, M. 2003. "Explaining Change in Established Migration Systems: The Movement of Algerians to France and the UK," Sussex Migration Working Paper 16, Migration Research Centre, University of Sussex, Brighton.
CONAIE 2004. See www.conaie.org
Connell, J. and D. Conway 2000. "Migration and Remittances in Island Microstates: A Comparative Perspective on the South Pacific and the Caribbean," *International Journal of Urban and Regional Research* 24(1): 52–78.
Conradson, D. and A. Latham 2005. "Transnational Urbanism: Attending to Everyday Practices and Mobilities," *Journal of Ethnic and Migration Studies* 31(2): 227–233.
Conway, D. 2000a. "The Importance of Migration for Caribbean Development," *Global Development Studies* 2(1/2): 73–105.
—— 2000b. "Notions Unbounded: A Critical (Re)read of Transnationalism Suggests that US–Caribbean Circuits Tell the Story Better," in Biko Agozino (ed.) *Theoretical and Methodological Issues in Migration Research: Interdisciplinary, Intergenerational and International Perspectives*. Aldershot: Ashgate, pp. 203–226.
—— 2005. "Transnationalism and Return: 'Home' as an Enduring Fixture and 'Anchor'," in R. B. Potter, D. Conway and J. Phillips (eds) *The Experiences of Return Migration: Caribbean Perspectives*. Aldershot: Ashgate, pp. 263–281.
—— and J. H. Cohen 1998. "Consequences of Migration and Remittances for Mexican Transnational Communities," *Economic Geography* 74(1): 26–44.
—— and J. H. Cohen 2003. "Local Dynamics in Multi-local, Transnational Spaces of Rural Mexico: Oaxacan Experiences," *International Journal of Population Geography* 9(1): 1–21.
Cooke, P., M. G. Uranga and G. Etxebarria 1997. "Regional Innovation Systems: Institutional and Organizational Dimensions," *Research Policy* 26(4/5): 475–491.
Cooper, M. 2001. *Pinochet and Me: A Chilean Anti-Memoir*. London: Verso.
—— 2002. "From Protest to Politics: A Report from Porto Alegre," *The Nation*, 11 March, pp. 11–16.
Corbridge, S. 1992. "Discipline and Punish: The New Right and the Policing of the International Debt Crisis," *Geoforum* 23(3): 285–301.
Cordero-Guzmán, H. R., R. C. Smith and R. Grosfoguel 2001. *Migration, Transnationalization and Race in a Changing New York*. Philadelphia, PA: Temple University Press.
Cormier, T. 2001. "Transnational Crime in a Borderless World," in R. McRae and D. Hubert (eds) *Human Security and the New Diplomacy*. Montreal: McGill-Queen's University Press, pp. 199–205.

Cowhey, P. and J. Aronson 1993. *Managing the World Economy*. New York: Council on Foreign Relations Press.

Cox, H. 1999. "The Market as God: Living in the New Dispensation," *Atlantic Monthly*, March, pp. 18–23.

Cox, K. 2002. *Political Geography: Territory, State and Society*. Malden, MA: Blackwell.

Cox, R. W. 1998. "Latin America's New Insertion in the World Economy: Towards Systematic Competitiveness in Small Economies," *Journal of InterAmerican Studies and World Affairs* 40: 127–130.

Crankshaw, O. and S. Parnell 2004. "Johannesburg: Race, Inequality, and Urbanization," in J. Gugler (ed.) *World Cities Beyond the West: Globalization, Development and Inequality*. Cambridge: Cambridge University Press, pp. 348–370.

Crevoisier, O. and D. Maillat 1991. "Milieu, Industrial Organization and Territorial Production Systems: Towards a New Theory of Spatial Development," in R. Cammagni (ed.) *Innovation Networks: Spatial Perspectives*. London: Belhaven Press, pp. 13–34.

Crockett, A. 2001. "In Search of Anchors for Financial and Monetary Stability," in M. Balling, E. H. Hochreiter and E. Hennessy (eds) *Adapting to Financial Globalization*. London: Routledge, pp. 5–14.

Cross, G. 2000. *An All-Consuming Century: Why Commercialism Won in Modern America*. New York: Columbia University Press.

Dalby, S. 1990. *Creating the Second Cold War*. London: Pinter.

Dallaire, R. 2003. *Shake Hands with the Devil: The Failure of Humanity in Rwanda*. Toronto: Random House.

Daly, H. 2003. "Globalization's Major Inconsistencies," *Philosophy and Public Policy Quarterly* 23(4): 22–27.

——and J. B. Cobb 1994. *For the Common Good: Redirecting the Economy Towards Community, the Environment and a Sustainable Future*, 2nd edn. Boston, MA: Beacon Press.

Danaher, K. 1994. *Fifty Years is Enough: The Case Against the World Bank and the International Monetary Fund*. Boston, MA: South End Press.

Dasgupta, S. 2004. *The Changing Face of Globalization*. New Delhi: Sage.

Daudelin, J. and W. E. Hewitt 1995. "Churches and Politics in Latin America: Catholicism at the Crossroads," *Third World Quarterly* 16(2): 221–236.

Davidson, B. 1992. "The Bones and Blood of Racism," *Race and Class* 33(3).

Debord, G. 1994. *Society of the Spectacle*. New York: Zone Books (trans. Donald Nicholson Smith).

DeFleur, M. H. and M. L. DeFleur 2002. "How We're Seen: Foreign Teens See an Uglier American," *The Tallahassee Democrat*, October 27, p. 1E.

de Goede, M. 2001. "Discourses of Scientific Finance and the Failure of Long-term Capital Management," *New Political Economy* 6: 149–170.

DeLong, B. 1998, "Robber Barons," in Anders Aslund (ed.) *Perspectives on Russian Economic Development*. Moscow: Carnegie Endowment for International Peace. www.j-bradford-delong.net/Econ_Articles/Carnegie/DeLong_Moscow_paper2.html

Desai, M. 1994. "Second-hand Dealers in Ideas: Think Tanks and Thatcherite Hegemony," *New Left Review* 27: 68.

——2002. *Marx's Revenge: The Resurgence of Capitalism and the Death of Statist Socialism*. London: Verso.

Dicken, P. 1992a. "International Production in a Volatile Regulatory Environment: The Influence of National Regulatory Policies on the Spatial Strategies of Transnational Corporations," *Geoforum* 23: 303–316.

—— 1992b. "Wheels of Change: The Automobile Industry," in P. Dicken (ed.) *Global Shift*. New York: Guilford Press, pp. 268–308.

—— 1998. *Global Shift*, 3rd edn. London: Paul Chapman.

—— 2000. "Places and Flows: Situating International Investment," in G. Clark, M. Gertler and M. Feldman (eds) *Handbook of Economic Geography*. Oxford: Oxford University Press, pp. 275–291.

—— 2002. *Global Shift*. London: Harper & Collins.

—— 2003. *Global Shift: Reshaping the Global Economic Map in the 21st Century*, 4th edn. New York: Guilford Press.

—— 2004. "Geographers and 'Globalization': (Yet) Another Missed Boat?" *Transactions, Institute of British Geographers NS* 29: 5–26.

—— and M. Malmberg 2001. "Firms in Territories: A Relational Perspective," *Economic Geography* 77: 345–363.

——, J. Peck and A. Tickell 1997. "Unpacking the Global," in R. Lee and J. Willis (eds) *Geographies of Economies*. London: Arnold, pp. 158–166.

Díez-Nicolás, J. 2002. "Two Contradictory Hypotheses on Globalization: Societal Convergence or Civilization Differentiation and Clash." www.worldvaluessurvey.org (accessed 5 October 2005).

Dixit, A. K. and V. Norman 1980. *Theory of International Trade*. Welwyn, Herts: James Nisbet & Co.

Dobson, W. and C. S. Yue 1997. *Multinationals and East Asian Integration*. Canada: International Development Research Center.

Dodds, K. 1999. *Geopolitics in a Changing World*. New York: Prentice Hall.

—— 2000. "The Globalization of Environmental Issues," in K. Dodds (ed.) *Geopolitics in a Changing World*. London: Pearson Education, pp. 108–125.

Dolowitz, D. *et al.* 1999. *Parliamentary Affairs* 52.

Dor, D. 2004. "From Englishization to Imposed Multilingualism: Globalization, the Internet, and the Political Economy of the Linguistic Code," *Public Culture* 16(1): 97–118.

Drakakis-Smith, D. 1996. "Less-developed Economies and Dependence," in P. Daniels and W. Lever (eds) *The Global Economy in Transition*. Essex: Addison-Wesley Longman, pp. 215ff.

Drake, C. 1994. "The United Nations and NGOs: Future Roles," in G. J. Demko and W.B. Wood (eds) *Reordering the World: Geopolitical Perspectives on the Twenty-first Century*. Boulder, CO: Westview Press, pp. 243–268.

Dummett, A. 1995. "Internal Movement in the European Community," in R. Cohen (ed.) *The Cambridge Survey of World Migration*. Cambridge: Cambridge University Press, pp. 481–485.

Dunning, J. 1993. *The Globalization of Business: The Challenge of the 1990s*. New York: Routledge.

During, A. and T. Ayers 1994. "The History of a Cup of Coffee," *World Watch* 7(5): 20–22.

Eagleton, T. 2000. *The Idea of Culture*. Oxford: Blackwell.

Eatwell, J. and L. Taylor 2000. *Global Finance at Risk: The Case for International Regulation*. New York: The New Press.

Economist, The 1984. "The World Upside Down, Inside Out," 22 December.

—— 2000. "The Andean Coca Wars," 4 March: 23–25.

—— 2001. "Drugs, War and Democracy: A Survey of Colombia," 21 April: 1–16.

—— 2002. "Brand Wars in the Middle East: Regime Change," 2 November: 65.

Editors 2002. "US Military Bases and Empire," *Monthly Review* 53(10): 1–14.
Edney, M. H. 1997. *Mapping an Empire: The Geographical Construction of British India, 1765–1843*. Chicago, IL: University of Chicago Press.
Edquist, C. and B. Johnson 1997. "Institutions and Organizations in Systems of Innovation," in C. Edquist (ed.) *Systems of Innovation: Technologies, Institutions and Organizations*. London: Pinter/Cassel Academic, pp. 41–63.
Edquist, C. and B.-Å. Lundvall 1992. "Comparing Small Nordic Systems of Innovation," in R. Nelson (ed.) *National Systems of Innovation: A Comparative Study*. Oxford: Oxford University Press, pp. 265–298.
Edwards, F. R. 1999. "Hedge Funds and the Collapse of Long-term Capital Management," *Journal of Economic Perspectives* 13: 189–210.
Ehrlich, P. R. 1968. *The Population Bomb*. New York: Ballantine.
Eichengreen, B. 1999. *Towards a New Financial Architecture: A Parochial Post-Asia Agenda*. Washington, DC: Washington Institute for International Economics.
Eisenburger, M. and R. Patel 2003. *Agricultural Liberalization in China: Curbing the State and Creating Cheap Labor*. Oakland, CA: FoodFirst Institute.
Ekins, P. 1993. *A New World Order: Grassroots Movements for Global Change*. London: Routledge.
—— and M. Max-Neef 1992. *Real-Life Economics: Understanding Wealth Creation* London: Routledge.
Elm, M. 2001. "New Indian Revolt in Bolivia," *Native Americas* 18(2): 5.
Elwood, W. 2001. *The No-Nonsense Guide to Globalization*. Toronto: New Internationalist.
Engardio, P. 2005. "A New World Economy: The Shape of the Future," *Business Week*, 22/29 August, pp. 52–58.
Engels, F. 1940. *Dialectics of Nature*. New York: International Publishers.
Escobar, A. 1992. "Planning," in W. Sachs (ed.) *The Development Dictionary: A Guide to Knowledge as Power*. London: Zed Books.
Esteva, G. 1992. "Development," in W. Sachs (ed.) *The Development Dictionary: A Guide to Knowledge as Power*. London: Zed Books.
Evans, G. 2003. "The US versus the World? How American Power Seems to the Rest of Us," *Fletcher Forum of World Affairs* 27(2): 99–113.
Fabian Global Forum 2003a. "Progressive Globalisation: A New Political Approach." London: Fabian Society for the Global Forum. www.fabianglobalforum.net/forum/article023.html
—— 2003b. "An Agenda for Progressive Globalisation." London: Fabian Society for the Global Forum. www.fabianglobalforum.net/forum/article024.html
Fahrtig, L. and B. Kohl 2001. "Bolivia's New Wave of Protest," *NACLA Report on the Americas*, March/April, 34(5): 4–8.
Faist, T. 2000. *The Volume and Dynamics of International Migration and Transnational Social Spaces*. Oxford: Clarendon Press.
Falk, R. 1999a. *Predatory Globalization: A Critique*. Cambridge: Polity Press.
—— 1999b. "Hans Küng's Crusade: Framing a Global Ethic," *International Journal of Politics, Culture, and Society* 13(1): 63–81.
—— 2003. *The Great Terror War*. New York: Olive Branch Press.
Fanon, F. 1963. *The Wretched of the Earth*. New York: Grove Press.
Farer, T. 1999. "Fighting Transnational Organized Crime: Measures Short of War," in T. Farer (ed.) *Transnational Crime in the Americas*. New York: Routledge, pp. 245–296.

252 References

Ferleger, L. and J. R. Mandle 2000. "Dimensions of Globalization," *Annals of the American Academy of Political and Social Science* 570, July.

Fernandez, E. and A. Varley 1998. *Illegal Cities: Law and Urban Change in Developing Countries*. London: Zed Books.

Fernandez-Kelly, M. P. 1982. *Feminization, Mexican Border Industrialization and Migration*. Berkeley, CA: Center for the Study, Education and Advancement of Women, University of California.

Ferrerya, A. and R. Segura, 2000. "Examining the Military in the Local Sphere: Colombia and Mexico," *Latin American Perspectives* 27(2): 18–35.

Fertl, D. 2004. "Indigenous Uprising Paralyses Ecuador," *Green Left Weekly*, Committees in Solidarity with Communities in Latin America and the Caribbean (CISLAC). www.cislac.org.au/index.php?option=com_content&task=view&id=23&Itemid=51

Ffrench-Davis, R. 2002. *Economic Reforms in Chile: From Dictatorship to Democracy*. Ann Arbor, MI: University of Michigan Press.

Finckenauer, J. O. 2001. "Russian Transnational Organized Crime and Human Trafficking," in D. J. Kyle and R. Koslowski (eds) *Global Human Smuggling: Comparative Perspectives*. Baltimore, MD: Johns Hopkins University Press, pp. 166–186.

Findlay, A. M. 1993. "New Technology, High-level Labour Movements and the Concept of the Brain Drain," in *The Changing Course of International Migration*. Paris: Organisation for Economic Co-operation and Development, pp. 149–159.

—— 1995. "Skilled Transients: The Invisible Phenomenon?" in R. Cohen (ed.) *The Cambridge Survey of World Migration*. Cambridge: Cambridge University Press, pp. 515–522.

Fine, B. 1997. "The New Revolution in Economics," *Capital and Class* 61(spring): 143–148.

—— and C. Stoneman 1996. "Introduction: State and Development," *Journal of Southern African Studies* 22(1): 5–26.

Fisher, W. and T. Ponniah 2003. *Another World is Possible: Popular Alternatives to Globalization at the World Social Forum*. London: Zed Books.

Fitzgerald, V. 1999. "Global Capital Market Volatility and the Developing Countries: Lessons from the East Asian Crisis," *Bulletin: Institute of Development Studies* 30: 10–25.

Fletcher, B. 2002. "Sweatshop Labor, Sweatshop Movement." (Book review of Miriam Ching Yoon Louie, 2001. *Sweatshop Warriors: Immigrant Women Workers Take on the Global Economy*. Cambridge, MA: South End Press.)

Flint, C. 2002. "Political Geography: Globalization, Metapolitical Geographies and Everyday Life," *Progress in Human Geography* 26(3): 391–400.

—— 2003. "Geographies of Inclusion/Exclusion," in S. Cutter, D. Richardson and T. Wilbanks (eds) *The Geographical Dimensions of Terrorism*. New York: Routledge, pp. 53–58.

—— 2004. "The 'War on Terrorism' and the 'Hegemonic Dilemma': Extra-territoriality, Re-territorialization and the Implications for Globalization," in J. O'Loughlin, L. Staeheli and E. Greenberg (eds) *Globalization and its Outcomes*. New York: Guilford Press, pp. 361–385.

Fog Olwig, K. 2001. "New York as a Locality in a Global Family Network," in N. Foner (ed.) *Islands in the City: West Indian Migration to New York*. Berkeley, CA: University of California Press, pp. 142–160.

Foray, X. and B.-Å Lundvall 1997. "Une Introduction à l'economic fondée sur la connaisance," in B. Guilhon (ed.) *Economie de la connaisance et des organisations*.

Paris: l'Harmattan. Cited in D. Foray and A. Grubler (1996) "Technology and the Environment: An Overview," *Technological Forecasting and Social Change* 53(1): 3–13.
Fortescue, A. 2003. "Catholic Encyclopedia: Eastern Schism." www.newadvent.org/cathen/13535a.htm
Frank, A. G. 1978. *Dependent Accumulation and Underdevelopment*. London: Macmillan Press.
Frank, T. 2002. "Enron: Elvis Lives," *Le Monde diplomatique*, 13 February, 12–13.
Fratianni, M. and J. Pattison 2001. "Review Essay. The Bank for International Settlements: An Assessment of its Role in International Monetary and Financial Policy Coordination," *Open Economies Review* 12: 197–222.
French, M. 2002. *Taking on the Golden Arches*. www.peak.sfu.ca/the-peak/2002-2/issue5/mcfeature.html
Friedmann, J. 1978. "On the Contradictions between City and Countryside," *Comparative Urban Research* 6(1): 5–41.
Friedman, T. L. 2005. *The World is Flat: A Brief History of the Twenty-first Century*. New York: Farrar, Straus & Giroux.
Friends of Earth Europe 2004. "European Regions Declare Themselves GM-free," *Environmental News Service*, April 22 – Earth Day. www.ens-newswire.com/ens/apr2004/2004-04-22-04.asp
Frobel, F., J. Heinrich and O. Kreye 1980. *The New International Division of Labor*. Cambridge: Cambridge University Press.
Fukuyama, F. 1992. *The End of History and the Last Man*. New York: Avon Books.
Fyfe, C. 1992. "Race, Empire and the Historians," *Race and Class* 33(4).
Galbraith, J. K. 1992. *The Culture of Contentment*. Boston, MA: Houghton Mifflin.
——— 2002. "A Perfect Crime: Inequality in an Age of Globalization," *Daedalus* 131: 11–25.
Gardener, E. P. M. and P. Molyneux 1990. *Changes in Western European Banking*. London: Unwin Hyman.
Garnsey, E. 1998. "The Genesis of the High Technology Milieu: A Study in Complexity," *International Journal of Urban and Regional Research* 22(3): 361–377.
GAWC 2005. *Globalization & World Cities Study Group & Network*, University of Loughborough, UK: www.lboro.ac.uk/gawc/
GCIM 2005. *Migration in an Interconnected World: New Directions for Action*. Switzerland: Report of the Global Commission on International Migration. www.gcim.org/attachements/gcim-complete-report-2005.pdf
George, E. A. J. 1997. Speech given at a dinner with the Lord Mayor for Bankers and Merchants of the City of London at the Mansion House, 12 June, and available from Bank of England, Threadneedle Street, London.
George, S. 1999. "A Short History of Neoliberalism," paper presented at the conference on Economic Sovereignty in a Globalising World, 24–26 March: Global Policy Forum. www.globalpolicy.org/globaliz/econ/histneo1.htm
Gereffi, G., M. Korzeniewicz and R. Korzeniewicz 1994. "Introduction: Global Commodity Chains," in *Commodity Chains and Global Capitalism*. Westport, CN: Greenwood Press.
Germain, R. 1997. *The International Organization of Credit: States and Global Finance in the World-Economy*. Cambridge: Cambridge University Press.
Gertler, M. 1995. "Being There: Proximity, Organization and Culture in the Development and Adaptation of Advanced Manufacturing Technologies," *Economic Geography* 71(1): 1–26.

Giddens, A. 2003. *Runaway World: How Globalization is Reshaping our Lives*. New York: Routledge.
Gill, S. 1990. *American Hegemony and the Trilateral Commission*. Cambridge: Cambridge University Press.
——"Economic Globalization and the Internationalization of Authority: Limits and Contradictions," *Geoforum* 23(3): 269–283.
Gills, B. K. 2000. *Globalization and the Politics of Resistance*. New York: St Martin's Press.
Gilmore, R. W. 1998. "Globalization and US Prison Growth: From Military Keynesianism to Post-Keynesian Militarism," *Race and Class* 40: 171ff.
——forthcoming. *Golden Gulag: Prisons, Surplus, Crisis, and Opposition In California, 1982–2000*. Berkeley, CA: University of California Press.
Glick-Schiller, N., L. Basch and C. Blanc-Szanton 1992. *Towards a Transnational Perspective on Migration: Race, Class, Ethnicity, and Nationalism Reconsidered*. New York: New York Academy of Sciences.
——1995. "From Immigrant to Transmigrant: Theorizing Transnational Migration," *Anthropological Quarterly* 68(1): 48–63.
Global Witness 2000. *Conflict Diamonds: Possibilities for the Identification, Certification and Control of Diamonds*. www.globalwitness.org/campaigns/diamonds/reports.html
——2004. *Time for Transparency: Coming Clean on Oil, Mining and Gas Revenues*. http://globalwitness.org/reports/show.php/en.00049.html
Glyn, A. *et al*. 1990. "The Rise and Fall of the Golden Age," in S. A. Marglin and J. B. Schor (eds) *The Golden Age of Capitalism: Reinterpreting the Postwar Experience*. Oxford: Clarendon Press.
Gold, M. 1984. "A History of Nature," in D. Massey and J. Allen (eds) *Geography Matters!* London: Cambridge University Press, pp. 24–43.
Gold, S. J. 2000. "Transnational Communities: Examining Migration in a Globally Integrated World," in P. S. Aulakh and M. G. Schechter (eds) *Rethinking Globalization(s): From Corporate Transnationalism to Local Interventions*. New York: St Martin's Press and Macmillan, pp. 73–90.
Goldsmith, E. 1997. "Can the Environment Survive the Global Economy?" *Ecologist* 27(6): 242–248.
Golini, A., A. Righi and C. Bonifazi 1993. "Population Vitality and Decline: The North–South Contrast," in *The Changing Course of International Migration*. Paris: Organisation for Economic Co-operation and Development, pp. 19–35.
Golub, P. S. 2005a. "United States: The Slide to Disorder," *Le Monde diplomatique*, July, pp. 1–2.
——2005b. "My Country 'Tis of Thee," *Le Monde diplomatique*, July, p. 3.
Gould, W. 1988. "Skilled International Migration," *Geoforum* 19: 381–386.
Graham, S. 1999. "Global Grids of Glass: On Global Cities, Telecommunications and Planetary Urban Networks," *Urban Studies* 36(5/6): 929–949.
Gramsci, A. 1971. *Selections from the Prison Notebooks*. New York: International Publishers.
Grant, R. and J. Nijman 2002. "Globalization and the Corporate Geography of Cities in the Less-developed World," *Annals, Association of American Geographers* 92: 320–340.
Greenspan, A. 1998. "Remarks Before the 34th Annual Conference on Bank Structure and Competition of the Federal Reserve Bank of Chicago," 7 May. Available from Board of Governors of the Federal Reserve System, Washington, DC 20551 (www.bog.frb.fed.us).

Greider, W. 1997. *One World, Ready or Not: The Manic Logic of Global Capitalism*. New York: Simon & Schuster.
—— 2002. "Wawasan 2020," in F. Lechner and J. Boli (eds) *The Globalization Reader*. Malden, MA: Blackwell, pp. 148–154.
—— 2004. "Under the Banner of the 'War' on Terror," *The Nation*, June.
—— 2005. "America's Truth Deficit," *New York Times*, 18 July.
Group of Seven 1998. "Strengthening the Architecture of the Global Financial System," Report of G7 Finance Ministers to G7 Heads of State or Government for their meeting in Birmingham, UK, May 1998.
Group of Thirty 1993. *Derivatives: Practices and Principles*. Washington, DC: Group of Thirty, 1990 M Street NW, Suite 450, Washington, DC, 20036.
—— 1997. *Global Institutions, National Supervision and Systemic Risk*. Washington, DC: Group of Thirty, 1990 M Street NW, Suite 450, Washington, DC, 20036.
Grundman, R. 1991. *Marxism and Ecology*. Oxford: Clarendon Press.
Guan, X. 2001. "Globalization, Inequality and Social Policy: China on the Threshold of Entry into the World Trade Organization," *Social Policy & Administration* 35(3): 242–257.
Guillén, M. F. 2001. "Is Globalization Civilizing, Destructive or Feeble? A Critique of Five Key Debates in the Social Science Literature," *Annual Review of Sociology* 27: 235–260.
—— 2005. "Mauro Guillén's Indicators of Globalization, 1980–2003"; www.management.wharton.upenn.edu/guillen/files/Global.Table.1980-2003.pdf
Gustafson, B. 2003. "Political Defense in the Chapara: Voices from Bolivia," *Cultural Survival Quarterly* 26(4): 49–54.
Gwynne, R. N., T. Klak and D. J. B. Shaw 2003. *Alternative Capitalisms: Geographies of Emerging Regions*. London: Arnold.
Habermas, J. 1973. *Legitimation Crisis*. Boston, MA: Beacon Press.
—— 1984. *The Theory of Communicative Action, Vol. 1*. Boston, MA: Beacon Press.
—— 1987. *The Theory of Communicative Action, Vol. 2*. Boston, MA: Beacon Press.
Hagstrom, P. 2000. "Relaxing the Boundaries of the Firm," in J. M. Birkinshaw and P. Hagstrom (eds) *The Flexible Firm: Capability Management in Network Organizations*. Oxford: Oxford University Press, pp. 201–212.
Hakansson, H. and J. Johansen 1993. "The Network as a Governance Structure," in G. Grabher (ed.) *The Embedded Firm: On the Socioeconomics of Industrial Networks*. London: Routledge, pp. 35–51.
Hall, D. 2001. *Water Privatization: Global Problems, Global Resistance*. Greenwich, UK: Public Services Research Unit. www.psiru.org/reports/2001-07-W-salb.doc
Hall, S. 1988. *The Hard Road to Renewal: Thatcherism and the Crisis of the Left*. London: Verso.
—— 1997a. "The Local and the Global: Globalization and Ethnicity," in Anthony D. King (ed.) *Culture, Globalization and the World System: Contemporary Conditions for the Representation of Identity*. Minneapolis, MN: University of Minnesota Press, pp. 19–39.
—— 1997b. "Old and New Identities, Old and New Ethnicities," in Anthony D. King (ed.) *Culture, Globalization and the World System: Contemporary Conditions for the Representation of Identity*. Minneapolis, MN: University of Minnesota Press, pp. 41–68.
Hamilton, K. and J. Yau 2004. *The Global Tug-of-War for Health Care Workers*, Migration Information Source. Washington, DC: Migration Policy Institute. www.migrationinformation.org/Profiles/display.cfm?ID=271

Hammar, T., G. Brochmann, K. Tamas and T. Faist 1997. *International Migration, Immobility and Development: Multidisciplinary Perspectives.* Oxford: Berg.
Hancock, G. 1989. *Lords of Poverty: The Power, Prestige and Corruption of the International Aid Business.* New York: Atlantic Monthly Press.
Hancock, W. M. and M. Zayko 1998. "Lean Production," *IIE Solutions* 30(6): 38–42.
Hanink, D. 2000. "Resources," in E. Sheppard and T. Barnes (eds) *A Companion to Economic Geography.* Oxford: Blackwell, pp. 227–241.
Hannertz, U. 1992. *Cultural Complexity.* New York: Columbia University Press.
—— 1996. *Transnational Connections: Culture, People, Places.* New York: Routledge.
Hansen, N. 1992. "Competition, Trust, and Reciprocity in the Development of Innovative Regional Milieux," *Papers in Regional Science* 71: 95–105.
Hardt, M. and A. Negri. 2000. *Empire.* Cambridge, MA: Harvard University Press.
—— 2004. *Multitude: War and Democracy in the Age of Empire.* New York: Penguin.
Harper, C. L. 2004. *Environment and Society: Human Perspectives on Environmental Issues*, 4th edn. Upper Saddle River, NJ: Pearson Prentice-Hall.
Harraway, D. 1991. *Simians, Cyborgs and Women: The Reinvention of Nature.* London: Free Association Books.
—— 1997 *Modest-Witness@Second-Millennium.FemaleMan©-Meets_OncomouseTM.* London: Routledge.
Harrison, B. 1994. *Lean and Mean.* New York: Guilford Press.
Harriss-White, B. 2002. *Globalization and Insecurity: Political, Economic, and Physical Challenges.* New York: Palgrave.
Hart, J. 1992. *Rival Capitalists.* Ithaca, NY: Cornell University Press.
Harvey, D. 1982. *The Limits to Capital.* Chicago, IL: University of Chicago Press.
—— 1989a. *The Condition of Postmodernity.* Oxford: Blackwell.
—— 1989b. "From Managerialism to Entrepreneurialism: The Transformation in Urban Governance in Late Capitalism," *Geografiska Annaler* 71B: 3–17.
—— 1996. *Justice, Nature and the Geography of Difference.* Oxford: Blackwell.
—— 2000. *Spaces of Hope.* Berkeley, CA: University of California Press.
—— 2001. *Spaces of Capital.* New York: Routledge.
—— 2003a. "Retrospective on the Limits to Capital," *Antipode.*
—— 2003b. *The New Imperialism.* Oxford: Oxford University Press.
—— 2005. *A Brief History of Neoliberalism.* Oxford: Oxford University Press.
Haughton, G. and C. Hunter 1994. *Sustainable Cities.* London: Jessica Kingsley.
Hawley, J. 1984. "Protecting Capital from Itself," *International Organisation* 38: 138–165.
Hay, C. and D. Marsh 2000. *Demystifying Globalization.* New York: St Martin's Press.
Heinrich Böll Foundation 2004. *Asian Modernity: Globalization Processes and Their Cultural and Political Localization.* www.robert-furlong.com/AsianModernity.pdf
Held, D. 1995. *Democracy and the Global Order.* Cambridge: Polity Press.
——, A. McGrew, D. Goldblatt and J. Perraton 1999. *Global Transformations.* Cambridge: Polity Press.
Helleiner, E. 1994. *States and the Emergence of Global Finance.* Ithaca, NY: Cornell University Press.
—— 1996. "Post-globalisation: Is the Financial Liberalisation Trend Likely to be Reversed?," in R. Boyer and D. Drache (eds) *States Against Markets.* London: Routledge, pp. 193–210.
Henderson, H. 1999. *Beyond Globalization: Shaping a Sustainable Global Economy.* West Hartford, CN: Kumarian Press.

Henderson, J., P. Dicken, M. Hess, N. Coe and H. Yeung 2002. "Global Production Networks and the Analysis of Economic Development," Global Production Network Working Paper 1.

Herb, G. H. and D. H. Kaplan (eds) 1999. *Nested Identities: Nationalism, Territory, and Scale*. Lanham, MD: Rowman & Littlefield.

Herod, A. 2002. "Global Change in the World of Organized Labor," in R. J. Johnston, P. J. Taylor and M. J. Watts (eds) *Geographies of Global Change: Remapping the World*, 2nd edn. Oxford: Blackwell, pp. 78–87.

——, S. M. Roberts and G. Ó Tuathail 1998. *An Unruly World?: Globalization, Governance, and Geography*. London: Routledge.

Hersh, S. M. 2005. "Up in the Air: Where is the Iraq War Headed Next?" *New Yorker*, 5 December. www.newyorker.com. Accessed 1 December 2005.

Hertz, N. 2001. *The Silent Takeover: Global Capitalism and the Death of Democracy*. London: William Heinemann.

Heynen, N. and H. Perkins 2005. "Scalar Dialectics in Green: Urban Private Property and the Contradictions of the Neoliberalization of Nature," *Capitalism, Nature, Socialism* 16(1): 99–113.

—— and P. Robbins 2005. "The Neoliberalization of Nature: Governance, Privatization, Enclosure and Valuation," *Capitalism, Nature, Socialism* 16(1): 5–8.

Higashi, C. and G. P. Lauter 1987. *The Internationalization of the Japanese Economy*. Boston, MA: Kluwer.

Higgott, R. and G. Underhill 2000. *Non-state Actors and Authority in the Global System*. London: Routledge.

Hills, C. A, P. G. Peterson and M. Goldstein 1999. *Safeguarding Prosperity in a Global Financial System: The Future Financial Architecture*. New York: Council on Foreign Relations.

Hirst, P. and G. Thompson 1999. *Globalization in Question: The International Economy and the Possibilities of Governance*, 2nd edn. Cambridge: Polity Press.

Holden-Rhodes, J. F. 1997. *Sharing the Secrets: Open Source Intelligence and the War on Drugs*. Westport, CT: Praeger.

Holton, R. 2000. "Globalization's Cultural Consequences," in L. Ferleger and J. R. Mandle (eds) "Dimensions of Globalization," *Annals, American Academy of Political and Social Science* 570: pp. 140–152.

Horkheimer, M. and T. Adorno 1994. *The Dialectic of Enlightenment*. New York: Continuum.

Hotz-Hart, B. 2000. "Innovation Networks, Regions, and Globalization," in G. Clark, M. Gertler and M. Feldman (eds) *Handbook of Economic Geography*. Oxford: Oxford University Press, pp. 432–450.

Hudson, A. 2000. "Offshoreness, Globalization and Sovereignty: A Postmodern Geopolitical Economy?," *Transactions, Institute of British Geographers NS* 25: 269–283.

Huertas, T. F. 1990. "US Multinational Banking: History and Prospects," in G. Jones (ed.) *Banks as Multinationals*. London: Routledge, pp. 248–267.

Hughes, J. 2000. *Ecology and Historical Materialism*. Cambridge: Cambridge University Press.

Hugo, G. 2003. "Circular Migration: Keeping Development Rolling?" Migration Information Source. Washington, DC: Migration Policy Institute. www.migrationinformation.org/feature/print.cfm?ID=129

Huntington, S. P. 1993. "The Clash of Civilizations?" *Foreign Affairs* 72(3): 22–49.

258 References

—— 1996. *The Clash of Civilizations and the Remaking of World Order*. New York: Touchstone.

—— 1999. "Robust Nationalism," *The National Interest*, winter. Washington, DC.

—— 2003. "The Clash of Civilizations," in G. Ó Tuathail, S. Dalby and P. Routledge (eds) *The Geopolitics Reader*. London: Routledge, pp. 159–169.

Hylton, F. and S. Thomson 2004. "The Roots of Rebellion. 1: Insurgent Bolivia," *NACLA Report on the Americas* 38(3): 15–20.

ICRC 2005. "Red Cross and Red Crescent Movement." www.redcross.int/en/history/movement.asp

IFRC 2003. "Red Cross, Red Crescent: A History." www.ifrc.org/who/history.asp

Ikenberry, G. J. and C. A. Kupchan 1990. "Socialization and Hegemonic Power," *International Organization* 44: 283–315.

Ikenberry, J. 2002. "America's Imperial Ambition," *Foreign Affairs* 81(5): 44–60.

ILO (International Labor Organization) 1997. *World Labor Report: Industrial Relations, Democracy and Social Stability*. Geneva: ILO.

—— 2000. *World Labor Report: Income Security and Social Protection in a Changing World*. Geneva: ILO.

—— 2004a. *Fair Globalization: Creating Opportunities for All*. Geneva: ILO, World Commission on the Social Dimension of Globalization. www.ilo.org/public/english/wcsdg/globali/globali.htm

—— 2004b. *Social Dimension of Globalization*. Geneva: ILO, World Commission on the Social Dimension of Globalization.

—— 2005. *A Global Alliance Against Forced Labour*. Geneva: International Labour Office.

Inglehart, R. and Baker, W. E. 2000. "Modernization, Globalization and the Persistence of Tradition: Empirical Evidence from 65 Societies," *American Sociological Review* 65: 19–55.

International Crime Threat Assessment 2000. *President's International Crime Control Strategy*, Interagency Working Group.

International Forum on Globalization 2002. *Alternatives to Economic Globalization: A Better World is Possible*. San Francisco, CA: Berrett-Koehler.

IOM (International Organization for Migration) 2003. "Facts and Figures on International Migration," Migration Policy Issues 2, March. Geneva: IOM.

—— 2005. *Migration in South East Asia*. Geneva: International Organization for Migration. www.iom-seasia.org

Jachimiwicz, M. 2003. "Foreign Students and Exchange Visitors," Migration Information Source. Washington, DC: Migration Policy Institute. www.migrationinformation.org/USfocus/display.cfm?ID=158

Jackson, P. 1989. *Maps of Meaning: An Introduction to Cultural Geography*. London: Unwin Hyman.

—— 1999. "Commodity Culture: The Traffic in Things," *Transactions, Institute of British Geographers* 24: 95–108.

Jacobs, J. 1984. *Cities and the Wealth of Nations: Principals of Economic Life*. New York: Vintage Books.

James, H. 2001. *The End of Globalization: Lessons from the Great Depression*. Cambridge, MA: Harvard University Press.

Jameson, F. 1991. *Postmodernism, Or the Cultural Logic of Late Capitalism*. London: Verso.

Jandl, M. 2003. "Estimates on the Numbers of Illegal and Smuggled Immigrants in Europe," Presentation at Workshop 1.6, 8th International Metropolis Conference, Vienna,

Austria: International Centre for Migration Policy Development (ICMPD). www.icmpd.org
—— 2004. "The Estimation of Illegal Migration in Europe," *Studi Emigrazione/Migration Studies* XLI(153): 141–155.
Jessop, B. 1994. "Post-Fordism and the State," in A. Amin (ed.) *Post-Fordism: A Reader*. Oxford: Blackwell, pp. 251–279.
—— 1997. "Capitalism and its Future: Remarks on Regulation, Government and Governance," *Review of International Political Economy* 4: 561–581.
—— 1999. "The Wealth of States: A Comparative Sociology of International Economic and Political Change," *American Political Science Review* 93: 240–241.
Jhaveri, N. J. 2004. "Petroimperialism: US Oil Interests and the Iraq War," *Antipode* 36(1): 12–23.
Jiminez, M. 2003. "200,000 Illegal Immigrants Toiling in Canada's Underground Economy," *The Globe and Mail* (Canada), news report, 15 November.
Johnson, N. C. 2002. "The Renaissance of Nationalism," in R. J. Johnston, P. J. Taylor and M. J. Watts (eds) *Geographies of Global Change: Remapping the World*, 2nd edn. Malden, MA: Blackwell, pp. 130–142.
Johnston, R. J., P. J. Taylor and M. J. Watts 2002. *Geographies of Global Change: Remapping the World*, 2nd edn. Malden, MA: Blackwell.
Jokisch, B. and J. Pribilsky 2002. "The Panic to Leave: Economic Crisis and the 'New Emigration' from Ecuador," *International Migration* 40(4): 75–99.
Jones, G. 1990. "Banks as multinationals," in *Banks as Multinationals*. London: Routledge, pp. 1–13.
Jones, G. A. 1994. "The Latin American City as Contested Space," *Bulletin of Latin American Research* 13(1): 1–12.
Jordan-Bychkov, T. G. and M. Domosh 2003. *The Human Mosaic: A Thematic Introduction to Cultural Geography*. New York: W. H. Freeman.
Jubilee 2000. *The Radical Agenda for Global Social Transformation*. www.jubilee2000.org/aganda.html
Kagan, R. 2003. *Of Paradise and Power: America and Europe in the New World Order*. New York City: Alfred A. Knopf at Random House.
—— and W. Kristol 2000. *Present Dangers: Crisis and Opportunity in American Foreign and Defense Policy*. San Francisco, CA: Encounter Books.
Kaplan, R. and W. Kristol 2003. *The War Over Iraq: Saddam's Tyranny and America's Mission*. San Francisco, CA: Encounter Books.
Kapstein, E. 1992. "Between Power and Purpose: Central Bankers and the Politics of Regulatory Convergence," *International Organisation* 46: 265–287.
—— 1994. *Governing the Global Economy: International Finance and the State*. Cambridge, MA: Harvard University Press.
—— 1998. "Can the Financial Markets Privately Regulate Risk? The Development of Derivatives Clearing Houses and Recent Over-the-Counter Innovations," *Journal of Money Credit and Banking* 31: 596–618.
Karasek, R. and T. Theorell 1990. *Healthy Work: Stress, Productivity and the Reconstruction of Working Life*. New York: Basic Books.
Karlsson, K.-G. 1995. "Migration and Soviet Disintegration," in R. Cohen (ed.) *The Cambridge Survey of World Migration*. Cambridge: Cambridge University Press, pp. 486–489.
Katz, C. 2001. "Vagabond Capitalism," *Antipode* 33: 709–728.
Kaufman, G. 1997. "Bank Failures, Systemic Risk and Bank Regulation," *Cato Journal* 16: xx.

Kay, C. 1993. "For a Renewal of Development Studies: Latin American Theories and Neo-liberalism in the Era of Structural Adjustment," *Third World Quarterly* 14(4): 691–702.

Keely, C. B. 1979. *US Immigration: A Policy Analysis*. New York: Population Council.

—— 2002. "Globalization Transforms Trade–Migration Equation," Migration Information Source. Washington, DC: Migration Policy Institute. www.migrationinformation.org/feature/print.cfm?ID=73

Keil, R. *et al.* 1998. *Political Ecology: Global and Local*. London: Routledge.

Kellner, D. 1992. *Persian Gulf TV War*. Boulder, CO: Westview Press.

Kelly, P. F. 1999. "The Geographies and Politics of Globalization," *Progress in Human Geography* 23(3): 379–400.

Kendall, R. E. 2001. "Responding to Transnational Crime," in P. Williams and D. Vlassis (eds) *Combating Transnational Crime: Concepts, Activities and Responses*. London: Frank Cass, pp. 269–275.

Kenen, P. 2000. "The New International Financial Architecture," *International Journal of Finance and Economics* 5: 1–14.

Kennedy, P. 2001. "Letters to the Editor," *Wall Street Journal*, 6 October.

Kepel, G. 2002. "From the Gulf War to the Taliban Jihad," *Jihad: The Trail of Political Islam*. Cambridge, MA: Harvard University Press.

Kiely, R. 2005. "Globalisation and the Third Way in the 1990s," in R. Kiely (ed.) *The Clash of Globalisations: Neo-liberalism, the Third Way and Anti-globalisation*. Leiden, Netherlands: Brill, pp. 81–125.

Kindleberger, C. P. 1974. "The Formation of Financial Centers: A Study in Comparative Economic History," *Princeton Studies in International Finance* 36. Princeton, NJ: University of Princeton.

—— 1984. *A Financial History of Western Europe*. London: George, Allen and Unwin.

King, A. 1997. *Culture, Globalization and the World System: Contemporary Conditions for the Representation of Identity*. Minneapolis, MN: University of Minnesota Press.

King, M. 2000. "Who Triggered the Asian Financial Crisis," *Review of International Political Economy* 8: 438–466.

Klare, M. 2001. *Resource Wars: The New Landscape of Global Conflict*. New York: Henry Holt & Co.

—— 2004. *Blood and Oil: The Dangers and Consequences of America's Growing Dependence on Imported Petroleum*. New York: Henry Holt & Co.

Klinenberg, E. 2002. *A Social Autopsy of Disaster in Chicago*. Chicago, IL: University of Chicago Press.

Knox, P. and S. Marston 2001. *Places and Regions in Global Context: Human Geography*, 2nd edn. Upper Saddle River, NJ: Prentice-Hall.

—— and P. J. Taylor 1995. *World Cities in a World System*. Cambridge: Cambridge University Press.

Knudsen, D.C., F. R. Jacobs, D. Conway and M. K. Blake 1994. "A Survey of Group Technology Adoption in the American Midwest," *Growth and Change* 25(2): 183–205.

Knuf, J. 2000. "Benchmarking the Lean Enterprise: Organizational Learning at Work," *Journal of Management in Engineering* 16(4): 58–61.

Korten, D. 1995. *When Corporations Rule the World*. West Hartford, CN: Kumarian Press.

Korzeniewicz, M. 1993. "Commodity Chains and Marketing Strategies: Nike and the Global Athletic Footwear Industry," in G. Gereffi and M. Korzeniewicz (eds) *Commodity Chains and Global Capitalism*. Westport, NJ: Greenwood.

Koslowski, R. 2001. "Economic Globalization, Human Smuggling, and Global Governance," in D. J. Kyle and R. Koslowski (eds) *Global Human Smuggling:*

Comparative Perspectives. Baltimore, MD: Johns Hopkins University Press, pp. 337–357.

Krippner, G. R. 2003. "The Fictitious Economy: Financialization, the State and Contemporary Capitalism," unpublished PhD thesis, Department of Sociology, University of Wisconsin-Madison.

Kristof, N. D. and D. E. Sanger 1999. "How US Wooed Asia to Let Cash Flow In," *New York Times*, 16 February, p. A1.

Kritz, M. M. 1987. "The Global Picture of Contemporary Immigration Patterns," in J. T. Fawcett and B. V. Cariño (eds) *Pacific Bridges: The New Immigration from Asia and the Pacific Islands*. Staten Island: Center for Migration Studies, pp. 29–51.

Kroszner, R. S. 1999. "Can the Financial Markets Privately Regulate Risk? The Development of Derivatives Clearinghouses and Recent Over-the-counter Innovations," *Journal of Money, Credit and Banking* 31(3): 596–623.

Kupchan, C. A. 2002. *The End of the American Era: US Foreign Policy and the Geopolitics of the Twenty-First Century*. New York: Knopf.

Kyle, D. J. and Z. Liang 1998. "The Development and Organization of Trans-national Migrant Trafficking from China and Ecuador," paper presented to the conference on Managing Migration in the Twenty-first Century, Hamburg, Germany, June.

—— and R. Koslowski 2001. *Global Human Smuggling: Comparative Perspectives*. Baltimore, MD: Johns Hopkins Press.

Laasko, L. 2000. "State Collapse and International Community," in Krishna-Hensel (ed.) *The New Millennium: Challenges and Strategies for a Globalizing World*. Aldershot: Ashgate, pp. 71–85.

Lanoszka, A. 2003. "There's No Trade Crisis," *The Globe and Mail*, 26 June, A15.

Lasserre, F. 2005. "The Blue Gold Rush," *Le Monde diplomatique*, March.

Law, L. 2003. "Transnational Cyberpublics: New Political Spaces for Labour Migrants in Asia," *Ethnic and Racial Studies* 26(2): 234–252.

Lawton Smith, H. 1997. "Regulatory Change and Skill Transfer: The Case of National Laboratories in the UK, France and Belgium," *Regional Studies* 31(1): 41–54.

League of Nations 2005. "League of Nations." http://en.wikipedia.org/wiki/League_of_Nations

Le Billon, P. 2001. "The Political Ecology of War: Natural Resources and Armed Conflicts," *Political Geography* 20: 561–584.

Lebow, J. 1990. "The Last Word on Lean Manufacturing," *IEE Solutions* 31(9): 42–45.

Lee, R. W. 1999. "Transnational Organized Crime: An Overview," in T. Farer (ed.) *Transnational Crime in the Americas*. New York: Routledge, pp. 1–38.

Le Galès, P. and C. Lequesne (eds) 1998. *Regions in Europe*. London: Routledge.

Leitner, H. 2001. "The Political Economy of International Labor Migration," in E. Sheppard and T. J. Barnes (eds) *A Companion to Economic Geography*. Oxford: Blackwell, pp. 450–467.

Le Monde 2002. "Enron: Elvis Lives," Tom Frank, *Le Monde Dipolomatique*, February.

Lenin, V. 1963. "Imperialism: The Highest Stage of Capitalism," in *Collected Works, Vol. 1*. Moscow: Progress Publishers.

Lewchuk, W. and D. Robertson 1996. "Working Conditions under Lean Production: A Worker-based Benchmarking Study," *Asia Pacific Business Review* 2(2): 60–81.

—— 1997. "Production Without Empowerment: Work Reorganization from the Perspective of Motor Vehicle Workers," *Capital & Class* 63(3): 37–64.

Lewis, M. K. and K. T. Davis 1987. *Domestic and International Banking*. Deddington: Philip Allen.

Ley, D. 2004. "Transnational Spaces and Everyday Lives," *Transactions, Institute of British Geographers NS* 29(1): 151–164.
Leyshon, A. and N. J. Thrift 1997. *Money/Space*. London: Routledge.
—— and A. Tickell 1994. "Money Order? The Discursive Constitution of Bretton Woods and the Making and Breaking of Regulatory Space," *Environment and Planning A* 26: 1861–1890.
Li, F., A. Findlay, A. Jowett and R. Skeldon 1996. "Migrating to Learn and Learning to Migrate: A Study of the Experiences and Intentions of International Student Migrants," *International Journal of Population Geography* 2(1): 51–67.
Liechty, M. 1997. "Selective Exclusion: Foreigners, Foreign Goods and Foreignness in Modern Nepali History," *Studies in Nepali History and Society* 2(1): 5–68.
Linard, A. 1998. *Migration and Globalisation: The New Slaves*. Brussels: International Confederation of Free Trade Unions. www.icftu.org/www/PDF/Migration-ENG.pdf
Lipsey, R. and I. Kravis 1987. "The Competitiveness and Comparative Advantage of US Multinationals," *Banca Nazionale del Lavoro Quarterly Review* 161: 147–165.
Lobe, J. 2004. "US: War is Bad for Business," *Foreign Policy in Focus*, 31 December. www.corpwatch.org/article.php?id=11771. Accessed 15 July 2005.
Lowell, L. B. 2003. "Skilled Migration Abroad or Human Capital Flight?" Migration Information Source. Washington, DC: Migration Policy Institute. www.migrationinformation.org/feature/print.cfm?ID=135
Lowell, L. B. and R. O. de la Garza 2000. *The Developmental Role of Remittances in US Latino Communities and in Latin American Countries*. Inter-American Dialogue and Tomás Rivera Policy Institute, Final Project Report.
Luke, T. W. 2003. "Global Cities vs. 'global cities': Rethinking Contemporary Urbanism and Public Ecology," *Studies in Political Economy*, spring: 11–33.
Lundvall, B.-Å. 1995. "The Learning Economy: Challenges to Economic Theory and Policy," BETA Working Paper 95-14, Strasbourg: University Louis Pasteur.
—— 1996. "The Social Dimension of the Learning Economy," DRUID Working Paper 96-1.
—— and B. Johnson 1994. "The Learning Economy," *Journal of Industrial Studies* 1(2): 23–42.
Luttwak, E. 1993. "The Coming Global War for Economic Power: There are No Nice Guys on the Battlefield of Geo-economics," *International Economy* 7(5): 18–67.
—— 1999. *Turbo Capitalism: Winners and Losers in the Global Economy*. New York: HarperCollins.
—— 2003a. "From Geopolitics to Geoeconomics: Logic of Conflict, Grammar of Commerce," in G. Ó Tuathail, S. Dalby and P. Routledge (eds) *The Geopolitics Reader*. London: Routledge, pp. 125–130.
—— 2003b. "Who Are We Trying to Scare?" *The Globe and Mail*, 27 May, p. A15.
McAfee, K. 1991. *Storm Signals: Structural Adjustment and Development Alternatives in the Caribbean*. Boston, MA: South End Press and Oxfam America.
McCaffery, B. R. 1998. "Organizing Drug Control Efforts Along the Southwest Border," Office of National Drug Control Policy. www.whitehousedrugpolicy.gov
McCarthy, J. 2004. "Privatizing Conditions of Production: Trade Agreements as Neoliberal Environmental Governance," *Geoforum* 35(3): 327–342.
McCarthy, T. 1984. "Translator's Introduction," in J. Habermas, *The Theory of Communicative Action, Vol. 1*. Boston, MA: Beacon Press, pp. v–xxxvii.
Macdonald, S. and C. Williams 1994. "The Survival of the Gatekeeper," *Research Policy* 23(2): 123–132.

Machimura, T. 1998. "Symbolic Use of Globalization in Urban Politics in Tokyo," *International Journal of Urban and Regional Research* 22: 183–194.

MacKenzie, D. 2000. "Long-term Capital Management and the Sociology of Finance," *London Review of Books*, 13 April, pp. 1–5. Available at www.lrb.co.uk/v22/n08/mack2208.htm

Mackinder, H. J. 1904. "The Geographical Pivot of History," *Geographical Journal* 23: 421–444.

MacLeod, G. 2000. "The Learning Region in an Age of Austerity: Capitalizing on Knowledge, Entrepreneurialism, and Reflexive Capitalism," *Geoforum* 31(2): 219–236.

McMichael, P. 1996. "Globalization: Myths and Realities," *Rural Sociology* 61: 25–55.

Mahbubani, K. 2000. "The Rest of the West." Lecture, BBC's World Lectures, pp. 1–14. www.bbc.co.uk/worldservice

Maier, C. S. 1978. "The Politics of Productivity: Foundations of American International Economic Policy after World War II," in P. J. Katzenstein (ed.) *Between Power and Plenty*. Madison, WI: University of Wisconsin Press.

Maillat, D., B. Lecoq, F. Nemeti and M. Pfister 1995. "Technology Districts and Innovation: The Case of the Swiss Jura Arc," *Regional Studies* 29(3): 251–264.

Maingot, A. P. 1993. "The Internationalization of Corruption and Violence: Threats to the Caribbean in the Post-Cold War World," in J. I. Dominguez, R.A. Pastor and R. DeLisle Worrell (eds) *Democracy in the Caribbean: Political, Economic, and Social Perspectives*. Baltimore, MD: Johns Hopkins Press, pp. 42–56.

Malecki, E. J. 1996. "Technology, Competitiveness, and Flexibility: Constantly Evolving Concepts," in D. C. Knudsen (ed.) *The Transition to Flexibility*. Boston, MA: Kluwer Academic, pp. 15–26.

Malmberg, A. 1996. "Industrial Geography: Agglomeration and the Role of Proximity," *Progress in Human Geography* 20(3): 392–403.

—— 1997. "Industrial Geography: Location and Learning," *Progress in Human Geography* 21(4): 573–582.

Malthus, T. R. 1992. *An Essay on the Principle of Population*, ed. D. Winch. Cambridge: Cambridge University Press.

Mannion, A. M. 1995. *Agriculture and Environmental Change*. Chichester: John Wiley.

Mansfield, D., A. Tickell and G. L. Clark 2001. "Hard Borders, Soft Geographies: The International Financial Architecture," Future Governance Working Paper 7, School of Geographical Sciences, University of Bristol.

Mao Tse-tung 1990. *Quotations from Chairman Mao Tse-tung*. San Francisco, CA: Foreign Languages Press.

Marsh, G. P. 1965. *Man and Nature*. Cambridge, MA: Belknap Press of Harvard University Press.

Martin, H.-P. and H. Schumann 1997. *The Global Trap: Globalization and the Assault on Democracy and Prosperity*. London: Zed Books.

Martin, J. M. and A. T. Romaro 1992. *Multinational Crime: Terrorism, Espionage, Drug and Arms Trafficking*. London: Sage.

Martin, P. and M. Miller 2000. "Smuggling and Trafficking: A Conference Report," *International Migration Review* 34(3): 969–975.

—— and J. Widgren 2002. "International Migration: Facing the Challenge," Population Bulletin 57, no. 1, Population Reference Bureau, Washington, DC.

Martin, S. 2001. "Global Migration Trends and Asylum," *Journal of Humanitarian Assistance: New Issues in Refugee Research*, Working Paper 41. www.jha.ac/articles/u41.htm

Martinez, E. and A. Garcia 1997. "What Is Neo-liberalism? A Brief Definition for Activists," *National Network for Immigrant and Refugee Rights*, 1 January 1997. www.corpwatch.org/article.php?id=376

Marx, K. 1973. *Grundrisse*. London: Penguin.

—— 1987. *Capital, Vol. 1*. New York: International Publishers.

—— and F. Engels 1845/1998. *The German Ideology*. New York: Prometheus Books.

—— and F. Engels 1848/1998. *The Communist Manifesto*. USA: Penguin Group.

Maskell, P. 1996a. "Learning in the Village Economy of Denmark: The Role of Institutions and Policy in Sustaining Competitiveness," DRUID Working Paper No. 96-6.

—— 1996b. "Localised Low-tech Learning in the Furniture Industry," DRUID Working Paper No. 96-11.

—— 1998. "Low-tech Competitive Advantages and the Role of Proximity: The Danish Wooden Furniture Industry," *European Urban and Regional Studies* 5(2): 99–118.

—— and A. Malmberg 1995. "Localised Learning and Industrial Competitiveness. Berkeley Round Table of International Economy (BRIE)," Working Paper 80, Berkeley University. server.berkeley.edu/brie/wplist.html#wp80

—— and A. Malmberg 1999. "Localised Learning and Industrial Competitiveness," *Cambridge Journal of Economics* 23(2): 167–185.

——, H. Eskelinen, H. Hannibalsson, A. Malmberg and E. Vatne 1998. *Competitiveness, Localized Learning and Regional Development: Specialization and Prosperity in Small Open Economies*. London: Routledge.

Massey, D. S. 1984. *Spatial Divisions of Labour: Social Structures and the Geography of Production*. London: Macmillan.

—— 1990. "The Social and Economic Origins of Immigration," *American Academy of Political and Social Sciences* 510: 60–72.

—— 1994. "A Global Sense of Place," in *Space, Place, Gender*. Minneapolis, MN: University of Minnesota Press, pp. 146–156.

—— and F. P. Espana 1987. "The Social Process of International Migration," *Science* 237: 733–738.

——, J. Arango, G. Hugo, A. Kouaouci, A. Pellegrino and J. E. Taylor 1998. *Worlds in Motion: Understanding International Migration at the End of the Millennium*. Oxford: Clarendon/Oxford University Press.

Mattelart, A. 2005. "Cultural Diversity Belongs to us All," *Le Monde diplomatique*, November.

Mazlish, B. 1993. "An Introduction to Global History," in B. Mazlish and R. Buultjens (eds) *Conceptualizing Global History*. Boulder, CO: Westview Press, pp. 1–24.

Mazrui, A. 2000. "Pretender to Universalism: Western Culture in the Globalising Age," Keynote Address, Royal Society of Art and the British Broadcasting Service, pp. 1–19. www.bbc.co.uk/worldservice

Meadows, D. H., D. L. Meadows *et al.* 1972. *The Limits to Growth*. New York: Universe Books.

Meltzer, A. 1988. "The Policy Proposals in the AEI Studies," in W. S. Havat and R. M. Kushmeider (eds) *Restructuring Banking and Financial Services in America*. Washington, DC: American Enterprise Institute.

Memmi, A. 1965. *The Colonizer and the Colonized*. Boston: Beacon Press.

Mendis, A. and C. van Bers 1999. "Bitter Fruit: Attractive Supermarket Displays of Tropical Fruit Conceal Ugly Environmental and Social Costs," *Alternatives Journal* 25(1): 18–23.

Menzel, S. H. 1997. *Cocaine Quagmire: Implementing the US Anti-drug Policy in the North Andes-Colombia*. New York: University Press of America.

Meyer, B. W. and B. L. Tuner 1995. "The Earth Transformed: Trends, Trajectories, and Patterns," in R. J. Johnston, P. J. Taylor and M. J. Watts (eds) *Geographies of Global Change*. Malden, MA: Blackwell.

Meyer, D. 2003. "The Predator Class," CBS, Against the Grain Commentary. www.cbsnews.com/stories/2003/11/19/opinion/meyer/main584424.shtml

Millennium Goals (UN) 2005. *Millennium Development Goals Report 2005*. http://unstat.un.org/unsd/mi/pdf/MDG%20Book.pdf

Miller, B. 2000. *Geography and Social Movements: Comparing Antinuclear Activism in the Boston Area*. Minneapolis, MN: University of Minnesota Press.

——2004. "Spaces of Mobilization: Transnational Social Movements in a Globalizing World," in C. Barnett and M. Low (eds) *Spaces of Democracy*. Thousand Oaks, CA: Sage.

Miller, M. 1995. "Illegal Migration," in R. Cohen (ed.) *The Cambridge Survey of World Migration*. Cambridge: Cambridge University Press, pp. 537–540.

Ministry of Finance 1995. *The Report of the Inspectors Appointed by the Ministry of Finance*. Government of Singapore, Singapore.

Mitchell, D. 1995. "There's No Such Thing as Culture: Towards a Reconceptualization of the Idea of Culture in Geography," *Transactions, Institute of British Geography* 20: 102–116.

Mofson, P. 1999. "Global Ecopolitics," in G. Demko and W. B. Wood (eds) *Reordering the World: Geopolitical Perspectives on the Twenty-first Century*. Boulder, CO: Westview Press, pp. 246–259.

Mohawk, J. 2004. "Bolivia's Indians Confront Globalization," *Indian Country Today* 24(11): 5–7.

Mokhiber, R. 2004. "Top 100 Corporate Criminals of the 1990s Decade," Corporate Predators. www.corporatepredators.org/top100.html

——and R. Weissmann 2004. *Corporate Predators: The Hunt for Mega-profits and the Attack on Democracy*. Monroe, ME: Common Courage Press.

Monbiot, G. 2003. "Globalisation/How to Stop America," *New Statesman*, 9 June. www.monbiot.com/dsp_article.cfm?article_id=583

——2004. *Manifesto for a New World Order*. New York: The New Press.

Moore, S. and A. Scott 1999. "Biotech Battle," *Chemical Week* 161(48): 23–27.

Moran, M. 1990. *The Politics of the Financial Services Revolution*. London: Macmillan.

Morgan, K. 1997. "The Learning Region: Institutions, Innovation and Regional Renewal," *Regional Studies* 31(5): 491–503.

——and J. Murdoch 2000. "Organic vs. Conventional Agriculture: Knowledge, Power and Innovation in the Food Chain," *Geoforum* 31(2): 159–173.

Morgenstern, O. 1959. *International Financial Transactions and Business Cycles*. Princeton, NJ: Princeton University Press.

Morley, D. and K. Robins 1995. *Spaces of Identity: Global Media, Electronic Landscapes, and Cultural Boundaries*. London: Routledge.

Muir, R. 1997. *Political Geography: A New Introduction*. New York: John Wiley.

Müller, A. R. and R. Patel 2004. *Shining India? Economic Liberalization and Rural Poverty in the 1990s*. Oakland, CA: FoodFirst Institute for Food and Development Policy.

Myers, N. and J. Kent 1995. *Environmental Exodus: An Emergent Crisis in the Global Arena*. Washington, DC: The Climate Institute.

NACLA 2004. "Bolivia Fights Back: An Introduction," *NACLA Report on the Americas* 38(3): 14.

—— 2005. "Social Movements: Building from the Ground Up," *NACLA Report on the Americas* 38(5).
Nader, R. and L. Wallach 1996. "GATT, NAFTA, and the Subversion of the Democratic Process," in J. Mander and E. Goldsmith (eds) *The Case Against the Global Economy*. San Francisco, CA: Sierra Clubs Books.
National Bureau of Statistics 2003. *China Statistics Yearbook on High Technology Industry*. Beijing: China Statistics Press.
Naylor, R. T. 2001. "The Rise of the Modern Arms Black Market and the Fall of Supply-Side Control," in P. Williams and D. Vlassis (eds) *Combating Transnational Crime: Concepts, Activities and Responses*. London: Frank Cass, pp. 209–235.
NEF (New Economics Foundation) 2002. *Five Brothers: The Rise and Nemesis of the Big Bean Counters*. Basingstoke: Palgrave Macmillan.
—— 2002–4. *Mergerwatch*: a bi-monthly publication of the New Economics Foundation. www.neweconomics.org
—— 2003a. *Return to Scale: Alternatives to Globalization*. Basingstoke: Palgrave Macmillan.
—— 2003b. *Real World Economic Outlook: The Legacy of Globalization: Debt and Deflation*. Basingstoke: Palgrave Macmillan.
Nevins, J. 2002. *Operation Gatekeeper: The Rise of the "Illegal Alien" and the Making of the US–Mexico Boundary*. New York: Routledge.
New American Century Report 2000. *Rebuilding America's Defenses: Strategy, Forces and Resources for a New Century*. Washington, DC: Project for the New American Century.
—— 2005. *Iraq: Setting the Record Straight*. Washington, DC: Project for the New American Century.
Newman, D. (ed.) 1998. *Boundaries, Territory and Postmodernity*. London: Frank Cass.
Nichols, J. 2002. "Enron's Global Crusade," *The Nation*, 4 March, pp. 11–19.
Nietschmann, B. 1987. "The Third World War," *Cultural Survival Quarterly* 11(3).
—— 1994. "The Fourth World: Nations versus States," in G. J. Demko and W.B. Wood (eds) *Reordering the World: Geopolitical Perspectives on the Twenty-first Century*. Boulder, CO: Westview Press, pp. 225–242.
Noble G. N. and S. Ravenhill 2000. *The Asian Financial Crisis and the Architecture of Global Finance*. Cambridge: Cambridge University Press.
NPR (National Public Radio) 2005. "Gaza Palestinians Vent Frustrations Through Rap" (reported by Ivan Watson), 6 October.
Nyberg-Sorensen, N., N. van Hear and P. Engberg-Pedersen 2002. *The Migration-Development Nexus: Evidence and Policy Options*. Geneva: International Organization for Migration.
Oas, I. 2002. "The Spatial Dementia of Geopolitics," Master's thesis, Department of Geography, Pennsylvania State University.
O'Connor, J. 1998. *Natural Causes: Essays in Ecological Marxism*. New York: Guilford Press.
O'Connor, M. 1994. *Is Capitalism Sustainable? Political Economy and the Politics of Ecology*. New York: Guilford Press.
Ohmae, K. 1995. *The End of the Nation State: The Rise of Regional Economies*. New York: Free Press.
Olds, K. 1997. "Globalizing Shanghai: The 'Global Intelligence Corps' and the Building of Pudong," *Cities* 14: 109–123.

O'Loughlin, J. 1989. "World-power Competition and Local Conflicts in the Third World," in R. J. Johnston and P. J. Taylor (eds) *A World in Crisis? Geographical Perspectives*. Oxford: Blackwell.

—— 2005. "The Political Geography of Conflict: Civil Wars in the Hegemonic Shadow," in C. Flint (ed.) *The Geography of War and Peace: From Death Camps to Diplomats*. Oxford: Oxford University Press, pp. 85–105.

—— and H. van de Wurston 1990. "The Political Geography of Panregions," *Geographical Review* 80(1): 1–20.

——, L. Staeheli and E. Greenberg 2004. *Globalization and Its Outcomes*. New York: Guilford Press.

Omelaniuk, I. and T. L. Weiss 2005. "Introduction: Migration Challenges in the 21st Century," in *World Migration 2005*. Geneva: International Organization for Migration.

One World Trust 1999. *Charter 99: A Charter for Global Democracy*. London: One World Trust. www.oneworldtrust.org/documents/charter99g.pdf

Oram, J. 2002. "Addicted to Profit: The Pharma Cartel," in *Corporate Breakdown*, 2nd edn. New Economic Foundation. www.neweconomics.org

Orozco, M. 2002a. "Globalization and Migration: The Impact of Family Remittances in Latin America," *Latin American Politics and Society* 44(2): 41–67.

—— 2002b. "Remittances to Latin America and its Effect on Development," presentation made at the Round Table on Remittances as a Development Tool in the Caribbean (Jamaica), held in Kingston, Jamaica, September.

Ottaway, M. 2001. "Corporatism Goes Global: International Organizations, Nongovernmental Organizational Networks and Transnational Business," *Global Governance* 7: 265–292.

Ó Tuathail, G. 1996. *Critical Geopolitics*. Minneapolis, MN: University of Minnesota Press.

—— 1998. "Political Geography III: Dealing with Deterritorialization," *Progress in Human Geography* 22(1): 81–93.

—— and S. Dalby 1998. *Rethinking Geopolitics*. London: Routledge.

Overbeek, H. (ed.) 1993. *Restructuring Hegemony in the Global Political Economy: The Rise of Transnational Neo-Liberalism in the 1980s*. London: Routledge.

Palast, G. 2000. "Tony Rushes in where Bill Fears to Tread: How US Business Sets the Globalisation Agenda for the World Trade Organisation," *Manchester Guardian Weekly*, 26–31 May, p. 14.

Papastergiadis, N. 2000. *The Turbulence of Migration: Globalization, Deterritorialization and Hybridity*. Cambridge: Polity Press.

Pape, R. 2003. "The Strategic Logic of Terrorism," *American Political Science Review* 97(3): 343–361.

Parsons, J. E. 1988. "Bubble, Bubble, How Much Trouble? Financial Markets, Capitalist Development and Capitalist Crises," *Science and Society* 52: 260–289.

Passas, N. 2001. "Globalization and Transnational Crime: Effects of Criminogenic Asymmetries," in P. Williams and D. Vlassis (eds) *Combating Transnational Crime: Concepts, Activities and Responses*. London: Frank Cass, pp. 22–56.

Passell, J. 2002. "New Estimates of the Undocumented Population in the United States," Migration Information Source. Washington, DC: Migration Policy Institute. www.migrationinformation.org/feature/print.cfm?ID=19

—— 2005 "Unauthorized Migrants: Numbers and Characteristics," Background Briefing Prepared for Task Force on Immigration and America's Future, Pew Hispanic Center: a Pew Research Center Project. www.pewhispanic.org

Patterson, O. 1987. "The Emerging West Atlantic System: Migration, Culture, and Underdevelopment in the United States and the Circum-Caribbean Region," in W. Alonso (ed.) *Population in an Interacting World.* Cambridge, MA: Harvard University Press, pp. 227–260.

Pattullo, P. 2005. *Last Resorts: The Cost of Tourism in the Caribbean,* new edn. New York: Monthly Review Press.

Pauly, L. 1997. *Who Elected the Bankers? Surveillance and Control in the World Economy.* Ithaca, NY: Cornell University Press.

Pearce, D. 2002. "Making Globalisation a Positive Force for Sustainable Development," paper prepared for the Commonwealth Secretariat, Commonwealth Consultative Group on Environment, Cartagena, Colombia, February.

Peck, J. A. 2001. *Workfare States.* New York: Guilford.

—— 2002. "Political Economies of Scale: Fast Policy, Interscalar Relations, and Neoliberal Workfare," *Economic Geography* 78(3): 331–360.

—— 2004. "Geography and Public Policy: Constructions of Neoliberalism," *Progress in Human Geography* 28(3): 392–406.

—— and A. Tickell 1994. "Searching for a New Institutional Fix: The After-Fordist Crisis and the Global-Local Disorder," in R. Lee and J. Willis (eds) *Geographies of Economies.* London: Arnold, pp. 280–315.

—— and A. Tickell 2002. "The Urbanization of Neoliberalism: Theoretical Debates Neoliberalizing Space," *Antipode* 34(3): 380–404.

Penrose, E. 1959. *The Theory of the Growth of Firms.* New York: Oxford University Press.

Perelman, M. 1998. *McDonald's Question.* http://csf.colorado.edu/mail/pen-l/dec98/0163.html

Petros, M. 2005. *The Costs of Human Smuggling and Trafficking,* Global Migration Perspectives no. 31. Geneva: Global Commission on International Migration.

Pettifor, A. 2003. *The Real World Economic Outlook: The Legacy of Globalization – Debt and Deflation, Vol. 1.* London: New Economics Foundation.

Pew Research Center for the People and the Press 2002. *What the World Thinks in 2002.* Washington, DC: Pew Research Center for the People and the Press.

—— 2003. *Views of a Changing World.* Washington, DC: Pew Research Center for the People and the Press.

Phillips, L. 1998. *The Third Wave of Modernization: Cultural Perspectives on Neoliberalism.* Wilmington, DE: Scholarly Resources.

Pieterse, J. N. 2004. *Globalization and Culture: Global Mélange.* New York: Rowman & Littlefield.

Piven, F. F. 1995. "Is it Global Economics or Neo Laissez-faire?" *New Left Review* 213: 107–114.

Portes, A. and L. E. Guarnizo 1991. "Tropical Capitalists: US-Bound Immigration and Small-Enterprise Development in the Dominican Republic," in S. Diaz-Briquets and S. Weintraub (eds) *Migration, Remittances, and Small Business Development: Mexico and Caribbean Basin Countries.* Boulder, CO: Westview Press, pp. 101–131.

Porter, M. 1990. *The Competitive Advantage of Nations.* London: Macmillan.

—— 2000. "Location, Competition, and Economic Development: Local Clusters in a Global Economy," *Economic Development Quarterly* 14: 15–34.

Porter, T. 1997. "NAFTA, North American Financial Integration and Regulatory Co-operation in Banking and Securities," in G. Underhill (ed.) *The New International Order in International Finance.* Basingstoke: Macmillan, pp. 174–192.

Portes, A. 1997. *Globalization from Below: The Rise of Transnational Communities.* Transnational Communities Research Programme WPTC-98-01. Oxford: ESRC.

Portnoy, B. 2000. "Alliance Capitalism an Industrial Order," in R. A. Higgott, G. Underhill and A. Bieler (eds) *Non-state Actors and Authority in the Global System*. London: Routledge, pp. 157–173.

Potter, G. A. 2003. "The Bolivian Coca-growers Movement," *Cultural Survival Quarterly* 26(4): 50–58.

Preet, S. A. and M. G. Schechter 2000. *Rethinking Globalization(s): From Corporate Transnationalism to Local Interventions*. New York: St Martin's Press.

Price, M. D. 1999. "Nongovernmental Organizations on the Geopolitical Front Line," in G. Demko and W. B. Wood (eds) *Reordering the World: Geopolitical Perspectives on the Twenty-first Century*. Boulder, CO: Westview Press, pp. 260–178.

Pritchett, L. 1997. "Divergence, Big Time," *Journal of Economic Perspectives* 11(3): 3–17.

Project for a New American Century 2000. *Rebuilding America's Defenses: Strategy, Forces and Resources for a New Century*. Washington, DC: Project for a New American Century.

Prudham, S. 2004. "Poisoning the Well: Neoliberalism and the Contamination of Municipal Water in Walkerton, Ontario," *Geoforum* 35(3): 343–360.

Pugh, J. and R. B. Potter 2003. *Participatory Planning in the Caribbean: Lessons from Practice*. Aldershot: Ashgate.

Putnam, R. 1993. *Making Democracy Work: Civic Traditions in Modern Italy*. Princeton, NJ: Princeton University Press.

Queen Noor 2000. "Globalization and Culture," address, 50th Anniversary Symposium of the Aspen Institute, pp. 1–7. http://yaleglobal.yale.edu

Rabino, S. 1984. "Foreign Competition for the US Banking World," *Long Range Planning* 17: 115–122.

Radio Project 2000. *National Radio Project*, Oakland, CA. www.radioproject.org/archive/2000/0020.html

Ramonet, I. 2004. "Resistance," *Le Monde diplomatique*, May.

Rankin, K. N. 2004. *The Cultural Politics of Markets: Economic Liberalization and Social Change in Nepal*. Toronto: University of Toronto Press.

Ransom, D. 1994. "The New Robber Barons," *New Internationalist*, issue 259, September. www.newint.org/issue259/keynote.htm

Rashid, A. 2001. *Taliban: Militant Islam, Oil, and Fundamentalism in Central Asia*. New Haven: Yale Nota Bene.

Reddy, P. 2000. *Globalization of Corporate R&D: Implications for Innovation Systems in Host Countries*. London: Routledge.

——2002. *Jihad: The Rise of Militant Islam in Central Asia*. New York: Penguin.

Reich, R. E. 1991a. *The Work of Nations: Preparing Ourselves for 21st Century Capitalism*. New York: Knopf.

——1991b. "The Myth of 'Made in the USA'," *Wall Street Journal*, 5 July, p. A6.

——2003. "Analysis: Power Americana." http://news.bbc.co.uk/2/hi/americas/2801349.stm

Robbins, P. 2004. *Political Ecology: A Critical Introduction*. New York: Blackwell.

Roberts, B. R. 2005. "Globalization and Latin American Cities," *International Journal of Urban and Regional Research* 29(1): 110–123.

Roberts, S. 1998. "Geogovernance in Trade and Finance and Political Geographies of Dissent," in A. Herod, G. Ó Tuathail and S. Roberts (eds) *An Unruly World?* London: Routledge, pp. 116–134.

——2002. "Global Regulation and Trans-state Organization," in R. J. Johnston, P. J. Taylor and M. J. Watts (eds) *Geographies of Global Change: Remapping the World*, 2nd edn. Malden, MA: Blackwell, pp. 143–157.

——, A. Secor and M. Sparke 2003. "Neoliberal Geopolitics," *Antipode* 35(5): 886–897.
Robertson, J. 1998. *Transforming Economic Life: A Millennial Challenge*. Dartington, Totnes: Schumacher Society and Green Books.
Robertson, R. 1992. *Globalization: Social Theory and Global Culture*. London: Sage.
—— 1997. "Social Theory, Cultural Relativity and the Problem of Globality," in A. King (ed.) *Culture, Globalization and the World System: Contemporary Conditions for the Representation of Identity*. Minneapolis, MN: University of Minnesota Press, pp. 69–90.
Robinson, W. I. and J. Harris 2000. "Towards a Global Ruling Class? Globalization and the Transnational Capitalist Class," *Science & Society* 64(1): 11–54.
Rodney, W. 1974. *How Europe Underdeveloped Africa*. Washington, DC: Howard University Press.
Rogers, A. 2000. *A European Space for Transnationalism?* Transnational Communities Programme Working Paper WPTC-2K-07. Oxford: University of Oxford.
—— 2005. "Observations on Transnational Urbanism: Broadening and Narrowing the Field," *Journal of Ethnic and Migration Studies* 31(2): 403–407.
Rogowski, R. 1989. *Commerce and Coalitions: How Trade Affects Domestic Political Alignments*. Princeton, NJ: Princeton University Press.
Rose, N. 1999. *Powers of Freedom*. Cambridge: Cambridge University Press.
Rosecrance, R. 1986. *The Rise of the Trading State: Commerce and Conquest in the Modern World*. New York: Basic Books.
Rosenau, J. N. 1997. *Along the Domestic–Foreign Frontier: Exploring Governance in a Turbulent World*. Cambridge: Cambridge University Press.
Rosenberg, E. 2003. "Army to Help Tell Jessica Lynch Story," *Syracuse Post-Standard*, 23 August, E1–E3.
Ross, G. 2000. "Labor versus Globalization," in L. Ferleger and J. R. Mandle (eds) "Dimensions of Globalization," *Annals, American Academy of Political and Social Science* 570: 78–91.
Roy, A. 2001. *Power Politics*, 2nd edn. Cambridge, MA: South End Press.
—— 2003. "Confronting Empire," *ZNet*, Foreign Policy. Speech given at the World Social Forum, Porto Alegre, Brazil, 28 January: www.zmag.org/content/showarticle.cfm?SectionID=51&ItemID=2919.
—— 2004. *Public Power in the Age of Empire*. New York: Seven Stories Press.
Rubin, R. 1998. Speech at Mansion House, London, 8 May. Available from www.treas.gov/press/releases/pr2428.htm
Rudolph, S. H. and J. Piscatori 1997. *Transnational Religion and the Fading States*. Boulder, CO: Westview Press.
Ruffin, R. J. 1974. "International Trade Under Uncertainty," *Journal of International Economics* 4: 243–259.
Ruggie, J. G. 1983. International Regimes, Transactions and Change: Embedded Liberalism in the Postwar Economic Order," in S. D. Krasner (ed.) *International Regimes*. Ithaca, NY: Cornell University Press.
Ruggiero, V. 2001. "Transnational Crime and Transnational Economies," in P. C. van Duyne *et al.* (eds) *Cross-border Crime in a Changing Europe*. Huntington, NY: Nova Science Publishers, pp. 229–240.
Rugman, A. 1999. "Do World Bank and IMF Policies Work?" *International Affairs* 75: 845.
Rupert, M. E. 1990. "Producing Hegemony: State/Society Relations and the Politics of Productivity in the United States," *International Studies Quarterly* 34: 427–456.
Sachs, W. 1992. *The Development Dictionary*. London: Zed Books.
—— 1993. *Global Ecology: A New Arena of Political Conflict*. London: Zed Books.

—— 1999. *Planet Dialectics: Explorations in Environment and Development*. London: Zed Books.
Said, E. 1979. *Orientalism*. New York: Vintage Books.
—— 1993. *Culture and Imperialism*. New York: Alfred A. Knopf.
Saith, A. 2004. "Social Protection, Decent Work and Development," Education and Outreach Programme, International Institute for Labour Studies, Discussion Paper DP/152/2004. Geneva, Switzerland.
Salt, J. 1997. "International Movements of the Highly Skilled," Organization of Economic Co-operation and Development, Occasional Paper 3, ACDE/GD(97)169. Paris.
Samuelson, P. A. 1952. "Spatial Price Equilibrium and Linear Programming," *American Economic Review* 42: 283–303.
Sassen, S. 1988. *The Mobility of Labor and Capital: A Study in International Investment and Labor Flow*. Cambridge: Cambridge University Press.
—— 1991. *The Global City*. Princeton, NJ: Princeton University Press.
—— 1998. *Globalization and its Discontents*. New York: New York Press.
—— 2000. *Cities in a World Economy*. Thousand Oaks, CA: Pine Forge Press.
—— 2001. *The Global City: New York, London, Tokyo*. Princeton, NJ: Princeton University Press.
—— 2002a. *Global Networks, Linked Cities*. New York: Routledge.
—— 2002b. "Global Cities and Diasporic Networks: Microstates in Global Civil Society," in H. K. Anheier *et al.* (eds) *Global Civil Society 2002*. Oxford: Oxford University Press, pp. 217–238.
Sayer, A. and R. Walker 1992. *The New Social Economy: Reworking the Division of Labor*. Cambridge, MA: Blackwell.
Scandinavian Design 1997. Poul Henningsen, Arne Jacobsen, Verner Panton. *From Consulate General of Denmark in New York*. www.scandinaviandesign.com
Schiller, D. 1999. "Deep Impact: The Web and the Changing Media Economy," *Journal of Policy, Regulation and Strategy for Telecommunications Information and Media* 1(1): 35–51.
Schindlmayr, T. 2003. "Sovereignty, Legal Regimes and International Migration," *International Migration* 41(2): 109–123.
Schlesinger, A. 2003. "Good Foreign Policy a Casualty of War," *Los Angeles Times*, 23 March, p. M1.
Schlesinger, S. and S. Kinzer 1982. *Bitter Fruit: The Untold Story of American Coup in Guatemala*. New York: Anchor Books.
Schlosser, E. 2002. *Fast Food Nation*. New York: HarperCollins.
Schoenberger, E. 2000. "Creating the Corporate World: Strategy and Culture, Time and Space," in E. Sheppard and T. Barnes (eds) *A Companion to Economic Geography*. Oxford: Blackwell, pp. 377–391.
Scholte, J. A. 2000. "Can Globality Bring a Good Society?," in P. S. Aulakh and M. G. Schechter (eds) *Rethinking Globalization(s): From Corporate Transnationalism to Local Interventions*. New York: St Martin's and Macmillan Presses, pp. 13–31.
—— 2002. "Civil Society and the Governance of Global Finance," in J. A. Scholte and A. Schnabel (eds) *Civil Society and Global Finance*. London: Routledge, pp. 13–32.
Schultz, J. 2000. "Bolivians Win Anti-privatization Battle," *NACLA Report on the Americas* 33(6): 44–47.
Schumacher, E. F. 1973. *Small is Beautiful: Economics as if People Mattered*. New York: Harper & Row.
Scott, A. J. 1998. *Regions and the World Economy*. Oxford: Oxford University Press.

Sears, P. (1956) "The Process of Environmental Change by Man," in W. L. Thomas (ed.) *Man's Role in Changing the Face of the Earth: Vol. 2*. Chicago, IL: University of Chicago Press, pp. 471–486.

Seis, M. 2001. "Confronting the Contradiction: Global Capitalism and Environmental Health," *International Journal of Comparative Sociology* 42(1/2): 123–144.

Sen, A. 1997. "Development Thinking at the Beginning of the XXI Century," in L. Emmerij (ed.) *Economic and Social Development into the XXI Century*. Baltimore, MD: Johns Hopkins Press, pp. 531–551.

—— 2002. "Globalization: Past and Present." Lecture 1. Ishizaka Lectures.

Sen, J., A. Anand, A. Escobar and P. Waterman 2004. *The World Social Forum: Challenging Empires*. New Delhi: Viveka.

Sequera, V. 2000. "Colombia Militias Tax Drug Trade," *Associated Press*, 10 January.

Sevareid, S. 2002. "US Troops Face Anger as War Talk Heats Up," *The Tallahassee Democrat*, November 3, p. 14A.

Shah, A. 2005. *Free Trade and Globalization: A Primer on Neoliberalism*. www.globalissues.org/TradeRelated/FreeTrade/Neoliberalism.asp

Shannon, S. 1999. "Prostitution and the Mafia: Involvement of Organized Crime in the Global Sex Trade," in P. Williams (ed.) *Illegal Immigration and Commercial Sex: The New Slave Trade*. London: Frank Cass, pp. 119–144.

Shapiro, M. J. 1997. *Violent Cartographies: Mapping Cultures of War*. Minneapolis, MN: University of Minnesota Press.

—— 2003. "Nation-States," in J. Agnew, K. Mitchell and G. Ó Tuathail (eds) *A Companion to Political Geography*. Malden, MA: Blackwell, pp. 271–288.

Sheppard, E. 2001. "The Spaces and Times of Globalization: Place, Scale, Networks and Positionality," paper prepared for "Geographies of Global Economic Change" Conference, Clark University, Worcester, MA.

Shiva, V. 1999. "The Historical Significance of Seattle," MAI-NOT List serve. http://lists.essential.org/mai-not/msg00181.html

Shorrock, T. 2003. "Selling (off) Iraq," *The Nation*, 23 June, 11–16.

Shrestha, N. R. 1988. "Historical Evolution of the World System," in T. A. Hartshorn and J. W. Alexander (eds) *Economic Geography*. Englewood Cliffs, NJ: Prentice-Hall.

—— 1995. "Becoming an Underdeveloped Category," in J. Crush (ed.) *The Power of Development*. London: Routledge.

—— 1997. *In the Name of Development: A Reflection on Nepal*. Lanham, MD: University Press of America.

——, W. I. Smith and K. R. Gray 2005. "A Multidimensional Approach to Understanding Cultural Landscapes for Global Business," *Proceedings of the Conference on Emerging Issues in Business and Technology*. Macomb, IL: College of Business and Technology, Western Illinois University.

Shurmer-Smith, P. and K. Hannam 1994. *Worlds of Desire, Realms of Power: A Cultural Geography*. London: Arnold.

Siedentop, L. 2000. *Democracy in Europe*. Harmondsworth: Penguin.

Simmons, B. A. 1993. "Why Innovate? Founding the Bank for International Settlements," *World Politics* 45: 361–405.

Simms, A., T. Bigg and N. Robins 2000. *"It's Democracy, Stupid": The Trouble with the Global Economy – The United Nation's Lost Role and Democratic Reform of the IMF, World Bank and the World Trade Organization*. London: New Economics Foundation.

Skeldon, R. 2004. "China: From Exceptional Case to Global Participant," Migration

Information Source. Washington, DC: Migration Policy Institute. www.migrationinformation.org/Profiles/print.cfm?ID=219

Sklair, L. 2002. *Globalization: Capitalism and its Alternatives*, 3rd edn. Oxford: Oxford University Press.

Sklar, R. L. 1976. "Post-imperialism: A Class Analysis of Multinational Corporate Expansion." *Comparative Politics* 9: 75–92.

Slotkin, R. 1992. *Gunfighter Nation: The Myth of the Frontier in Twentieth Century America*. New York: Atheneum.

Small Arms Survey 2003. Oxford: Oxford University Press. www.smallarmssurvey.org/publications/yb_2003.htm

Smith, M. P. 2000. *Transnational Urbanism*. Thousand Oaks, CA: Sage.

—— 2001. *Transnational Urbanism: Locating Globalization*. Malden, MA: Blackwell.

—— 2003. "Transnationalism and Citizenship," in B. S. A. Yeoh, M. W. Charney and T. C. Kiong (eds) *Approaching Transnationalisms: Studies on Transnational Societies, Multicultural Contacts and Imaginings of Home*. Boston, MA: Kluwer, pp. 15–37.

—— 2005. "Transnational Urbanism Revisited," *Journal of Ethnic and Migration Studies*, 31(2): 235–244.

—— and L. E. Guarnizo 1998. *Transnationalism from Below*. New Brunswick, NJ: Transaction Publishers.

Smith, N. 1990. *Uneven Development*, 2nd edn. Oxford: Blackwell.

—— 2002. "New Globalism, New Urbanism: Gentrification as Global Urban Strategy," in N. Brenner and N. Theodore (eds) *Spaces of Neoliberalism: Urban Restructuring in North America and Western Europe*. Malden, MA: Blackwell, pp. 80–103.

Soros, G. 1997. "The Capitalist Threat," *The Atlantic Monthly* (digital edition: www.theatlantic.com). Accessed 7 July 2005.

—— 1998/9. "Capitalism's Last Chance?" *Foreign Policy* 113: 55–66.

Sparke, M. and V. A. Lawson 2003. "Entrepreneurial Geographies of Global–Local Governance," in J. Agnew, K. Mitchell and G. Ó Tuathail (eds) *A Companion to Political Geography*. Malden, MA: Blackwell, pp. 315–334.

Speth, J. G. 2003. *Worlds Apart: Globalization and the Environment*. Covelo, CA: Island Press.

Srinivasan, T. N. 2000. "The Washington Consensus a Decade Later: Ideology and the Art and Science of Policy Advice," *World Bank Research Observer* 15(2): 265–270.

Stafford, L. 1992. London's Financial Markets: Perspectives and Prospects," in *Global Finance and Urban Living: A Study of Metropolitan Change*. London: Routledge, pp. 31–51.

Stalker, P. 1994. *The Work of Strangers: A Survey of International Labor Migration*. Geneva: International Labour Office.

—— 2000. *Workers without Frontiers: The Impact of Globalization on International Migration*. Boulder, CO: Lynne Rienner.

Standing, G. 1999. *Global Labour Flexibility: Seeking Distributive Justice*. New York: St Martin's Press.

Steinert, H. 2003. "Unspeakable September 11th: Taken-for-Granted Assumptions, Selective Reality Construction and Populist Politics," *International Journal of Urban and Regional Research* 23(3): 651–665.

Stevenson, M. 1992. "Columbus and the War on Indigenous People," *Race and Class* 33(3).

Stiglitz, J. 2002. *Globalization and Its Discontents*. New York: W. W. Norton.

—— 2003. *The Roaring Nineties: A New History of the World's Most Prosperous Decade*. New York: W. W. Norton.
Stohr, W. B. 1981. "Development from Below: The Bottom-up and Periphery-inward Development Paradigm," in W. B. Stohr and D. R. Frazer Taylor (1981) *Development from Above or Below? The Dialectics of Regional Planning in Developing Countries*. New York: John Wiley, pp. 39–72.
Storper, M. 1997. *The Regional World: Territorial Development in a Global Economy*. New York: Guilford Press.
Strange, S. 1986. *Casino Capitalism*. Oxford: Blackwell.
Sum, N.-L. 2000. "Globalization and Its 'Other(s)': Three 'New Kinds of Orientalism' and the Political Economy of Trans-border Identity," in C. Hay and D. Marsh (eds) *Demystifying Globalization*. Basingstoke: Macmillan, pp. 105–126.
Suskind, R. 2003. *The Price of Loyalty: George W. Bush, the White House and the Education of Paul O'Neill*. New York: Simon & Schuster.
Swyngedouw, E. 1996. "The City as a Hybrid: On Nature, Society and Cyborg Urbanisation," *Capitalism, Nature, Socialism* 7: 65–80.
—— 1997. "Neither Global or Local: 'Glocalization' and the Politics of Scale," in K. R. Cox (ed.) *Spaces of Globalization*. New York: Guilford Press, pp. 137–166.
—— 2005. "Dispossessing H_2O: The Contested Terrain of Water Privatization," *Capitalism, Nature, Socialism* 16(1): 81–98.
—— and N. C. Heynen 2003. "Urban Political Ecology, Justice and the Politics of Scale," *Antipode* 35(5): 898–918.
Takaki, R. 1989. *Strangers from a Different Shore: A History of Asian Americans*. New York: Penguin.
Tapinos, G. 1999. "Clandestine Immigration: Economic and Political Issues," *SOPEMI, Trends in International Migration*, annual report. Paris: OECD, pp. 229–251.
Taran, P. A. 2000. "Human Rights of Migrants: Challenges of the New Decade," *International Migration* 38(6): 7–46.
—— 2005. *Migration and Labor Solidarity*. Ithaca, NY: ILO–Cornell University. www-ilo-mirror.cornell.edu/public/english/dialogue/actrav/publ/129/5/pdf
Taylor, J. E., J. Arango, G. Hugo, A. Kouaouci, D. S. Massey and A. Pellegrino 1996a. "International Migration and National Development," *Population Index* 62(2): 181–212.
—— 1996b. "International Migration and Community Development," *Population Index* 62(3): 397–418.
Taylor, L. 1997. "The Revival of the Liberal Creed: The IMF and the World Bank in a Globalised Economy," *World Development* 25: 145–152.
Taylor, P. J. 1982. "A Materialist Framework for Political Geography," *Transactions, Institute of British Geographers NS* 7: 15–34.
—— 1993. *Political Geography: World Economy, Nation-State, and Locality*. Harlow: Longman Scientific & Technical.
—— 1994. "World Cities and Territorial States: The Rise and Fall of their Mutuality," in P. Knox and P. J. Taylor (eds) *World Cities in a World System*. Cambridge: Cambridge University Press, pp. 48–62.
—— 1996. *The Way the Modern World Works: World Hegemony to World Impasse*. Chichester: John Wiley.
—— 1999. *Modernities: A Geohistorical Interpretation*. Minneapolis, MN: University of Minnesota Press.

—— 2000. "Geopolitics, Political Geography and Social Science," in K. Dodds and D. Atkinson (eds) *Geopolitical Traditions: A Century of Geopolitical Thought*. London: Routledge, pp. 375–379.

—— 2004. *World City Network: A Global Urban Analysis*. London: Routledge.

——, D. R. F. Walker and J. V. Beaverstock 2000. "Firms and their Global Service Networks," in S. Sassen (ed.) *Global Networks, Linked Cities*. New York: Routledge, pp. 93–115.

Thomas, B. 1961. *International Migration and Economic Development*. Paris: UNESCO.

—— 1993. *The Industrial Revolution and the Atlantic Economy*. London: Routledge.

Thomas, W. L. 1956. *Man's Role in Changing the Face of the Earth: Vol. 1*. Chicago, IL: University of Chicago Press.

Thomas-Hope, E. 2003. "Skilled Labour Migration from Developing Countries: Study of the Caribbean Region," International Migration Programme, IM Paper 50. Geneva: International Labour Office.

Thornton, W. 2003. "Cold War II: Islamic Terrorism as Power Politics," *Antipode* 35(2): 205–211.

Thoumi, F. E. 1995. *Political Economy and Illegal Drugs in Colombia*. Boulder, CO: Lynne Rienner.

Thrift, N. J. 1983. "On the Determination of Social Action in Space and Time," *Environment and Planning D: Society and Space* 1(1): 23–57.

—— 1987. "The Fixers: The Urban Geography of International Commercial Capital," in J. Henderson and M. Castells (eds) *Global Restructuring and Territorial Development*. London: Sage, pp. 219–247.

—— 1998. "The Rise of Soft Capitalism," in A. Herod *et al.* (eds) *An Unruly World?: Globalization, Governance and Geography*. London: Routledge, pp. 25–71.

—— 2000. "Geography of Consumption," in R. Johnston, D. Gregory, M. Watts and G. Pratt (eds) *Dictionary of Human Geography*, 4th edn. Oxford: Blackwell, pp. 108–110.

—— 2002. "A Hyperactive World," in R. J. Johnston, P. J. Taylor and M. J. Watts (eds) *Geographies of Global Change: Remapping the World*, 2nd edn. Oxford: Blackwell, pp. 29–42.

—— and A. Leyshon 1994. "A Phantom State? The De-traditionalization of Money, the International Financial System and International Financial Centres," *Political Geography* 13(4): 299–327.

Thurow, L. C. 2000. "Globalization: The Product of a Knowledge-based Economy," in L. Ferleger and J. R. Mandle (eds) "Dimensions of Globalization," *Annals, American Academy of Political and Social Science* 570: 19–31.

Tickell, A. 1996. "Making a Melodrama Out of a Crisis: Reinterpreting the Collapse of Barings Bank," *Environment and Planning D: Society and Space* 14(1): 5–33.

—— 1999. "Unstable Futures: Controlling and Creating Risks in International Money," in L. Panitch and C. Leys (eds) *Socialist Register 1999*. Rendlesham: Merlin Press, pp. 248–277.

—— 2000. "Global Rhetorics, National Politics: Pursuing Bank Mergers in Canada," *Antipode* 32: 152–175.

—— 2001. "The Transformation of Financial Regulation in the UK," in M. Bovens, P. T. Hart and G. Peters (eds) *Success and Failure in Public Governance: A Comparative Analysis*. Aldershot: Elgar, pp. 419–436.

—— 2002. "Cultures of Money," in K. Anderson, S. Pile and N. J. Thrift (eds) *A Handbook of Cultural Geography*. London: Sage.

—— and J. Peck 1995. "Social Regulation after Fordism: Regulation Theory, Neo-liberalism and the Global–Local Nexus," *Economy and Society* 24: 357–386.

—— and J. A. Peck 2002. "Making Global Rules: Globalisation and Neoliberalisation?" in J. Peck and H. W.-C. Yeung (eds) *Making Global Connections*. London: Sage.

—— and J. A. Peck 2003. "Making Global Rules: Globalisation or Neoliberalisation?" in J. Peck and H. Yeung (eds) *Remaking the Global Economy*. London: Sage, pp. 163–182.

Tietmayer, H. 1997. "Globalisation of Financial Markets and the Need for International Standards and Harmonisation of Prudential Agreements," speech presented at the "Financial Stability and Prudential Standards" conference, Hong Kong, 22 September. Available from Deutsche Bundesbank, Wilhelm-Epstein-Str. 14, P.O.B. 10 06 02, D-60006 Frankfurt am Main, Germany.

Tiryakian, E. 1999. "War: The Covered Side of Modernity," *International Sociology* 14(4): 473–489.

Tokar, B. 1997. *Earth for Sale: Reclaiming Ecology in the Age of Corporate Greenwash*. Cambridge, MA: South End Press.

Toporowski, J. 2000. *The End of Finance: Pension Funds, Derivatives and Capital Market Inflation*. London: Routledge.

Triffin, R. 1960. *Gold and the Dollar Crisis*. New Haven, CT: Yale University Press.

Turner, F. J. 1896. "The Problem of the West," *The Atlantic Monthly* 78: 289–297.

—— 1920. *The Frontier in American History*. New York: Henry Holt.

Twitchell, J. B. 1999. *Lead Us Into Temptation: The Triumph of American Materialism*. New York: Columbia University Press.

UNESCO 2003. "What Is UNESCO?" www.unesco.org/general/eng/about/what.shtml

UNHCR 2003. *Asylum Levels and Trends in Industrialized Countries: January to July 2003*. Geneva: UNHCR.

UNICEF UK 2004. *Faces of Exploitation: End Child Exploitation*. www.endchildexploitation.org.uk/issue_child_labour_asp

United Nations Security Council 2002. *Final Report of the Panel of Experts on the Illegal Exploitation of Natural Resources and Other Forms of Wealth of the Dem. Rep. of Congo*.

Valdés, J. 1995. *Pinochet's Economists: The Chicago School in Chile*. Cambridge: Cambridge University Press.

Van Duyne, P. C. 2001. "Cross-border Crime: A Relative Concept and Broad Phenomenon," in P. C. Van Duyne *et al.* (eds) *Cross-border Crime in a Changing Europe*. Huntington, NY: Nova Science, pp. 1–14.

Van Ham, P. 2003. "War. Lies and Videotapes: Public Diplomacy and the USA's War on Terrorism," *Security Dialogue* 34(4): 427–444.

van der Pijl, K. 1998. *Transnational Classes and International Relations*. London: Routledge.

—— 2001. "Restoring the Radical Imagination in Political Economy," *New Political Economy* 6: 380–390.

Varney, W. and B. Martin 2000. "Net Resistance, Net Benefits: Opposing MAI," *Social Alternatives* 19(1): 47–52.

Vidal, G. 2002. *Perpetual War for Perpetual Peace*. New York: Thunder's Mouth Press/Nation Books.

Voigt-Graf, C. 2004. "Towards a Geography of Transnational Spaces: Indian Transnational Communities in Australia," *Global Networks* 4(1): 25–49.

Wachtel, H. M. 1986. *The Money Mandarins: The Making of a New Supranational Economic Order*. New York: Pantheon.

Wacquant, L. 2000. "The Coming of the Penal State is not Inevitable," *Working Papers in Local Governance and Democracy* 4, November 2000.

Wade, R. 1998/9. "The Coming Fight Over Capital Flows," *Foreign Policy* 113: 41–54.

—— 1998. "The Asian Debt-and-Development Crisis of 1997: Causes and Consequences," *World Development* 26: 1535–1553.

—— 2000. "Wheels Within Wheels: Rethinking the Asian Crisis and the Asian Model," *Annual Review of Political Science* 3: 85–115.

—— 2001. "Showdown at the World Bank," *New Left Review* 7: 124ff.

—— and F. Veneroso 1998. "The Asian Crisis: The High Debt Model versus the Wall Street Treasury IMF Complex," *New Left Review* 228: 3–22.

Walcott, S. 2002. "Growing Global: Learning Locations in the Life Sciences," *Growth and Change* 33: 511–532.

—— 2003. *Chinese Science and Technology Industrial Parks*. Aldershot: Ashgate.

Walker, R. 1999a. "The Americanisation of British Welfare: A Case Study of Policy Transfer," *International Journal of Health Services* 29: 679–697.

—— 1999b. "Putting Capital in its Place: Globalization and the Prospects for Labor," *Geoforum* 30: 263–284.

Wallerstein, I. 1976. *The Modern World System: Capitalist Agriculture and the Origins of the European World Economy in the Sixteenth Century*. New York: Academic Press.

—— 1979. *The Capitalist World Economy*. Cambridge: Cambridge University Press.

—— 1980. *The Modern World System. II: Mercantilism and the Consolidation of the European World Economy: 1600–1750*. New York: Academic Press.

—— 1989. *The Second Era of Great Expansion of the Capitalist World Economy, 1730–1840s*. San Diego, CA: Academic Press.

—— 1992. *Geopolitics and Geoculture*. Cambridge: Cambridge University Press.

—— 1996a. "The Global Picture, 1945–90," in T. K. Hopkins and I. Wallerstein *et al.* (eds) *The Age of Transition: Trajectory of the World System 1945–2025*. London: Zed Books, pp. 209–225.

—— 1996b. "The Global Possibilities, 1990–2025," in T. K. Hopkins and I. Wallerstein *et al.* (eds) *The Age of Transition: Trajectory of the World System 1945–2025*. London: Zed Books, pp. 226–243.

—— 2000. "Globalization or the Age of Transition? A Long-term View of the Trajectory of the World System." http://yaleglobal.yale.edu. Accessed 17 July 2005.

Wall Street Journal 2003. "World Economic Forum's Three Decades of History," *Wall Street Journal*, 20 January.

Warf, B. 2000. "Telecommunications and Economic Space," in E. Sheppard and T. Barnes (eds) *A Companion to Economic Geography*. Oxford: Blackwell, pp. 484–498.

Waters, J. 2003. "Flexible Citizens? Transnationalism and Citizenship amongst Economic Immigrants in Vancouver," *The Canadian Geographer* 47(3): 219–234.

Watkins, S. 2004. "A Weightless Hegemony: New Labour's Role in the Neoliberal Order," *New Left Review* 25: 5–33.

Watson, C. A. 2000. "Civil–Military Relations in Colombia: A Workable Relationship or a Case for Fundamental Reform?" *Third World Quarterly* 21(3): 529–548.

Watson, J. (ed.) 1998. *Golden Arches East: McDonald's in East Asia*. Cambridge: Cambridge University Press.

Webber, M. J. and D. L. Rigby 1996. *The Golden Age Illusion: Rethinking Postwar Capitalism*. New York: Guilford Press.

Weber, A. 1929. *Theory of the Location of Industries*. Chicago, IL: University of Chicago (trans. C. J. Friedrich).

Webster, F. 2001. *Culture and Politics in the Information Age: A New Politics?* New York: Routledge.

WEF (World Economic Forum) 2004. *Annual Report: Global Governance Initiative*. Geneva: WEF. www.weforum.org

Weil, P. 2002. "Towards a Coherent Policy of Co-development," *International Migration* 40(3): 41–53.

Weinberg, W. 2000. *Homage to Chiapas: The New Indigenous Struggles in Mexico*. London: Verso.

Weiner, M. 1995. *The Global Migration Crisis: Challenges to States and Human Rights*. New York: HarperCollins.

—— and S. S. Russell 2001. *Demography and National Security*. New York: Berghahn.

Weiss, L. 1998. *The Myth of the Powerless State*. Cambridge: Polity Press.

Whatmore, S. 2002. *Hybrid Geographies: Natures, Cultures, Spaces*. London: Sage.

White House 2002. *The National Security Strategy of the United States of America*, 17 September.

Whitwell, C. 2002. "'New Migration' in the 1990s: A Retrospective," Migration Research Centre, University of Sussex, Working Paper 13, Brighton.

WHO 2005. *The Migration of Health Workers: An Overview*. Geneva: World Health Organization.

Wickramasekera, P. 2001. *Asian Labour Migration: Issues and Challenges in an Era of Globalization*. Geneva: International Labour Office.

Widgren, J. 1993. "Movements of Refugees and Asylum Seekers: Recent Trends in a Comparative Perspective," in *The Changing Course of International Migration*. Paris: OECD.

Willett, S. 2002. "Globalization and the Means of Destruction: Physical Insecurity and the Weapons Industry at the Turn of the Millennium," in B. Harriss-White (ed.) *Globalization and Insecurity: Political, Economic, and Physical Challenges*. New York: Palgrave, pp. 184–201.

Williams, P. 1999. *Illegal Immigration and Commercial Sex: The New Slave Trade*. London: Frank Cass.

—— 2002. "Organizing Transnational Crime: Networks, Markets, and Hierarchies," in P. Williams and D. Vlassis (eds) *Combating Transnational Crime: Concepts, Activities and Responses*. London: Frank Cass, pp. 57–87.

Williams, R. 1977. *Marxism and Literature*. New York: Oxford University Press.

—— 1980. *Problems in Materialism and Culture*. London: Verso.

—— 1983. *Keywords*. London: Fontana.

—— 1989. *Resources of Hope*. London: Verso.

Williams, W.A. 1969. *The Roots of Modern American Empire: A Study of the Growth and Shaping of Consciousness in a Marketplace Society*. New York: Random House.

Wilson, D. and R. Purushothaman 2003. "Dreaming with BRICs: The Path to 2050," Global Economics Paper 99. Goldman Sachs global economics website: www.gs.com

Wisner, B. 1978. "Does Radical Geography Lack an Approach to Environmental Relations?" *Antipode* 10(1): 84–95.

Womack, J. P., D. Jones and D. Roos 1990. *The Machine that Changed the World*. New York: Rawson Associates, pp. 48–191, 277.

Wood, R. 1986. *From Marshall Plan to Debt Crisis: Foreign Aid and Development Choices in the World Economy*. Berkeley, CA: University of California Press.

Woods, N. 2000. *The Political Economy of Globalization*. New York: St Martin's Press.

Woodward, B. 2000. *Maestro*. New York.

Woodward, D. 1998. *Globalization, Uneven Development and Poverty: Recent Trends and Policy Implications*. United Nations Development Programme, Social Development and Poverty Elimination Division.

World Bank 2003. "Welcome to World Bank Group." http://web.worldbank.org/

World Economic Forum 2004. *World Economic Forum's Annual Meeting 2004: Fact Sheet*, 20 January – Davos, Switzerland: www.weforum.org/site/homepublic.nsf/Content/World+Economic+Forum%27s+Annual+Meeting+2004%A+Fact+Sheet

World Watch Institute 1990. *State of the World in 1990*. Washington, DC: World Watch Institute.

—— 1993. *State of the World in 1993*. Washington, DC: World Watch Institute.

—— 2003. *State of the World in 2003*. Washington, DC: World Watch Institute.

—— 2004. *State of the World in 2004: Special Focus, the Consumer Society*. Washington, DC: World Watch Institute.

Wright, R. 2002. "Transnational Corporations and Global Divisions of Labor," in R. J. Johnston, P. J. Taylor and M. J. Watts (eds) *Geographies of Global Change: Remapping the World*, 2nd edn. Malden, MA: Blackwell, pp. 68–77.

—— and J. Austen 1993. "'It's Gotta Be Da Shoes': Domestic Manufacturing, International Subcontracting, and the Production of Athletic Footwear," *Environment and Planning A* 25(8): 1103–1114.

Wrigley, N. 2000. "The Globalization of Retail Capital: Themes for Economic Geography," in G. Clark, M. Gertler and M. Feldman (eds) *Handbook of Economic Geography*. Oxford: Oxford University Press, pp. 292–316.

Yapa, L. 1992. "Why Do They Map GNP per Capita," in S. K. Majumdar, G. S. Forbes, E. W. Miller and R. F. Schmalz (eds) *Natural and Technological Disasters: Causes, Effects and Preventive Measures*. Easton, PA: Pennsylvania Academy of Sciences.

—— 1999. "Rediscovering Geography: On Speaking Truth to Power," *Annals, Association of American Geographers* 89(1): 151–155.

Yeoh, B. S. A. 1999. "Global/Globalizing Cities," *Progress in Human Geography* 23(4): 607–616.

—— 2005. "Observations on Transnationalism: Possibilities, Politics and Costs of Simultaneity," *Journal of Ethnic and Migration Studies* 31(2): 409–413.

Yergin, D. 1992. *The Prize: The Epic Quest for Oil, Money and Power*. New York: The Free Press.

Yeung, H. W.-C. 1994. "Critical Reviews of Geographical Perspectives on Business Organizations and the Organization of Production: Towards a Network Approach," *Progress in Human Geography* 18(4): 460–490.

—— 1998. "Capital, State and Space: Contesting a Borderless World," *Transactions, Institute of British Geographers* 23(3): 291–309.

Yingling, J., R. Detty and J. Sottile 2000. "Lean Manufacturing Principles and their Applicability to the Mining Industry," *Mineral Resource Engineering* 9(2): 215–238.

Young, D. and R. Keil 2005. "Urinetown or Morainetown? Debates on the Reregulation of the Urban Water Regime in Toronto," *Capitalism, Nature, Socialism* 16(2): 61–83.

Zhou, Y. 2005. "The Making of an Innovative Region from a Centrally Planned Economy: Institutional Evolution in Zhongguancun Science Park in Beijing," *Environment and Planning A* 37: 1113–1134.

Zibechi, R. 2005. "New Challenges for Radical Social Movements," *NACLA Report of the Americas*, special issue, 38(5): 14–21.

Zlotnik, H. 2003. "The Global Dimensions of Female Migration," Migration Information Source. Washington, DC: Migration Policy Institute. www.migrationinformation.org/feature/print.cfm?ID=109

Zolberg, A. R. and P. Benda 2001. *Global Migrants, Global Refugees: Problems and Solutions*. New York: Berghahn.

Zukin, S. 1995. *Cultures of Cities*. New York: Routledge.

Index

activist 14, 31, 145, 197, 198, 199, 212, 213, 214, 215, 216, 217, 218, 219, 220, 222, 223, 224, 225, 235
agency 8, 33, 79, 124, 222, 224
agriculture 85, 194,
al-Qaeda 162, 164, 167
alternative "spaces of resistance" 215
American/US: domestic policies 23, 28, 42; economy 132, 133, 134, 135, 136, 137, 138; foreign policies 23, 130, 132, 144, 165, 169, 207; "frontiers" 129, 130; globalization 130, 201; hegemony 23, 41, 42, 128, 129, 131, 139; imperialism 124, 128, 150, 171, 238; international agenda 23, 129, 131; neo-imperialism 109
Amsterdam Treaty 92
anti-globalization 215, 217, 218, 219, 221, 223, 224, 225, 236
anti-immigration lobby 92
anti-terrorism 82, 172
anti-war 23, 213, 217, 218, 225, 237
arms: race 22, 118, 125, 162, 236; trafficking 97
Asian crisis/meltdown 139, 233, 234
asylum-seekers 83, 89, 90, 92, 93, 103, 122, 141, 216

Barings Bank 39, 43
"Battle for Seattle" 31, 215, 227
biodiversity 192, 193, 217
biological and chemical weapons 170
"boom–bust" economic cycles 43, 53
border enforcement 59, 79, 80, 87, 103
Bretton Woods Agreement 18, 22, 23, 31, 40, 41, 63, 133, 134, 143, 219, 239

capital-intensive production 65, 66, 72, 73, 74, 75, 235

capitalism's: contradictions 5, 17, 18, 20, 23, 32, 47, 152, 154, 159, 185, 190, 192, 194, 228; hyper-mobility 4, 5, 9, 94, 233, 234; "time–space compression" 3, 5, 20, 127; unruliness 5, 80, 226; volatility 5, 31, 80, 233, 234
CARICOM 28
Catholic Church 111, 112,120
central banks 19, 47, 233
Chicago School of Monetarists 24, 145, 146
children 81, 83, 113, 114, 125, 194, 224; exploitation of 81, 91, 93, 97, 234, 235
city systems 12, 33, 110, 111, 120, 124
civil society 13, 30, 83, 144, 218, 225, 237, 238
civil war 21, 80, 82, 89, 234
Cold War 14, 21, 22, 23, 82, 85, 89, 90, 92, 96, 100, 115, 118, 127, 130, 134, 137, 138, 139, 142, 166, 236
colonialism 20, 128, 131, 163, 197, 198, 200, 205, 208
commodity chains 9, 13, 53, 54, 64, 199, 229
communications 3, 4, 5, 8, 13, 42, 50, 69, 81, 86, 98, 114, 123, 151, 156, 163, 164, 201, 222, 224, 225, 236
Communism 23, 128, 205
"conflict" diamonds 14, 95
"consumerscapes" 229
coral reef damage 193
corporations: corruption 11, 16; mergers 5, 10, 43, 52, 62, 63, 131, 233; multi-national 25, 27, 41, 52, 73, 123, 137, 191, 199, 233; Top 200 62, 63; transnational 6, 10, 13, 27, 31, 42, 49, 50, 52, 63, 73, 74, 75, 81, 82, 89, 120, 122, 123, 137, 139, 141, 183, 190, 218, 221, 222, 223, 230, 233, 238
craft-based production 69, 70, 73, 74, 75

crimes against humanity 114, 169
criminal: commodities 96; economies 95, 96, 97, 98, 99, 103, 105; enterprises 95, 98, 100, 103; markets 96; organizations 96, 97, 100, 101, 102, 103
cultural: contestations 206, 207; convergence 201, 206; divide 204, 209; identity 204, 205, 206, 207, 208, 209, 229; proximity 71; transformations 17
culture 5, 14, 29, 54, 88, 104, 114, 117, 122, 129, 130, 144, 145, 146, 147, 148, 149, 150, 151, 152, 153, 154, 155, 156, 157, 158, 159, 160, 163, 164, 183, 192, 196, 197, 199, 200, 201, 202, 203, 204, 205, 206, 207, 208, 212, 229, 236, 237, 238, 239

debt crisis 26, 44
democracy 22, 30, 132, 146, 159, 172, 176, 215, 230, 232, 236, 237, 238, 241
deregulation 24, 25, 26, 27, 39, 40, 43, 45, 100, 101, 141, 181, 182, 227
development: economic 49, 65, 71, 128, 142, 149, 189, 205, 221; era 89; -induced displacement 89, 90; models/strategies 22, 75; uneven 3, 4, 7, 9, 15, 17, 20, 21, 32, 59, 81, 99, 119, 152, 154, 163, 182, 183, 185, 226, 227, 228, 230; urban 54
developing countries 10, 55, 65, 72, 74, 85, 101, 227
developmental state 16, 109, 231
downsizing 10, 62, 63, 227, 233
drug(s) 14, 33, 81, 95, 96, 97, 103, 105, 119, 234; crops 99, 101; interdiction efforts 104, 234; legalization of 105; markets 96; production 101; smuggling/trafficking 89, 97, 105

East–West 21, 22, 236
economic liberalism 18, 19, 127, 128
economies of scale 66, 137
education 4, 74, 75, 83, 85, 86, 113, 114, 130, 144, 151, 152, 197, 198, 199, 200, 210, 220, 230, 235, 236, 238, 239
emerging markets 28, 29, 42, 227
emigration 83, 85, 88, 94
endangered species 193, 212, 214, 217
environmental 63, 80, 119, 125, 163, 164, 181, 182, 183, 185, 186, 187, 188, 189, 190, 191, 192, 193, 194, 195, 214, 215, 216, 217, 218, 223, 228, 235, 236, 238, 240; change 183, 184, 185, 186, 187, 194; crisis 15, 185, 187, 216; deterioration/degradation 5, 82, 89, 90, 91, 93, 119, 182, 188, 189, 194, 212, 216, 236; disasters 89, 228; justice 194, 241; protection 16, 114, 115, 182, 193, 212, 215, 216, 217; refugees 90; regulations 52, 145, 193, 216, 217; sustainability 16, 125, 194, 220, 230
environmentalism 125, 193, 194, 213, 216
ethnic 21, 80, 90, 91, 93, 100, 111, 141, 142, 185, 187, 199, 203, 208, 213, 216, 223, 224, 234; cleansing 80, 115; conflicts 82, 91; minorities 90, 122, 163
Eurocurrency markets 41
European Union 30, 44, 59, 92, 110, 113, 115, 116, 136, 139, 141, 229, 230
everyday things 153, 202
Exclusive Economic Zones (EEZs) 73
extraordinary things 153, 154, 156

"failed states" 100
Federal Reserve Board 42, 44
financial institutions 22, 39, 40, 41, 42, 44, 45, 229, 234
financial markets 39, 43, 44, 45, 46, 47, 122, 141, 234
Financial Sector Assessment Program (FSAP) 45, 47
First World 21, 53, 54, 194, 233
flexible regimes 63
Fordism 67, 134
foreign direct investment 26, 52, 56, 57, 58, 131, 133, 134, 136, 137, 141, 143, 229, 232, 233
fragmentation 128, 139, 141, 142, 208
free trade 15, 19, 29, 30, 33, 63, 72, 103, 124, 128, 135, 139, 191, 212, 223, 227, 233
freedom 19, 22, 41, 79, 83, 114, 130, 159, 161, 164, 229

General Agreement on Tariffs and Trade (GATT) 10, 22, 28, 31, 47, 59, 63, 128, 133, 139, 170, 190, 233, 237
genocide 82, 89, 163, 218
geo-economic(s) 122, 123, 124, 125, 126, 228; interdependency 49; outcomes 48; relationships 49
geography: of globalization 7; of labor 79
geopolitical 5, 7, 9, 11, 12, 14, 16, 17, 21, 22, 23, 28, 32, 33, 39, 46, 48, 49, 55, 80, 81, 82, 85, 109, 110, 111, 115, 116, 117, 119, 120, 121, 122, 123, 124, 125, 127, 128, 130, 132, 134, 137, 139, 144, 158, 162, 166, 170, 172, 202, 206, 208, 209,

211, 215, 221, 226, 228, 229, 236, 237, 240; regions 118; strategies 85, 119, 162
geo-strategic 109, 118, 119, 120; power 109
global: communication networks 86; governance 12, 170, 171, 175, 176, 216, 220, 236, 240, 241; media 146, 151, 157; redistribution 239; sex trade 91
global cities 8, 44, 55, 110, 117, 120, 121, 122, 123, 125, 155, 185, 224, 228, 229; *see also* world cities
Global North 21, 25, 26, 29, 31, 33, 39, 50, 53, 54, 64, 81, 86, 87, 89, 93, 109, 110, 119, 120, 122, 125, 164, 193, 200, 213, 214, 215, 216, 219, 227, 229, 230, 235; Core countries/ 10, 11, 12, 18, 23, 25, 26, 27, 29, 30, 31, 42, 44, 52, 54, 64, 85, 103, 105, 109, 110, 119, 120, 122, 125, 133, 151, 164, 165, 166, 209, 210, 228, 231, 232, 233; Europe, North America and Japan 88
Global South 9, 11, 21, 26, 28, 29, 30, 31, 42, 53, 65, 81, 83, 85, 86, 87, 89, 90, 93, 109, 110, 111, 114, 119, 122, 123, 124, 125, 134, 149, 172, 175, 188, 213, 214, 215, 216, 219, 220, 228, 229, 230, 232, 235; LDCs 21, 49, 73, 74, 75, 186, 187, 188, 189, 190, 191, 192, 193; Periphery 10, 11, 12, 25, 30, 54, 100, 103, 133, 151, 165, 166, 206, 209, 210, 228, 231, 233; Third World 9, 10, 11, 13, 20, 21, 53, 90, 119, 130, 134, 176, 184, 192, 216, 231, 232, 233
globalization: from above 15, 213, 214, 221, 225, 236; from below 5, 15, 33, 125, 213, 214, 215, 216, 222, 224, 236
globalization *passim*: of capital 4, 5, 6, 9, 13, 20, 33, 49, 55, 57, 65, 79, 94, 116, 122, 123, 124, 137, 166, 186, 188, 204, 205, 206, 214, 218, 221, 223, 228, 233; corporate 5, 6, 10, 11, 13, 24, 26, 27, 33, 49, 50, 51, 52, 53, 54, 55, 59, 62, 63, 64, 85, 94, 120, 122, 123, 147, 148, 190, 194, 213, 214, 215, 218, 220, 223, 226, 227, 230, 232, 233, 238; of culture 3, 5, 14, 114, 122, 144, 145, 146, 151, 152, 153, 154, 155, 156, 157, 159, 183, 192, 196, 197, 199, 200, 202, 203, 204, 205, 206, 207, 229, 236, 237; of fear 5, 161, 162, 163, 164, 165, 166, 167, 169, 170, 171, 172, 176; grassroots 33, 125, 182, 213, 214, 215, 217, 218, 221, 223, 224, 225, 228, 241; of labor 5, 9, 10, 13, 19, 20, 25, 27, 28, 52, 54, 63, 73, 79, 81, 82, 83, 85, 87, 88, 91, 92, 94, 104
global-to-local 3, 5, 8, 20, 32, 33, 224, 229, 240; *see also* local-to-global
"Glocalization" 240; from below 220, 221
government: corruption 11, 99, 231, 237; subsidies 64
grassroots: movements 182, 213, 214, 217, 228, 241; organizations 214, 217, 218; resistance 182, 193, 195, 214, 221, 223, 224, 225, 235, 241
Great Depression 18, 132
greenhouse gas(es) 186, 193
Group of Eight (G-8) countries 24, 30, 42, 46, 47, 62, 212, 214, 218, 220, 226, 227, 232, 233, 237
Group of Seven (G-7) countries 24, 227, 237
guest-worker program 83, 92

hegemonic: cultural homogenization 198, 199, 200, 201, 203, 207; power 14, 33, 109, 110, 119, 124, 207
homeland security 92, 94, 225
hub-and-spoke systems 98
human rights 5, 15, 27, 80, 81, 86, 87, 90, 91, 93, 112, 114, 115, 119, 164, 213, 214, 216, 218, 221, 222, 230, 236, 238
human smuggling/trafficking 5, 89, 91, 92, 93, 97, 234, 237
hybridization 5, 15, 16, 151, 197, 199, 201, 202, 203, 207, 208, 209, 210, 211
"hyperglobalizers" 8

illegal migration 80, 86, 87
immigration 13, 79, 83, 84, 87, 92, 94, 229
imperial(ism) 133, 134, 151, 155, 158, 166, 186, 198, 199, 200, 218, 219; cultural 124, 210; new 11, 134, 230, 236, 238; reach 206
incentives 55, 57, 59, 72, 104, 105
indebted countries 22, 184, 232
indigenous peoples 90, 212, 215, 218, 221, 222, 233; resistance movements 221, 237; human rights 221
information technology (IT) 5, 28, 54, 122, 226
inter-governmental organizations/ institutions 40, 46
internally displaced persons (IDPs) 81, 89, 90
international aid 83, 159, 231, 232
International Bank for the Reconstruction and Development (IBRD) 22, 116

international banks 40, 41, 43
International Criminal Court (ICC) 114, 169, 171
International Labor Organization (ILO) 62, 87, 91, 116, 239
International Monetary Fund (IMF) 12, 22, 26, 28, 30, 31, 32, 39, 40, 42, 45, 46, 47, 63, 95, 110, 116, 128, 133, 141, 142, 143, 163, 170, 212, 214, 219, 220, 226, 227, 232, 237, 241
international non-governmental organizations (IGOs) 113, 193, 194, 213, 215, 217, 220, 228
International Organization for Migration (IOM) 87, 92
International Red Cross 27, 112
international trade 28, 31, 72, 104, 132, 190
International Trade Organisation (ITO) 40
Internet 4, 54, 70, 86, 155, 213, 225
irregular migration 81, 87, 88, 94
Islam 11, 119, 120, 161, 162, 164, 165, 166, 172, 198, 207

jihad 209
justice 62, 114, 149, 169, 187, 194, 212, 214, 232, 234, 241; global 15, 30, 164, 214, 215, 222; social 15, 30, 125, 214
just-in-time methods 25, 67, 68, 69

Keynesian 18, 19, 21, 23, 24, 25, 27, 32, 42, 63, 133, 231, 241
knowledge-based: economy 3, 4, 26; services 81
Kyoto protocol 186

labor 9, 10, 13, 19, 20, 24, 25, 27, 28, 30, 43, 52, 54, 55, 58, 63, 65, 66, 67, 68, 69, 73, 74, 75, 79, 81, 82, 83, 85, 87, 89, 91, 92, 93, 94, 96, 97, 103, 104, 105, 111, 112, 113, 122, 135, 136, 149, 150, 151, 152, 153, 163, 181, 189, 190, 200, 217, 227, 228, 229, 230, 235, 237, 238, 239, 241
labor intensive production 63, 65, 66, 69, 72, 74
labor markets 27, 82, 87
language 4, 159, 169, 224
law enforcement 96, 97, 98, 99, 103, 104
lean production 66, 67, 68
liberation theology 111
less-developed countries (LDCs) 21, 49, 73, 74, 75, 186, 187, 188, 189, 190, 191, 192, 193; Global South 9, 11, 21, 26, 28, 29, 30, 31, 42, 53, 65, 81, 83, 85, 86, 87, 89, 90, 93, 109, 110, 111, 114, 119, 122, 123, 124, 125, 134, 149, 172, 175, 188, 213, 214, 215, 216, 219, 220, 228, 229, 230, 232, 235; Periphery 10, 11, 12, 25, 30, 54, 100, 103, 133, 151, 165, 166, 206, 209, 210, 228, 231, 233; Third World 9, 10, 11, 13, 20, 21, 53, 90, 119, 130, 134, 176, 184, 192, 216, 231, 232, 233
local-to-global 11, 220, 229; *see also* global-to-local

machinofacture 66, 67, 68, 72, 73, 74, 75
macroeconomic structures 12
McWorld 209
market access regime 127, 135, 137, 138, 143
market liberalization 42, 239
Marshall Plan 21, 130, 212
media 4, 74, 86, 93, 122, 130, 146, 151, 152, 153, 155, 156, 157, 158, 162, 167, 168, 169, 200, 217, 221, 225, 229
MERCOSUR 28
migrant(s) 10, 13, 53, 80, 81, 83, 84, 86, 87, 88, 89, 90, 92, 93, 94, 103, 111, 122, 129, 141, 223, 224; global recruitment of 88; irregular 80, 81, 87, 88, 94, 122, 216, 229; laborers 96, 97, 103; trafficking 81, 89, 91, 92, 93, 234, 235, 237
migration 5, 13, 14, 28, 79, 80, 81, 82, 83, 84, 85, 86, 87, 88, 89, 90, 91, 92, 93, 94, 103, 105, 119, 140, 147, 222, 229, 239; commodification of 88, 91, 93; forced 81, 89, 90, 93, 94; global 79, 81, 93; illegal 80, 87; international 13, 14, 28, 80, 81, 84, 85, 93, 103, 229; North-to-South 84; rural-to-urban 79; transnational 84; unauthorized 86, 87, 92; undocumented 86
militarism 20, 33, 172, 216, 236
military intervention 33, 90, 115, 134, 138, 158, 235
military–industrial complex 85
Millennium Development Goals 220, 230
Ministry of Overseas Development (ODM) 28
modernization 17, 20, 21, 22, 33, 58, 111, 123, 128, 130, 163, 164, 165, 176, 182, 203, 204, 205, 208, 209, 210, 225, 231, 237, 241; "theory" 231; Western 197, 198, 201

nationalism 21, 117, 120, 205, 208
nation-state(s) 6, 8, 9, 10, 12, 14, 19, 21, 23, 26, 33, 40, 41, 46, 47, 49, 52, 55, 57, 59,

62, 63, 64, 79, 80, 82, 88, 90, 91, 103, 109, 110, 111, 113, 114, 115, 117, 118, 119, 120, 121, 124, 142, 162, 166, 169, 184, 193, 201, 208, 222, 228, 229, 231, 233, 237, 241
national governments 6, 142, 163, 221
National Security Strategy of the United States 171
natural resource extraction 29, 31, 163, 165, 188, 217
natural resources 189, 200
neoconservative 32, 110, 158, 169, 170, 214, 215, 217
neoliberalism *passim*: capital 8, 9, 11, 15, 16, 17, 18, 20, 21, 30, 31, 33, 42, 110, 123, 181, 182, 183, 185, 186, 189, 190, 194, 195, 205, 223, 226, 227, 230, 232, 241; deregulation 39, 43, 45; militarism 33; roll-back 25, 39, 44, 47; theory 19
network(s) 6, 8, 9, 11, 14, 33, 43, 50, 52, 54, 55, 69, 73, 74, 79, 84, 86, 89, 94, 96, 97, 98, 99, 101, 111, 121, 122, 123, 125, 128, 135, 137, 138, 153, 155, 156, 158, 167, 169, 171, 186, 187, 199, 206, 210, 212, 220, 221, 222, 223, 224, 234; actor 8, 97; all-channel 98; chain 98; governance 98; interconnected 96; transnational 33, 86, 94, 111, 120, 124, 222, 223; underground 96, 98
networks: of communication 50, 123; of production 6, 33, 135
new age of migration 80, 81, 83, 93
new imperialism 11, 230
New International Division of Labor (NIDL) 25, 27
new slavery 91, 234
new world (dis)order 4, 31, 111, 124, 241
9/11 5, 14, 81, 82, 92, 158, 169, 170, 172, 207, 211
Non-Aligned Movement 22, 27, 219, 237
non-governmental organizations (NGOs) 27, 122, 193, 194, 207, 213, 215, 216, 217, 218, 228, 232, 237
North American Free Trade Agreement (NAFTA) 28, 29, 103, 141, 238
North Atlantic Treaty Organization (NATO) 9, 115
nuclear weapons 118, 132, 166, 170, 172

Oil Producing and Exporting Countries (OPEC) 24
oil/petroleum industry 24, 53, 85, 96, 101, 162, 165, 188, 221, 234, 235

offshore financial centers (OFCs) 102
Organization for Economic Co-operation and Development (OECD) 41, 62, 44, 46, 62, 83, 226
organized crime 11, 13, 89, 91, 93, 95, 96, 97, 104, 234
outsourcing 52, 54, 85
ozone 190, 193

pax Americana 170, 175
Pearl Harbor 169, 172
Pentagon 119, 157, 158, 160, 167, 176
Periphery 10, 11, 12, 25, 30, 54, 100, 103, 133, 151, 165, 166, 206, 209, 210, 228, 231, 233; Global South 9, 11, 21, 26, 28, 29, 30, 31, 42, 53, 65, 81, 83, 85, 86, 87, 89, 90, 93, 109, 110, 111, 114, 119, 122, 123, 124, 125, 134, 149, 172, 175, 188, 213, 214, 215, 216, 219, 220, 228, 229, 230, 232, 235; LDCs 21, 49, 73, 74, 75, 186, 187, 188, 189, 190, 191, 192, 193; Third World 9, 10, 11, 13, 20, 21, 53, 90, 119, 130, 134, 176, 184, 192, 216, 231, 232, 233
post-colonial 22, 87, 187, 201, 204, 209, 210, 211, 231, 232, 236; states 22
post-Fordist 52, 125
poverty 34, 75, 81, 89, 146, 163, 212, 214, 216, 218, 220, 221, 225, 230, 232, 235
private sector 24, 40, 46, 125, 212, 232
Project for the New American Century (PNAC) 169
prostitution 91, 235
public services 20, 27, 30, 123
public–private partnerships/institutions 7, 24, 26, 32, 33, 52, 239
pull production 67, 69

rainforest 192, 194
refugee 81, 82, 83, 87, 89, 90, 92, 111, 113, 114, 119, 141, 234
remittances 84, 86, 223
Report on the Observation of Standards and Codes (ROSC) 45
restructuring 3, 11, 14, 28, 32, 33, 52, 54, 64, 80, 82, 95, 111, 118, 119, 142, 183, 200, 232, 236; cultural 202, 209; financial 13, 45, 47, 94; global 4, 9, 10, 13, 17, 21, 119, 122, 124; industrial 13, 25, 26, 29
"roll-back" neoliberalism 25, 39, 44, 47
Roman Catholic Church 111, 112, 120

scale 7, 8, 12, 23, 33, 49, 50, 52, 59, 64, 66, 74, 95, 97, 104, 109, 110, 115, 116, 117, 121, 124, 127, 132, 134, 137, 142, 143, 147, 149, 151, 156, 176, 182, 183, 184, 185, 187, 189, 191, 194, 209, 210, 213, 215, 222, 223, 230, 240
separatist movements 82, 101
social *passim*: civil rights 23, 164; environmental 63, 80, 119, 125, 163, 164, 181, 182, 183, 185, 186, 187, 188, 189, 190, 191, 192, 193, 194, 195, 214, 215, 216, 217, 218, 223, 228, 235, 236, 238, 240; human rights 5, 15, 27, 80, 81, 86, 87, 90, 91, 93, 112, 114, 115, 119, 164, 213, 214, 216, 218, 221, 222, 230, 236, 238; inequality 16, 34, 81, 89, 93, 94, 124, 129, 142, 165, 182, 189, 192, 212, 213, 220, 236; justice/global justice 15, 30, 62, 114, 149, 164, 169, 187, 194, 212, 214, 215, 222, 232, 234, 241; movements 3, 5, 13, 74, 82, 100, 101, 125, 141, 142, 164, 182, 213, 214, 215, 217, 218, 219, 220, 221, 222, 228, 237, 241; nationalism 21, 117, 120, 205, 208; reproduction 149, 151, 153, 156; welfare 7, 18, 24, 25, 27, 30, 61, 62, 94, 100, 109, 112, 114, 123, 125, 132, 133, 145, 193, 212, 227, 228, 232, 238, 240; women's 84, 164, 214, 215, 216, 218, 221; social services 158
socialism 24, 30, 117, 142, 149
"soft capitalism" 5, 13, 26, 227, 231
sovereignty 14, 79, 99, 100, 102, 103, 104, 110, 112, 115, 116, 118, 172, 195, 205, 206, 211, 241
spatial proximity 71
Special Economic Zones 57
state *passim*: "hollowed out" 64, 102, 125, 162
state governments 25, 27, 52, 105, 120
structural adjustment programs (SAPs) 10, 220, 232
structural processes 124, 185, 189, 194
supranational: global capital 6; governance 6, 238
sustainability 15, 16, 64, 114, 124, 125, 138, 194, 215, 216, 220, 230, 236
sustainable 53, 125, 143, 159, 190, 194, 215, 236, 237, 240, 241; development 62, 194, 220, 230, 239, 240; urbanism 125

Taylorism 163
technology 5, 7, 9, 11, 24, 43, 53, 54, 65, 67, 74, 98, 101, 127, 164, 184, 187, 200, 202, 227, 228, 235, 236; change 4, 17, 121, 143; diffusion 7, 229; innovation 21, 22, 29, 75, 81, 86, 122, 202, 203, 204, 205, 222
"ten plagues of globalization" 81
terrorism 81, 82, 96, 119, 125, 161, 162, 166, 167, 169, 170, 171, 172, 175, 176, 207
theory of competitive advantage 70, 74, 124, 135, 137, 227
Third World 9, 10, 11, 13, 20, 21, 53, 90, 119, 130, 134, 176, 184, 192, 216, 231, 232, 233; Global South 9, 11, 21, 26, 28, 29, 30, 31, 42, 53, 65, 81, 83, 85, 86, 87, 89, 90, 93, 109, 110, 111, 114, 119, 122, 123, 124, 125, 134, 149, 172, 175, 188, 213, 214, 215, 216, 219, 220, 228, 229, 230, 232, 235; LDCs 21, 49, 73, 74, 75, 186, 187, 188, 189, 190, 191, 192, 193; Periphery 10, 11, 12, 25, 30, 54, 100, 103, 133, 151, 165, 166, 206, 209, 210, 228, 231, 233
time–space compression 3, 5, 127
"transformationalists" 6, 7, 8
transnational 10, 12, 13, 16, 25, 33, 42, 48, 50, 63, 81, 82, 84, 93, 94, 95, 102, 103, 104, 117, 120, 121, 122, 123, 137, 139, 141, 162, 187, 208, 209, 215, 221, 222, 223, 224, 225, 229, 230, 233; corporations 6, 10, 13, 27, 31, 42, 49, 50, 52, 63, 73, 74, 75, 81, 82, 89, 120, 122, 123, 137, 139, 141, 183, 190, 218, 221, 222, 223, 230, 233, 238; crime 96, 98, 99, 104, 105; elites 124, 224; migrants 84, 223, 224; networks 6, 9, 33, 86, 94, 111, 124, 222, 223; organized crime 13; urbanism 33, 216, 223, 224; workers 57
transnationalism 81, 84, 208, 222, 223, 224
transportation 4, 16, 27, 53, 73, 86, 88, 95, 97, 123, 125, 136, 139, 163, 164, 167
Treaty of Rome 83
Treaty of Westphalia 118

underdevelopment 20, 128, 230
underside of globalization 91, 95
unemployment 19, 82, 83, 131
uneven development 3, 152, 154, 185
unions 63, 145, 218
United Nations 27, 101, 109, 110, 112, 113, 114, 115, 116, 125, 165, 170, 171, 176, 211, 212, 218, 237; Development Program (UNDP) 114 Environment Program (UNEP) 62, 114; High

Commission for Refugees (UNHCR) 90, 114; Security Council 101, 113, 114, 115, 237
United States: Agency for International Development (USAID) 28, 220, 231; Department of Homeland Security 92
unruly spaces 12, 13, 14, 93, 95
urban 5, 8, 11, 14, 16, 22, 32, 33, 54, 64, 83, 96, 109, 111, 122, 123, 124, 125, 126, 184, 185, 186, 187, 213, 215, 216, 221, 223, 224, 229, 230, 234; development 54; entrepreneurialism 32
urbanization 13, 14, 111, 186, 211

Vietnam War 23

Wal-Mart 62
war on terror(ism) 33, 81, 119, 158, 172, 175, 207, 208
warfare 21, 90, 93, 118, 119
Washington consensus 10, 194, 212, 214, 220, 237, 240
weapons 101, 102, 118, 163, 166, 167; manufacturers 101; of mass destruction 22, 132, 163, 166, 170, 172, 177
Weberian location theory 71
welfare 7, 18, 24, 25, 27, 30, 61, 62, 94, 100, 109, 112, 114, 123, 125, 132, 133, 145, 193, 212, 227, 228, 232, 238, 240

women 48, 117, 163, 164, 187, 196, 212, 214, 215, 216, 218, 220, 221, 228, 230, 234, 235; changing roles 83; egalitarian rights 84; exploitation of 81, 82, 89, 91, 93, 97
World Bank 12, 18, 22, 28, 30, 31, 40, 45, 46, 47, 63, 110, 116, 128, 133, 141, 142, 143, 163, 170, 212, 214, 219, 221, 226, 227, 231, 232, 237, 241
World Business Council for Sustainable Development 62
world cities 121; *see also* global cities
World Economic Forum (WEF) 24, 62, 141, 214, 215, 218, 220, 227, 232
World Health Organization (WHO) 110, 116
World Social Forum (WSF) 211, 215, 218, 219, 220
world system 3, 17, 109, 119, 121, 165, 206
World Trade Center 157, 162, 166, 176
World Trade Organization (WTO) 28, 31, 47, 63, 116, 136, 139, 163, 170, 190, 212, 237
World War II 17, 20, 21, 23, 29, 40, 41, 109, 113, 114, 118, 128, 130, 132, 133, 143, 170, 200, 204

xenophobia 93, 196

eBooks – at www.eBookstore.tandf.co.uk

A library at your fingertips!

eBooks are electronic versions of printed books. You can store them on your PC/laptop or browse them online.

They have advantages for anyone needing rapid access to a wide variety of published, copyright information.

eBooks can help your research by enabling you to bookmark chapters, annotate text and use instant searches to find specific words or phrases. Several eBook files would fit on even a small laptop or PDA.

NEW: Save money by eSubscribing: cheap, online access to any eBook for as long as you need it.

Annual subscription packages

We now offer special low-cost bulk subscriptions to packages of eBooks in certain subject areas. These are available to libraries or to individuals.

For more information please contact webmaster.ebooks@tandf.co.uk

We're continually developing the eBook concept, so keep up to date by visiting the website.

www.eBookstore.tandf.co.uk